BETWEEN FREEDOM AND SUBSISTENCE
China and Human Rights

BETWEEN FREEDOM AND SUBSISTENCE

China and Human Rights

ANN KENT

HONG KONG
OXFORD UNIVERSITY PRESS
OXFORD NEW YORK

Oxford University Press

Oxford   New York
Athens   Auckland   Bangkok   Bombay
Calcutta   Cape Town   Dar es Salaam   Delhi
Florence   Hong Kong   Istanbul   Karachi
Kuala Lumpur   Madras   Madrid   Melbourne
Mexico City   Nairobi   Paris   Singapore
Taipei   Tokyo   Toronto

and associated companies in
Berlin   Ibadan

Oxford is a trade mark of Oxford University Press

First published 1993
Second impression 1995

Published in the United States
by Oxford University Press, New York

British Library Cataloguing in Publication Data
available

Library of Congress Cataloging-in-Publication Data

Kent, A. E. (Ann E.)
Between Freedom and Subsistence/Ann Kent.
p. cm.
Includes bibliographical references and index.
ISBN 0-19-585519-1 (HB).
ISBN 0-19-585521-3 (PB)
1. Human rights—China.
I. Title.
JC599.C6K46   1992
323.4'90951–dc20
92-19756
CIP

Cover painting 'The Third Generation' by Ho Duoling

Printed in Hong Kong
Published by Oxford University Press (China) Ltd
18/F Warwick House, Taikoo Place, 979 King's Road, Quarry Bay, Hong Kong

*For my father, the late J. M. Garland,
and for my mother, Nancy Jean*

The question of human rights is a very sensitive one in China at the moment . . . I prefer to talk of 'civil rights', since if you say 'human rights' you are regarded as an agent of Carter. Some people say that the main thing now is to work to modernize China. For the time being we should not bother about affairs of state. But, in that case, how are the people to express their power? Is the aim to turn the Chinese into conveyor-belt workers, like in Chaplin's *Modern Times*? What then is the point of human intelligence? . . . A person who cannot think freely feels wounded. Only a minority are allowed to express their views. It is impossible to modernize the country unless you let the intelligence of a thousand million individuals unfold. So the problem of freedom of thought is more serious than that of physical attacks on people.

Xu Wenli, February 1980

Although the sun of democracy and human rights has risen, we in China can barely see the light. While most of mankind has already awakened from the bad dream of superstition and dictatorship, we are still sound asleep and suffering nightmares. What is our future? What can it give us? Do we have to be exploited and suffer for our entire lives? Will our ideals be mere spirits wandering among the pages of books? No. All this must come to an end.

'On Human Rights', *Enlightenment*, 1979

Preface

THE understanding of a given country's human rights condition requires a mix of institutional documentation, cultural explanation, and social, economic, and political analysis. It also requires a comparative framework which enables the theory and practice of that country's human rights to be located squarely within the context of international human rights norms.

Within these guidelines it is possible to say what this book is not. It is neither a moral tract nor a prescription for Chinese practice. It takes neither a Western view of human rights, viewing rights mainly as civil and political rights, nor a cultural-relativist approach which sees Chinese values, including their approach to rights, as separate and discrete from international mores. It is not designed primarily as a detailed report on the empirical condition of human, and especially civil, rights in China, nor does it seek to separately document the related and important issue of minority rights: such reports are more properly left in the efficient hands of International Non-Governmental Organizations like Amnesty International, Asia Watch, Lawasia and the Tibetan Information Network, or of governmental human rights delegations visiting China. At the same time, it recognizes that empirical evidence must form the basis of theory, or the human rights analyst falls into the sad category defined by Marjorie Agosin:

> When they began
> to define terrorism
> they used the lofty
> language
> of the demagogue
> disguised
> as a teacher.
> they enumerated
> quotes and
> bibliographies,
> documents sealed
> in the sad imbecility
> of those who define,
> of those who control,
> of the mediocre,

defending themselves in the
superfluous shelves
of encyclopedias . . .
they forgot about
the children with heads split open
their brains turned into puddles of moss
mixed up with the earth.[2]

This book therefore, at the risk of trying to be all things to all
people, represents an attempt to combine theory with practice. It
seeks both to stand back and assess the overall condition of human
rights in China since 1949, at the formal institutional level and at
the informal level of rule application, with its social and political
implications, and to provide a comparative theoretical framework
relating Chinese domestic human rights practice and norms to the
international standards of human rights. It is clear, whatever the
current legal controversies, that the prevailing international definition
of human rights includes both the civil and political rights emphasized in Western liberal democracies, and the social, economic,
and developmental rights which are stressed by socialist, developing nations like China. The discussion which follows will therefore comprehend both of these categories of rights. The idea of
cultural relativism is not accepted, but the analysis of a political
culture is seen as the prerequisite to an understanding of the content and background of a state's human rights perceptions. Objective
cultural understanding, rather than sanctimonious moralizing, is
therefore the appropriate environment within which to observe
the Chinese state's dynamic role in shaping its human rights policies to reconcile the often conflicting pressures of its ideology, its
finite resources, the rising expectations of its people, and the
increasingly rigorous international standards of human rights.

This book is the perfect example of the production imperative.
It emerged from a report on human rights in China commissioned
by the Australian Parliamentary Research Service in early March
1989. The completion of this report, published in August 1989,
was naturally hastened by the developments which took place in
China between April and June 1989. It assumed another shape in
May 1990, as an expanded and updated monograph published by
the Peace Research Centre of the Australian National University.
The final metamorphosis, the present volume, represents a matura-
tion of my thinking on the subject and has benefited enormously
from the comments of my colleagues on the earlier versions.

When a book has such an extensive biography, it is obvious that the list of colleagues to whom I have been indebted over the past three years would be too long to be contained here. Were I to mention them all, too much would be expected of the work. But some of them must not be missed. I am grateful to the Contemporary China Centre of the Australian National University, headed by Jonathan Unger, and to all my colleagues there, including Dianne Stacey and Elizabeth Kingdon, who breathed humour and humanity into my closeted existence, and constantly compensated for my technological incompetence. The original parliamentary paper had its origins, appropriately, in a Canberra bus ride when Frank Frost, director of the Foreign Affairs Group in the Parliamentary Research Service, and I discussed the latest news about Wei Jingsheng, and the absence of news about Wang Xizhe, and deplored the lack of international interest in the issue of China's human rights. Apart from Frank, Brian Martin and Dennis Argall of the Parliamentary Research Service made helpful comments on the original paper. Throughout the three productions, Andrew Chin of the Parliamentary Reference Service gave me invaluable assistance. In the Peace Research Centre, I benefited from the support of Professor Andrew Mack, Graeme Cheeseman, Richard Leaver, and members of the Centre staff.

The present book has been enriched by discussions with members of the Law Faculty of the Australian National University, Professor Philip Alston, Peter Bailey and J.-P. Fonteyne, and with Professor Paul Finn of the Division of Philosophy and Law, Research School of Social Sciences. I am particularly indebted to Professor James Crawford, now Whewell Professor of Law at Cambridge University, whose succinct comments on an earlier draft of Chapter 1 stripped away any legal solecisms. I also gained from discussions about rights with Professor Barry Hindess and Jack Barbalet of the Sociology Department, and Thomas Mautner of the Philosophy Department, The Faculties. Among China scholars, apart from those whose work is cited in the following pages, I wish to thank Professor David Goodman, who read the first three chapters, and Barrett McCormick, who read two chapters. Others who helped, either with comments on a chapter or in book reviews or in other ways, were James Cotton, Cao Yong, Michael Dutton, Peter Van Ness, Garry Woodard, Geremie Barmé, Boerge Bakken, Chris Buckley, Chen Weidong, Keith Forster, John Girling, Hong Lijian, Terence Hull, Linda Jaivin, Penny

Mlakar, Lisa Pola, Ian Wilson, and You Ji. Needless to say, none of these colleagues may be held responsible for the errors which, apart from being entirely my own responsibility, are also the unintended consequences of the production imperative.

Aside from these colleagues, I am grateful to Professor Michel Oksenberg, whose ever generous comments on the monograph gave me the thought to proceed towards a larger undertaking. And I am indebted to members of the Australian Human Rights Delegation to China, in particular Professor Stephen FitzGerald, Senator Chris Schacht, and Professor Alice Tay, for sharing their findings and widening my knowledge of the issue.

In the last three years I could not have done without the efficient and patient service of librarians of the National Library of Australia, both in the Petherick Room and in the Asian Collections Reading Room. I thank in particular Jean James and C. P. Tang. I am also grateful to the librarians of the Asian collection, headed by Y. S. Chan, in the Menzies Library, Australian National University. Officers of the Australian Department of Foreign Affairs and Trade, the Treasury, and relevant embassies, and representatives of Amnesty International and Asia Watch were also helpful in supplying information and material. I am grateful to Marian Robson, who offered me assistance over the Christmas break. I have also enjoyed amicable and constructive working relationships with all my editors at Oxford University Press.

Particularly helpful in the last few months of writing was a period doing research in the Universities Service Centre, the Chinese University of Hong Kong, where I was extended the warm hospitality and professional assistance which has been the hallmark of its director, Jean Xiong.

Finally, I wish to remember scholars who have influenced me in the writing of this book. The late Professor John Vincent, whose imprint is strongly felt throughout, sent me a copy of his *Human Rights and International Relations* just before his premature death. It is a sad irony that in that volume, he himself referred to the untimely death of Professor Hedley Bull, mentor of all of us who passed through the Department of International Relations, Australian National University, in the late 1960s and early 1970s. I can only hope that in some small way I can continue to carry their flag. I also wish to remember a Chinese friend who would have understood the struggle for human rights. Finally, along with many others, I am grateful to my former teacher, Professor Benjamin

Schwartz, and to Professor Wang Gungwu who, although having no hand in this book, have been enduring influences.

My greatest debt, however, is to Bruce Kent, my good companion, and to Rohan and Cris, for waiting.

ANN KENT
January 1992

Contents

Contents

Introduction

THE events of China's 1989 Democracy Movement have now receded to a point where it is possible to obtain some historical perspective on them and make some tentative judgements. In themselves, they serve both as a dramatic manifestation of popular discontent with the overall conditions of human rights in China, and as the symbol of a further loss of civil rights. As such, they provide a point of departure for a study not only of China's civil and political rights, the main focus of recent international attention, but of the broader condition of its social and economic rights. For those months were the culmination of growing mass dissatisfaction not only with the inadequacy of China's civil and political rights, of which most outside observers were aware, but with the diminution of social and economic rights over the previous decade, which had escaped general attention. Those forty-nine days of open debate and demonstration of popular feeling will be shown to have been the unique outcome of a revolution of rising expectations in the arena of civil and political rights, and of rising expectations and relative deprivation in the area of social, economic, and cultural rights.[1]

The decision by the Chinese government to suppress the Democracy Movement rather than initiate the desired reforms had important short-term and long-term consequences. First, it saw the return to a process of purge and denial of civil rights of those seen as dissenters, a process which has become a permanent backdrop to domestic policies since June 1989. Secondly, it halted the informal process of the expansion of civil and political rights in China since the late 1970s and led initially to a new series of hardline policies. June 4 represented the crucial point at which the Chinese leadership signalled its intention not to change but to maintain itself: regime legitimation was reasserted through a reemphasis on economic and social rights, and, six months later, with a reaffirmation of the need for limited political reform and a slight expansion of civil rights at the informal level. The June 4 action also served to institutionalize the formation of Chinese dissident organizations seeking to expand human, and in particular, civil and political rights in China, and it led to the diaspora of opposition groups outside China. Finally, it galvanized international attention, long dormant, to the pressing question of human rights in China.[2]

In an instrumentalist sense, the fall-out from the June crack-down in the shape of countless refugees stranded outside China, and the freezing of the location of Chinese students abroad obliged many Western governments to concern themselves with the plight of those Chinese resident within their own territory.[3] It also pro-voked grave concerns in Hong Kong, whose own lack of formal human rights protection made it potentially vulnerable after the handover to China in 1997.[4] In a normative sense, members of international bodies like the United Nations Commission on Human Rights and the International Labour Organization, as well as individual governments imposing economic and symbolic sanctions, were obliged for the first time to publicize their criticism of China's human rights.

Such disapproval, and the imposition of economic sanctions, led to China's protests of interference in its internal affairs. At the same time, these protests were clothed in the language of human rights rather than in the form of a rejection of such standards, suggesting that the Chinese government had already moved some distance from the Mao era towards an acceptance of the validity of civil and political rights. Other indications that China had moved closer to international standards were its release of some political prisoners in early 1990 and in 1991, and its invitation to Australian, French, and other governments to send delegations to monitor the condition of its rights. Whatever its initial reasons, the latter action served to substantially modify China's earlier insistence on the overriding importance of the principle of state sovereignty in this sphere of policy. Perhaps the most positive sign, however, was the publication in November 1991 of China's White Paper, *Human Rights in China (Zhongguo de renquan zhuangkuang)*,[5] which was the signal of the current regime's intention to take part in serious debate, as well as to scrutinize its civil and political rights record. At the same time, the emphasis in the Paper on the right to sub-sistence was suggestive of a bid to spearhead a renewed effort by non-Western states to redefine the human rights discourse.

Against these ambiguous signs must be counterposed the failure of the United Nations Commission on Human Rights, at its forty-sixth session from February to March 1990, to condemn the abuse of civil rights in Beijing in June 1989 and its aftermath, and the lifting of most international economic sanctions on China in 1991.

China's co-operation in other fields of international activity, notably relating to the Gulf crisis, also enabled it to regain its international credibility, despite the evasion of its human rights responsibility. On the other hand, domestic pressures in the form of economic problems which provided obstacles to the expansion of economic and social rights, required the regime to make at least formal gestures in the direction of renewed political reform. And, despite the overall failure of the international community to continue sanctions, the threat in 1991 and 1992 by the US Congress to withdraw Most Favoured Nation status from China in bilateral trade relations, refocused China's interest on the human rights issue.

The assumption of this book is that human rights constitute an international regime which transcends state boundaries and provides individual citizens of the sovereign state with a link to international bodies. In order to locate the universal character of rights connecting Chinese experience and belief systems with those of other nations, an attempt is made to establish a basic 'core' of rights against which to measure Chinese performance. Above all, the book seeks to indicate the complexity and the dynamic nature of China's human rights, particularly in the changing economic, social, and political context of the modernization decade. The expansion and contraction over time of China's human rights policies is in dramatic contrast to the apparently unyielding and unchanging official position. This dynamic condition, which in itself offers the greatest hope for China, is best illustrated within a comparative international human rights framework.

Consequently, this book focuses in Chapter 1 on theoretical issues, discussing the international law of human rights in relation to the culture and concepts of developing and socialist states like China. While outlining areas of convergence in North–South theories, it discusses the major obstacles to obtaining universal acceptance for the whole gamut of internationally supported human rights, in view of certain philosophical and theoretical objections of developing states. This first chapter also introduces the principal methodology employed in the book: to analyse the interplay between international human rights norms, Chinese constitutional, legal, and institutional provisions, and the informal condition of the rights actually enjoyed by Chinese citizens. Chapter 2 sets the scene for the later chapters, and describes the historical and cultural background of Chinese policies, assessing the traditional relationship between individual, society, and the state, and the

4 CHINA AND HUMAN RIGHTS

attitude towards law and human rights in the first half of the twentieth century.

Because the emphasis here is on the dynamic relationship between international norms and Chinese domestic practice and theory at the international and domestic level, the remaining chapters are arranged chronologically according to the principal phases of human rights. Chapter 3 provides the background to the reform era by describing the congruence of the formal constitutional and institutional framework of rights and their substantive content in the Maoist and early post-Maoist era of 1949–1978. Chapter 4 analyses the formal and informal civil and political rights of the modernization decade 1979–1989, documenting the evolution of China's official attitudes in response to domestic developments and China's membership of the United Nations and human rights forums. It also discusses the ongoing debate over human rights in this decade among Chinese scholars at the semi-official and unofficial levels. Chapter 5, on the other hand, describes the formal and substantive condition of economic, social, and cultural rights of Chinese citizens in the same period.

In both cases, the substantive or informal rights enjoyed by citizens present a dramatic contrast with formal provisions: civil and political rights are discovered to have expanded, while the economic and social rights still given precedence in China's 1982 Constitution are seen to have contracted. Chapter 6 provides a background to the June crisis, delineating the main features of the internal and external critique of China's human rights record up until 1989. In Chapter 7, the impact of the April–June 1989 Democracy Movement is described. This chapter also charts the immediate international reaction to the June crisis, which began a new era in the international attitude to China's human rights, and placed new pressures on the Chinese government to review its policies. The final chapter surveys the changes to China's practice of human rights after June 1989, describing the attempts by China's leaders to restore a combination of socio-economic and corporatist political arrangements aimed at mobilizing popular support and maintaining the power of the Party. It distinguishes between three main, if overlapping, phases in the 1989–1991 period; and it details the continued involvement of the international community in monitoring China's human rights conditions. The Conclusion summarizes the findings of the book, and ends with a discussion of the future of human rights in China.

1   China and the International Law of Human Rights

THE problem of human rights lies at the heart of modern political discourse. On the one hand, human rights are a compelling part of international political rhetoric, on the other so diverse and abstract in content as to be easily dismissed in competing claims for government attention. Human rights raise questions about the essential values of society, about the relationship between the state and the individual, between the international community, the state, and individual, and between international and domestic law. At stake are issues of state sovereignty and the place of cultural relativism in the determination of human rights values. Because human rights as a standard must command universal consensus, because in this modern era they are so crucial to the life of the individual and yet so challenging to the authority of the state, and because they are so varied, they present peculiar problems of definition, priority, jurisdiction, and enforcement. Moreover, the complex triangular relationship between international authority, domestic institutions and legislation, and the individual citizen as recipient of rights gives rise to methodological problems in the analysis of human rights conditions in particular states.

The importance of these issues and the urgent need to grapple with them have been highlighted by developments in the late 1980s and early 1990s in Eastern Europe, the Soviet Union, and China, when the popular demand for human rights became a driving force for political change. In the case of Eastern Europe and the Soviet Union, these demands brought the desired change: in the case of China, they led to the reassertion of authoritarian leadership and the abuse of civil rights. This outcome focused international attention, so long averted, on the condition of China's human rights. But at the same time, the ability of the United Nations, if not of the international community as a whole, to respond to human rights abuses was in some respects diminishing.

Along with the newly enhanced importance of human rights as a public policy and international relations issue came evidence of the increased dangers which it faced in the coming decade.[1] The newly independent countries, or Group of 77, pressed for, and in 1990 obtained, an enlargement of the UN Commission on Human

Rights from forty-three members to fifty-three. All the new seats were allocated to developing countries, which then acquired voting control in the Commission. These countries, ambivalent, to say the least, about United Nations efforts to investigate and act on violations of human rights, now had a decisive voice over whether a country could or should become the subject of investigation for such violations. On the other hand, in late November 1991, the United Nations General Assembly, in an action which reflected the new seriousness of international attitudes, adopted without a vote a resolution on human rights in Myanmar (Burma), which noted with concern 'a grave human rights situation in Myanmar' and called upon the Government of Myanmar 'to take firm steps towards the establishment of a democratic state'.[2] Neither China nor the ASEAN states raised any formal objection.

The following discussion seeks to locate the issue of China's human rights in the context of this new international environment in which human rights have both assumed greater importance and are more at risk. It sets out the problems of definition and priority which the issue of human rights raises, and describes attempts which have been made to establish a core of rights to be used as a minimum international standard. It also delineates the international framework for the monitoring of human rights; outlines opposing political views on the question of ultimate jurisdiction in the case of human rights abuses; and analyses the difficulties raised by lack of an international enforcement agency. In the light of these problems, it discusses the issues involved in achieving a balanced assessment of substantive human rights in any given country, and in particular establishes a framework for the analysis of the situation in China.

Problems of Definition and Priority

Human rights are rights of individuals in society which are regarded as universal and inalienable. They are universal in the sense that they are to be enjoyed by all human beings on an equal basis.[3] They are inalienable, not because they cannot be alienated but because if they are, 'the life left is not fully human life'.[4] The essence of a human right is that the right holder has a claim to some good or substance which may be asserted against some bearer of the correlative duty, on the basis of particular grounds.[5] All basic human rights are said to have three correlative duties:

to avoid depriving (negative rights), to protect from deprivation, and to aid the deprived (positive rights).[6] Rights exist by virtue of moral entitlement, legal or positive entitlement, and, in the empirical sense, as they are observed to be implemented.[7]

Human rights being universal, their justification is not ultimately based in municipal law or custom, for human beings can be said to have these rights whether or not they are lodged in domestic instruments.[8] Their justification lies rather in regional international law, as in the European Convention on Human Rights, or in their ultimate location, the International Covenant on Civil and Political Rights (ICCPR) and the International Covenant on Economic, Social, and Cultural Rights (ICESCR). Although there are important differences between these human rights instruments, the broad moral, as opposed to legal, justification of human rights lies in the authority provided by the Universal Declaration of Human Rights, a document described by Gerald Draper as 'a transitional instrument somewhere between a legal and a moral ordering'.[9] The wide ambit of the contemporary usage of the term 'human rights', embracing as it does civil, political, economic, social, cultural, collective, and developmental rights, is partly a result of the particular chronological development of these human rights instruments.[10] Before World War II, in so far as the term 'human rights' was used, it was taken to refer to the civil and political rights deriving from the ancient notion, of Greek origin, of the 'natural' rights of the individual. Articulated in the American Declaration of Independence (1776) and the French Declaration of the Rights of Man and of the Citizen (1789), as well as in other bills of rights, these 'human' or 'natural' rights became known as the 'first generation' of rights and were regarded by socialist and developing nations as expressions of Western culture and notions of individualism.

The full text of the Universal Declaration of Human Rights of 1948, however, did not limit itself to the elaboration of the classical principles, but added to the civil and political rights in the first twenty-one articles a set of new 'economic and social' rights, or the second generation of human rights. Following the adoption of the Declaration, the two International Covenants (ICCPR and ICESCR) were adopted in 1966 and came into effect ten years later. These both contained statements that human beings form peoples who are entitled to political self-determination and control over their own natural resources as well as to live in a peaceful, healthy, and economically developing environment. Such principles formed the basis for the subsequent formulation of a third generation of rights, known collectively as the right to development. The Universal Declaration of Human Rights, which, as Peter Bailey remarks, was 'almost miraculously' agreed to in 1948 by the United Nations General Assembly with 48 supporting votes and no dissent (but 8 abstentions), together with the two Covenants and the two Optional Protocols on Civil and Political Rights, today form the definitive statement of the International Bill of Rights.[11] In addition to this Bill of Rights are the 1986 Declaration on the Right to Development and many other similar declarations, which deal with different aspects of the two groups of rights, civil/political and social/economic/cultural, and which emphasize their indivisibility.[12]

Any objective, universal definition of human rights must therefore focus on the rights articulated in these international instruments. 'Civil rights' may be understood as conferring rights of immunity upon the individual, as requiring non-interference from others, and as 'not normally dependent upon general social conditions'.[13] They include freedom of thought, conscience and religion, expression and association, residence and movement; every person's right to life, free from arbitrary killing, torture or mistreatment; freedom from slavery, arbitrary arrest or detention; and equality before the law.[14] They may be loosely divided into two main categories: the rights of freedom of expression, and rights of immunity, which include the right to life, personal freedoms, and the right to impartial justice.[15] Political rights may be defined as rights of participation and include the individual's right to 'take part in the conduct of public affairs, directly or through freely chosen representatives'; the right of access to public service; and the right of election and recall of government on the basis of 'universal and equal suffrage' by secret ballot.[16]

Social and cultural rights, in the form of claims to benefits from the state, may be understood as rights of consumption or positive rights, allowing access to social security, to education and to 'the cultural life of the community'. Social rights include 'the right (of everyone) to a standard of living adequate for the health and wellbeing of himself and of his family, including food, clothing, housing, and medical care and necessary social services, and the right to security in the event of unemployment, sickness, disability, widowhood, old age or other lack of livelihood in circumstances beyond his control'.[17]

Economic rights, which suggest not only the right of consumption but also the more active right of participation in the workforce, include the right to work, to free choice of employment, to equal pay for equal work, and the right to 'reasonable limitations of working hours and periodic holidays with pay'.[18] They also include the right to strike which, together with the civil right of freedom of association underlying the right to join trade unions, comprise a special category of industrial rights. Although civil and political rights are generally categorized as individual rights, while economic, social, and cultural rights are described as collective rights, some of the latter category may also be defined as individual rights.

Collective rights may be said to include the rights of peoples to self-determination and equality of rights, rights relating to international peace and security, the right of permanent sovereignty over natural resources, developmental rights, environmental rights, and the rights of minorities.[19] The principle of 'external self-determination' has been emphasized in the practice of the United Nations since the drafting of the international covenants and the Declaration on the Granting of Independence. 'Internal self-determination', or the right of peoples within states to choose their form of government, has been correspondingly downplayed.[20]

The problem of human rights, however, lies precisely in the number and diversity detailed above. Their comprehensive nature is seen as a source of weakness. The increasingly broad interpretation of the concept means that 'it no longer indicates minimum conditions for an existence worthy of human dignity, but is beginning to include practically everything which is considered desirable for human development': thus its very success 'threatens to rob it of part of its operational significance'.[21]

Furthermore, the diversity of rights has created internal contradictions within the Bill of Rights itself. The rights formulated in the Universal Declaration of Human Rights are seen by Eugene Kamenka as 'conceptually disparate and muddled, containing rhetoric and crucially important conflicts with each other'. Most importantly, they fail to consider 'the sharp and fundamental clash between civil and political rights, that limit the power of the state, and social, economic and cultural rights that positively demand an ever-increasing state organization of society'.[22] The only constitutions which resolve this contradiction, Kamenka observes, are the communist constitutions which provide that 'all rights granted by the constitution or in the codes shall be exercised only in conformity with the social, economic and political system of the country and the purposes of building socialism'.[23] Peter Bailey, among others, disputes the existence of such a clash, and claims that both groups of rights, civil/political and economic/social/ cultural, involve claims on the state, citing the right to a fair trial as an example of a very expensive claim.[24] Nevertheless, he points out that inconsistencies do exist at the level of basic principles, between the right to life and capital punishment (in Article 6 of the ICCPR); between the right to privacy and the right to freedom of expression and information (Articles 17 and 19, ICCPR); between the right to freedom of movement and the right to work (Article 12, ICCPR and Article 6, ICESCR); and between the right to self-determination and the right to an adequate standard of living (Article 1, ICCPR and Article 11, ICESCR).[25]

Such diversity is the inevitable outcome of the need to encompass, if not reconcile, a variety of views on human rights reflecting different political philosophies and systems. However, the politicization of human rights has meant that this rich variety of rights has resolved itself into a crude polarity between civil/ political/individual rights and economic/social/collective rights. It is perhaps of less consequence to us today that 'the great political controversy between liberal democracy and communism is pursued under the rubric of human rights'.[26] But this controversy has also been joined by many Third World states, thereby perpetuating the problem of the manipulation of human rights as 'a weapon in competition between states and ideologies . . . a calculated arm in foreign policy'.[27]

The apparent conflict between the Third World and remaining socialist countries, most of whom emphasize the social and economic aspects of human rights and consider the aspirations of their peoples as realizable mainly through collective social and economic action, and the advanced Western nations which emphasize individual civil and political rights, has both an economic and a political source. In developing countries, faced with major prob- ms in transforming backward economies, economic and collec- e rights take priority over the rights of the individual and of freedom. Socialist countries generally concur with Marx's view that political rights and political equality, or 'bourgeois right', are the manifestation of social and economic inequality; this materialist philosophy interprets true rights as arising from state ownership of the means of production and the equal distribution of wealth.[28] Thus, as Alice Tay has observed, 'the socialist court of appeal, for much of the history of socialism, was the public welfare, or the needs of the working class, or the demands of the collective or of history'.[29]

Both North–South and East–West relations have been characterized by the tension between individualism and liberty on the one hand, and collectivism and equality on the other: civil and political rights compete with economic and social rights. The difference is that the East–West debate has taken place through established systems, between two varieties of 'have' countries, whereas the North–South disagreement is between 'haves' and 'have-nots'.[30] This neat development-determined compartmentalization, of course, has its inevitable fuzzy edges: for China, as part of the Third World and as one of the few remaining countries claiming to be socialist, falls into the categories of both East and South.

The obvious problem with such polarity is that 'one is offered bread or freedom but never both'.[31] Even if both are offered, they are not awarded equal status. At issue is the question of whether 'human rights begin with breakfast' or whether human rights begin with the right to request breakfast. The question is not just one of the precise sequence of the evolution of the different categories of human rights, but of the relationship between them. Both T. H. Marshall and R. P. Claude, for instance, claim that, in the case of developing states, the chronological stages exhibited in Western liberal democracies, of civil and political rights preceding economic and social rights, may be, and often are, reversed.[32] On the other hand, both C. B. Macpherson and Marshall warn of the dangers of the 'trade-off' which is often made by countries emphasizing one category of rights over another.[33] As R. J. Vincent observes, 'the assertion of a right to a decent standard of living presupposes a system in which having a right to anything means something, including the freedom to assert the right'.[34] Equally, it is clear that a basic minimum standard of living is required for freedom to be effective.[35] All arguments, in other words, including the familiar chicken and egg conundrum, point to the interdependence, rather than the mutual exclusiveness, of these two generations of rights.[36]

Whether or not this interdependence is accepted, it is important to acknowledge the areas of convergence, as well as the differences, in human rights thinking between liberal-democratic and socialist political systems. On the socialist side, areas of convergence include the at least nominal recognition of the notion of a citizen's civil and political rights. Before the transformation of the Soviet political system, it was significant that both the Soviet Union and China had incorporated into their constitutions support for the civil rights of freedom of speech, press, and association as well as for other 'negative' rights or rights of immunity. Although these rights will be shown to have been purely nominal ones, the fact that they were included could be interpreted as reflecting a basic belief in the universality of a core of human rights which, in Maurice Cranston's words, 'belong to a man simply because he is a man'.[37] David Lane, among others, has argued that the fact that Marx regarded human rights as emancipation of people in a social and economic sense did not imply the absence of rights under socialism in a legal and political sense — Marxism had a humanistic human rights tradition as well as an authoritarian one.[38] Istvan Kovacs has claimed that it was '*not the fundamental rights and liberties* which were attacked in the Communist Manifesto but their *bourgeois construction and practice*'.[39] The promise of the Paris Commune to unfold the natural abilities of French citizens was seen as having approached 'not only . . . the modern requirements of personality but also . . . a wider and richer list of fundamental rights'.[40] It thus came close to fulfilling the young Marx's concept of self-realization — the creation of a fully developed, unalienated, free, and conscious individual.

However — and here socialist ideas diverge from liberal-democratic assumptions — the socialist notion that there is no unhistorical human nature in general and no pre-social individual has challenged the notion of 'abstract human rights preceding social arrangements and capable of acting as courts of appeal against such arrangements'.[41] Natural rights, in the sense of rights raised above the state and its legal system, are rejected in socialist theory. Socialist theory claims that in capitalist systems, 'in reality there was never a question of "natural" or "human" rights but always of citizens' rights, rights which were established by the state, enforcing the will of the ruling class, determined in the last

analysis by a class-will embodied in the capitalist relations of production'.[42] Similarly, human rights in socialist systems are seen as
determined by the state and as having no autonomous existence.

Furthermore, while in a socialist society political (including civil)
rights are seen as a legitimate category of rights separate from
economic rights, they are also conceived as a function of the economic base, which in turn transmutes and modifies them. With
the socialization of the means of production, it has been claimed,
the character of production changed, as did the position of individuals in their relation to the means of production. The result
was a new kind of economic and social rights, and a change in
the political organization of society, which lent a new substance
to the citizens' political rights.[43] This claim of the transformation
of the nature of rights under socialism is similar to that of Chinese
analyses which state, for instance, that 'our country's socialist ownership of the means of production, distribution according to work,
system of people's congresses, socialist democracy and socialist
legal system, and so on, our economic, political, and legal systems, have brought our country new forms, new content and new
avenues for the guarantee of human rights'.[44]

The 'new substance' with its capacity for transformation, is the
socialization, and hence politicization, of all individual activity,
the effect of which has been significantly to transform the content
and purpose of the rights of free speech, assembly, association,
and collective bargaining. Thus, it has been argued:

it is ... clear that it does not belong to the content of the right of assembly and association under socialist conditions that the working masses,
the citizens of the socialist state, create organisations *against* the socialist state. The fact that the citizens of the socialist state form numerous
social, cultural and other associations, societies, and organisations and
that they make an extensive use of the right of assembly involves a
changed political meaning of these terms. These social and mass organisations, together with the trade unions and co-operatives are participating
to an increasing extent in the conduct of political, government affairs ...
These organizations are part of the self-administration of society which
will eventually replace the administration by government organs after
communist society will have been fully established.[45]

What is not acknowledged here, however, is the fact that this new
political function of social organizations, a necessary prerequisite
for the final dissolution of the state, would have been understood

by Marx as only feasible if established on the basis of a developed economic infrastructure. The imposition of such a burden of political responsibility on an impoverished and inadequately educated population would have been seen by him as encouraging total dependence on an educated vanguard of the proletariat, with the resulting development of a privileged stratum of society, and, as in fact occurred, the creation of gross inequalities between different sections of the people. Such was the dilemma which, among other causes, led to the final dissolution of the communist system in Eastern Europe and the former Soviet Union, and to the Chinese decision to return to a 'primary stage of socialism', based on some of the market practices of capitalism, and designed to build up the economic base.

As a result of this conception of the relationship between man and state, the rights of man, in the negative sense of freedom from the incursions of the state, although formally recognized by socialist governments, have until recently been effectively relocated in socialist theory away from the domestic arena of state–citizen relations to the international arena marked by the struggles of peoples against imperialism and colonialism and for self-determination. The increasing emphasis in the post-war world on individual human rights within the overall international community, and the increasing international activity in relation to human rights have, however, obliged socialist states to extend nominal recognition, at least in international forums, to the importance of individual civil and political rights.

Equally, Western liberal democracies have moved in post-war years to blur the dualism of civil/political and social/economic rights by extending their instrumentalities as welfare states to the protection of the individual's well-being. The concern has been not only to cushion the individual from the fall-out effects of the *laissez-faire* economy but, through a more egalitarian distribution of resources, to give 'social and economic content to the concept of equality'.[46] These socio-economic concerns have coincided with an extraordinary flowering within western nations of the consciousness of individual rights, with their extension to every type of minority group.[47] Thus the two traditions, of natural rights centred on the individual, and of group and community rights invoked by socialist and developing nations, are now brought together, if not reconciled, within western states.

This coincidence of two traditions, it must be emphasized, is not unique. As R. J. Vincent reminds us, these two traditions are both the product of western thought, reaching back to the enclosed notion of community in the Greek *polis* and the challenge by the Stoics who upheld the notion of the individual as independent moral agent. As the thinking of the Stoics underpinned the French and American Revolutions, so the writings of Burke and Hegel, Bentham and Marx, despite their differing political standpoints, drew from the original notion of the Greek community. In romantic German thought, the individual was not, however, rendered inconsequential. Individual freedom was the end product, rather than the precondition, of the historical process, to be achieved in the political community through the mechanism of the *Geist*, the cosmic spirit linking man and society. With Hegel and Marx, as in the Greek *polis*, man and citizen were reconciled.[48] Thus man's attachment to the community, as opposed to the individual liberties associated with eighteenth-century thinkers, became the basis on which Marxist economic and social rights, and group rights such as that to self-determination, were subsequently built.[49]

Despite these areas of convergence between North–South and East–West thinking on human rights, it must be acknowledged that the diversity of human rights and the differences in political culture and political philosophies between nation states pose a challenge to the notion of the universal nature of human rights and to the normative solidarity of the world community. And yet, it has been argued, it is precisely in the Third World that a 'global consciousness' must and can be moulded, because the Third World is 'the centre of the anticolonial and developmental process in which the two streams of individualistic and social human rights flowing from the first two worlds have met'.[50] A number of human rights thinkers and activists have grappled with this problem. The most effective effort to locate an area of common ground between the attitudes of Western liberal democracies and socialist and Third World states like China on the issue of human rights has been the attempt, initiated by Henry Shue and endorsed by Vincent and others, to establish a core of 'basic rights' which recognizes the priority of certain rights within the three generations of rights rather than, as some writers have done, allocating preference to any one set.[51]

Henry Shue has identified the guaranteed right to physical security and the guaranteed right to subsistence as 'inherent necessities' for the exercise of any other right.[52] The right to physical security is defined by him as a 'right that is basic not to be subjected to murder, torture, mayhem, rape, or assault'.[53] The right to subsistence, on the other hand, is the right to adequate food, clothing, shelter, and minimal preventive health care. The 'right to life' of the person, which is not to be confused with the complex issue of the right to life of the foetus, thus assumes significance as the basic right, since enjoyment of it, in the sense both of a right to security against violence and of a right to subsistence, is essential to the enjoyment of all other rights.[54] It is also a basic right in the sense that it represents 'everyone's minimum reasonable demands upon the rest of humanity'.[55] The 'right to life', which has 'as much to do with providing the wherewithal to keep people alive as with protecting them against violent death' asserts the equal value of civil/political and social/economic rights: it is both a positive right, requiring action by others and a negative right, requiring non-interference by others.[56]

Other writers have attempted to reduce the number of rights to a basic workable minimum. They include Fouad Ajami, who identifies four basic rights which will achieve 'maximum feasible consensus at this time': the right to survive; the right not to be subjected to torture; the condemnation of apartheid; and the right to food.[57] Another model, originally proposed by Yougindra Khushalani, invokes the same basic concept of the right to life as Shue and Vincent. By drawing a distinction between 'le droit à la vie' ('the right to life') and 'le droit de vivre' ('the right to live'), however, it seeks to conceptualize the difference between essential basic rights and the remainder of the rights contained within the International Bill of Rights.[58] As Olivier Veyrat has suggested, 'the right to life could appear as the lowest common denominator, the "right to live" as the highest'.[59]

According to this distinction, the right to life can be seen as a simple given, largely outside of the individual's control, of which the individual is sole beneficiary. It has been defined as involving the protection of the person and the related freedoms from want and from fear.[60] It thus can be understood to include not only the right to exist but also the right to freedom from torture and other physical violations of the person. The right to live, on the other hand, depends on a combination of factors for which the individual bears some responsibility, and which can benefit both the individual and collective. The right to live implies satisfactory conditions of life, geographical, socio-cultural, political, and economic, which favour the flourishing and dignity of the human being: specifically it presupposes the possibility of finding decent work, of enjoying a satisfactory diet, access to one's own culture, the right to a safe homeland which one can freely leave and return to, and the right to an adequate education and health care.[61] The right to live thus presupposes the basic rights and goes beyond them. Whatever its conceptual limitations, it allows for the progressive expansion of economic and social rights. Yougindra Khushalani has divided the right to live into three components: life rights; work rights; and social and political rights.[62]

The interesting point to note about Henry Shue's thesis of the inherent necessity of the guaranteed right to physical security and the guaranteed right to subsistence is that these rights may already be said to enjoy customary support. There are certain elementary rules which all societies do in fact endorse, and of these the 'right to life' is central.[63] As Hedley Bull has pointed out, 'there is not a natural right to security of the person, or to have one's property respected or to have contracts honoured, but because *a posteriori* we know these rights to enjoy something like universal support, it is possible for practical purposes to proceed as if they were natural rights'.[64] Equally, the right to subsistence is a basic assumption in traditional societies that are commonly regarded as backward and primitive.[65] Whether treated as 'natural' rights, or as customary law established by the practice of states, it is widely accepted that 'it is now a violation of international law for any state to practise or condone genocide, slavery or slave trade, killing or causing the disappearance of persons, torture, prolonged arbitrary detention, comprehensive and systematic racial discrimination, and perhaps other consistent patterns of gross violations of internationally recognised rights'.[66] Equally, there is a general recognition of the moral obligation on the part of governments to assist their poorer citizens, and an acceptance of the duty of developed states to extend material assistance and aid to developing states, particularly in times of natural disasters.

In other words, there is already customary universal acceptance of the priority of 'the right to life' and its associated civil rights of freedom from torture and other threats to life. Where the initiators of the notion of 'basic rights' have made a conceptual contribution to Western thinking about rights is in their claim that within the 'right to life', the right to subsistence deserves an equal place to the civil rights of immunity of the person, and in their plea for universal acceptance of the notion that 'a death from hunger or thirst is not preferable to a death under bombing or torture'.[67] It is within this dual character of the right to life that the main contradiction between Western and socialist/Third World notions of rights is played out. And the challenge facing those seeking universal consensus on human rights in the next decade is to obtain from North, South, East, and West the acknowledgement that these two different aspects of the right to life are but two sides of a single coin.

In maintaining the priority of 'basic rights', it should not be supposed that with their realization all endeavour should cease. On the contrary, as Khushalani has shown, to emphasize a lowest common denominator of rights is to simultaneously assert that the other rights are already in the process of realization or will continue as programmatic rights. For in the case of most countries many rights still remain aspirations, and it is precisely changes in social, economic, and political contexts which enable aspirations to be realized. Thus, the increase in affluence of a particular state may allow it to progress from the ideologically neutral or 'core' rights to such peripheral rights as that of 'periodic holidays with pay'.[68] Likewise, it could be argued that the moves in the last decade in China to modernize and develop the economy, which have led to calls from within China, arguably inappropriate at an earlier stage, to match modernization of its economy with greater freedom of thought and political self-expression, represent a similar extension of programmatic rights. So Chinese dissident Xu Wenli argued as early as 1980 that 'it is impossible to modernize the country unless you let the intelligence of a thousand million individuals unfold'.[69] So former Premier Zhao Ziyang conceded at the Thirteenth Party Congress in October 1987:

We can never go back to the closed society of the past, when people were forbidden contact with ideological trends of different sorts . . . The process of reform and opening to the outside world liberates people's thinking to an extraordinary degree, and that is a good thing and a natural historical phenomenon.[70]

There is, however, one fault with this line of reasoning — currently, the freedoms of thought and expression in China are inextricably linked with the right to physical security. As Xu Wenli again pointed out, 'the problem of freedom of thought is more serious than physical attacks on people'. Despite the preparedness of political dissidents in China to make this heroic choice, it is clear that the physical implications of exercising freedoms of thought and expression in China mean that the latter freedoms do not fall simply into the category of 'programmatic' rights. Rather, they form part of the core right to life. The deliberate exercise of the rights of freedom of expression by Chinese dissenters should also be seen for what it ultimately becomes — an effort to extend the meaning of the basic right to life, from its original Chinese interpretation as a 'subsistence' right, as the economic right not to starve, to its cognate meaning, the civil right to enjoy physical security.

Problems of Jurisdiction and Enforcement

The aim of identifying a basic core of rights is first to locate areas of convergence between human rights thinking in states based on different political philosophies and secondly, in view of the conflict between the various rights, to establish a 'short list' of rights from the International Covenant of Civil and Political Rights and from the International Covenant of Economic, Social, and Cultural Rights, whose universality and validity are already indisputably determined, both in custom and law. These basic and undisputed rights may then be legitimately used by the international community, and by human rights analysts, to monitor the human rights conditions within a sovereign state in any part of the globe. It is at this point that the second set of problems arises.

The problem of the jurisdiction and enforcement of human rights may be said to lie in their abstract and supranational character. It has been claimed that 'the revolutionary contribution to international law by the human rights doctrine has been a recognition that the treatment of individuals within a state is a matter of international concern'.[71] Human rights are thus seen as providing a lifebelt between the international community and the individual which by implication bypass the authority of the state. However, in opposition to this notion of supranational authority is the principle of self-determination, itself related to the notion of cultural relativism.

The argument of cultural relativism or cultural pluralism has already been alluded to. It is based on the assumption that each culture is a discrete and self-contained entity which does and should remain isolated from supranational mores and international influences.[72] The notion of cultural relativism has been accepted by some human rights analysts because of its explanatory power, since it involves a recognition not just of the cultural relativity of Third World attitudes, but also of the relativity of Western approaches to human rights.[73] But it is important here, as Vincent argues, to distinguish explanation and description from prescription, or the 'is' from the 'ought'. 'Practical anthropology' should not be confused with 'morals': statements about how people should behave should not be equated with statements about how they do behave.[74] To uphold cultural relativism is to contend that every culture is equally valid and that no external values should contaminate it. The first case is fallacious, the second morally reprehensible, as well as demonstrably untrue. Apart from the moral objection that it smacks of cultural discrimination, racism, and intellectual apartheid, such an argument flies in the face of the existence of supranational bodies and value systems which are generally endorsed. In fact, what has happened in the realm of human rights values is that over time different cultures have both expanded and exerted mutual influence on each other. In other words, 'the emergence of the new states, and the associated revival of suppressed cultures, has not in fact meant the jettisoning of Western doctrine. What it has meant is, in part, the use of Western principles against their authors, and in part the accommodation of a Western tradition to these new arrivals'.[75]

Yet at the same time as one rejects the doctrine of cultural relativism as an argument against the acceptance of an international standard of norms, one must accept its uses as a behavioural explanation for the analysis both of Western and non-Western approaches to human rights. Thus, on the one hand, the universal acceptance of certain 'basic rights' norms proclaims a state's membership of the international community and the universality of a basic morality: on the other hand, the same nation's practice in respect of human rights cannot be fully understood except with reference to its cultural character. Thus, for instance, one may examine the way in which China's understanding of rights, and particularly civil rights, has presented an obstacle to its adjustment to international norms.[76]

This practice of mutual adaptation and evolution of ideas has affected the principle of self-determination, initially a Western principle encapsulated in the first article of both International

Covenants. These announce that all peoples have the right to self-determination, whereby they may 'freely determine their political status and freely pursue their economic, social and cultural development', and that the remaining colonial countries should promote its realization. This principle was first invoked by Third World states as the means to liberation from colonialism, then as the source of freedom from racial oppression. Finally it became the basis for the contemporary assertion of the primacy of economic and social rights, which are also seen as collective rights and are associated with the right to development.

The problem, already touched upon, is that the doctrine of self-determination has been narrowly interpreted by states in accordance with its 'external' rather than its 'internal' implications. Its meaning as the right of peoples within states to choose their form of government has been neglected. The paradoxical consequence is that the principle of self-determination, which originated in an effort to protect the rights of peoples, has been used to undermine precisely those rights in the case of states such as China containing significant minority populations. Yet international lawyers argue that the right of 'peoples' to self-determination should not be conflated with the right of governments.[77] The use of the principle of self-determination to justify the 'statist' argument against the international jurisdiction of human rights law, in fact, is open to the same criticism as cultural relativism, of which it is an outgrowth. Thus,

States' fears of secession and governments' fears of revolution have combined to restrict the right to self-determination to little more than a right to sovereignty for those states (and colonies) that currently exist. Given that the right to self-determination emerged as part of the struggle against Western imperialism, this is not surprising, but . . . linking human rights with the rights of states is extremely dangerous.[78]

The implication of such linkage is that 'self-determination, considered as the right to non-intervention, means the right that foreign states shall not interfere in the life of the community against the will of the government'.[79] This view of self-determination is implicit in the socialist concept of the primordial role of the state. The state is seen as the embodiment of the interests of the proletariat and as such the citizen cannot have interests that conflict with it. The sovereign state can admit of no tension between sovereignty and human rights and cannot embrace the cause of human rights to the point where foreign interference may threaten its sovereignty. Apart from invoking the principle of self-determination, socialist and Third World countries like China cite as authority for their statist position Article 2 (7) of the UN Charter which forbids interference in matters 'which are essentially within the domestic jurisdiction of any state'.[80] Nevertheless, the paradox remains that one of China's principal arguments against the right of the international community to monitor its human rights, the principle of self-determination, was originally aimed at protecting the rights of peoples such as Tibetan and Muslim minorities.

This assertion of ultimate state responsibility for the implementation of human rights obviously conflicts with the general principle accepted by UN members that cases characterized by 'a consistent pattern of gross violations of human rights' should be lifted from the area of domestic jurisdiction to the international arena. As Henkin has observed, 'such violations surely are not a matter of domestic jurisdiction. Whether an alleged infringement is such a violation is a question of international law, not one for an accused state to determine finally'.[81] Furthermore, 'if human rights were always a matter of domestic jurisdiction and never a proper subject of external attention in any form, provisions of the UN Charter, the Universal Declaration of Human Rights, the various international covenants and conventions, and countless activities, resolutions, and actions of the United Nations and other international bodies would be *ultra vires*'.[82] The difficulty, of course, for states like China which have insisted that human rights are primarily a matter for domestic jurisdiction, is to distinguish between those cases deserving international attention and those which do not.[83]

On the other hand, in matters of jurisdiction and enforcement, there is one obvious and crucial sticking point: the international human rights movement has not basically changed the international system as a system of states, lacking any central authority, with each state responsible for its own affairs and citizens.[84] In other words, apart from its effect in challenging the ingrained assumption of the state as the carrier of values and as ultimate source of authority, the new transnational concern with the rights of the individual is not bolstered by the existence of any independent enforcement agency. Since rights, unlike domestic laws, are not enforced on the state by any legal agency, their actual enforcement is thus ultimately dependent on the political will of the state. Although in principle the remedies for a violation of international human rights obligations are the same as for violations of other international obligations, in practice, with notable exceptions, 'states have been reluctant to expend political capital and good will and jeopardize friendly relations to vindicate the human rights of nationals of other countries against their own governments'.[85]

In considering the question of China's international obligations in respect of its human rights practice, one must take into account both the formal legal position and the customary response. As noted, the international law of human rights is contained essentially in the two international covenants, which together legislate what the Universal Declaration declared. In the International Covenant on Civil and Political Rights, each state undertakes 'to respect and ensure to all individuals within its territory and subject to its jurisdiction the rights recognized in the present Covenant'.[86] In the Covenant on Economic, Social, and Cultural Rights each state undertakes to 'take steps . . . to the maximum of its available resources, with a view to achieving progressively the full realization' of designated rights.[87] B. G. Ramcharan has suggested the following legal propositions:

(a) the human rights provisions of the Charter represent binding legal obligations for all states;

(b) some parts of the Universal Declaration and the International Covenants represent international customary law, and thus are binding on all states;

(c) in all other respects the International Covenants (which China has not yet signed or ratified) are legally binding only on states that have ratified or acceded to them; for these states they give rise to State Responsibility; and

(d) in addition, the International Covenants and the Universal Declaration represent 'minimal standards of conduct for all peoples and all nations', thereby leading to 'the expression of views which might not necessarily give rise to questions of responsibility'.[88]

States have been willing to accept these high international standards: about half the states in the world are parties to the International Covenants and virtually all the rest have either signed and not ratified (in particular, the United States), or otherwise expressed acceptance of or commitment to their norms. Those same states who have signed or ratified have, as already suggested, been less willing to allow international scrutiny of their compliance with, or implementation of, these standards. The UN Charter did not appear to anticipate the necessity of sanctions against the violators of the covenants. Under the International Covenant on Civil and Political Rights, all state parties are required to report to a Human Rights Committee. The deliberations of this Committee are marked by a shifting debate between those who wish to use these reports to monitor the human rights conditions of states and those who believe that such scrutiny does not fall within the Committee's terms of reference.[89] The Committee, moreover, is not entitled to make specific changes to findings and can only make 'general comments'.

Under the International Covenant on Economic, Social, and Cultural Rights, states are required to report on their compliance through the UN Economic and Social Council to the UN Commission on Human Rights 'for study and general recommendation'. Since 1986, a Committee on Economic, Social, and Cultural Rights has existed in parallel to the Human Rights Committee. Apart from these two bodies, the UN Commission on Human Rights, established in 1946, has been active in setting human rights standards and promoting human rights norms, and has been granted limited monitoring powers.[90] These enable it to investigate complaints that 'appear to reveal a consistent pattern of gross and reliably attested violations of human rights'. However, under this charter particular violations cannot be covered; and its promotional capacity exceeds its monitoring powers. Added to these constraints are the recent changes to the power balance within the Commission, which have undermined its capacity for action.

As well as the two International Covenants and the two Optional Protocols, particular conventions such as those on issues of racial discrimination, torture, and women's rights, have provided additional enforcement mechanisms. Yet even ratification of these international instruments has not been an infallible guide to a country's commitment to human rights: for the absence of any likelihood of enforcement has made it feasible for some governments to ratify agreements they cannot keep, while other governments which are more committed to human rights are prevented from becoming parties to conventions by the theoretical possibility of enforcement.[91] As a result, the general conclusion has been that 'despite the accumulation of declarations, resolutions, rules, standards, and guidelines within the framework of the United Nations, the abiding weakness is that of implementation, and at the same time politics may cut across the functions of promotion of human rights cast upon the Economic and Social Council and the Human Rights Commission by the Charter'.[92]

No better illustration could be found of the pessimistic outlook for the UN effort to balance its dual functions of protecting human rights and upholding state sovereignty than its attempt to broker a peace settlement in Cambodia that includes Pol Pot, the Khmer Rouge leader.[93] However, if international enforcement has been less effective on the global stage, it has brought notable success at a regional level, in the European human rights system which has a more effective system of remedies, in the American human rights system, and the African system.[94] Moreover, for 'single issue' human rights such as workers' rights, which include important civil rights issues such as the right of association, the right to organize and bargain collectively, the right to equality of remuneration, the issue of forced labour and some social rights, the International Labour Organization and its Committee of Experts have been highly successful.[95] For less specific human rights issues, however, it is clear that the most important guarantees of human rights remain national commitment, cultural community, and the dominant national ideology.[96] Despite these imposing constraints, the crucial fact remains that:

No one now objects to the category 'human rights' on the ground that the level of actual protection of those rights in many countries remains problematic, that the machinery for their protection remains embryonic, or that there are still important areas of uncertainty about the content and application of those rights. These things may be true, but they are taken either as reasons for improving the articulation and enforcement of international human rights standards, or at least as inevitable concomitants, in a diverse, disorganised, and disorderly international community, of recognising human rights at all.[97]

The above discussion has centred on some of the main issues and difficulties involved in the problem of human rights. It suggests that 'international human rights', or human rights as a subject of international law and politics, are distinct from individual rights under national legal systems. The distinction has been clearly drawn:

the international movement accepts human rights as rights that, according to agreed-upon moral principles, the individual should enjoy under the constitutional–legal system of his or her society. But national protections for accepted human rights are often deficient; international human rights were designed to remedy those deficiencies . . . The international law of human rights is implemented largely by national law and institutions; it is satisfied when national laws and institutions are sufficient.[98]

This distinction raises the final issue for discussion: how, given the lack of necessary correlation between these laws, can one properly analyse the condition of human rights in a given country? Already a comparative framework seems necessary. But to fully explore the dynamic relationship between international standards and the realization of those same standards at the domestic level, a third dimension is implicit, that of the actual implementation of these rights, of their substantive reality within each society.

Strouse and Claude have observed that, 'although the human aspirations underlying various rights may reflect perennial high goals, and although human rights depend on formal legal and institutional endorsement, modern social scientists must inquire into the underlying social forces generating human rights development'.[99] Human rights should not be conceived 'as little more than the documentary results of enlightened processes'.[100] Human rights exist as abstract principles but also as empirically verifiable facts, reflected in the actual exercise of these rights by individuals as the subject of these rights. In any society there is a distance between the theory of its human rights policy encapsulated in its constitutions, bills of rights, legislation, and formal institutions, and the reality of its practice. Whether conceptualized as the difference between legal and empirical (or substantive) rights, between the 'instrumentation' of rights and compliance in honouring them, between the 'theory' and practice of rights, between *de jure* rights and *de facto* rights, or between formal and informal rights, the existence of this gap must be acknowledged and defined.[101] In China's case the most appropriate distinction, for reasons which will become clear, is between formal and informal civil/political rights and between formal and substantive economic/social/cultural rights.

To move from a comparison of formulated standards of human rights in the different legal instruments and in formal domestic structures and institutions to their informal practice is to leave the rocky terrain of international law for the even less certain environment of the social sciences. The need for a greater inter-penetration of these different disciplines in research on human rights has already been the subject of some discussion.[102] It is clear that analysis of the triangular relationship between formal rights at an international and national level and informal rights facilit-ates the understanding of the human rights situation in any given country: it also complicates the process. Yet both the common methods, of comparing international legal norms with national provisions, or of applying an international model of human rights directly to a country's actual situation of rights, appear incom-plete. Any methodology should accurately reflect the dynamic relationship between international norms, national norms and institutions, and empirical reality. Consequently, the most useful methodology should involve a comparison between international standards of human rights and national norms, most accurately reflected in a state's constitution and laws. This should be accom-panied by a second step, an examination of the relationship between the constitutionally guaranteed and legally supported rights, the formal enabling institutions, and changing informal reality.[103]

Such is the approach which has been adopted in this analysis of human rights in China, an approach which also exploits the potential of human rights to serve as an instrument to monitor the changing political, social, and economic conditions of the nation state. It thus facilitates, *inter alia*, an understanding of some of the tensions which led to the 1989 Democracy Movement in China.

It must be observed that this approach, although using China's constitutions as a central point of reference, does not ignore the limits of constitutionalism in China. Yash Ghai's findings on the limits of constitutionalism and the rule of law in Africa are also applicable to China.[104] Ghai points out that in Third World coun-tries the burden placed on the constitution in creating political order, providing for equitable development, promoting national unity and loyalties, and protecting national minorities and safe-guarding human rights, has been much heavier than in the West. On the other hand, the objective social and economic conditions of these countries make it difficult to establish a social order on the basis of general rules. The circumstances in which the state arose make it a central force in the process of accumulation and reproduction, and the nature of that accumulation reinforces the authoritarian nature of the state, leading to corruption and repression. Moreover, the ideological function of constitutions is less important than in the West, and other competing ideologies — developmentalism, religion, or racism — antithetic to democratic practices, are invoked as legitimation. In addition, in China, the Marxist view of law as part of the superstructure determined by the economic base serves to undermine the importance of the constitution.

However, if constitutions are acknowledged to be frail vessels, they are nonetheless the best available guides to a state's social and political norms and institutions. In China, which has had four state constitutions since 1949, each promulgated in a distinctive social and political policy environment, constitutions tend to be more like political programmes. But precisely because socialist constitutions like China's are more sensitive to a government's will, they act as guides to the state's prevailing values and intentions, against which the current political and social condition can be measured.

Secondly, it should be emphasized that the analysis of the relationship between constitutions and informal reality does not assume a fixed causal link between the nature of that relationship and the fact of social and political unrest. The main pressures for political and social disaffection come from disturbances deep within the society: but radical divergence of constitutional guarantees of rights from the reality of their exercise in society is at the very least a barometer of those tensions.

Finally, the focus on China's constitutions should not suggest that constitutions are the only source of legally guaranteed rights. Just as in China the state has the power to expand rights by law so, it shall be seen, the state has the power to limit constitutional rights by law. Thus any analysis of China's formal human rights conditions must also take into account both existing laws and regulations and the formal structures and institutions which facilitate the exercise of these rights. As the constitutions themselves point out, Chinese constitutions remain the primary source and inspiration of legally guaranteed rights in the People's Republic. However, as William Safran has observed: 'A constitutional civil rights provision is often an emptying vessel if left unattended, that is, if not associated with an appropriate statute law.'[105]

At the same time as one gives recognition to formal provisions and structures, however, it is essential to acknowledge the significant role of the informal, particularly in China's case, in determining the degree of liberalization within the society. In an authoritarian state like China, where constitutional provisions are open to the Party's rights of interpretation, where the judiciary enjoys nominal but not actual independence, where the general public is acutely sensitive and responsive to the least shift in elite political attitudes, where the character and preferences of the leader of a work unit are major determinants of the degree to which new policies are enforced in the workplace, where the work-force itself has no direct means of communicating its reactions, but many indirect means, the gap between formal provisions and structures and informal behaviour and responses is both wide and significant. To properly reflect the dynamic nature of China's human rights, therefore, these three dimensions, the formal international norms, the formal national norms and structures, and the informal or substantive reality, must be given due and equal weight.

2 Human Rights from Imperial to Communist China

Slowly, quietly, but unmistakably, the Chinese renaissance is becoming a reality. The product of this rebirth looks suspiciously occidental. But, scratch its surface and you will find the stuff of which it is made is essentially Chinese.

Hu Shi, *The Chinese Renaissance*

The previous chapter identified a core of internationally endorsed rights which must be the basis for an objective analysis of human rights in China. The right to life, it was argued, is both a civil and an economic right, which transcends political cultures and state boundaries. At the same time, one must simultaneously acknowledge the nature of the differences in outlook and culture which give rise to different human rights approaches and which provide an explanation for the human rights practices and priorities in different states. To recapitulate, if one were to characterize the main differences between human rights philosophies and systems in the West and in China, it would be that the former emphasizes the universal and abstract nature of the individual's civil and political rights, with social rights as secondary, concrete, non-universal and contingent, and that the latter emphasizes social and economic rights, but views all rights as collectively based, concrete, non-universal, and subordinate to state sovereignty.

Looking more closely at China's concept of civil and political rights, it can be seen to assume a different relationship between the citizen, the state, and the law, from that which pertains in the West. Thus, while in the West the legal system, through the individual's invocation of his civil rights, intercedes between the sovereign individual and the state, claiming for the individual rights of immunity, as well as of political participation and welfare consumption, in China the legal system, to the extent that it is invoked, intervenes on behalf of the collective interest of all individuals, vested in the sovereignty of the state.

Not only is the relationship between individual, state, society, and the law very different in the two political systems, but each concept is separately defined. In China, traditional concepts of the individual, the state, and the law have reinforced Marxist concepts. The view of society as an organic whole whose collective rights prevail over the individual, the idea that man exists for the state rather than vice versa and that rights, rather than having any absolute value, derive from the state, have been themes prevailing in old as well as new China. According to the Confucian precepts of traditional China, society was seen as the source of essential unity and harmony, within which the individual was subsumed. The concept of the individual was not absent: but it was of an order of importance secondary to a family-based community system which differentiated between roles and abilities.[1] A harmonious hierarchical order consisted of an order of social relations in which the ruler related to his kingdom as a kind of extended *pater familias*; the relationship between father and son, marked by filial piety (*xiao*) was paralleled by the relationship between ruler and subject, marked by loyalty (*zhong*). Government was seen as the necessary instrument of this social order, although in an ideal society it was never egregious. Similarly, the individual was a cog in the machine of social harmony, contributing through his own moral self-cultivation to the social betterment.

The individual's rights and duties were conditional on their contribution to the good of society: ideally, the individual's good was seen as coterminous with society's good, and his interests with those of society. There was not the separation characteristic in Western societies between the moral and religious and the social and political spheres of life, although, as will be suggested, there was a separation between the formal and informal system of ideas and lifestyles. The atomization of society in the West is the product of a long and complex history of state–church conflict, the rise of the bourgeoisie, the decline of monarchical absolutism, the development of parliamentary politics and, finally, the extension of civil and political rights to the lower classes after the Industrial Revolution.

Such pressures leading to individualism had no equivalent in China. The adversarial Western tradition of the individual wresting concessions from an absolutist state was replaced in Chinese tradition by the kinship family, the basic social, economic, and *de facto* political unit sheltering the individual from the intrusions of the imperial state. For although a despotic state, traditional Chinese government allowed 'zones of indifference', personal spaces between the reach of the state and the grass-roots community.[2] Because of this group framework, any emphasis on the compartmentalized individual as the subject of separate rights would be seen as potentially destructive of social harmony. Harmony could only be encouraged by a socially responsible adjustment of personal needs and claims to the needs of others, achieving through mediation and conciliation and the readiness to yield (*rang*) the socially oriented compromise which could never be reached through hostile confrontation.

The principle on which this social order was based was propriety (*li*), norms of conduct governing the relations between men and women in their social roles, or rather, 'the relations of persons acting according to norms prescribed by social roles'.[3] *Li* was associated with moral rather than physical force and provided rules internalized by the gentleman (*junzi*) through education. This education came both through example, with the ideal government providing the model of proper behaviour, and precept, through education by the government. Thus the ruling elite was ideally both a source of education for this moral force and its basis.[4] The *li* were thus not positive laws; as 'more or less tacit models of exemplary conduct' they were not universalistic or abstract, but related to concrete situations.[5] They were at once the expression and the underpinning of a traditional social context of community and shared norms.

It is from this notion of *li* that some idea of the give and take between the state and the individual may be inferred. Although it was the source of social order, Wang Gungwu has argued that *li* involved the extension of a qualified idea of 'rights' to the subjects. In fact, the word for rights, *quan*, which also means power, was the sole prerogative of the ruler.[6] Nevertheless, while it was the duty of the subjects to show loyalty to the ruler, that duty was understood to be dependent on the ruler treating his subjects with propriety, which included a sense of enabling them to maintain their livelihood. Unlike the Western notion of equal rights, however, these duties and implicit rights were seen as obtaining between unequals. Hence, embedded in the very concept of reciprocity was the idea that the shares of both duties and rights were necessarily unequal.[7] Moreover, the notion of reciprocity in *li* did not entail the Western sense of insisting on one's rights.[8] It was not explicit since it sought not to legislate for specific circumstances but to provide an attitudinal framework that would facilitate concessions in the event of any type of conflict of interest. The implications for rights of such an approach are self-evident, as Alice Tay and Eugene Kamenka observe:

A social ethic oriented towards mediation and compromise, towards recognising the extent to which another's emotions and dignity are involved
in his claim, rather than towards the abstract question of the justice of
his claim, is likely to avoid any clear, uncompromising definition of rights
or claims *ab initio*. Where Western legal procedures tend to deperson-
alise claims in order to bring out more sharply the question at issue,
Chinese tradition personalises all claims, seeing them in the context of
a social human relationship. It thus rejects the notion that a sharp legal
distinction or a formal legal pronouncement can by itself resolve the dis-
pute between the parties by re-establishing harmony and mutual respect
and treats justice as above all a form of fireside equity.[9]

At the same time, the *li* were not merely self-regulating principles: they were supported even in pre-Qin times by the household registration system, which was necessary not only for the
extraction of taxes, levies, and *corvée*, but also for the ordering,
surveillance, and detailing of hierarchical systems of power relations.[10] This system, which also had the effect of binding the
peasant to the land, later developed into the intricate network of
mutual surveillance and controls within the kinship family known
as the *baojia* system. Despite these structural controls, which
reached down to the lowest level of sub-administration, events
and human beings often fell short of the ideal social order regulated by *li*. To obtain order in all circumstances where *li* was
powerless to prevail, penal law or *fa* was invoked in criminal cases
to induce fear of punishment. The Confucian acknowledgement
that *fa* was a necessary, if regrettable, device compensating for
the weakness of human nature was later subsumed and developed
by a school of *fa*, or Legalists, who believed not only that social
order could only be maintained by *fa*, but that through reliance
on *fa* the ruler could use his subjects to expand the power and
scope of the state. The meaning of *fa* was thus extended from
penal law to bureaucratic law, encompassing the rationalization
of the social order.[11]

A dynasty based on the principles of *fa*, the Qin dynasty, which
united China in the third century BC into a centralized bureaucratic empire, established the basic principles later understood to
be associated with the rule of law (*fazhi*). These were an assumption of the sanction of force, the external rather than internal
reform of men based on reward and punishment and the neglect
of *li*.[12] By the end of the Qin, numerous aspects of social life were
regulated by these written laws, which had the defining qualities

of bureaucratic law: they were both positive and public.[13] Such laws were necessitated by the disintegration of community resulting from the breakdown of the feudal system; the dissolution of the traditonal system of ranks was paralleled by the destruction of the common value system.[14] The *fa* were also policy dependent. They were as general or as particular as policy objectives required, and lacked any distinction between administrative commands and legal rules. There was no concept of separation between the functions of policing and of the administration of justice.[15]

In later years, under Confucian influence, law in imperial China developed as an amalgamation of Legalism and Confucianism. Confucian influence controlled and inhibited the expansion of the ambit of *fa* and encouraged the resort to custom in civil law disputes. Thus, the harshness of the law was mitigated. On the other hand, the egalitarian insistence of the Legalists that all men should conform to a single law whatever their status was modified by the Confucians to take legal cognizance of status, and a graded unequal society was matched by a graded, unequal law.[16] Furthermore, it ensured the establishment of a social tradition in which the rule of law and litigation had socially pejorative connotations. A clear picture of the relationship between the *Gemeinschaft* (community) normative social order, emphasizing mediation, conciliation, social harmony, and hierarchical relationships, and the function of law is obtained from Michael Dutton's detailed examination of the *baojia* system:

The *baojia* system inserted itself between family and society and designated the appropriate way of organising family order. It thus established anti-social behaviour as anti-familial. A crime by a family member not only broke the law of the land but also threatened the power of the family. If it were a serious crime and was not rectified by family action, it proved that the family itself was unable to 'order its household' and was, therefore, in need of state intervention. A crime thus constituted a threat not only to law, the state and the emperor but also to the family order. It took away from the household the right to govern its own affairs. A magistrate adjudicating a case, while empowered to do so by the state was, by that intervention in family affairs, disempowering the family head and taking over his role. The criminal paid then, not only for the crime committed but also for their crime against the family order — that is, the crime of forcing the state to intervene and, in so doing, to disempower the family. Thus, the crime was doubled and the punishment was harsh.[17]

Law was thus used as an instrument to control crime and contained no concept of protecting the rights and interests of the subjects.[18] In any case, the individual was not thought of as an independent entity, but as the member of a group. Consequently, attempts by some China scholars to link *ren* ('humanity') and *yi* ('justice'), the humanist ethics of traditional China, with the notion of 'human rights as founded in the well-being of the people as individual moral beings' involve a qualitative logical leap from the collective notion of 'well-being of the people', which they represent, to the notion of the quintessential value of the individual, which they do not.[19] The only channel for seeking individual protection was the customary right of people to address letters of appeal to officials calling for justice or appealing for clemency.

In cases of extreme and intolerable abuse of power by the ruler, however, two other mechanisms could be invoked to protect the people. Political power was normally restrained under the Confucian order by a panoply of customs, rites to be observed, rules and procedures. When despotic rulers waived these norms, the literati had a duty to criticize their excesses, even at the risk of their lives.[20] In an extreme situation, a successful rebellion was the sign that the emperor had lost the mandate of Heaven, which was often then transferred to the leader of the rebellion. But this form of governance, whether benevolent or tyrannical, rested on a system of ethics and on custom, rather than on a system of formal, legal safeguards: it was a rule of man (*renzhi*), not a rule of law (*fazhi*).[21]

In normal times, however, stability was ensured, not just by the quasi-customary law of *li*, by the grass-roots *baojia* system, by the fine mesh of bureaucratic controls, and by the integrating force of the kinship family, but by the existence of the 'subsistence rights' which Henry Shue and others have identified as typical of traditional societies. 'Village egalitarianism', which James Scott has described as 'conservative, not radical', and as claiming that 'all should have a place, a living, not that all should be equal', had the function of 'informal social control'.[22] Similarly, Benedict Kerkvliet has characterized the 'strong patron–client relationship' of traditional Asian societies as 'a kind of all-encompassing insurance policy whose coverage, although not total and infinitely reliable, was as comprehensive as a poor family could get'.[23]

In China, the ruling elite of emperor, officials, and gentry maintained the tradition of ensuring a basic subsistence level for the common people. The gentry maintained emergency grain stores, while merchants and craftsmen ensured employment, training, and injury compensation to those working within their trade and craft monopolies.[24] Gentry and officials combined to plan and finance the building of roads, bridges, and irrigation and water conservation systems. These public works were, of course, undertaken by the peasants themselves; and the peasants' surplus labour was extracted for the benefit of the elites.[25] Nevertheless, within this unequal, clientelist relationship marked by paternalistic benevolence, the lower socio-economic orders were given basic means of subsistence which served to maintain social and political stability during normal times. The traditional association in Chinese minds between the occurence of natural disasters and the end of a dynasty was undoubtedly partly related to the deleterious impact which such events had on the elite's ability to sustain these subsistence rights.

The roots of Chinese political culture are not thoroughly addressed without reference to the 'two cultures' of China identified by Lucian Pye. Pye discusses the polarity in Chinese culture between, on the one hand, an emphasis on conformity, repressive centralized controls, and orthodox beliefs and, on the other, a greater tolerance for private initiatives, for decentralization, and a liberation from orthodoxy. This dual condition was best exemplified in traditional China by the contrast between 'an elitist high Confucian culture that glorified the established authority of the better educated and rationalized their claims of superiority on the basis of possessing specialized wisdom, and a passionate, populist heterodox culture that glorified the rebel and trusted magical formulas to transform economic and social reality'.[26] Both cultures, however divided, were united in the belief that the ruler had a divine or mystical dimension and both idealized harmony as a supreme value.[27]

Pye observes correctly that more historically significant than these similarities is the fact that these two cultures remained essentially separate and distinct. He is on less certain ground when he suggests a link between the traditional popular rebel culture and Maoism on the one hand, and between China's high political culture and Deng Xiaoping's pragmatism on the other.[28] The significance of the co-existence of these opposing traditions in China would appear to lie rather in the habit it established for tolerating the dualism of an official, formal sphere of existence

and thought, and an informal, more individualistic and free thinking reality. The space created between these two spheres to a
certain extent made up for the absence of formal legal and institutional structures separating the powers of government from the
rights of the citizen.

In turning to the modern period of Chinese history, the traditional notions of society, the state, the individual, and the law can
be seen to have exerted a powerful influence on the precise interpretation given by Chinese thinkers to the new ideas flooding into
China from the West. The three main periods of Chinese response
to the West — the Self-Strengthening Movement (1861–95), the
period between the Sino-Japanese war (1894–5) and the post-
Imperial era of the Republic, and the May 4 Movement (1919)
— saw the rapid influx of Western ideas of liberty, equality, constitutionalism, citizenship, the rule of law, the separation of
powers, and parliamentary government.[29] Kang Youwei and Liang
Qichao, two of the last literati opinion makers who sought to
influence the Qing emperor, advocated constitutional monarchy,
the separation of powers, and a concept of civil rights. Yet even
Liang's notion of citizens' rights did not correlate with the Western
notion of claims against the state: it assumed that the citizens'
pursuit of their own affairs would not clash with the general interest. Indeed, the rights of the individual were seen to add up to
the power of the state interest.[30]

In general, Chinese thinkers in this period sought consonance
between Western and Chinese ideas by drawing on minor strands
of Chinese thought which were then developed in accordance with
Chinese interpretations of the Western concepts. They also drew
from those strands of Western thought that were most in sympathy with Chinese ideas and most useful to the needs of the
Chinese state. In both cases, even when they were being used to
challenge the assumptions of Chinese tradition, Western ideas had
first to pass through a Chinese filter or 'mind set' whose chief reference point was the priority of the collective interests of society.
Thus, the source of both the development of the *minben* concept
in twentieth-century China and the interest in utilitarianism was
not the self-interested claims of individualism but the public good.
To adapt to the Western notion of citizens' rights, Chinese reformers separated out a minor strand of Confucian thought that
the people were the basis of the state (*min wei bang ben*) and
developed from it the idea of *minben sixiang* (the notion of

people-as-the-basis).[31] But again this new notion was interpreted not as a means of bolstering the interests of the individual against the state but as a way of enabling the individual to make a more effective contribution to strengthening the state.[32]

According to this newly developed tradition, people became the active instrument of state power rather than being passively compliant to it. The rights they enjoyed though were still best determined and channelled by the state. Chinese thinkers like Liang Qichao and Yan Fu, although working from different premises, transmuted the original purpose of Jeremy Bentham's utilitarianism, to justify the conduct of government in terms of its benefits to the people, into the Chinese version of justifying the benefits of the people to the state.[33] While Liang stressed the need for people to sacrifice their personal interests for the state, Yan saw the value of individual interests as a vehicle for achieving collective ends.[34] Even in the early 1920s when there were calls for individual rights, women's rights, political, and legal rights, it was recognized that the struggle to wrest stability and order from the troubled condition of corruption and military anarchy took precedence over the issue of rights and duties: 'finer issues of rights and duties would simply have to wait'.[35]

Even where claims of modernization required the open rejection of the assumptions of traditional thought, the new concepts were heavily overlaid with traditional nuances. Following the overthrow of the Qing government in 1911 and its replacement by a Republic, Sun Yat-sen introduced the Three People's Principles of National Consciousness, People's Rights, and People's Livelihood. By people's rights (minquan), Sun did not mean personal or civil liberties. The rights of the individual were not seen as autonomous, but as subordinated to the rights of the group he belonged to, be it scholar literati, merchant guild, or local organization; at the same time the individual could invoke the rights of his group.[36] Thus, by minquan Sun meant, as did other intellectuals of his generation, the political power due to the people, their part in determining the destiny of China.[37] Sun's three stage programme for China's political transformation had traditional authoritarian overtones. The first stage of military government to unite the country in preparation for democracy was to be followed by a period of 'tutelage' under the Kuomintang preparing the people for democracy; the final stage of constitutional government provided for the separation of powers and popular sovereignty.

In assessing the potential which Chinese political culture had for absorbing such individualistic concepts as democracy and civil rights, the difficulty facing China scholars has been that the forces for liberalism which flourished in the early twentieth century were 'without power in any real sense in a time when power was computed almost exclusively in terms of physical force'.[38] In the face of the great potential for disorder among China's huge population of peasants and workers, the political theories of Chinese intellectuals were subject to the persuasive language of military power. The debate before and after the establishment of the Republic in 1911 between revolutionaries and constitutionalists reflected the dilemma faced by intellectuals inspired by Western ideas of liberalism and democracy, and yet intimidated by the physical constraints imposed by the country's enormous, poor, and, for the most part, illiterate population. Because of the important input of power and circumstance into the eventual outcome of the failure of liberalism in China, it is difficult to judge the crucial question of whether yet another constraint existed, in the shape of a deeply rooted cultural resistance to individualistic liberal politics.[39] Supporters of constitutional government like Song Jiaoren and Zhang Shizhao reflected elite concern to ensure that executive strength was not eroded by representative control; they therefore chose as their model the English parliamentary system, whose strength, they believed, lay in the unity of parliament and cabinet.[40] These constitutionalists were not committed to the values of individual and personal liberty, but nevertheless sought a system in which the government was accountable to the people. Their ultimate weakness, however, lay in 'the fear that elite and national interests would suffer more from domestic strife than from dictatorial rule'.[41]

National and elite interests were not, however, simply forces of political restraint. They were also facilitators of change. The period of greatest Western influence on China followed the May 4 Movement of 1919, a basically anti-imperialist movement tripped off by a popular reaction against the capitulation of a corrupt Chinese government to Western powers at the Paris Peace Conference. Students attacked the government's preparedness to allow the transfer of German rights in Shandong province to Japan. This movement, with its calls for 'democracy and science', prepared the way for the erosion of the Confucian system and for the gradual influx into China of Western Marxist and liberal ideas.

It has thus been called 'the first ever "human rights movement" in Chinese history'.[42] The founding of the Chinese Communist Party (CCP) in 1921 was the beginning of a confrontation between two major Chinese parties, in effect representing different strands of Western thought, which only ended with the communist take-over in 1949. The main and obvious difference between the two parties was, of course, the effort by the Communist Party to combine the elite vertical control characteristic of Kuomintang rule with the horizontal mobilization of workers and peasants. But, once again it is important to note that, whether of Marxist or liberal persuasion, China's main political parties had important structural similarities: both were organized as revolutionary parties with authoritarian structures and based on political principles of democratic centralism.[43] Furthermore, both favoured small parties co-opted by the main party, discouraged the formation of interest groups, and controlled the press through legal and extra-legal means; they both maintained party control over the executive, and gave the executive, which was independent of the legislature, control over the judiciary. Most importantly, both regarded democracy as 'a means to national wealth and power rather than a method of public control of government'.[44] Finally, although both were committed to reversing the Confucian attitude towards the rule of law (*fazhi*), their notion of that rule was quite different from its Western counterpart. The rule of law was seen as essential to the development of a modern, industrializing, and bureaucratic state: but again, its chief function was not to meet the needs or protect the rights of the individual, but to increase the power of the state.

It was in response to the authoritarian one-party rule of the Kuomintang, and to the blatant disregard of human rights it entailed, that the first formal human rights movement in China was established in 1929. The leaders of the group, Hu Shi, Luo Longji, and Liang Shiqiu were all professors who had studied in the United States. The unification of the country under the Kuomintang in 1928 after a long period of fighting among warlords, and the establishment of a central government in Nanking was followed by the introduction of the system of 'political tutelage'. Despite a 1929 governmental decree that 'no individual or group shall by unlawful acts violate the person, freedom, or property of other individuals', the Nationalist government continued to protect its power through censorship, arbitrary arrests, and party interference with the judicial process.[45] In his article, 'Human

Rights and the Provisional Constitution', Hu Shi, China's leading liberal thinker, therefore argued that it was insufficient to prohibit 'individuals and groups' from violating the rights of man, if that prohibition were not also extended to the government and its agencies. Furthermore, there was no law to provide sanctions against the government when it infringed on civil rights.[46] To protect the citizen's rights Hu also argued for the promulgation of a constitution even during the period of tutelage,[47] and called for a bill of rights to guarantee the basic rights of human beings to life, liberty, and property.[48]

The main theorist of the Human Rights Movement, Luo Longji, was influenced by Jeremy Bentham, Thomas Paine, and Harold Laski. He believed that the function of the state was to protect human rights and that its purpose was to attain the greatest happiness of the greatest number. He rejected Hobbes' theory of rights as the satisfaction of desires because of its destructive implications; he did not accept Rousseau's theory of natural rights; and he rejected Bentham's idea that rights were dependent on law.[49] His conception of human rights was one of 'social functionalism' — rights had a meaning in that they had a direct impact on society.[50] Thus, as Terry Narramore points out, he was identifying with a tradition of English political thinking which went back to John Stuart Mill.[51]

On the basis of social utility, human rights were seen as a necessary precondition for social well-being, as well as a goal to be striven for in the common good.[52] In his essay, 'On Human Rights', Luo set out a list of thirty-five rights currently lacking in China which were 'necessary conditions of being human'.[53] They included the sovereignty of the people, the rule of law, equality before the law, equal applicability of the law, and the independence of the judiciary. He continually emphasized the accountability of government, of the armed services, and the bureaucracy to the people. The government had the responsibility to educate the people, and the people would progressively contribute their talents to the benefit of society: but they could only do this if they could enjoy the freedoms of thought, belief, speech, publication, and assembly. Above all, Luo laid stress on the welfare rights of traditional thought:

The function of the state is to protect human rights; and the most basic principle of human rights is to protect the people's lives. The means by which citizens maintain their lives is by exchanging labour power for clothing, food, and shelter. So the citizen has the right to work, and the state has the obligation to provide him with the opportunity to work. If the citizen is unemployed (*shiye*), that is proof that the state has failed in its duty. It is proof that the state has failed to assume its duty towards human rights . . . [A]ll aid for natural disasters which afflict the citizen is the state's human rights responsibility; it is not a matter of government charity towards its citizens. This kind of duty comes before all others, because the fundamental human right is life.[54]

The Human Rights Movement lasted only three years; it ended after the 18 September 1931 incident, when the Japanese invaded Manchuria, and the cause of patriotism became stronger than the call for freedom of speech. Its ideas, however, were taken up by others during the anti-Japanese war, and promoted as a powerful weapon to aid in the overthrow of the Japanese and the strengthening of the Chinese state.[55]

Over half a century later, Chinese communist scholars assessed the historical significance of the movement. It was seen as a basically bourgeois reform movement which, although critical of the Kuomintang, in its opposition to one-party rule and to violent revolution, sought to undermine communism in China.[56] Of particular concern to contemporary Chinese scholars were Hu Shi's ideas of 'peaceful revolution', or evolution, and his theory of the five evils, which identified the source of China's problems as poverty, disease, ignorance, corruption, and social disorder, rather than as feudalism.[57] From an objective, historical point of view, however, the Human Rights Movement was seen as having helped to expose the 'decadent and reactionary' nature of the Kuomintang, and to have mitigated to some extent the oppression of the people. Its particular strengths, within the context of Kuomintang rule, were seen as its insistence on the rule of law, its emphasis on equality before the law, and on the equal applicability of the law to administrators and the ordinary people; other strengths were its opposition to military rule, its insistence on a bureaucracy selected on the basis of talent, its opposition to the unification of thought and to the suppression of freedom of speech, and its support for popular supervision over the state.[58]

Despite the areas of congruence between the Kuomintang and the communists which the Human Rights Movement served to highlight, the year 1949 brought a qualitative change in official Chinese attitudes to human rights. The advent of a communist government to power brought a move away from the earlier official endorsement of 'human rights' as an explicit, if nominal, part of China's political agenda.[59] National goals were now articulated not in terms of human rights, which were identified with the civil or 'natural' rights advocated in Western liberal thought, but with Marxist goals of equal distribution and the socialist ownership of the means of production. As a socialist country, China now conformed with the view of other socialist and Third World countries which emphasized the social and economic aspects of 'human rights' and considered the aspirations of their people as realizable mainly through collective social and economic action. The basic content of economic and social rights was encompassed in Marxist theory in the form of the more equal distribution of resources and the guarantee of the right to work through which citizens had access to social welfare and social security, as well as of the universal right to education. In other words, although its policies were not normally articulated in the precise terms of 'human rights', the Chinese leadership, however authoritarian, legitimized its rule by one part of the content of human rights. Thus the strand of subsistence rights, now channelled through the work unit rather than through the traditional kinship family, was woven into the social texture of the new political era.

On the other hand, Western notions of civil and political rights, to the extent that they were referred to at all, were pilloried as an instrument 'to conceal the real encroachment upon the rights and freedoms of the labouring people by the bourgeoisie (and to) provide pretexts for imperialist opposition to socialist and nationalist countries'.[60] They had relevance to China only in so far as human rights could be defined as freedom from class and imperialist oppression. Thus:

Under the socialist system, the elimination of the system of private ownership of the means of production has led to the elimination of the economic basis which gives rise to political and legal inequality, and thereby guarantees the genuine realisation of the human rights of the vast labouring people. The rights of landlords and bourgeoisie arbitrarily to oppress and enslave labouring people are eliminated; the privilege of imperialism and its agents to do mischief, kidnap, rob, rape, and massacre is also eliminated. To the vast masses of the people . . . this is genuine protection of human rights.[61]

This view of human rights was a reflection of Chinese communist notions of the relationship between the state, society, the individual, and the law. These were in turn a complex amalgam of socialist and Maoist ideas, and of traditional thought and practices, as well as of the historical experience of the Chinese revolution.[62]

The Chinese Communist Party came to power through violent revolutionary struggle based on a strategy of mass mobilization: the united front, armed struggle, and Party building were seen by Mao Zedong as the 'three magic wands' for defeating the enemy.[63] Although the external enemies, the Japanese and the Kuomintang, were now vanquished, the struggle was to continue against the 'enemy within', or the class enemy. Embracing the Leninist notion of the Party as vanguard of the proletariat, Mao nevertheless betrayed no hint of Marx's notion of the withering away of the state or of the millenarianism evident in Lenin's *State and Revolution*. Far from withering away, the state was to be the instrument whereby victory over the class enemy was to be achieved:

What is under discussion here is the question of 'state system'. Though this question of the state system has been wrangled over for several decades since the end of the Manchu dynasty, it is still not clarified . . . A dictatorship of all the revolutionary classes over the counter-revolutionaries and collaborators is the kind of state we want today.[64]

The 'state system' or '*guoti*' indicated not only the class nature of the state but the mode of rule, and was to be distinguished from the system of government or '*zhengti*':[65]

The state system is the class essence of the state. The question of the state system is the question of the place of the various social classes in the state, that is, it is the question of which class controls the political power of the state. For the most part, the state systems of the various countries of the world at the present time can be divided into three types: (1) the capitalist state system, marked by the dictatorship of the reactionary bourgeoisie; (2) the socialist state system, marked by the dictatorship of the working class; and (3) the new-democratic system, marked by the joint dictatorship of the various revolutionary classes, led by the working class and with the worker-peasant alliance as the foundation.[66]

China, as a society in transition and an economically backward state, was to be ruled by the third category of state system, a people's democratic dictatorship, with democratic centralism as its system of government. In essence, the democratic dictatorship was seen by Mao as consisting of democracy for 'the people' and dictatorship over the class enemy or 'reactionaries'. The notion of continuing class struggle under socialism was based on the future possibility of 'capitalist restoration'. Class struggle was to be waged on two fronts: by handling 'contradictions between ourselves and the enemy' (antagonistic contradictions) and 'contradictions among the people' (non-antagonistic contradictions).[67] The methods of dictatorship meted out to the class enemy involved serious sanctions including the deprivation of political (including civil) rights, while contradictions among the people were to be handled by the democratic methods of persuasion, criticism, and education.

The identification of the individual with his class and the linkage of classes with political power served to diminish the traditional ability of Chinese citizens to preserve an individual and personal sphere in their lives. The Communist Party's vanguard role as the custodian of truth, which made it the ultimate arbiter in deciding the precise identity of the class enemy at different historical periods, and its invasive organizational structure reaching to the grass roots of society, further diminished that space. The normal dividing line between state and society became blurred, and the dissenting opinion and plurality of ideas which maintained that division themselves became the object of class struggle.

Consequently, the notion of human rights as a matter of 'natural' rights which were universal, transcendent, and intrinsic to the individual was rejected by the new communist leadership, which regarded the individual as a social being achieving self-realization and material satisfaction through the collective, and political expression through his class nature.[68]

On the other hand, despite its formal position after 1949, China, if not itself a member of the United Nations, was now operating as a sovereign state within an international system, which, within the post-World War II environment, exhibited a new awareness and concern with the principles of human rights. In line with the majority of other states established in the post-war era, and following the precedent of the Soviet Constitution, China therefore incorporated in its first Constitution of 1954 the majority of the human rights principles identified in the Universal Declaration of Human Rights. The interesting feature of China's four constitutions since 1949 is that, in spite of their changing character, they have all provided guarantees not only of economic, social, and cultural rights, but of civil and political rights. Over time, some rights have been added and some subtracted, but they have all included guarantees for the freedoms of speech, correspondence, press, assembly, association, procession and demonstration, and for freedom of the person, freedom of religious belief, the right of appeal against state functionaries, and the autonomy of national minorities. Political rights have been guaranteed under the Chinese constitutions to all citizens aged 18 and over as 'the right to vote and stand for election'.[69] Civil rights not contained in the constitutions, it should be noted, have included rights laid down in the Universal Declaration and International Covenant on Civil and Political Rights, such as freedom of residence or movement, the right to choose one's work, freedom from forced labour, freedom from torture, and the presumption of innocence, though there is a right to defence and to a public trial.[70]

This formal guarantee of civil and political rights was, in any case, subject to a number of crucial limitations. First, like other communist countries, China was a state operating not on a common law basis but according to concepts of civil law. Thus, the constitution was directed not at the courts but at the legislator, establishing the parameters of permissible action. But, since the constitution was not judicially actionable, the state was not obliged to put the rights guaranteed into action: in any case, civil law 'sees law itself, much more so than common law tradition does, as rooted in the will of the state and the legislative provisions made by it'.[71]

Secondly, the socialist emphasis upon the supremacy of the state over the individual had certain consequences both for the guarantee and the realization of civil and political rights. These effects were manifested in three main areas: the dependence of the individual on the state for rights; the view of law as an instrument of the state; and the view of human rights as a matter of domestic jurisdiction as well as an issue potentially threatening to state sovereignty.

Since the state was the source of rights, it could grant them to the people; it could equally deny them to the class enemy. Moreover, because the rights of the state predominated over those of the individual, as in the earlier part of the century, the duty of the Chinese citizen to the state took priority over his rights. Thus, every right conceded the Chinese citizen had a corresponding duty, and in the event of that duty being threatened, it took precedence over the right. As the 1982 Constitution stated, 'the exercise by citizens of the People's Republic of China of their freedoms and rights may not infringe upon the interests of the state, of society and of the collective, or upon the lawful freedoms and rights of other citizens'.[72]

The Chinese communist view of the law as an instrument of the state was early observed by Benjamin Schwartz, who noted the 'strong kinship (probably not conscious) to the legalist conception of the function of law', and warned that 'it would be extremely foolhardy to assume that, in China, the growing emphasis on the role of legality in the communist sense must inevitably lead to the freedom of the individual under law. Certainly other factors must also intervene if this end is ever to be achieved.'[73] What these factors are will be the subject of later speculation. Writing over a decade later, Richard Pfeffer was also to describe the Chinese judicial system in terms reminiscent of traditional forms. Thus 'under the Communists the criminal process is arbitrary, highly politicised and responsive to class and status differences in its treatment of targets . . . Laws in China not infrequently are applied retroactively and analogically or, to put it most crudely, on an *ad hoc* basis. Application of what we would classify as criminal law, especially of the law of minor crimes, tends to be by administrative rather than judicial institutions'.[74]

This view of the law as an instrument of the state meant that not only was there no promise of remedies to ensure the citizens' enjoyment of their rights, but also that the rights themselves could be cancelled (or expanded) by state laws. Moreover, state laws could be overruled by Party fiat. This flexibility was not simply a function of the state's will: under Mao, legality was governed, much as it had been in imperial China, both by legal codification and by extra-legal norms, such as ideology, prevailing state and Party policies, and the continuing *Gemeinschaft* tendency to resort to mediation and conciliation rather than judicial action. The fledgling development of a *Gesellschaft* system of law, based on individualism and competition and drawing its provisions from Anglo-American and continental civil law, did not supersede the traditional Chinese practices of *Gemeinschaft* customary law and bureaucratic law, but, rather, was superimposed upon them.[75]

The resultant condition of law has been conceived as a complex intertwining of the jural (formal) and the societal (informal) models of law, with one model or the other dominant at a particular period of communist history.[76] Although some Western theorists argue the need to bolster the formal role of law in maintaining political order and social progress by means of institutions of mediation and conciliation, the Chinese experience showed how easily institutions of popular justice could be politically manipulated.[77] In the most extreme expression of the societal model, such as during the Cultural Revolution, the authorities suspended rights for groups of people or the whole population without resort to due legal process. Moreover, as will be seen, in periods when the jural form dominated, judges were still influenced by the traditional view of law as policy dependent. The Party's influence was felt through a system of political-legal committees composed of Party and government legal figures, which operated at all levels of the Party independent of the court system. In important criminal cases these committees enforced the interests of the Party and state. Moreover, China's judicial system was not structured to favour protection of the rights of the individual.[78]

The third major impact of the state's predominance over the individual and his rights was expressed in the Chinese emphasis on the principle of state sovereignty in relation to human rights issues and in its insistence that only states could be subjects of international law, while individuals were subjects only of municipal law:

As to the protection of 'fundamental human rights' (Preamble) and respect for 'fundamental freedoms' (Article 62) emphasised in the United Nations Charter, the fact that the United Nations General Assembly has adopted the 'Declaration of Human Rights' and 'Draft Covenant of Human Rights' does not mean, as described by certain bourgeois jurists (such as Lauterpacht and Jessup), that the United Nations Organisation, its Economic and Social Council, or its Commission on Human Rights can bypass states to protect the 'human rights' of individuals in the various states and thus make individuals subjects of international law. As a matter of fact, the principle concerning fundamental human rights prescribed in the United Nations Charter is that the various member states are obligated to guarantee that individuals under their rule enjoy certain rights. But the fundamental human rights enjoyed by individuals are not conferred on them by an international organisation, but rather by the municipal law of the various member states which undertake such obligations . . . All individuals, whether citizens within a state or aliens, are under the sovereignty of the state and are not subjects of international law.[79]

Thus, while China early recognized a state's obligation to guarantee its citizens certain rights, it could not embrace the cause of

human rights to the point where international claims regard
the rights of Chinese citizens threatened the sovereignty, or se___
rity, of the Chinese state.[80]

   In imperial China, then, the notion of human, or civil, rights in
the sense of the individual's right to protection from the incursions of the state, did not exist. Nevertheless, the unquestioned
duty of the community and the individual to the state was accompanied by an implicit sense of the state's responsibility to the
people to maintain stability and guarantee basic subsistence rights.
Social order was maintained through a normative system which
emphasized a hierarchy of duties reaching from the individual to
the emperor, and by the intermeshing of a plethora of customary
norms and bureaucratic laws which gently mediated social discord
while severely sanctioning criminal, politically subversive, or anti-
social behaviour.
   Within the context of the collectively based normative uniform-
ity characteristic of a patrimonial state, and the unequal, graded
nature of the law, existed an informal arena of personal space, in
which eccentricity, initiative, new ideas, and deviant social behaviour,
such as a hermit's existence, were tolerated. The impact of the
West on China in the late nineteenth and early twentieth centuries saw a continuation of the priority accorded to the collective over the individual, and to the idea of subsistence rights.
Western liberal ideas, not in the shape of *laissez-faire* liberalism
but in line with the social utilitarian stream of British liberal
thought, took a tenuous hold on the minds of Chinese intellectuals: but at the same time, the traditional Chinese utilitarian
notion of political ideas as a means to strengthen the Chinese
state, rather than as a good in themselves, persisted. Consequently,
a gap developed between the human rights norms professed by
the incumbent Kuomintang government and the reality of its
authoritarian military rule.
   With the advent to power in 1949 of a new communist government, this gap between political form and informal reality dis-
appeared, and civil and political rights lost their status as part of
the national rhetoric: but the traditional notion of subsistence
rights, as an integral part of the new political doctrine, re-emerged
as a dominant theme. In the ideology and practice of the new
socialist system, however, these subsistence rights were transferred
away from their strong traditional basis in the family, to the work

unit or *danwei*. At the same time, with the rejection of civil rights as a bourgeois concept and of liberal notions of popular sovereignty, the law, in actual terms, retained its status of a graded, unequal, and policy-based instrument promoting state interests. Within a context of substantial political and social change, therefore, two threads of continuity, if not identity, with the Chinese past, of subsistence rights and of an unequal and marginalized bureaucratic legal system coexisting with traditional *Gemeinschaft* practices of mediation and conciliation, assumed a dominant pattern in the texture of the new communist society.

3 Human Rights in China, 1949–1979

> What are human rights? They are the rights of how many people, of a
> majority, a minority, or of all the people? What the West calls human
> rights and what we call human rights are two different things, with dif-
> ferent standpoints.
>
> Deng Xiaoping

Jerome Cohen has remarked upon the yawning gap that existed
in the republican era between 'on the one hand, constitutional
documents that called for representative democratic institutions
and individual liberties and, on the other, a personalised party-
military dictatorship maintained over a non-Western populace that
was for the most part poor, illiterate, disorganised and impotent'.[1]
After 1949, however, under the Common Programme of 1949 and
accompanying laws, and the new communist government's first
state Constitution of 1954, the groundwork was laid for a constitutional and legal framework whose provisions, unlike those under
the Kuomintang constitutional documents, correlated closely with
the reality of a heavily monitored and intricately controlled
society.

In the Maoist era, and the early post-Mao period preceding the
modernization decade, China's three state constitutions in their
different forms reflected the broad hierarchy of socialist rights,
emphasizing economic and social rights in preference to, and even
exclusion of, individual civil and political rights. As Andrew Nathan
has noted, 'where the republican constitutions had purported to
fit the institutions of the state to citizens' rights, rights were now
framed to suit the purposes of the state'.[2] The lack of civil and
political rights effectively guaranteed in these three constitutions
was, of course, in conflict with the requirements of international
human rights instruments, the Universal Declaration of Human
Rights, and the International Covenant on Civil and Political
Rights. In spite of outward adherence to international requirements, in the sense of the constitutional listing of a number of
civil and political rights, these rights were simultaneously cancelled out by other constitutional provisions and by already existing laws. On the other hand, the economic and social rights in
China's constitutions largely conformed with the requirements of
the International Covenant on Economic, Social, and Cultural Rights.

It was not until the 1982 Constitution of the modernization decade that the lack of congruence between constitutionally guaranteed rights and substantive rights, so characteristic of the Kuomintang constitutional documents, once again exhibited itself. This question of congruence, or lack of congruence, between China's national norms and formal guarantee of rights, and the substantive content of these rights will, as already suggested, be one of the recurring themes in succeeding chapters. Although there is in all countries a gap between ideals and practice, socialist constitutions can be said to exhibit two principal relationships with empirical social reality. They may converge, in the negative sense that the provisions of the constitution are close to the reality of a strictly regimented society, or in the positive sense that existing constitutional norms are maintained and the Party and general populace are encouraged to adhere to them.[3] On the other hand they may diverge, in that they provide obstacles to, or anticipate and seek to shape, that reality. The broad thesis maintained here is that close convergence in either sense is symptomatic of a more stable social condition, even though that cohesion may also be a product of coercion. Wide divergence, however, is indicative of either rising social expectations or a popular sense of relative deprivation, both situations being conducive to social unrest or even to revolution.[4]

As has been suggested, with the proclamation of the People's Republic of China in October 1949, the limited autonomy from the state which existed for the individual and the group in traditional local society was increasingly whittled away. The unequal privileges based on wealth and social status of traditional society were transmuted into the inequality of privileges accorded political status and class.[5] The 5 per cent of the people deemed reactionary (the landlord class, the bureaucrat-capitalists, and members of the Kuomintang) were separated from 'the people' who had catapulted the communists to power (the working class, peasantry, the urban petty bourgeoisie, and the national bourgeoisie) and denied access to political (including civil) rights. The formal Leninist concepts of political organization — democratic centralism, the 'mass line' of political participation, and the vanguard Party — were invoked as legitimation for a political condition in which the individual's loyalty and subordination to the Party were seen as synonymous with his loyalty to the state and the collective national interest.[6] The interests of the individual were identified with the maximization of state power and the massive effort to rescue China from grinding poverty. The rewards for this communal effort were both spiritual and material: the honour and glory accorded the spirit of self-sacrifice were accompanied by a more equal distribution of resources which topped and tailed the highest and lowest socio-economic strata, raising the general living, health and educational standards of the majority of Chinese citizens.

For a number of reasons the policies and goals of the new regime commanded substantial popular support. The unification of the Chinese nation brought a welcome relief from the civil war, financial instability, social disorder, and factional and party rivalries of the previous decades. Important sources of continuity with Chinese tradition were the collectivist attitudes of the new and imported political culture, its authoritarian nature, and its emphasis on the duty of the state to ensure social stability and maintain the welfare of its people. On the other hand, as has been observed, there were also important areas of discontinuity. Welfare was transferred from a traditional community and family-based system to a state-based welfarist intervention, and the family was replaced by the work unit as the main source of housing, welfare, and social security services.[7] A crucial factor in support of the government was the coincidence of the impoverished condition of the majority of Chinese citizens with that of the Chinese state. Despite the violence of the suppression of landlords in the initial years, the unpopularity of the collectivization movement, and the upheavals caused by later politico-economic campaigns like the Great Leap Forward, the majority of Chinese citizens, particularly the urban workers and the poor and lower middle peasants, conformed with the prevailing political climate, at least until the Cultural Revolution, and adapted to it. Heavily monitored by an invasive state and Party system, they were in any case given few opportunities for dissent.

Civil and Political Rights: Formal and Informal

The Common Programme of the Chinese People's Political Consultative Conference of September 1949 which, until 1954, served in lieu of a constitution for the new communist government, decreed the abolition of all laws, decrees, and judicial systems of the Kuomintang government, and their replacement with 'laws and decrees protecting the people . . . and the people's judicial system'.[8] Although a number of acts and regulations were adopted in the early years, such as the Act for the Punishment of Counter-revolution (1951) and the Provisional Act on Guarding State Secrets (1951), it was not until 1954 that the first communist constitution, providing for the guarantee of civil, political, economic, and social rights of the citizen, was promulgated.[9] But the earlier legislation and enactments had already heavily circumscribed the civil freedoms of the people. The Provisional Act on Guarding State Secrets defined state secrets as including 'all state affairs which have not yet been decided on or which have been decided on but which have not yet been made public; and all other state affairs which should be kept secret'.[10] The Act for the Control of Counter-revolutionaries (1952) defined 'counter-revolutionary purpose' as a major determinant of serious crime, and under Article 10 identified the act of provocation of 'conducting counter-revolutionary propaganda and agitation and making and spreading rumours' as punishable by anything from three years' imprisonment to life imprisonment or death.[11] Thus, by 1953 freedom of speech had already been undermined by a lack of information as to what constituted a 'secret', by the absence of legislative guidelines, and by the fear of arbitrary government and Party decisions as to what constituted 'counter-revolutionary purpose'.

Within this restrictive environment for civil and political rights, the 1954 Constitution represented an attempt to regularize and institutionalize the political and legal structures of the new Chinese state, with the aim of facilitating the task of economic reconstruction.[12] The People's Republic was characterized as a 'people's democratic dictatorship' and as a 'people's democratic state led by the working class and based on the alliance of workers and peasants'.[13] The National People's Congress (NPC) was described as the 'highest organ of state authority' and, with its Standing Committee, exercised broad powers of legislation, amendment, and appointment. Chapter 3 (Articles 85 to 103) enumerated the people's rights as equality before the law; freedom of speech, of the press and publication; and the freedoms of association, assembly, procession, demonstration, and religion.[14] There were rights of appeal against state officials and the right to compensation for loss at the hands of state employees. Protection against arbitrary arrest was provided in Article 89, which guaranteed that freedom of the person was inviolable and that no arrest could occur except by decision of a people's court or with the sanction of a people's procuratorate, the legal supervisory organ of the state. Although the 1954 Constitution did not grant that rights could be restricted by law, this power was in fact exercised through laws promulgated before and after the 1954 Constitution.

In September 1954, the judicial system was given a permanent structure by the promulgation of the organic laws of the people's courts and of the people's procuratorates. Together with the Constitution, these laws introduced new features such as the right to legal defence, the principles of public (open) trial, and the right to appoint and withdraw judges. However, these nominal freedoms were effectively and simultaneously neutralized by corresponding duties, the existence of laws overriding rights, the limitation of the exercise of rights to situations which did not infringe upon the 'interests of the state, of society and the collective, or upon the lawful freedoms and rights of other citizens', and the continuing tendency to restrict these rights through changes in Party and state policies. Even the Constitution's guarantee of equality before the law, which appeared inconsistent with the deprivation of the political rights of feudal landlords and bureaucrat-capitalists as well as with the realities of life in everyday China, did not apparently mean that 'when the state enacts law, it would treat individuals from different classes equally in legislation'.[15]

The same restrictions on constitutional guarantees applied to the treatment of ethnic minorities, of women, and of religious groups within China. A requirement common both to the ICCPR and the ICESCR was that the rights enunciated should be exercised 'without discrimination of any kind as to race, colour, sex, language, religion, political or other opinion, national or social origin, property, birth or other status'.[16] These rights of non-discrimination were reflected in the provisions of China's 1954 State Constitution, as in those of subsequent constitutions. Article 3 in the General Principles stated that 'all the nationalities are equal. Discrimination against or oppression of any nationality, or any act that undermines the unity of nationalities, is prohibited'. Women were declared in Article 96 to 'enjoy equal rights with men in all aspects — political, economic, cultural, social, and domestic'; and in Article 88, citizens were guaranteed 'freedom of religious belief'. But these articles, like all others, were open to reinterpretation by laws and by Party and state policies. In practice, discrimination based on ethnicity, sex, and religious beliefs persisted in respect of civil and political rights, as well as in respect of housing, employment, education, and access to culture and religion and other aspects of economic, social, and cultural life.[17]

Political rights were guaranteed citizens under the 1954 Constitution (and subsequently under the 1975 and 1978 Constitutions) as 'the right to vote and stand for elections' for 'all citizens of 18 or over', with the exception of those persons deprived by law. Below the national level, the Constitutions required all three governmental levels of provincial, county, and basic level to have their own people's congresses (legislature) and people's councils (executive). At the basic level, deputies for people's congresses were to be directly elected by universal adult suffrage, while the next level would be indirectly elected by deputies at the previous level.

The guaranteed rights of the 1954 Constitution closely corresponded with the prevailing authoritarian reality. There was however an even closer correspondence between the 1975 and 1978 Constitutions and the realities of the late Maoist and post-Maoist periods. Adopted in January 1975 at the end of the later phase of the Cultural Revolution, the 1975 Constitution was heavily imbued with Maoist ideas in its emphasis on mass politics and the centrality of the Party. As Jerome Cohen has put it, in the 1975 Constitution the Party 'narrowed the gap that has existed between modern China's constitutions and the reality of a personalised Party–military dictatorship'; and the 1978 Constitution did 'not significantly widen the gap'.[18] Cohen's point is that in eliminating the 1954 declaration of equality before the law, the 1975 and 1978 Constitutions came close to the reality of the denial of political rights to 'class enemies', unreformed landlords, rich peasants, and reactionary capitalists.[19] They also deleted the nominal 1954 constitutional guarantee of 'freedom of residence and freedom to change . . . residence'; and although retaining the freedom to believe in religion they were more realistic in adding, 'and freedom not to believe in religion and to propagate atheism.'

The 1975 Constitution was, however, much more restrictive of citizens' rights than either its predecessor or successor. It deleted the 1954 reference to freedom of scientific research, and literary and artistic creation, requiring all cultural activity to 'serve proletarian politics, serve the workers, peasants and soldiers and be combined with productive labour';[20] and it omitted the 1954 commitments to workers' supervision in factories, and privacy of correspondence. It also deleted the right to compensation for loss caused to citizens by state employees' abuse of their rights.[21] More importantly, it provided institutional confirmation of the downgrading of the legal and judicial process which had begun in 1957 but was completed in the Cultural Revolution. It deleted the provision for the procuracy, and the constitutional provisions of equality before the law, the right to a public trial, the right to defence, and to protection against arbitrary arrest.[22] The provision guaranteeing judicial independence was dropped and the people's courts were to be subjected to the control of local political leadership.[23] The 1975 Constitution also introduced mass trials for 'major counter-revolutionary criminal cases'.[24] The functions and powers of the procuratorial organs were to be exercised by organs of public security at various levels.

The 1975 Constitution formally proclaimed the Party's leadership over the National People's Congress with the words, 'the Communist Party of China is the core of the leadership of the whole Chinese people'. Otherwise, it retained the same political rights, although describing the method of selection of people's congress deputies as elected 'through democratic consultation'. Even the extra rights provided in the right to strike and the 'four great freedoms' reflected the reality of the historical context of the Cultural Revolution in that they confined the exercise of civil rights to those 'among the people'. Just as the right to strike was interpreted as a political weapon for mobilizing the masses to undermine the power and privilege of the bureaucracy, rather than as an economic weapon to further the masses' material interests, so the 'four great freedoms' of 'speaking out freely, airing views fully, holding debates and writing big character posters' were seen as empowering the masses to overthrow enemies within the Party and the bureaucracy.[25]

The 1978 Constitution has been described as a compromise between the 1954 and 1975 Constitutions. Just as the 1975 Constitution was an attempt to preserve the Cultural Revolution's environment and mores, so the 1978 Constitution heralded an attempt, in the post-Mao period when Deng Xiaoping had not yet achieved supremacy, to move away from that era. Thus the 1975 Constitution, which emphasized Party supremacy, was more restrictive of political and cultural rights than its 1978 successor. The 1978 Constitution contained a number of aspects of the 1975 Constitution, including the description of the People's Republic of China as a socialist state of the dictatorship of the proletariat, and of the Party as the core of leadership.[26] It also maintained the right to strike and the 'four great freedoms'. It failed to restore the 1954 provisions on equality before the law and the independence of the courts. However, it restored many of the 1954 provisions on legality, reinstated the procuracy, and introduced individual rights absent from the 1975 document, such as the right of the accused to defence, and an open trial.[27] It restored the people's right to supervise the bureaucracy and the principle of election of deputies to people's congresses 'by secret ballot after democratic consultation'.[28] It also enlarged the citizen's right of appeal in Article 55 and appeared to restore the workers' right to supervise production found in the 1954 Constitution.[29] But in all cases the differences between the 1975 and 1978 Constitutions reflected the difference in the immediately preceding political and social environments — even if the inclusion in the 1978 Constitution of the right to strike and the 'four great freedoms' was somewhat anachronistic.

There is, as others have observed, a certain appropriateness to China of Max Weber's appraisal of the traditional legal system as 'a type of patriarchal obliteration of the line between justice and administration'.[30] There are, moreover, similarities between the traditional and Maoist systems of sanctions, as Jerome Cohen has suggested:

Both in basic assumptions and in institutions and practices, there are some obvious parallels between the traditional and the Chinese communist sanctioning systems. Many of these parallels derive from the great extent to which interests of the Chinese state have always prevailed over those of the individual. Thus, it has been assumed that justice in Chinese courts is the exclusive preserve of the state; that no independent actors such as lawyers should be permitted to intrude; that the accused is generally a bad person and would not make proper use of a meaningful opportunity to defend himself; that he is the best source of evidence and should be interrogated according to inquisitorial procedures likely to elicit his confession; and that confessions, if not legally required, are at least eminently desirable. A substantive criminal law that is of uncertain application, that is status oriented, and discriminates against certain classes of people, and that permits proscriptions to be applied both by analogy and retroactively has deep roots in China.[31]

In the Maoist era, China's legal system, which underwrote the condition of the citizens' civil rights, was not based on any substantive or procedural criminal code, but rather on a large number of laws, regulations, and decrees of various kinds.[32] According to these documents, the three law enforcement agencies, the courts, the procuracy, and the police, were subject to a constitutional separation of powers, and the independence of the courts. In fact, they served as 'constituent units of a single administrative structure'.[33]

The court system established by the Organic Law of 1954 was composed of the Supreme People's Court and Local People's Courts (divided into higher, intermediate, and basic levels). Below the basic courts were 'people's conciliatory committees', charged with the responsibility of settling civil disputes and minor criminal law cases by means of conciliation.

The People's Procuracy, an independent and highly centralized organization, consisted of the Supreme People's Procuratorate, local people's procuratorates and special people's procuratorates. Its functions were to exercise supervisory power over the execution of the law, deal with reinvestigation and review of cases, to oversee observance of the law, and prosecute counter-revolutionary and other criminal elements.[34]

Within the court system, the socialist principle of 'collective leadership' was implemented through judicial committees, usually comprising the court president, division chief, and judges of the court. Their functions included the review of judgements and the summary of judicial experience, but they also ensured political guidance of the courts and the correct execution of Party policy.[35]

Apart from the courts, justice in Maoist China was administered by a number of administrative agencies and social organizations, chief of which were the police, consisting of both public and secret units. These were organized into a hierarchy of public security organs headed by the Ministry of Public Security in the State Council. Together with the courts, they formed the 'judicial organs', seen as 'weapons' of the people's democratic dictatorship to be used against class enemies. Their numerous functions included the arrest, detention, and investigation of suspected counter-revolutionaries and other criminals; the imposition and administration of punishment; the direction of the system of reform through labour; and responsibility for traffic control, public health, census registration, and protection of important military and economic establishments.[36] But once again, the nominal independence of the public security organs from the courts and procuratorates was undermined by the political and judicial committees

responsible to the Communist Party which operated at every level
of organization and co-ordinated their activities.[37]

Extra-judicial agencies forming part of the highly articulated
system of social and legal control at the local level were street
offices, residents' committees (100 to 600 households), and residents' groups (15 to 40 households). In the countryside, these
functions were assumed by the people's communes, production
brigades, and production teams. They, together with state organs,
schools, work units, political parties, and mass organizations, had
the power not only to handle disputes through mediation and conciliation, but also to impose administrative and disciplinary sanctions on offenders, such as criticism and struggle sessions, and
demotion or dismissal from jobs.[38] Two specialized committees in
the residents' committees, the mediation committee and the security defence committee, were particularly crucial to the process
of monitoring citizens' activities and passing on information to
public security officials.[39]

Central to the control of the individual was the citizen's personal dossier (*dang'an*), which provided a record of his activities
through life from early school days, and which could be used
against him during political campaigns, or when seeking work
transfers, or opportunities for outside study or movement. However,
the most effective source of social control was the *hukou*, a form
of household registration introduced after 1949 which was based
not on family as in the past, but on work unit organization.[40] Since
the basic, as opposed to the more differentiated, categories of
hukou were *nongcun hukou* (rural) and *chengshi hukou* (urban),
this institution was a primary source of urban–rural differentiation and inequality. Related to the traditional *baojia* system, it
was 'a citizen's passport into direct relations with the welfare state'
and could not be used outside the place of one's registration.[41]
Moreover, on the *hukoubu* was printed the holder's class origins,
reflecting whether one belonged to the 'five red categories' or the
'five black categories'.[42] Consequently, the *hukou* was a most powerful instrument of social control and mobility.

Informal sanctions were not, however, the only forms of punishment open to extra-judicial agencies. For more serious offences, which were not considered 'criminal', a large category of
administrative penalties (*xingzheng chufen*) existed, which could
be invoked either by police order or the decision of a work/
neighbourhood/Party unit, without a court decision.[43] These administrative penalties included warnings, fines, short detention,

supervised labour without detention, as well as rehabilitation through labour (*laodong jiaoyang* or *laojiao*). This last penalty was provided for by the State Council's Decision Relating to Problems of Re-education through Labour in 1957, and involved incarceration in special labour camps.[44] It was often quite similar to reform through labour (*laogai*), but offered better conditions. It applied to vagrants, to counter-revolutionaries whose crimes were minor, to those who refused to work, or were fired, and to trouble-makers who failed to respond to repeated efforts at re-education.

Criminal penalties (*xingshi chufen*), on the other hand, were imposed by a court, during closed trials, open trials (where the defendant had the nominal right to defence), or mass public trials involving up to tens of thousands of people. Criminal sanctions involved a term of imprisonment, usually carried out in a reform through labour (*laodong gaizao*) institution (camp, prison, or farm); life imprisonment, generally served in prison; the death penalty suspended for two years, which generally meant life imprisonment; or the death penalty, followed by immediate execution.[45]

Penal institutions were defined as 'instruments of the people's democratic dictatorship'. They were run by the Public Security bodies at the level at which they were established, and armed guards were supplied by the Public Security armed units.[46] Different categories of prisoners were often sent to the same institution, but the different institutions had their own procedures. They consisted of detention centres, corrective institutions for juvenile offenders, rehabilitation through labour groups, reform through labour brigades, and prisons.[47] Detention centres (*kanshousuo* or *juliusuo*) were established at all administrative levels, and were mainly for offenders who had not been tried, but could include those convicted for two years imprisonment or less. Political offenders were often kept in solitary confinement at the beginning of their detention. Detainees as yet unconvicted received only two meals a day. A frequent complaint was the overcrowding of cells, particularly during political campaigns.[48]

Corrective centres carried out 'reform through education' for juvenile offenders between 13 and 18. Such offenders were sentenced to criminal punishment, but the emphasis was on education rather than labour. Juvenile offenders transferred from overcrowded reformatories to adult prison-farms, however, spent half the day studying and the other half in manual labour. Labour re-education groups included those sent to farms holding only prisoners serving terms for administrative punishment, or to penal institutions holding other categories of offenders.

Although in theory a distinction was made between administrative and criminal forms of punishment, in practice the work and discipline required under both were the same. The labour reform brigades were often part or the whole of a prison farm, factory or camp, set up to build factories, railways, or bridges. Labour-reform prisoners were given the hardest work and acted as a mobile, unpaid labour force; they were often transferred from camp to camp. These camps frequently contained different categories of prisoners. In 1967, for instance, the Yingde camp in Guangdong province contained more than 10,000 workers, including convicted prisoners, labour-rehabilitation offenders, 'free workers' who had finished their sentence but were detained in the camp, and ordinary workers.[49] On the other hand, according to the law, prisons were intended mainly to house major offenders sentenced to long-term imprisonment: in fact, most prisons were also factories and included other types of offenders. Major offenders were not supposed to work until they had completed a reform programme which included repeated self-examination sessions, with confessions, self-denunciations, and denunciations of others.

According to the 1978 Amnesty International report on political imprisonment, in the Maoist era there were large numbers of penal institutions spread throughout the country, particularly in the north-east, in Heilongjiang province, Inner Mongolia, and Liaoning province. There were also large labour-reform settlements in the Uighur Autonomous Region of Xinjiang (northwest), in Qinghai province and Tibet in the west, and in Yunnan province (south). Conditions for prisoners of conscience were later chillingly evoked by Wei Jingsheng of the Democracy Wall Movement.[50] Near Beijing, the largest corrective farm was Qinghe, said in the 1960s to house some 10,000 convicted prisoners and *laojiao* detainees. About ten smaller labour-reform farms and factories outside Beijing were supervised by the city's Public Security Bureau. In 1960 Beijing's Prison No. 1 reportedly contained 1,800 prisoners, 40 per cent of whom were political prisoners. In Shanghai there were reported to be at least eighteen detention centres and three labour-reform farms.[51]

Political offenders liable to conviction included 'all counter-revolutionary criminals whose goal is to overthrow the people's democratic regime or to undermine the undertaking of the people's democracy'.[52] In all other legal documents the definition was of equal looseness and arbitrariness. The scope was further widened by the establishment in Article 16 of crime by analogy, allowing that those who, 'with a counter-revolutionary purpose', committed crimes not covered by the Act, should be punished according to comparable crimes in the Act. Political offenders fell into three main categories: historical counter-revolutionaries (*lishi fangeming*), members of former political parties and organizations, and members of former privileged classes involved in organized opposition to the Chinese Communist Party before 1949; active counter-revolutionaries (*xianxing fangeming*), guilty of offences ranging from expressions of dissent to politically motivated common law offences; and dissenters, consisting of those who occasionally voiced criticisms of government policy.[53]

The crime of counter-revolution, and indeed the concept of human rights itself, only achieved coherence within the overall prism of class. The inevitable continuation of class struggle after the victory of the socialist revolution made the definition of the identity of the class enemy a crucial issue. This enemy was defined by Mao in 1957 as the 'five black elements', or 'landlords, rich peasants, counter-revolutionaries, rightists, and other bad elements'.[54] Although the exploiting classes by definition were 'objects of dictatorship', any individual could become an object of its control and, depending on the exigencies of different political periods, be deprived of freedom. Erroneous political tendencies and beliefs thus served as an extension of class characteristics and were often partly defined by them. Thus the same offence was punished differently, depending on the offender's social class and political background: in the case of a bad class background, the crimes would be deemed political in nature.[55] The concept of equality before the law, despite its inclusion in the 1954 Constitution, had no part in this class-based criminal law system of Maoist and early post-Maoist China.

The restrictive nature of the constitutional and legal provisions, backed up by equally restrictive institutions in this era, thus closely conformed with the empirical condition of civil and political rights in the society at large. Within the broadly restrictive context, different phases of the administration of justice in the Maoist and early post-Mao period are generally distinguished:[56]

(a) the terror of 1949-53 when the Chinese leadership resorted freely to extra-judicial processes for imposing major sanctions;

(b) the 1953–7 period in which the establishment of a frame-
    work for a formal judicial system was briefly interrupted by a
    period of extra-judicial terror;
(c) the 1957–65 period, characterized by increasing Party control
    over the judiciary and the continuing decline of the import-
    ance of China's legal system;
(d) the 1966–76 period, characterized by the dismantling of the
    law enforcement apparatus, the use of mass line devices, and
    the imposition of military control over the *gongjianfa* (police,
    procuracy, and courts);
(e) the return after 1976 to a stable legal order and a regular
    criminal justice system, marked by the codification of impor-
    tant laws, the restructuring of the judicial system, and the
    expansion of legal education and research.

These alternating phases of 'societal' and 'jural' models of law
reflected in the judicial arena the alternating phases of political
mobilization and consolidation. Periods of mass campaigns against
class enemies were often characterized by the overriding of the
legal norms and judicial procedures characteristic of the jural
model and the dispensation of a summary people's justice through
the revolutionary tribunals and public security organs. The ease
with which political leaders switched from one mode to another,
moreover, was itself an indication of the inefficacy of institutions
and structures in the face of challenge by the sovereign Party. It
was also an indication of the inherent flexibility, ambiguity, and
arbitrary nature of the existing system of laws.

Informal revolutionary justice was invoked during nationwide
mass campaigns such as Land Reform, the Three-Antis and the
Five-Antis Movements, and the Suppression of Counter-revolutionaries Movement in 1950–2.[57] It was also a feature of the Anti-
Rightist Movement which followed trenchant criticisms of the
Party during the Hundred Flowers Movement of 1956–7. This
phase saw an attack both on those with bad class backgrounds
and on intellectuals who expressed non-violent opposition to the
regime.[58] Many of the 'rightists' were detained under the administrative sanction of *laojiao*; since there was then no time limit for
placing a person under re-education, many remained in detention
for about twenty years before their release in the post-Mao
period.[59] One schoolteacher imprisoned in south-west China for
twenty-one years from 1958, for instance, reported that tens of
thousands of political prisoners and intellectuals at the camp over

this period worked seven days a week for up to twenty hours a day, hauling coal or collecting manure. Thousands were said to have died of mistreatment, and malnutrition in periods of food shortages and extreme weather conditions.[60] In the period prior to the Anti-Rightist Campaign, from 1949 to 1957, according to a report by Premier Zhou Enlai, 16.8 per cent of counter-revolutionaries were sentenced to death, most between 1949 and 1952; 42.3 per cent had been sentenced to terms of reform through labour, of whom 16.7 per cent were still detained in 1957; 32 per cent had been put under control, with 9.1 per cent remaining in control in 1957; 8.9 per cent had been released after a period of re-education; and 48.5 per cent of those sentenced to reform through labour or put under control had been released by 1957.[61] Han Chinese were not the only objects of these draconian policies. Chinese suppression of the 1959 uprising in Lhasa was followed by the imprisonment of Tibetan ecclesiastical and government officials, aristocrats, affluent socialites, and all those suspected of having links with the rebel movement.[62]

It was not, however, until the Cultural Revolution that the full implications of the class nature of China's legal system for the citizens' exercise of civil rights became apparent. Launched against the 'bourgeois headquarters' by an aging Mao resolved to rekindle the revolutionary fervour of the civil war period and to prevent bureaucratism from hardening the arteries of the revolution, the Cultural Revolution witnessed the use of the mass line against the institutions of Party and state and even against the revolutionary leaders themselves. In a period of violence and chaos, the judiciary was dismantled and the Public Security organs were attacked by the Red Guards. The most minute details of citizens' political and class backgrounds became the object of public attack and 'struggle meetings', and many leading cadres and intellectuals were humiliated, summarily tortured, killed, or driven to commit suicide. Even in the case of long detention or sentences, normal legal procedures were ignored. Law and order was ultimately only restored after military intervention, and then at the cost of considerable bloodshed.[63]

A further campaign towards the end of 1968 to 'clean up the class ranks' (qingli jieji duiwu) targeted those who had attacked Chairman Mao and Vice Chairman Lin Biao; those cadres who had not properly participated in the Cultural Revolution; those who had caused the deaths of people during the Cultural Revolution or who had destroyed equipment; those among the 'five bad elements' who had not reformed properly; and those cadres downgraded or dismissed during the 1964 'four clean-ups campaign'.[64] It was only between 1970 and 1973 that military control over law enforcement gave way to more normal legal practices. The Procuracy, however, eliminated under the 1975 Constitution, did not return until it was reinstituted in Article 43 of the 1978 Constitution. The role of the courts, until the death of Mao in September 1976, has been described as merely a 'subsidiary or ceremonial' one. According to the Indictment of the Trial of the Gang of Four (November 1980–January 1981), from the years 1966–76 a total of 729, 511 people were framed and persecuted, of whom 34,800 were persecuted to death.[65] Between 1977 and mid-1980, more than 2,800,000 people reportedly had their unjust verdicts from the previous three decades reversed. Some, like Liu Shaoqi, were rehabilitated posthumously.[66]

The nature of these campaigns, whereby certain classes of citizens, under the guidance of their leaders, obtained the right to speak out and censure others, raises the general question of the relationship between mass campaigns in China and 'civil' and 'political' rights. If one were to interpret political rights in the broader sense of the 'right to participate in the exercise of political power' rather than in the more technical, democratic sense of the right to vote and act to influence the choice of government leaders and policies, it could be claimed that some Chinese citizens enjoyed a degree of political rights. Mao's mass line in politics meant mass political participation. As has been suggested, during these political campaigns and movements, some citizens enjoyed the civil rights of freedom of speech, press, movement, and association to a certain extent. The aim, if not the effective result, of such mass movements as the Cultural Revolution was to enable the masses to exert some control over their leaders, and to prevent the emergence of a 'new class' of elites enjoying excessive privilege.

However, the mass line in Chinese politics first developed in the 1930s and 1940s in a situation in which there was a high correlation between leadership objectives and those of the ordinary people.[67] By the mid-1950s, the situation had altered, and application of the same formula, whereby education from above, exhortation, and leadership took priority over electoral and representative institutions in the leaders' relations with the people, no longer had the same effect. Constant repetition of outworn slogans of unity containing such descriptions of the relations between the leadership and the masses as *'xin lian xin'* ('heart to heart'), and a succession of political campaigns which called on ever-lagging mass enthusiasm, had the paradoxical effect of gradually opening up the gap between state and society which had been almost closed after 1949. Political forms were maintained, but they became ritualized as political theatre, as part of a symbolic act which all recognized as ensuring the protection of inner heart and mind from political intrusion. At certain political high points, such as the death of Zhou Enlai in January 1976 and the Tiananmen Square incident which followed in April, the tension between appearance and reality became so great that the masses took spontaneous action.[68] Moreover, ritual could not protect those who became the victims in this political theatre, or those who belonged to the 'five black categories'. They felt the actual wound of political and social ostracism, and the loss of civil, political, and even economic, rights.

Thus, the important thing to note about these excursions into the arena of 'civil and political' rights during mass campaigns in China, is that they were initiated, guided, and revoked by the political leaders. They had no permanent legal structures to underwrite them. The infrequency and impermanence of these phases served to highlight the absence of rights in normal times. Exercise of these rights by one group usually led to the restriction of the civil rights of others and was punishable after the event. Political campaigns aside, a further argument along these lines could be that the large and ubiquitous Party organization, reaching out from the Party centre to branches and groups at the most local level in enterprises and villages, guaranteed widespread political participation, but this participation was neither universal nor direct. And for political participation to be defined as a right, it must be universal.

Economic, Social, and Cultural Rights: Formal and Substantive

In contrast to the ambiguities and limited provision of civil and political rights in the pre-modernization constitutions, the guarantee of economic, social, and cultural rights in the first three constitutions was less equivocal. Randle Edwards has observed that Chinese constitutional guarantees of these rights incorporated every major category of the International Covenant on Economic, Social, and Cultural Rights.[69] Thus the economic and social rights of fair wages, equal remuneration, safe working conditions, rest, the rights to social welfare and social insurance, the right of everyone to an adequate standard of living, to physical and mental health care, and to education, provided for in the ICESCR, all had their echo in China's first three post-1949 constitutions, even though these rights were not guaranteed to 'everyone', but to 'working people'. On the other hand, Chinese constitutions did not include the right 'of everyone to form trade unions' required by Article 8 in the ICESCR, nor did the 1954 Constitution contain the right to strike.

From 1949 the legitimation of the People's Republic of China was articulated chiefly in terms of the achievement of social and economic goals. The priority of these goals was emphasized in the first paragraph of the Preamble to the 1954 Constitution: 'The system of People's Democracy — New Democracy — of the People's Republic of China guarantees that China can peacefully banish exploitation and poverty and build a prosperous and happy socialist society'.[70] The character of the regime was also suggested by the fact that, although landlords and bureaucrat-capitalists were deprived of political and civil rights, the 1954 Constitution still provided them with 'a way to live, in order to enable them to reform through work and become citizens who earn their livelihood by their own labour'.[71] Thus the concept of citizenship in post-1949 China, which was broader than the political concept of 'the people', was defined not by access to civil and political rights, as in Western societies, but in terms of access to the economic right to work.[72]

It was a feature of China's first three constitutions that social and economic rights were peculiarly conjoined, in that the right of access to social security was associated with the right to work. Thus, the 'iron rice bowl', or the right to work, was generally regarded as China's effective social welfare system. Social rights, which included access to medical and retirement benefits, as well as to subsidized housing, were thus inextricably attached to the work unit (*danwei*). In fact, a research project of the China Economic System Reform Research Institute, working directly for the State Council, found in 1986:

China's social security system is actually not a 'social system'. There is no national system covering retirement pensions or medical care. Instead,

China's social security system is largely realized by means of employment. Anyone will have welfare benefits and security so long as he or she gets a job. Peasants fall completely outside this welfare net. In addition, collective enterprises offer fewer benefits than state enterprises.[73]

This analysis, although otherwise valid, exaggerates the exclusion of the peasantry from the social welfare system — until recently they were guaranteed a basic rice ration, and, on a collective basis, limited health and education services. The state channelled welfare benefits through state enterprises, while the slack in the welfare system catering for the majority of the population not employed in the state system was taken up by the collective net, thereby ensuring a reasonably egalitarian social welfare and social security system. The focus of social and economic rights on the worker was explicable in terms of the Marxist tenet that labour was the true source of value. The right to work, which was guaranteed Chinese citizens under all constitutions, had the effect of compensating for the limitation to 'the working people' of access to some social rights. At the same time, it must also be noted that the right (and duty) to work was counterbalanced by the absence of some significant rights, such as freedom to choose one's job and the constitutional right for workers to engage in equal bargaining *vis-à-vis* their employer — two rights laid down in the International Covenant on Economic, Social, and Cultural Rights. The right to work also accounted for the failure of the Chinese constitutions to provide for the right to unemployment relief, as stipulated in Article 25 (1) of the Universal Declaration of Human Rights.[74]

Since the provision of economic and social rights was pivotal to the legitimation of the communist regime, both from the point of view of ideological credibility and of performance, there was less variation in their guarantees between the first three constitutions than there was in the case of civil and political rights. Under the 1954 and 1978 Constitutions all citizens of the country were guaranteed the right to work, and promised the future expansion of this right through state mediation to develop the national economy, create more employment, improve working conditions, and increase wages, amenities, and benefits.[75] The 1975 Constitution took this guarantee to its logical extreme in the statement, 'he who does not work, neither shall he eat', by assuming that all citizens could and should be found work.[76]

Another universal right, not linked to the workplace, was

education. However, this was not explicitly a 'free' education, and was also posited on the assumption of future expansion by the state. The 1954 and 1978 Constitutions also guaranteed the right to engage in scientific research, literary and artistic creation, and other cultural activity, encouraged and assisted by the state.[77] This latter right was not, however, guaranteed in the section on Fundamental Rights and Duties of Citizens in the 1975 Constitution. In the section on General Principles, moreover, it stated that 'culture and education, literature and art, physical education, health and scientific research work must all serve proletarian politics, serve the workers, peasants and soldiers, and be combined with productive labour'.[78]

On the other hand, the 1975 Constitution, and the 1978 Constitution after it, guaranteed citizens the right to strike. Although this right was meant to be invoked in the context of the Cultural Revolution to correct mistaken policies or bureaucratic misman-agement rather than to secure higher wages, it could also in the-ory be used to protect individual workers against bureaucratic injustice. This protection, although seldom exercised, was import-ant in a society where any conflict with leaders or cadres, whether personal or political, could lead not only to a loss of political rights but also to the effective loss of economic and social rights.[79]

Social rights guaranteed 'working people' in all three constitu-tions included 'the right to rest and the right to material assist-ance in old age and in case of illness or disability'.[80] The other two constitutions expanded these basic rights by itemizing the state's obligation to increase them.[81] Moreover, the 1978 Constitution implicitly accepted state responsibility for the non-state sector of employment in its pledge to 'gradually expand social insurance, social assistance, public health services, co-operative medical ser-vices and other services' so that the right of the working people to 'material assistance in old age and in case of illness or dis-ability' could be enjoyed.[82]

Just as the effective constitutional denial of civil and political rights in the pre-1979 period was an accurate reflection of a closely controlled society, so the guarantees of economic, social, and cul-tural rights under the pre-modernization constitutions were matched in practice by an attempt to balance national economic develop-ment strategies with a social policy requiring a more equitable distribution of resources. If the result was, as some claim, an equal-ity of poverty, it was a poverty padded with important economic and social safeguards against destitution, starvation, ill health, and ignorance.[83] In a few decades, China was transformed from a war-torn and poverty stricken society to a stable environment where the people were guaranteed at least a minimum of economic security, employment, good health, basic education, the opportunity to obtain work skills, and state or collective assistance in case of illness, disability, or old age.

Measuring China's achievement according to the Physical Quality of Life Index (PQLI), which combines life expectancy, infant mortality, and literacy into one indicator on a scale of 1 to 100, the Overseas Development Council found in 1981 that China had an average per capita income of $310, a life expectancy of 67, an infant mortality rate of 71 per thousand, and a literacy rate of 69 per cent. Thus China's PQLI in 1981 was 75 on a scale of 1 to 100, higher than all low-income countries measured except Sri Lanka. China had a PQLI that was 15 points higher than the average for the low-income countries ($280 average per capita) and 10 points lower than the lower middle-income countries ($665 average per capita).[84] The crucial function of economic and social rights in pre-1979 China was retrospectively recognized by China's State Statistical Bureau in a 1988 survey. While basic wages remained low and increased only gradually in this period, it stated, the principal ways in which urban living standards were raised was by increasing job opportunities and providing greater social welfare.[85]

By the mid-1970s, China was increasingly seen as providing a model for social experimentation that attacked the roots of the problems besetting modern industrialized and industrializing nations: bureaucratization; urban decay; pollution; inflation and unemployment; inadequate medical care for lower socio-economic groups; the abuse of drugs and the rise of crime.[86] As Gordon White has observed:

For socialists . . . the 'Maoist' experiment represented a serious attempt to . . . establish a new pattern for the 'transition to socialism' based on original socialist values of equality, participation and collectivism. In the world of 'development studies' . . . Chinese experiments in mass mobilisation, debureaucratism, educational redistribution, appropriate technology and local or national 'self-reliance' struck responsive chords. The 'Chinese model' was widely cited by development theorists and practitioners alike, as suitable for emulation and transfer to other Third World countries.[87]

This view of China's pre-modernization achievements has since been questioned, *inter alia*, by Alan Liu and Ramon Myers.[88] Liu concedes the improved life expectancy and the increased economic growth rate, claimed by Chinese authorities to have comprised a growth from 1949–78 in heavy industry of 90.5 times, in light industry of 19.7 times, and in agriculture of 2.4 times.[89] He also concedes a superficially excellent record of the Maoist leadership in terms of education and health. But both he and Myers emphasize the constant and even declining average food consumption in this period, and the unchanged income distribution. Liu cites Mao's comments on popular living standards which suggest that in Mao's eyes, improvement in the people's livelihood came second to the priority of increased production, and that achievement of the latter goal depended to a large extent on popular self-reliance and even self-sacrifice.[90]

The point is well made that an appraisal of China's social and economic rights in this pre-modernization era must be seen in the context of an economic development strategy requiring a high rate of capital investment and with consequently fewer resources available for social and individual consumption.[91] The goals of rapid industrialization and economic self-reliance set a limit to the potential for enjoyment of economic and social rights, as they restricted the amount of goods and services available for mass consumption.[92] Thus, while between 1952 and 1977 China's national income increased at an average rate of 6.2 per cent, between 1955 and 1977 the total disposable income of the peasants was estimated to have only increased by 17 yuan.[93] On the other hand, within the rural sector the relative differences were small. Thus it has been estimated that in 1978 the average annual income of 'rich' peasant households was only 1.9 times that of poor households.[94]

Within the overall constraint of only a slight rise in average per capita incomes, official emphasis was on social consumption as a means of redistribution, rather than on individual consumption. Although the problems in China of privilege, disparities of income, the stratification of society, and over-bureaucratization remained, there were strong social and political pressures to reduce them, and the virtues of egalitarianism and the willingness to serve society were promoted.[95] The simultaneous pursuit of economic and social goals necessarily involved 'a quest, a desire to reconcile the seemingly irreconcilable'.[96] Just as Mao sought a society that was both democratic and centralized, so he sought a developed, industrialized society that was also based on socially egalitarian principles. In a dialectical process, these potentially contradictory goals were pursued in zig-zag fashion.[97] Political policies alternated between periods of mobilization, emphasizing social change and conflict, and periods of consolidation, emphasizing institutional structures, central planning, and reconciliation. In similar fashion, developmental strategies alternated between periods of consolidation based on rational industrialization and planning mechanisms, and of mobilization, characterized by attempts to break down distinctions between mental and manual labour and the inequalities between urban and rural areas.

The positive side of these efforts has been emphasized in a number of World Bank reports and, to a lesser extent, in US Congressional reports.[98] Thus, at least up until the mid-1970s, China was able to underwrite the constitutional guarantee of the right to work through a number of devices — high levels of investment in industrialization, the subsidizing of non-financial industrial enterprises, the policy of sending unemployed urban youth into the remote rural areas, and the widespread resort to 'underemployment', a traditional feature of Chinese society. The disadvantage of such policies was economic inefficiency. Their positive side was that the crucial problem of unemployment was reduced.

Just and favourable conditions of work, at least in urban areas, were also reasonably well protected from 1949–78.[99] Although wages increased only gradually, basic needs of state workers and staff (*zhigong*) in housing, grain, clothing, and medical care, were state subsidized, while the needs of peasants were less well supplied by the collective. Urban–rural inequalities were somewhat reduced by the policy of investing in poorer agricultural regions, and by a system of rural relief for the most deprived.[100] Women, on the other hand, although promised equal pay for equal work, were often employed in the lower paid workshops within the industrial enterprises.

Membership of trade unions was also encouraged, except during the period of the Cultural Revolution, 1965–76. The function of Chinese trade unions did not, however, comply with International Labour Organization (ILO) standards. There was no right of industrial bargaining, no freedom to form and join a trade union, no effective right of association, nor the right to leave one's job and seek other employment.[101] The trade union, on the contrary, was used as a mechanism to exhort workers to increase production: the worker was encouraged to obey the rules of the enterprise and accept the guidance of the Party and of management.[102]

The right to social welfare and social security was constitutionally guaranteed to 'working people', and was covered by comprehensive laws and social welfare legislation. A large proportion of the labour force in urban areas was covered by these provisions, but, as already indicated, employees in state enterprises enjoyed the greatest benefits.[103] These employees were paid fixed wages on the basis of length of service, skills, experience, and responsibilities. Their jobs were secure, and they were eligible for such benefits and services as sickness and maternity leave, low-rental housing, retirement and death benefits, and access to nurseries, kindergartens, and social clubs.[104] These rights were channelled through the workplace and therefore encouraged overdependence on the *danwei*.[105] Distribution of welfare benefits through the work unit thus became another instrument of social control.

The allocation of health services also excessively favoured urban areas. Peasants obtained basic health care in return for a contribution to the collectively run welfare fund. The cost of old age and disability, on the other hand, were normally borne by the family, although the policy of 'five guarantees' was meant to cover the needy with provision of food, clothing, housing, medical care, and burial service in the countryside. In both the city and countryside, however, there was a financial subsidy for those unable to work, and if the income of a family dropped below the minimal level, the enterprise or commune was encouraged to provide them with support.

Numerous Western medical reports have testified to the effective public health system which eliminated past public health threats such as VD, TB, yellow fever, diphtheria, polio, and smallpox.[106] This was achieved by the focus on three particular areas of health care: preventive measures and vaccination programmes; the wide diffusion of basic curative care; and continued reliance on traditional Chinese medicine, personnel, and drugs.[107] Continuous public health campaigns led to the elimination of the four pests: flies, rats, bedbugs, and mosquitoes. The innovative introduction of 'barefoot doctors' to the countryside during the Cultural Revolution helped further universalize basic health care and provided services of physical examination, general immunization, and distribution of birth control devices, while referring patients to local hospitals for more specialized treatment. The 1983 World Bank report on Chinese conditions in 1980 commented that the gain of twenty-eight years in life expectancy in China between 1949 and 1978 was well above the average for both lower and middle-income countries: in fact it was sixteen years greater than would be anticipated in a country at its income level.[108] In terms of the broader services contributing to general health and welfare, cotton goods were in short supply, and rationed, but most people were adequately clothed. Housing was also in short supply (estimated to have declined from 4.5 square metres per capita in 1952 to 3.6 metres in 1978).[109] Yet urban dwellers at least enjoyed exceedingly low rents. Peasants, on the other hand, owned and built their own houses, but labour, and to a lesser extent, materials, were cheap and plentiful. The World Bank report drew the following conclusions:

The determinants of health — measured by illness as well as death rates — are much broader than is sometimes supposed. One determinant is people's consumption of certain goods and services, including food, housing, fuel, soap and water, as well as medical care. Another is the health environment — climate, standards of public sanitation, and the prevalence of communicable diseases. A third is people's understanding of nutrition, health and hygiene. Chinese health policies reflect an unusually good and early grasp of these determinants, in combination with a strong commitment to improve the health of the mass of the people under tight financial constraints.[110]

Educational policies in China tended to follow the general political and economic pattern of mobilization and consolidation: 'redness' and 'expertise' were qualities given emphasis at different periods. Egalitarian and socially oriented policies alternated with a more elitist, specialist focus. The primary goal, however, of providing every child with four to six years of primary education continued throughout the Maoist quarter century. The World Bank mission to China in 1980 estimated that the literacy rate among the population aged over fifteen years was about 66 per cent, an increase of over 46 percentage points since 1949. It compared with literacy rates on the Indian subcontinent of from 21 per cent to 33 per cent.[111] The most radical alteration of the educational system took place during the Cultural Revolution. Vocational education was emphasized over theoretical studies. Political indoctrination and study and work within the society at large were stressed. University and school courses were shortened and tertiary level entrance examinations were abolished. Political criteria predominated in student selection. The status and role of teachers was reduced and the management of universities transferred to revolutionary committees consisting of students, revolutionary cadres, and workers. By the end of the late Cultural Revolution period, as in the industrial arena, the cadres had emerged as the main power holders within universities, controlling not only administration but almost all academic decisions.[112]

Although later described as the 'ten lost years' in Chinese education, Cultural Revolution policies sought the further universalization of education and its increased socio-economic relevance. As in many other fields, however, the desired economic and social goals did not always correlate with the final result. Nevertheless, progress in the field of education was considered sufficient to justify the following appraisal by the World Bank:

The development of education in China has been impressive, despite the disruption during the Cultural Revolution. The number of primary school graduates has increased by 305 million from the 1949 figure of 70 million. Since 1949, senior secondary schools have graduated 51 million students, compared to 4 million during the previous 30-year period; for university graduates, the corresponding figures are 3 million and 185,000. Two out of three adult Chinese are now literate . . . Qualitative developments have been less satisfactory, since expansion was sometimes achieved at the expense of quality . . . Attempts have been made to bridge the gap between school and the world of work during most of the period since 1949, notably through the schools in factories and factories in schools. These attempts have contributed to China's impressive development of nonformal education opportunities, especially at the university level where enrolments totalled almost 0.9 million students in 1979. The types of education offered include night school and correspondence courses, spare-time university programs, and training given to workers and peasants at institutions run by their factories, enterprises and counties.[113]

Such achievements should not disguise the continued inequalities in standards of living experienced by different sectors of the population, the continued problem of social stratification which impeded mobility between socio-economic groups, and the existence of the abuse of power and privilege in Maoist China. A gradation of 30 levels in the state bureaucracy, of 18 grades among technical personnel and of 8–10 grades among industrial workers in state enterprises made such differentials inevitable.[114] Between urban and rural areas, the income differential was estimated at around 2:1.[115] Within communes, the differential was estimated at between 63 yuan to 454 yuan per labourer.[116] Even within the state sector, the abolition of bonuses and salary increases during the Cultural Revolution introduced new inequality and financial hardship into the industrial system; and industrial organization became more bureaucratic than it had been before the events of the 1960s.[117] The most fundamental differential, however, was between urban living standards, particularly for those employed in the state sector, and rural living standards. Thus, the state sector received almost all state investment, almost all the subsidized welfare and educational services and benefited from state-subsidized rations of grain, edible oil, meat, and fish, usually purchased from the peasants at prices set by the state. The remaining 80 per cent of the population, who were mostly peasants, received some cloth and other rationed items and the minimum of social services.[118]

Thus, there is some merit to Martin Whyte's argument that in Mao's China, 'the distinctiveness of Chinese egalitarianism (was) to be found not so much in its reduction or elimination of differences in income, power and educational skills, although some of this has occurred, but in its attempt to mute the consequences, in terms of matters like life styles, consumption patterns and interpersonal deference, of the inequalities that do exist'.[119] Nevertheless, it must be stressed that these differentials were of a relative, rather than absolute or qualitative kind. They avoided the extremes of wealth and poverty increasingly apparent in the post-Mao era. By 1976 the lower socio-economic groups had been raised to a tolerable level of subsistence in comparison to pre-1949 China, and the higher socio-economic groups had been shorn of their affluence. In general, apart from the Great Leap Forward period which led to great loss of life, and apart from the consistent inequities of distribution between the state and collective sectors of the economy, China's guarantees of social welfare and social security in the Maoist era, even if minimal, helped to overcome past patterns of disease, starvation, ignorance, and material need. As the World Bank concluded:

China's most remarkable achievement during the last three decades has been to make low-income groups far better off in terms of basic needs than their counterparts in most other poor countries. They all have work, their food supply is guaranteed through a mixture of state rationing and collective self-insurance; most of their children are not only at school, but being comparatively well taught; and the great majority have access to basic health care and family planning services. Life expectancy — whose dependency on many other economic and social variables makes it probably the best single indicator of real poverty in a country — is (at 64 years) outstandingly high for a country at China's per capita level.[120]

The expansion of economic and social rights under the Maoist era was therefore extraordinary in terms relative to the deprivation and destitution characterizing the preceding political era. These achievements, however, should not disguise the substantial inequities between urban and rural China that were tolerated and even encouraged by China's socialist government for reasons of capital formation in a period of rapid industrialization. Nor should they disguise the concomitant loss of civil rights such as freedom of movement, as well as of economic rights such as the freedom to choose employment, both of which were required under international human rights law. Therefore, whatever the ethics of the situation, it must be acknowledged that a substantial trade-off was made in the Maoist years between the values of equity and some civil, industrial, and economic rights. More importantly, in terms of official socialist norms, a trade-off was made between national developmental requirements and the greater equity which could have resulted from a less punitive milking of rural resources. On the other hand, even within the fluctuations between more authoritarian and less authoritarian political environments, and between the expansion and contraction of civil and political rights in the three constitutions of the Maoist years, the lack of civil and political rights in this period was self-evident, and was contrary to all requirements of the International Bill of Rights. The congruence between official norms as proclaimed in the constitutions, and their exercise in reality, was thus a close one. The resulting political and social stability was only achieved at the substantial cost of civil and political rights, and, less abstractly, in periods of revolutionary mobilization, at the cost of nation-wide mental anguish and widespread loss of life.

4 Civil and Political Rights in China, 1979–1989

ANDREW WALDER has written of the 'fatal interconnectedness of all aspects of industrial reform'.[1] Without adopting a simplistic position of economic determinism, the same fatal interconnectedness exists between industrial reform and the political and social systems in China. The modernization process which was initiated in December 1978 began a complex chain of restructuring in the economic, social, and political systems which has had unintended, and, since 1989, often fatal consequences for the condition of human rights in China. These consequences were mediated by the personal space which had continued to exist in the Mao era and which expanded in the modernization decade, and by the increasing gap which the modernization process opened up between state and society in China. An informal process of political communication evolved, whereby some citizens succeeded in protecting economic rights enjoyed in the Maoist era, and thereby undermined the effectiveness of the economic restructuring process, while others enjoyed an expansion of civil rights which, though nominally guaranteed under the constitution, were not in fact underwritten by any enabling laws.

Thus, the actual condition of civil and political rights in the modernization decade from 1979–89 has been the product of a number of complex developments, some of them the offshoots of structural changes in the economy, or the results of changes in administrative regulation, others the outcome of less tangible psycho-cultural factors. The expansion of publication rights, for instance, has been explained in administrative terms as due to a change in regulations, or in terms of the commercialization of the publishing process which followed the introduction of market principles into many facets of Chinese life.[2] Yet human beings are not simply creatures of structures. Institutional reforms of themselves do not create democracy.[3] The urge, and the confidence, to express opinions and to publish in China is the product not merely of institutional reform but of an environment of tolerance and enhanced public awareness. It was, paradoxically, the lack of democratic and legal structures in China which encouraged the continuation and development of the informal political condition facilitating communication between the leadership and the masses. This condition, an outgrowth of the traditional co-existence of the formal and informal spheres of life, worked primarily to convey the leaders' wishes to the people, but also operated in the reverse direction.[4] The alteration of public perceptions, as has already been suggested, could be the result of leadership decisions conveyed downwards and outwards through Party channels in many discrete ways to which the general populace was highly sensitive. Likewise, the tightening of policy could be immediately inferred by the people's sensitive political antennae, and resulted in self-censorship, whereby citizens adjusted their own behaviour, and even thoughts, to reflect the prevailing political line.

Although facilitating political communication, this resort to informal political channels has made policy-making an arbitrary, personalized, and unregulated affair. Even where formal institutions have existed, their original function has often been so distorted that it has become necessary to revert to informal channels to restore their original purpose. In the industrial arena, for example, the power of trade unions has not since 1982 been bolstered by the right to strike or engage in collective bargaining. Passive forms of communication, such as the withdrawal of effort and efficiency, have therefore been the main method whereby workers have placed pressure on management.[5] Thus, worker opposition to the loss of other rights such as the right to work has been expressed through informal means, has modified official policy and has thereby prolonged access to these rights, if only for workers already employed in state enterprises.[6] This pressure in turn has made it difficult for the leadership to proceed with policies encouraging the rationalization of labour and the expansion of the labour market. On the other hand, the increased freedom of movement which has been the consequence of a freer labour market, has not only bestowed a new right on Chinese citizens which will have profound sociological consequences, but it has provided new information and experiences to the people, and the rural population in particular, which are bound to have a political flow-on. Whatever the formal legal and institutional provisions of human rights, in other words, rights may be modified or liberalized, either by the pressure of formal, structural changes, or by informal devices.

The beginning of the modernization era in China is normally dated by Chinese and foreign analysts from the Third Plenum of the Eleventh Central Committee in December 1978, although calls for modernization had been initiated by Premier Zhou Enlai in 1964 and 1975. The two years following the death of Mao and the arrest of the radical leaders, the Gang of Four, in 1976, were a period of political and economic compromise, providing a bridge between the Mao era and a new emphasis on the increase of overall productivity. Economic policies were based on the assumption that China's problems would be resolved by the move away from radical policies and the Maoist edict of 'politics in command'. But China's planners were faced with a situation where the average grain ration for the peasant and the average wage of the worker had declined below the level of 1956 and 1957, and the supply of subsidiary food products in cities had decreased.[7] As well, the pace of economic advance was erratic, investment funds were used inefficiently, and the high levels of investment, 'in terms of consumption foregone', meant that people's incomes were stagnant or rising only slowly and labour productivity was static or declining.[8] The recovery in 1977 and 1978, moreover, led to the stockpiling of products not needed in the market-place.

In addition, there were numerous problems characteristic of the command economy: the difficulty of complex planning; the problem of regulating supply and demand through the planning system instead of the market; the indifferent quality of goods; the lack of innovation; and the inefficient use of capital, energy, and other scarce goods.[9] These problems were seen by Xue Muqiao as the product of two decades of economic imbalance, manifested by requisition purchase, state monopoly, and the rationing of more and more items, and resulting from the failure to give priority to agriculture and light industry over heavy industry.[10] Liu Guoguang, on the other hand, paid due deference to the economic achievements made prior to 1965 but blamed the ten years of the Cultural Revolution for the drop in growth, the decrease in agricultural and industrial production and in the national income, the worsening of the imbalance between the different economic sectors, and a drop in the real wages of workers and staff (*zhigong*), with a purely nominal rise in peasant incomes.[11]

The proposals issuing from the December 1978 Plenum reflected the views of Xue Muqiao in that they signified the realization that China's economic problems were not just a function of the chaos of the Cultural Revolution and of radical economic policies. The Third Plenum involved a decision to profoundly restructure China's economic and political system in the pursuit of economic modernization. It was announced that class contradiction was no longer the main contradiction in Chinese society and that economic construction was to be emphasized over class struggle. The mass political campaigns of the past were renounced and the development of socialist democracy and a socialist legal system proposed.[12] Politics thus became the handmaiden of economics, and the Party's function as an agent of economic development took priority over its other roles.[13] The ideological underpinning for these reforms was the notion of 'underdeveloped socialism', later reformulated by Premier Zhao Ziyang as China's 'primary stage of socialism'.[14] According to Zhao this stage would last in China for 100 years. It was characterized by the predominance of public ownership, with the simultaneous expansion of co-operative, individual, and private sectors of the economy in both rural and urban areas.

The notion of underdeveloped socialism carried with it two important implications. The first was that, since China was underdeveloped because of its backward productive forces, the state of the productive forces was the main determinant of the stage of socialism. Secondly, the implication was that China would modernize and industrialize under restricted market conditions, adapting to its purposes a number of capitalist economic devices. This rationale neglected the diverse effects of the socialist and capitalist systems on the developmental process, and treated the developmental process almost as 'neutral'.[15] Rather than giving priority to the social aim of full employment, for instance, it was argued that 'employment is, in the final analysis, contingent on production, and any attempt to isolate it from production must be discouraged'.[16] Employment was seen as an economic rather than a social problem, and employment made secondary to production, although both were seen as mutually reinforcing processes — hence, 'progress in production creates employment, and the expansion of employment pushes production forward'.[17]

The economic and social benefits to citizens resulting from the modernization process were seen more as an improved standard of living resulting from the trickle-down effects of increased overall economic prosperity, than, as in the past, one of the primary goals of socialist economic development to be achieved through redistributive mechanisms. The stress was on direct gain sharing rather than indirect gain sharing and on the improvement of real income and consumption levels rather than on the right to work and on social services *per se*, although the social services guaranteed to state workers were maintained. The egalitarianism of the 'iron rice bowl' was rejected in favour of a new policy, first applied to the peasantry and later imposed universally, sanctioning the right to get rich first. As Xue Muqiao observed: 'It is wrong to artificially level off the differences in living standards among the peasants. We should encourage a section of them to become prosperous first, for this will impel others to improve their livelihood through labour, helping to narrow the said differences'.[18]

This reordering of the state's priorities to a concentrated pursuit of economic prosperity through combined planning and market mechanisms in the shape of a socialist planned commodity economy with Chinese characteristics had a profound effect, partly intended, partly unanticipated, on China's economic, political, legal, and social organization, as well as on the social value system. The change from a centrally planned economy to a 'socialist commodity' economy brought the decollectivization of agriculture, a diversification of ownership systems, the decentralization of economic decision making, the separation of ownership and management within enterprises, some market-based pricing policies, and a freer labour market, as well as a new emphasis on the importance of expertise over 'redness' and of competition over egalitarianism. It brought a new focus on the individual, and on the benefits to the community of tapping the individual's resources. The increasing reliance on market forces challenged the Maoist value of self-sufficiency by implying the need to exploit the economic benefits of international markets and to integrate with the world economy. It also implied the reduction of the economic role of the state.[19] It revolutionized the system of communications, introducing sophisticated technology which transcended the national barriers which had hitherto acted as a filter to censor the content of materials and the type of information which could be imported and purveyed around the country. It also made inevitable the general freeing up of the political system, for a degree of democracy was seen both as the prerequisite and as the inevitable outcome of the economic liberalization process.[20] Civil freedoms at an informal level expanded in the gap which began to emerge between state and society. Finally, the move towards the market system and the integration with the world economy increased pressures to institutionalize and regularize the marketing process, and to replace the existing flexibility in the system of social control with a degree of predictability and dependability, thereby necessitating the development of a coherent legal system.[21]

Such profound structural and normative changes inevitably affected the general condition of human rights. The economic changes, as suggested, turned welfare services from a redistributive mechanism into a commodity, and placed the onus for redistribution on improved income and on consumer spending. The downgrading of class struggle made civil and political rights formally accessible to large groups of people hitherto denied them. Increased legislation promised legal support for constitutionally guaranteed civil rights, and the promise of socialist democracy in theory extended the ambit of civil and political rights. In terms of both civil/political and social/economic rights, political promises raised mass expectations. Subsequent moves to rehabilitate large numbers of people purged during the Cultural Revolution appeared to vindicate the promise of enhanced civil and political rights. The early surges in GNP and the increasing prosperity of China's citizens, in particular the peasantry in the suburbs around the big cities, seemed to vindicate the economic promise.

The challenges posed by the modernization era to China's one party system represented the process of China's adjustment to this Western developmental model. Thus, along the lines suggested by Richard Lowenthal, Chinese leaders were obliged to attempt to make structural adaptations to the requirements of an efficient and rational industrial order and to develop political forms sensitive to changing group interests in an increasingly differentiated society, while maintaining ultimate decision-making authority. They were obliged to develop new and credible forms of legitimation and to develop the capacity to cope with the unintended consequences of structural change.[22]

The formal framework incorporating the structural and institutional changes, and expanding the basic citizens' rights in the modernization era, was the 1982 Constitution. As early as 1980 the Chinese leadership had decided that the provisions of the 1978 Constitution did 'not conform to the conditions and needs of the current new period of historical development'.[23] A Committee for the Revision of the Constitution, established in September 1980, drew up the Draft of the Revised Constitution of the PRC which was circulated for discussion in April 1982. Finally, after a period of lengthy discussions and redrafting, the Constitution was adopted by the National People's Congress in December 1982.[24]

Formal Civil and Political Rights

In its provision of civil and political rights, the 1982 Constitution fulfilled the conservative function of underwriting social stability. This role was consistent with its official representation as a significant break with the mores of the Cultural Revolution. On the other hand, it was also represented as a return to the values of the 1954 Constitution. The assertion of unambiguous control by the Deng Xiaoping leadership was reflected in the identification of economic construction as the main task of the new era, in the downgrading of the role of class struggle, and the regulation of the Party's role as leader but not usurper of the role of the state.[25] The description in Article 1 of the Chinese political system as a 'socialist state under the people's democratic dictatorship' instead of a 'socialist state of the dictatorship of the proletariat' appeared symptomatic of a more liberalized political condition, as did the positioning of the chapter on rights and duties of citizens, containing twenty-four articles as against sixteen in the 1978 Constitution, near the beginning of the Constitution.

Foremost among the civil rights provisions was the restoration of the 1954 constitutional provision of equality before the law, already included in the Organic Law for the People's Courts adopted on 1 July 1979.[26] In line with the reaction against Cultural Revolution practice, emphasis was placed on the freedom of Chinese citizens, with new prohibitions on the unlawful search of their persons or homes.[27] New articles determined that the 'personal dignity of citizens was inviolable' and that 'insult, libel, false charge or frame-up of citizens (was) prohibited'.[28] In addition to the guarantee in Article 55 of the 1978 Constitution of a citizen's right to appeal to organs of state against violation of the law or neglect of duty was the guarantee that citizens who suffered losses through infringement of their civic rights by any state organ or functionary had the right to compensation in accordance with the law.[29] A further protection for civil rights was the restoration in Article 126 of the principle of independence of the judiciary, while the procuracy was also said to exercise its authority independently.[30]

On the other hand, it could not be said that the 1982 Constitution was a liberal document. The right to strike guaranteed in the 1975 and 1978 Constitutions was eliminated, together with the 'four great freedoms' which had been deleted in September 1980 when Article 45 of the 1978 Constitution had been amended. Justifying the elimination of the right to strike, Hu Sheng stated that 'working people can utilize means other than striking to express their demands and achieve their aims' and that 'in socialist society striking is not only disadvantageous to the state, but also harmful to the interests of the workers'.[31] Under Article 34 citizens were still able to be deprived of their political rights by law, and the state's right to limit rights by law was effectively continued. The freedoms of publication and residence were dropped and a number of other basic rights made subject to qualification. Thus, the freedom and privacy of correspondence formally guaranteed under the previous two constitutions was made subject in the 1982 Constitution to cases where 'the needs of state security or of investigation into criminal offences' required censorship by public security or procuratorial organs 'in accordance with procedures prescribed by law'.[32] State protection for 'normal religious activities' was subject to the qualification that 'no one may make use of religion to engage in activities that disrupt public order, impair the health of citizens, or interfere with the educational system of the state' and that 'religious bodies and religious officers are not subject to any foreign domination'.[33] The statement in Article 53 of the 1978 Constitution that 'the state advocates family planning' was replaced in the 1982 Constitution with the directive in Article 49 that 'both husbands and wives have the duty to practise family planning'.[34] And the right to make complaints to state organs was offset by a prohibition on 'fabrication or distortion of facts with the intention of libel or frame-up'.[35]

The 1982 Constitution, like its predecessors, also contained other articles cancelling out or jeopardizing guaranteed rights: for instance, it stipulated the duty to safeguard state secrets and to refrain from 'infring[ing] upon the interests of the state, of society, and of the collective or upon the lawful freedoms and rights of other citizens when exercising their freedoms and rights'.[36] It also stated that 'the state . . . suppresses treasonable and other counter-revolutionary activities', although it did not automatically deprive all persons with bad class backgrounds of their rights.[37] Finally, two new additions to the 1982 Constitution introduced potential restrictions on civil freedoms. Article 67 (20) introduced a new role for the Standing Committee of the National People's Congress which had destabilizing implications for civil and political rights: the power 'to decide on the enforcement of martial law throughout the country or in particular provinces, autonomous regions or municipalities directly under the Central Government'. This provision, which was contained in the 1954 Constitution, had been dropped from the 1975 and 1978 Constitutions.

An even greater restriction on civil freedoms in the 1982 Constitution was embedded in the preamble with the inclusion of the ideas underlying the 'four basic principles', first coined by Deng Xiaoping in response to the Democracy Wall Movement of 1978–81. According to these principles, no exercise of democracy could contradict the socialist road, the people's democratic dictatorship, the Communist Party leadership, and Marxist-Leninist-Mao Zedong thought. These principles formed the backbone of the conservative stabilizing force of the new constitution and were frequently invoked to restrain subsequent moves towards the informal expansion of civil and political rights.

In contrast to its restrictive impact on civil rights, the 1982 Constitution provided for a limited expansion of political rights. The new political regime it introduced has been summarized by Michel Oksenberg and Richard Bush: 'In 1972, totalitarian revolutionaries ruled the nation: by 1982 China's rulers had become authoritarian reformers'.[38] The Constitution sought to create 'a more predictable system based on a clearer separation of roles and functions and a system of clearly defined rules and regulations applicable to everyone'.[39] First, it made a clear distinction between the functions of state and Party and moved to limit the Party's control of state affairs.[40] It restored the position of President of the State and established a Central Military Commission to lead the armed forces, thus in theory removing command of the PLA from the Party.[41] It also required in Article 5 that 'all state organs, the armed forces, all political parties and public organizations, and all enterprises and undertakings must abide by the Constitution and the law.'

Secondly, the Constitution provided for increased powers of the state system by extending protection from arrest or trial to deputies of the National People's Congress, unless with the assent of the presidium of the NPC or its Standing Committee. It also required that NPC deputies not be called to legal account for speeches or voting at its meetings.[42] More importantly, it affirmed the power of the Standing Committee to make laws. The rights to vote and stand for office were to be enjoyed without reference to class background. NPC and local people's congress deputies were to be selected 'through democratic election' rather than, as in the 1978 Constitution, through 'secret ballot after democratic consultation'.[43] New provisions, incorporating the provisions of the Organic Laws of the National People's Congress and of the Local People's Congresses and Governments, and the Electoral Law for the National People's Congress and the Local People's Congresses of 1979, required direct election of deputies to local people's congresses at county, city, district, and township levels.[44] Popular supervision and political accountability were stressed in Articles 2, 27, 76, 77, and 102. The rights of national minorities listed in the 1954 Constitution, and their power of self-government, were restored and expanded.[45]

At the local level, the organizational system of township administration was reinstated, to overcome the perceived problems of democratic management and the supervision of organs of state power, which were involved in the over concentration of power in the people's communes.[46] The powers of the local people's congresses were expanded to allow them greater autonomy, with the right to promulgate local regulations and to 'adopt and issue resolutions and examine and decide on plans for local economic and cultural development and for the development of public services'.[47] Residents' and villagers' committees were described as 'mass organizations of self-management at the grass-roots level'.[48]

However, constitutional analysts have also pointed out that the powers of the people's congresses remained unchanged, and other suggestions to strengthen their role such as direct election of the NPC and extension of deputies' rights to question government beyond the period of the congressional session, were not accepted.[49] Moreover, while Article 5 stated that no laws, rules, or regulations should contravene the Constitution, the power to interpret the constitution and enforce its provisions did not lie with the courts or procuracy, but with the supreme legislature itself, thereby giving it power to repudiate its own laws or annul administrative acts.[50] There was thus no effective, independent mechanism to interpret and supervise the enforcement of the Constitution.[51]

Although the 1982 Constitution defined itself as 'the basic norm of conduct' and as 'the fundamental law of the state' with 'supreme legal authority', it was not, as we have already indicated, the only source of formal rights. Despite the claim of Article 5 that 'no law or administrative rules and regulations shall contravene the Constitution', the state continued to exercise the power to limit and expand rights by law. In addition, the significance of constitutional guarantees can only be understood in terms of the relationship between constitutional provisions and ordinary laws and statutes. For until an ordinary law is enacted to regulate a particular constitutional provision, that right may not be enforceable in a court of law.[52]

Thus, a development of considerable significance for human rights in China was the early recognition in the modernization decade that the rule of law was an indispensable accompaniment of economic development and expanded international trade. The initial emphasis on legal reform was related to introducing predictability and regularity into the areas of law dealing with foreign trade and joint ventures. But the recognition of the importance of strengthening the legal foundations of the state was in part born of a reaction against the lawlessness of the Cultural Revolution era and the loss of protection to the citizen that this lawlessness entailed. A legal system was seen as necessary, not only to guard against crime but to protect citizens from arbitrary official treatment. Consequently, in early 1979, the NPC Standing Committee established a Legal Affairs Commission headed by Peng Zhen, former Mayor of Beijing. A Chinese legal manual encapsulated the function of the new legal system which emerged from its deliberations:

(a) to organize and develop economic, cultural, and educational enterprises, and to protect and promote the building of the Four Modernizations;

(b) to punish the enemy and handle the contradictions between the enemy and the people; and

(c) to protect 'people's democracy' and handle the contradictions among the people.[53]

In the early years of modernization, economic legislation dominated, so that of 300 laws issued by 1982, nearly 250 were concerned with economic matters.[54] But these economic laws had many ramifications for human rights. The law was used to redefine China's socialist system of ownership by placing some public property under the effective control of private persons, and to facilitate the play of market forces within the centrally planned economy. At the same time it served to assert not only the significance of the role of the individual within the economy, but of his rights within the political system.[55] Both the General Provisions of Civil Law, promulgated in 1986, and their exegesis and supplement, the

iasic Principles of Civil Law, were positioned at the interface
vetween the individualistic *laissez-faire* values of foreign free-
market economies and the home-grown norms of China's socialist commodity economy. They thus contained, in the interests of
trade and economic development, concessions to the values intrinsic to a liberal democratic political system. For instance, the Basic
Principles of Civil Law adopted the Western concept of the 'absolute' (*juedui*) nature of personal rights, defined as a mixture of
civil and economic rights — the right to life, to health, freedom,
happiness, one's name, likeness, rights of status, and rights of
authorship.[56] In fact, China's human rights theory had never sub-
scribed to the 'absolute' nature of human rights, so that in the
process of economic legislation China's own human rights concepts were extended.

Specific laws covering civil and political rights were the Criminal
Law, the Criminal Procedure Law, the Organic Law of the Local
People's Congresses and Local People's Governments, the Election
Law for the National People's Congress and the Local People's
Congresses, the Organic Law of the People's Courts, and the
Organic Law of the People's Procuratorate, adopted by the Fifth
National People's Congress in July 1979. In December 1982 the
fifth session of the Fifth National People's Congress adopted four
new or revised laws: The Organic Law of the National People's
Congress, the Organic Law of the State Council, the Organic Law
of the Local People's Congresses and Governments, and the Electoral Law for the National People's Congress and the Local People's
Congresses. Jerome Cohen has subsequently referred to the 'remarkable decade of progress towards creating a credible rule of law'
in the period immediately preceding June 1989. Before June, judicial review of the legality of administrators' decisions was being
considered, and the National People's Congress was even on the
verge of abolishing the category of 'counter-revolution' as a crime.[57]
Predictably, this new emphasis on legal codification produced
expectations of, and calls for, the realization of constitutional civil
and political rights.

In some ways, the new laws implemented and extended constitutionally guaranteed civil rights. Here it is necessary to distinguish between, on the one hand, civil rights of expression, which
before 1989 lacked enabling legislation, and, on the other hand,
rights of immunity, which to some extent were protected by law.
Rights of immunity, contained in Articles 5–11 of the Universal

Declaration of Human Rights, include the right to life in its broadest sense, the right not to be tortured, the right not to be subjected to arbitrary arrest, detention or exile, the right to a fair and public hearing by an independent tribunal, the right to be presumed innocent, and the right to remedy by a competent tribunal for acts violating fundamental rights. The Criminal Law implemented the constitutional protection of personal freedom by making it an offence to detain or search a person unlawfully, and the Criminal Procedure Law and the Arrest and Detention Act of 1979 regulated the procedures for arrest and detention.[58] Labour rights guaranteed in the constitution were also amplified in administrative regulations.[59] The Criminal Law and the Criminal Procedure Law also institutionalized new rights not guaranteed in the constitution, such as the right to defence and the prohibition of torture. In terms of political rights, the precise ambit of the general constitutional provision of the right to elect and be elected was fleshed out in the Election Law and in the regulations on the direct election of NPC deputies at *xian* (county) level and below, promulgated by the Fifth NPC.

To a considerable extent, however, the expectations raised by these new laws were dampened by the revisions and amendments made between June 1981 and September 1983 to the Criminal Law, the Criminal Procedure Law, the Organic Law of the People's Courts, and the Organic Law of the People's Procuratorates, which diluted the protection of the individual's rights, and enhanced the flexibility of law as an instrument of the state.[60] In particular, revisions to the Criminal Law and the Criminal Procedure Law adopted by the second session of the Standing Committee of the Sixth National People's Congress in September 1983 allowed that, in serious cases, 'where the main criminal facts are clear and the evidence irrefutable and the people's indignation is very great, the case should be rapidly and promptly adjudicated and (the people's courts) may not be bound by the restrictions stipulated by Article 110 of the Criminal Procedure Law regarding the time limit for delivery to the defendant of a copy of the bill of prosecution and the time limits for the delivery of various subpoenas and notices'. The time limit for appeal for such cases was also changed from the ten days stipulated in the Criminal Procedure Law to three days.[61] In particular circumstances, time limits for handling cases were extended, and in the case of certain crimes, the right of approval for death sentences could be delegated by the Supreme People's Court to the high people's courts of the provinces.[62] Amendments to the Criminal Law also made a wide range of new offences punishable by death; and they made possible summary executions and limited the right to defence.[63] Increasing petty criminal activities throughout China, a by-product of social and economic dislocation, produced stiffer criminal penalties, and between 1983 and 1988 Amnesty International documented 1,500 executions and also unofficial estimates of 30,000 executions.[64] In Amnesty's view, the appeal procedure and the trial itself continued to be largely formalities, death sentences were often excessive and often inappropriate and arbitrary arrest and torture continued to be widespread.[65]

In similar vein, the government acted to reissue previous laws restricting civil rights, with or without revision. These included the 1957 Security Administration Punishment Act (SAPA) in February 1980, the 1957 Decision of the State Council on Reeducation through Labour, republished with revisions in November 1979, and the 1951 Provisional Act on Guarding State Secrets, republished in April 1980.[66]

The function of these revisions was to limit the civil freedoms guaranteed in the Constitution, particularly freedom of speech. Similarly, the Criminal Law itself contained provisions which authorized the imprisonment of people for the peaceful exercise of their human rights, specifically the rights of assembly, association, and freedom of speech and publication. Articles 98 and 102 of the Criminal Law provided imprisonment for the 'counter-revolutionary crimes' of taking part in a 'counter-revolutionary group', or for propagandizing for and inciting the overthrow of the political power of the dictatorship of the proletariat and the socialist system 'through counter-revolutionary leaflets and other means'. Under Article 103, 'when the harm to the state and the people is especially serious and the circumstances particularly odious', these crimes warranted the death penalty.[67] This failure of the legal system to uphold and enforce the informal condition of civil rights which evolved during the modernization decade, led many to describe the new legal system as rule by law rather than of law.[68]

The condition of China's civil rights of immunity resulting from this legislation was reviewed by Amnesty International:

(The laws) give insufficient protection against arbitrary arrest and fail to guarantee a fair trial. For example, they do not guarantee the right to receive visits from relatives and legal counsel shortly after arrest and regularly thereafter, the right to adequate time and facilities for preparation of the defence; and the right to be presumed innocent until proved guilty in a court of law.[69]

Most importantly, the Criminal Law listed seven ordinary offences and fourteen 'counter-revolutionary' offences punishable by death; and on 2 September 1983 the NPC Standing Committee introduced further amendments to the Criminal Law which made seven new categories of offence liable to the death penalty, bringing to over forty the total number of offences punishable by death.[70]

Structural changes made to the policing system since the Mao era included the establishment in 1983 of the Ministry of State Security. According to its own description, it was responsible for 'safeguarding state security, exercising the people's democratic dictatorship, crushing espionage, and safeguarding and promoting socialist modernization and national unification'.[71] Although its functions were shrouded in mystery, some outside observers believed that it was drawn from the third arm of the Public Security Ministry which formerly dealt with matters of state security, espionage, and counter-revolution.

In the modernization decade, the organs of the state and Party apparatus concerned with the legal, judicial, and administrative arrangements for dealing with cases bearing on and affecting the citizens' civil rights were many and varied. Apart from the Communist Party, the People's Liberation Army, and the Militia they included: the People's Armed Police (part of the state armed forces as well as of the public security organs), who escorted criminals and manned the reform through labour and re-education through labour centres, and had crack units to deal with 'extraordinary incidents'; the Ministry of Public Security which, with its network of bureaux and departments, penetrated Chinese society down to the level of neighbourhood and street committees; the Ministry of Justice, operating *inter alia* the national administration of police affairs and administering the nationwide work of lawyers and public notaries; the State Nationalities Affairs Commission, administering the over fifty separate minority groups scattered over some 50 to 60 per cent of China's territory and comprising 6 per cent of its population; the Bureau of Religious Affairs attached to the State Council, containing Department One in charge of Buddhism, Daoism, and Islam, and Department Two in charge of Catholicism and Protestantism; the People's

Procuratorates; the People's Courts, nominally independent of the government and State Council but overseen by the Politics and Law Leading Group of the Party Central Committee; and the Judicial Committees, usually composed of the President of the Court, chief judges of divisions and other judges, who exercised leadership over the court's judicial activities and whose decisions had to be carried out by the collegiate bench of the court.[72]

Finally, there were the penal institutions, the *laogai, laojiao* and prison systems of detention. Under the *laogai* system were the detention centres (*kanshousuo*), prisons (*jianyu*), disciplinary teams (*laogai gaizao guanjiao du*), and the juvenile detention centres (*shaonianfan guanjiao suo*).[73] The *laojiao* system operated under the Decision of 1957, republished in 1979, and also under the January 1982 regulation, 'Trial Implementation on *Laojiao*'. Its targets, as in the Maoist era, included counter-revolutionaries whose crimes were minor, those who did not engage in proper employment or who did not obey work assignments, those expelled from their work unit, and those who behaved like hoodlums.[74]

This network of institutions formed the structural underpinning of the 1982 Constitution and related legislation, according to which the overall condition of the citizens' civil rights was highly ambiguous. While there was formal legislation covering civil rights of immunity, there was no enabling legislation for the constitutional guarantees of freedom of expression. In terms of the civil rights of immunity, although there was no right of the presumption of innocence, various procedural rights such as independence of the judiciary, the right to defence and appeal, protection against arbitrary arrest and detention and public trial, were formally guaranteed. Other improvements included stricter limits on police–procuratorial action, a prohibition on requiring confessions for conviction, and the constitutional right to secure compensation for loss suffered through infringement of the citizen's rights.[75] And yet, as has been shown, other laws, state and Party policies as well as informal practice, frequently prevailed over these constitutional provisions.

Thus, notwithstanding attempts to formalize the administration of justice, in practice the judicial system failed to achieve autonomy. As one observer concluded at the time:

in practice the judicial system retains significant elements of a public security orientation. First, the system as implemented leaves the greater portion of justice outside of the formal judicial system. Most justice is still dispensed by informal authorities, such as the committees at the grassroots level of the urban political hierarchy, or by the public security bureaus without consulting the courts or the procuratorate. Second, while in theory the public security bureaus, procuratorates, and courts offer a system of checks and balances, in practice they form a hierarchy, with each level increasingly likely to approve decisions made at lower levels. Finally, procedural guarantees considered important in Anglo-Saxon law are missing, which allows for a very high rate of guilty verdicts and the use of trials for public propaganda.[76]

The paradoxical situation was that, while there was legislation to cover civil rights of immunity, it was precisely those rights which, during the modernization decade, were most threatened. Under this legal condition, political dissenters like Wei Jingsheng, Wang Xizhe, and Xu Wenli remained in detention and, in some cases, solitary confinement. In 1983, a wave of executions occurred throughout China as the result of an anti-crime campaign. Moreover, despite the nominal expansion of minority rights in the 1982 Constitution, it was in this period, on 7 March 1989, that martial law was declared in Tibet, following a number of demonstrations in Lhasa. During these demonstrations on 1 October 1987, 5 March 1988, and 5–7 March 1989, Chinese security forces fired directly into demonstrating crowds, killing and wounding Tibetans.[77] There was also overwhelming evidence that torture and other forms of cruel, inhumane, and degrading treatment or punishment were a routine part of detention in police stations, detention centres, labour camps, and prisons in Tibet.[78] On the other hand, civil rights of expression (apart from rights of assembly and association), which were not underwritten by laws, were in this decade expanded at an informal level throughout China. However, Chinese law retained its unstable character, its flexibility and ambiguity which allowed sudden changes to the rights of citizens at the whim of the state. It was this flexibility which underlay the weakness in the implementation of the laws by the judiciary and the police.[79]

The same ambiguity was evident in the political reforms, first institutionalized by the Election and Organic Laws passed by the NPC in June 1979, which, according to one analyst, represented 'relatively cautious attempts to restrain the use of state power'.[80] These sought to change the political structure in China's 2,757 county-level governments, through the use of secret ballots, with more candidates than positions. They extended citizens the right to nominate candidates for deputy positions at the county level; affirmed the right of deputies to query state administrators and submit motions to congresses; and empowered people's congresses at county level to establish standing committees.[81] Yet, once again, these were reforms initiated and organized from above by central Party leadership which were vulnerable to the Party's changing policies.

Informal Civil and Political Rights

It has been observed that, in contrast to the restrictive nature of the 1982 Constitution, and to the laws which were invoked to limit civil rights of immunity, civil rights of expression, relative to the past, underwent an enormous expansion at the informal level. China's citizens began to enjoy increased civil liberties in the form of freedoms of speech, publication, association, and movement (although the latter freedom was not constitutionally guaranteed). A burgeoning of publications in all disciplines, a network of associations and of semi-official consulting and research organizations providing advice to government, brought relatively open policy debate, and a new development in China's social and political life. Increased investment and commercial interchange between China and the West was paralleled by an unprecedented growth in cultural, educational, and scientific interchange, in the form of visiting delegations, businessmen, tourists, and student exchanges. Foreign films, TV programmes, books, and news flooded the Chinese market, open public and private information channels proliferated. Occasional political campaigns — the 1983 anti-spiritual pollution campaign and the early 1987 anti-bourgeois liberalization campaign — sought to neutralize the impact of this exposure to foreign culture, but they were short-lived and ultimately ineffectual.

In this new period of liberalization, the area of personal space, already prised open by the Cultural Revolution, expanded to a hitherto unprecedented extent. Both in the area of literature and the arts, and in the area of popular choice in culture and lifestyle, the state's reach was attenuated by the increasingly invasive pressures of a more pluralist society. In literature, the post-Mao decade initiated an intellectual liberalization that first produced 'scar' literature criticizing the excesses of the Cultural Revolution, and then the 'New Realism' of the years 1979–81.

The traditionally close links of Chinese literature to politics made literature an acceptable and indirect medium through which political dissent could be expressed. The hand-copied literature, including spy stories, detective stories, and love stories, which had abounded in the Cultural Revolution, now came to life in open, unexpurgated versions.[82] An openly critical popular film industry flourished, particularly in the years between the fall of the Democracy Wall in 1980 and the launching of the campaign against spiritual pollution in 1983.[83] Artists and writers were encouraged to experiment with modern techniques, as well as to creatively adapt traditional styles. In the area of personal freedom, the right to wear fashionable clothes and jewellery, as well as to pursue a wide variety of personal hobbies, made a dramatic contrast with the Mao years. Expanded opportunities for travel, not only outside China but within it, stimulated interest in, and knowledge of, the world outside the village and work unit.[84]

That this liberalization represented a change in kind rather than simply of degree was well illustrated by a book published in China devoted entirely to the new concepts and value systems which were a product of the modernization decade. The concepts listed were economic, political, educational, scientific, cultural, social, and ethical. They included a new concept of value, of time and space; the concepts of efficiency, of the market, and competition; equality before the law, separation of Party and state; new concepts of marriage, divorce, of care for the aged, and new lifestyles; and they involved the rejection of old concepts, such as the idea that power prevailed over the law, and the notion of personal dependency.[85] This alteration in the value system reflected the profound changes which had occurred in the arena of politics, the economy, and social structures. But the new ideas did not replace, but co-existed with, old assumptions from the Maoist era. These assumptions were not articulated or even consciously conceptualized as 'rights' by Chinese citizens, who were more conversant with duties: but the social and economic rights, the 'implicit social contract' which had been part of the fabric of their lives before 1979, were assumed to be the indispensable basis on which this newly promised prosperity and freedom would be built.[86]

Expectations were further enhanced by the new commitment to the rule of law which produced calls for the realization of constitutional civil and political rights. The change from collective to individual consciousness was symbolized by the increasing use of the term *gongmin* (citizen), as against the earlier ubiquitous reference to *renmin* (people) or *qunzhong* (masses), in legal and constitutional documents and in ordinary parlance. A number of books on human rights were published and commercially distributed, one of which itemized a broad spectrum of civil, political, social, and economic rights as being the entitlement of every Chinese citizen.[87] Through the decade, Chinese intellectuals began increasingly to make claims on the state to honour the guarantee of the nominal civil rights itemized in every constitution. They thus sought to infuse life and meaning into these hitherto token guarantees.

The greater informal access to civil rights of expression in an overall sense in this period, most strongly reflected in the 1978–80 Democracy Wall Movement, was later demonstrated in the 1986 and 1989 student demonstrations. For although expressions of dissatisfaction with the rate of change, these movements can also be understood as symptoms of an increased popular confidence in the reality and prospect of improved civil rights. Moreover, the exercise of these rights of expression demonstrated the leeway which existed between the essentially conservative function of the formal legal system in enforcing stability and the more liberal unofficial social and political consensus which supported qualified expressions of dissent. Part of this atmosphere of tolerance for divergent opinions was the discussion which developed in the late 1970s and the 1980s on human rights.

A substantial degree of liberalization was also evident in Chinese political life in the 1980s. The 1979 Electoral Law of the PRC for the National People's Congress and the Local People's Congresses of All Levels provided for direct election of people's congresses not only at the township but also at the county level.[88] Although the NPC in 1982 adopted several amendments to the election law to limit the exercise of 'extreme democracy' which had occurred in the 1980 elections, the process of gradual liberalization at an informal level was undeniable. Thus, at an enlarged Politburo meeting in August 1980, Deng Xiaoping suggested the separation of the power of Party and state, the establishment of an independent judiciary, the introduction of measures enabling public criticism and the recall of corrupt leaders, and limited elections for leaders in grass-roots level organizations.[89] The goal of political reform was pursued with the establishment in 1986 of political reform research groups (*zhengzhi gaige yanjiu xiaozu*) in each Party Committee at Central Committee, provincial, and city level.

The 1980 policy directives also provided the basis for Acting General Party Secretary Zhao Ziyang's later initiatives expanding civil and political rights at the Thirteenth Party Congress in October 1987. The reform agenda included the separation of the functions of Party and state, reform of the cadre system and governmental structures, increased popular participation in politics, and the strengthening of the socialist legal system.[90] In his opening speech to the Congress, Zhao said that the government should 'guarantee the citizens' rights and freedoms as stipulated in the constitution' and enact laws governing the press and publications, association and assembly, and freedom of belief.[91] Discussion and drafting of these proposed laws were reportedly well under way by the end of 1988.[92] Furthermore, in his speech Zhao announced that it was 'necessary to respect the will of the voters and ensure that they have more options in elections'.[93]

In the next few years the need for 'political supervision' became a popular catchword within the Chinese leadership. News conferences by top leaders became an important source of information dissemination and political supervision, and numerous polls were taken to assess popular opinion.[94] Within the National People's Congress, the Party's willingness to allow limited political liberalization was demonstrated at its seventh congress, held in the spring of 1988. The Chinese press called this the 'most open and democratic' NPC congress since 1954, and reform was the 'centre of all undertakings'.[95] A majority of the delegates were newcomers, and they were selected from local level congresses, which for the first time had more candidates than seats. They stressed reform and debated a wide range of crucial issues, such as the problem of inflation and inequities of economic development. Domestic and foreign journalists were also allowed to cover major segments of the session.[96] At the second session in April 1989 a bill on special legislative rights for Shenzhen was passed by a vote of 1,609 in favour, 274 against, and 805 abstentions.[97] And it was reported that 120 changes had been made to Premier Li Peng's report on government work in response to the views of deputies to the NPC.[98]

Nevertheless, in contrast to the expansion of civil rights, political reform was more limited, precisely because of the need to carry out lasting structural reform to achieve it. The more lively appearance of NPC sessions, and especially of the NPC Standing Committee, has been interpreted as 'a manifestation of inner Party struggle' rather than an indication of the strengthening of popular participation.[99] At the grass-roots level, the high rate of participation in the elections to local people's congresses in 1980 revealed 'both the symbolic quality of the elections and the regime's mobilizational capacity'.[100] The separation of Party and state, which required a complex restructuring process, was resisted by entrenched Party interests, especially in local Party committees. The streamlining of the bureaucracy, reflected in the newly pared-down State Council, proved a long term problem because of the in-built momentum for bureaucratic proliferation, and the informal channels of bureaucratic resistance.[101] Moreover, the decentralization of political control led to the ambiguous result that 'the simple relations between state and society based on unconditional obedience to the central authorities (were) superseded in most cases by an unregulated bureaucratic process'.[102] Finally, although attempts were made to regularize procedures among the top leadership in running state affairs, the events of May–June 1989 revealed how limited the results were.

China's Changing International and Domestic Position on Human Rights

A further dimension to the formal condition of human rights in the modernization decade was provided by Chinese official pronouncements and activities in respect of human rights in the international arena. As the point of contact between national and international norms and activities, and as a formative influence on China's international reputation, the United Nations and its community placed pressures on the Chinese government to respond to, and accommodate, a wide variety of international norms and practices, including the concept of human rights.[103] In its official pronouncements and activities in international forums, therefore, China was more responsive to making formal adjustments to the international law of human rights than its domestic legislation or domestic human rights policies would suggest. Prior to its entry into the United Nations in 1971, as suggested, China did not normally legitimate its policies in terms of human rights, but rather in terms of the achievements of the revolution in ending class exploitation, and promoting the material needs and welfare of the working people. This was notwithstanding retrospective justifications of China's policies which have cited Zhou Enlai's 1955 statement of respect for human rights.[104] In the late 1970s, however, the rather crude Chinese analyses of the differences between the capitalist and socialist theories of human rights were replaced by a more sophisticated and differentiated view of human rights and of their significance for China and the international community. China also began to cautiously participate in human rights activities in international bodies. This alteration in attitude was due to a complex of factors, including China's entry into the UN, domestic reactions to the civil rights abuses of the Cultural Revolution, and economic developments arising from the Four Modernizations and increasing levels of international trade.

In joining the United Nations in 1971, China became in theory a party to the basic human rights principles embodied in the UN Charter. It also became subject to the general principle accepted by UN members that cases characterized by the gross and persistent violation of human rights should be lifted from the area of domestic jurisdiction to the international arena. However, China did not sign or ratify the basic UN human rights instruments, the 1966 International Covenant on Civil and Political Rights and its Optional Protocol, and the 1966 International Covenant on Economic, Social, and Cultural Rights. At first, it was not prepared to become a member of the UN Commission on Human Rights and attended as observer at the Commission's sessions in 1979, 1980, and 1981. China appeared to be feeling its way, wishing neither to flout UN conventions nor to conform to any identifiable position on human rights, adopting in preference an 'evasive position of non-committal'.[105] Human rights issues raised in the UN General Assembly (UNGA) were initially supported primarily in terms of the right of peoples not to be discriminated against on the basis of race or sex. Until 1980, China supported UNGA resolutions on self-determination, on the granting of independence to colonial countries and on opposition to apartheid, racial discrimination, and discrimination against women. It absented itself, however, from resolutions on human rights in Chile and El Salvador, as well as on questions of drugs and the elimination of religious intolerance. On the other hand, it supported UN peacekeeping and UN sanctions against South Africa, if not against Cuba and Libya.[106]

By 1977 China had modified its refusal to cite UN standards on civil and political rights by its public criticism of the Soviet Union for the imprisoning and exiling of dissidents, and of Taiwan for the suppression of democracy supporters.[107] By 1981, China had changed its 'absent' vote on human rights in Chile and El Salvador to an abstention, thus at least indicating a preparedness to be involved in the consideration of civil and political rights issues.[108] In 1984, it supported the appointment of a rapporteur to examine the human rights situation in Afghanistan, despite Soviet and East European protests that this would constitute interference in internal affairs, and it also supported a 1985 Human Rights Commission resolution for a similar investigation in Chile, although not in El Salvador and Iran.[109]

In the same year China voted for an UNGA resolution, 'The Indivisibility and Interdependence of Economic, Social, Cultural, Civil and Political Rights'. Although meant to redress the imbalance between rights in favour of social and economic rights, this resolution implied acceptance of the need for civil and political rights.[110] In the Human Rights Commission, which China joined in 1982, resolutions adopted without a vote in 1989, following preliminary amendments contributed to by China, included decisions and resolutions on human rights in Burma and Chile and on a host of civil and political rights issues: the 'Right to Freedom of Opinion and Expression'; 'Human Rights in the Administration of Justice'; 'Independence and Impartiality of the Judiciary, Jurors and Assessors and the Independence of Lawyers'; 'Administrative Detention without Charge or Trial'; 'The Right of Everyone to Leave any Country, Including his Own, and to Return to his Country'; 'Political Prisoners'; 'Enhancing the Effectiveness of the Principle of Periodic and Genuine Elections'; and 'Summary or Arbitrary Executions'.[111]

Activities encompassing civil and political rights were paralleled by appropriate statements. In a speech to the forty-first session of the United Nations General Assembly in 1986, the Chinese Foreign Minister, referring to the twentieth anniversary of the International Covenant on Civil and Political Rights and the International Covenant on Economic, Social, and Cultural Rights, pointed out that 'the two covenants have played a positive role in realizing the purposes and principles of the UN Charter concerning respect for human rights. The Chinese Government has consistently supported these purposes and principles'.[112] In September 1988, at the forty-third session of the United Nations General Assembly, the Chinese Foreign Minister described the Universal Declaration of Human Rights as 'the first international instrument which systematically sets forth the specific contents

regarding respect for and protection of fundamental human rights
Despite its historical limitations, the Declaration has exerted a
far-reaching influence on the development of the post-war international human rights activities and played a positive role in this
regard'.[113]

China's preparedness to accept international standards of human
rights was underlined by its decision to join the UN Human Rights
Commission. It also joined the Sub-Commission on Prevention of
Discrimination and Protection of Minorities, the panel of human
rights experts, as well as the Commission on the Status of Women.
China successively signed, ratified, and acceded to seven human
rights conventions: the International Convention on the Elimination
of all Forms of Racial Discrimination; the International Convention
on the Suppression and Punishment of the Crime of Apartheid;
the Convention on the Elimination of all Forms of Discrimination
against Women; the Convention on the Prevention and Punishment
of the Crime of Genocide; the Convention against Torture and
other Cruel, Inhuman, or Degrading Treatment or Punishment;
the Convention Relating to the Status of Refugees; and the Protocol
Relating to the Status of Refugees. China actively participated in
working groups to draft and formulate international human rights
instruments such as the Convention against Torture and Other
Cruel, Inhuman, or Degrading Treatment or Punishment and the
Declaration on the Protection of Rights of Persons Belonging to
National, Ethnic, Religious, and Linguistic Minorities.[114] Under
the Racial Discrimination Convention, China was obliged to report
on, and receive criticisms of, its treatment of national or ethnic
minorities to an international committee of eighteen states. In
1988, it took a further step in the direction of human rights by
commemorating, for the first time, the anniversary (fortieth) of
the Universal Declaration of Human Rights. This activity, in the
form of a symposium and publication of some commemorative
articles, lasted one week, from 4–10 December 1988.[115]

Such participation in UN human rights activities and resolutions obviously crossed the theoretical divide between external
inquiries into matters involving the self-determination of peoples,
which China regarded as legitimate, and international inquiry
into matters of domestic civil rights, which in theory it proscribed. Whether expressed in terms of acquiescence or merely
passive involvement, China's participation increased its vulnerability to similar investigations into its own activities. Other areas

of involvement in international instrumentalities related to human rights included participation in the International Labour Organization (ILO), which brought China under the scrutiny of the Committee on Freedom of Association; co-operation with the International Committee of the Red Cross (ICRC); extension of permission to the World Food Programme to visit poor areas in China; and agreement in 1985 that the International Atomic Energy Agency could inspect its nuclear facilities.[116]

By 1989, therefore, China had become absorbed in numerous ways into a web of involvement and obligation in the international human rights arena. Yet it continued to stress notions of state sovereignty and non-interference, and had not signed or ratified the two international covenants of 1966 or the Optional Protocol. Moreover, its support in the UN for issues of civil and political rights was arbitrary and erratic. Nevertheless, China had modified its position on human rights over the years since entry into the United Nations and, in those forums at least, had come closer to accepting a basic core of universally accepted human rights. The challenge for the international community was to achieve a greater congruence between China's more liberal formal international position on human rights and its inflexible formal domestic position, and to break through the compartmentalization existing between them.[117]

Apart from China's formal activities and pronouncements in respect of human rights in international organizations, a changing attitude towards such issues in this post-Mao decade was reflected in the writings of individual Chinese scholars publishing in such formal and semi-formal media as *Red Flag, People's Daily, Xuexi yu Tansuo* ('Study and Exploration') and *Beijing Review*, as well as in citizens' handbooks, encyclopedias, and legal textbooks. Although conducted at a diminished level of formality, and although of a less homogeneous nature than official pronouncements, these theoretical discussions were part of the pattern of officially tolerated public discourse, which caught, filtered, and disseminated different, and sometimes opposing, strands of official opinion.

The era of the first democracy movement was a period of extensive intellectual ferment. Between 1979 and 1980, a plethora of issues that had been taboo in the Maoist era were freely debated in the press and in society at large. A number of conservative articles rehearsed the old arguments on human rights.

Thus, a 1979 *Red Flag* article by Xiao Weiyun, Luo Haocai, and Wu Xieyin, 'How Marxism Views the Question of "Human Rights"', stated that the issue of human rights was a question of principle differentiating between socialist democracy and capitalist democracy.[118] The article attacked the current supporters of human rights in China as being neither Marxist nor nationalist — they did not want socialism, the dictatorship of the proletariat, Communist Party leadership, or Marxism-Leninism-Mao Zedong Thought. The authors argued that only under a socialist state could there be extensive democratic rights. These, they claimed, had been achieved in China.

According to their views, China had eliminated private ownership of the means of production and the class basis of man's exploitation of man, and had implemented the principle of 'he who does not work, neither shall he eat'. The people were now the masters of the state, enjoying supervision over the state, enterprises, and cultural–educational affairs. The constitution guaranteed every political right and freedom, the right of election and recall, the right to work, the right to education, and the freedoms of expression, publication, assembly, association, procession, and demonstration, as well as the freedom to strike. It provided, moreover, for the equality of men and women and of minority peoples, and prohibited racial discrimination and oppression. The state expanded access to social security, to emergency relief, free medical services, and collective medical enterprises, and made available the material conditions of rest and recuperation for workers. Moreover, although the political rights of criminals and counterrevolutionaries were suspended, if they did not engage in wrongdoing they would be given land, work, and the means to live, so that they might reform and become new men. Although problems remained, in that the democratic and legal systems needed strengthening, these were problems which could be overcome under Party leadership: only thus could the Four Modernizations be realized. Those who used 'democracy' to create trouble, on the other hand, would have to be severely punished.

It will be noted that, while this article rehearsed the standard interpretation of bourgeois human rights, it did not reject human rights *per se*, claiming rather that only under a socialist system could democratic rights be realized. By contrast, the outer limits of the human rights debate in this period were established in an article, 'Human Rights and the Legal System', which publicized the human rights abuses in the case of Zhang Zhixin, executed for alleged criticism of the Cultural Revolution and of Mao.[119] In her criticisms of the Cultural Revolution, Lin Biao, and Jiang Qing, the article stated, Zhang was only exercising her civil rights guaranteed under the constitution. Her only crime was to think and to express her political convictions. If people were not allowed to use their freedom to debate, how could they be said to have freedom of speech and thought? If they could only praise and not criticize leaders, how could one talk of popular supervision? Was not the state constitution just an empty document? After the smashing of the Gang of Four, and the appearance of cases like Zhang Zhixin's, the author maintained, the people had realized they must change their powerless condition and fight for the sacred rights given them in the constitution, so they naturally discussed human rights.

The article concluded with a bold prescription for avoiding a recurrence of the tragedy of Zhang Zhixin: to develop socialist democracy and the socialist legal system; to implement the right to vote, using it as a mechanism to put arbitrary dictatorship to the test; to protect the people's right of supervision and recall of cadres; to change the situation whereby basic level cadres had the power of life and death over the people, against which the people had no recourse; to guarantee that the rights of the person were not violated; and to truly implement the principle of equality before the law.

Although the period of the Democracy Wall Movement was the most fertile source of human rights literature, scholarly interest in the subject continued throughout the decade. From constitutional legal texts, to 'citizens' handbooks, to articles on human rights published in journals and newspapers of varying degrees of official status, a certain consensus emerged. Over the decade, human rights were seen in an increasingly positive light. First, it was claimed that the human rights doctrine itself had changed, from its narrow, bourgeois, individual-based origins in civil and political rights, to broader and internationally accepted principles emphasizing the second and third generations of rights. Secondly, while a generally consistent case was made that under bourgeois rule civil and political rights in the guise of equality and freedom had disguised effective inequality and unequal access to material goods and opportunity, and led to exploitation, the historical revolutionary contribution made by human rights in the period of bourgeois ascendancy was increasingly acknowledged.[120]

Thus the traditional priority of economic and social rights and of the collective rights of self-determination and development was maintained, while the parameters of discussion of civil and political rights were broadened. Human rights, in the general view, were seen as neither abstract nor natural — they were contingent and cumulative. But civil and political rights were accepted as legitimate items on the human rights agenda and as a necessary corollary (along with their associated duties) to the Four Modernizations. Even the principle of non-interference was not consistently adhered to. Thus a *Peking Review* commentary criticized the Soviet condition of civil rights and implicitly condoned political dissent:

On this issue [of civil rights], the US attitude seems more candid, since Washington admitted: 'We are ourselves culpable in some ways', while Moscow pretended to have a clear conscience and boasted about the right to work, education, social welfare, vote . . . in the Soviet Union, to make itself out to be the champion of 'human rights'. But as the Soviet Union today has become a land of KGB agents, bristling with prisons full of its citizens while many others have been exiled, what 'human rights' can it talk about? An important reason for the growing number of 'dissidents' there in recent years is the Soviet revisionist ruling clique's unjust and oppressive rule which has roused the Soviet people's discontent and resistance. The Soviet revisionists' unbridled trampling on human rights while feverishly prettifying themselves precisely shows social-imperialism's hypocrisy and knavishness.[121]

In other basic ways, writings on human rights in the 1979–89 decade revealed differences of analysis, interpretation, emphasis, and outlook. In contrast to the 1979 *Red Flag* article analysed above, an article by Xu Bing, 'The Origins and Historical Development of the Theory of Human Rights', claimed that human rights were above class.[122] 'Human rights in its current legal usage has a clear class character and a clear supra-class character, one aspect cannot be stressed over another', it insisted. 'To deny the supra-class nature of human rights and to insist on its class character, to advocate that rights should only be given to the people and not to the enemy would lead to the fallacy of totally denying human rights, with the result that they would be trampled on'. Xu also disputed the generally held thesis that human rights were identical with citizens' rights, suggesting that rights had an abstract character: 'Human rights are not at all the equivalent of citizens' rights. Human rights mean the rights which should be enjoyed by man, while citizens' rights indicate the concrete man — the rights which the citizen can enjoy in real life. Human rights has its ideal quality'.

Despite unanimity about the desirability of the expansion of human rights in China, both for domestic reasons and because human rights were now an essential and inescapable part of the international political agenda, writers differed in their estimate of their potential for development in China. Lin Rongnian and Zhang Jinfan, for instance, suggested that 'the struggle to establish social-ist democracy and a rule of law and to guarantee human rights in China' would take a relatively long period, in view of the lack of democratic traditions, the backward economy, and the fact that Chinese socialism was established on the 'ruins' of a semi-feudal, neo-colonial state.[123] Another problem was seen to be the exist-ence of special privileges and of an ideology of special privileges in China. Adopting an economic determinist approach, the authors claimed that only after the development of the modernization pro-cess could democratic rights be properly guaranteed, because 'democracy needs the guarantee of a rule of law, a rule of law requires the appropriate cultural conditions'.

On the other hand, scholars were unanimous about the neces-sity of supporting human rights in the international arena. A 1982 article, 'On the Question of Human Rights in the International Arena' argued that despite the politicization of the issue of human rights, it was the duty of the Third World to support them. Moreover, it claimed, 'socialism and human rights are one (*shi yizhi de*)'.[124] And an article by Guo Shan, 'China's Role in the Human Rights Field', gave qualified support to the notion of inter-national involvement in human rights situations.[125] Even the hith-erto unchallenged priority of the collective interpretation of human rights came under question in a *Beijing Review* article in which Ma Jun stated: 'China maintains that human rights should in-clude both the rights of the individual and the rights of the col-lective and that a citizen's political right is as important as his economic, social, and cultural rights'. He further drew a tenuous distinction between appropriate and inappropriate areas of inter-national jurisdiction in matters of human rights:

China has no objection to the United Nations expressing concern in a proper way over consistent and large-scale human rights violations in a given country, but it opposes the interference in other countries' internal affairs under the pretext of defending human rights.[126]

Finally, at the symposium in December 1988 to celebrate the fortieth anniversary of the Universal Declaration of Human Rights in Beijing, Professor Wei Min concluded that although human rights involved collective and individual rights, 'the collective cannot be stressed to the neglect of the individual. The guarantee of fundamental individual rights constitutes the basis for practising democratic politics'.[127]

It has emerged that until 1982 the civil and political rights guaranteed to Chinese citizens under their constitutions remained reasonably consistent with the actual exercise of these rights — always excepting the token repetition of the standard civil rights — in the negative sense that the provisions of the constitution were close to the reality of a heavily controlled society. The 1982 Constitution, however, diverged sharply from informal reality.

In terms of civil and political rights, as a response to the official repudiation of the 1978–80 democracy movement, the Constitution curbed the expression of the qualified and circumscribed freedoms of thought, speech, assembly, and association allowed under the two previous constitutions by eliminating the 'four great freedoms' from its provisions and replacing them with the 'four basic principles' — that no exercise of democracy could contradict the socialist road, the people's democratic dictatorship, the Communist Party leadership, and Marxism-Leninisim-Mao Zedong thought. It also dropped the freedom to strike. In its formal reality, it therefore provided a clear contrast with later developments in Chinese society wherein all these freedoms were exercised to a hitherto unprecedented extent.

Some rights not constitutionally guaranteed, such as the right to freedom of movement and choice of job, were also exercised in the 1980s. Paradoxically, however, it was in the area of civil rights of expression, where there were no laws underwriting the informal freedoms, that civil rights were most freely enjoyed. Civil rights of immunity, on the other hand, which did have accompanying legislation, were the most abused. In contrast to civil rights, political rights showed less divergence between theory and practice, both because political rights in the 1982 Constitution and in the election laws were somewhat expanded and because their meaningful exercise in reality was more heavily circumscribed.

In contrast to the illiberal condition of human rights at the formal domestic level, Chinese official activities and statements in the international arena showed a more cosmopolitan acceptance of the status of civil and political rights as an essential component of the International Bill of Rights, as did the semi-formal discussion in the Chinese press and scholarly literature. The liberalization of China's international and theoretical stance on human rights thus formed a contrast to the subsequent events of June 1989, and helped shape the international reaction to those events.

5 Economic, Social, and Cultural Rights, 1979–1989

Although we make it our long-term task to raise efficiency by widening income gaps, it is not really our final goal. It is only a means to the end. By widening income gaps and raising efficiency, we eventually will usher in a new stage when genuine social equality can be realised.

Liu Guoguang, Liang Wensen, and others[1]

The civil and political rights embodied in the 1982 Constitution can be seen as the ambiguous product of conflicting urges to stabilize society and to liberalize it in the interests of economic development. The Constitution's provision of economic, social, and cultural rights was equally ambiguous, reflecting as it did a contradictory attempt to maintain the priority of rights characteristic of a socialist society while at the same time foreshadowing the changes which would be the outcome of economic restructuring. As a result, many of the clauses were anachronistic, granting rights that no longer existed in reality, or programmatic, containing rights that were not currently realizable. The rights promised either no longer conformed to the existing structure of Chinese society, or anticipated the new structure, but were not subsequently implemented or institutionalized.

The failure to match structural change in China's economy with appropriate political structural change was paralleled in this decade by a failure to effect appropriate changes in the infrastructure of China's economic and social rights. In any developing country, economic modernization under market conditions involves social change.[2] As Jack Donnelly has argued, development planning involves social choices and redistributive policies, even if they are not conscious ones.[3] The distribution of national income is determined by the central government, which decides the precise balance to be struck between social and individual consumption. Even if the government does not directly or consciously make these redistributive decisions, they may be the unintended consequences of its new development strategies. If in a socialist system these strategies involve market mechanisms, the unintended consequences can be destructive of socialist values and institutions. Whether conscious or unintended, the result is the same. Three trade-offs have been widely argued by governments to be the prerequisite of development — the needs trade-off, the equality trade-off, and the liberty trade-off.[4] Because of the trickle-down theory of growth, these trade-offs have been seen as temporary and self-correcting, as Liu Guoguang has suggested in the above citation. But, as Donnelly shows in his study of economic development in South Korea and Brazil, 'it is the initial distribution of assets which sets the pattern for growth. If asset distribution is unequal, it is probable that the additions to income from growth will be distributed unequally'.[5]

These observations are borne out by the impact of the modernization decade on China's economic and social rights. The new socialist commodity economy with market characteristics developed in China after 1978 represented a blend of socialist planning mechanisms which, in conjunction with an economic arena responsive to market pressures, was devised to suit Chinese conditions. Although many have argued that this development represented the dilution of socialist principles, it did not represent their formal abandonment.

The architects of this developmental strategy, the moderate/conservative reformers and the radical reformers, agreed to the necessity of such reforms but differed in regard to their timing and degree, as well as to the relative weighting to be placed on planning and the market.[6] The reform process in China thus proceeded in zigzag fashion depending on which reform policy won the day. The process of modernization was also characterized by an incremental and experimental approach, beginning with programmes designed to raise production and living standards. It also subjected potentially controversial policies to local experimentation, with adoption at a national level occurring only when the economic and political acceptability of these policies had been established.[7]

This politically sensitive approach had the virtue of allowing reform to proceed without excessive political repercussions. On the other hand, it held up the more controversial reforms, and allowed those reforms already in place to be undermined by informal obstruction. Even more importantly for the condition of economic and social rights, it engendered a piecemeal rather than a holistic approach to the developmental process, preventing the integration of structural economic change with appropriate changes in the social welfare and social security infrastructure.

The simultaneous operation of the dual economy of planning and market, moreover, whatever the relative strengths of each, facilitated the development of corrupt practices within the gaps or interstices between the two systems, thus increasing the problem of unequal and unproductive redistribution of resources. In China's case, this problem was recognized by the World Bank, which warned against the 'informal income redistribution' that was occurring in the country, and suggested that 'since these and similar practices quickly become well known, their social benefits are temporary, while they seem to have a high long-term cost in terms of corruption and the evolution of a society based on special privileges'.[8]

Two other inherent limitations on the success of economic modernization were also relevant to the condition of China's economic and social rights. The introduction of a strategy of maximizing economic growth can lead to serious economic problems which, when considered together with other socialist principles such as equality and collectivism, render problematic any cost–benefit analysis.[9] Secondly, the basis of the Leninist concept of leadership is the principle of one party dominance in a centrally planned and administered economy. Therefore, any reform programme which exceeds the acceptable limits to the point of challenging these basic principles will be resisted, whatever the economic consequences.[10] As a result, the shift in social welfare philosophy from indirect to direct gain sharing which is the consequence of the new economic policies, is rendered of doubtful value in the long term.

China's new economic development strategy launched in 1978 has been divided into two distinct phases, moderate (1978–84) and radical (1984–9).[11] The moderate reforms, which provided a baseline for economic modernization up to the present, assigned a greater role to economic incentives in both rural and urban sectors, encouraged a 'get rich first' mentality, stimulated the development of private and collective ownership in both arenas and expanded the role of market forces in the production, circulation, and pricing of goods. The radical phase not only involved more radical market reforms, but anticipated the pluralization of politics, the freeing of the press, and more competitive elections. This strategy affected economic and social rights by diminishing their accessibility, particularly for certain social groups.

The extent of this diminution of rights is brought into focus by a number of World Bank reports and, on the Chinese side, in a retrospective survey by Liu Guoguang of the achievements of the Maoist era:

> In spite of the negative phenomena that kept recurring in China's economic life, the many social evils seen in the course of industrialization in many developing countries such as inequality in distribution, constant unemployment, sustained inflation and increasing foreign loans that are all supposed to accompany the conventional strategy, have been either non-existent in China or have existed only as exceptional cases. In China's past practice, remarkable successes were scored in meeting the people's basic needs including nutrition, public health service, education, and so on.[12]

The extent of change was brought into prominence by the chasm which developed between the economic, social, and cultural rights guaranteed in China's constitutions, and the substantive rights that the majority of the people could enjoy. Liu Guoguang's analysis forms the necessary backdrop to this comparative framework.

Formal Economic, Social, and Cultural Rights

Classical Marxist theory maintains that the constitution is part of the superstructure which reflects and expresses the economic base, a position still endorsed by Chinese constitutional and legal theorists. Since 1949, however, Chinese constitutions have also had the function of determining the nature of the economic base.[13] Thus, the 1982 Constitution provided the structural underpinning for the new socialist commodity economy, with its expanded forms of ownership, its market orientation, decentralization of economic decision making, and its strengthened links with the international economy. For instance, while upholding the system of 'socialist public ownership', it pledged protection for 'the lawful rights and interests of the urban and rural collectives' as well as 'the lawful rights and interests of the individual economy', describing them as 'a complement to the socialist public economy'.[14] The state also pledged protection by law to 'the right of citizens to inherit private property'.[15]

The two main characteristics of economic, social, and cultural rights — the contingency of rights and state responsibility for their expansion — were set out in Article 14 under the heading of General Principles:

The state properly apportions accumulation and consumption, pays attention to the interests of the collective and the individual as well as of the state and, on the basis of expanded production, gradually improves the material and cultural life of the people.

In view of the expanded forms of ownership and the devolution of the state's actual political and economic authority in the modernization decade, the continuity in the provision of economic and social rights in the 1982 Constitution with those of previous constitutions was just as significant as the additional rights it guaranteed. In this respect it provided a contrast with the provision of civil and political rights, where the significance lay in the new rights which were guaranteed. Thus Article 42 of the 1982 Constitution continued to maintain the citizen's 'right as well as the duty' to work. Under Article 43, 'working people' were guaranteed the right to rest, with prescribed working hours and vacations, while under Article 44 a system of retirement was 'prescribed by law' for all state workers, and the livelihood of 'retired persons' ensured. As in previous constitutions all citizens had the 'duty as well as right to receive education' and the 'freedom to engage in scientific research, literary and artistic creation and other cultural pursuits'.[16] Women were guaranteed equal rights with men in all spheres of life and the principle of equal pay for equal work was reiterated.[17]

Where the 1982 Constitution diverged from previous constitutions was in the extension of social security rights from 'working people' to 'citizens'. Article 45 stated that 'citizens of the People's Republic of China have the right to material assistance from the state and society when they are old, ill, or disabled'. Moreover, the state undertook to 'develop the social insurance, social relief, and medical and health services that are required to enable citizens to enjoy this right'. This formal universalization of social rights signalled the end of the close nexus between social rights and the workplace which had been an integral feature of socialist rights, and implied acceptance of the existence of unemployment.

The expansion of economic, social, and cultural rights was also foreshadowed in the section 'General Principles'. New undertakings included the state's responsibility for developing medical and health services, promoting modern and traditional medicine, and 'sanitation activities of a mass character', as well as for developing physical culture and promoting mass sports activities.[18] The state also undertook the promotion of the development of literature and art, the press, broadcasting and TV, publishing and distribution services, libraries, museums and cultural services, and sponsored mass cultural activities.[19] The new emphasis on specialization and technical requirements was reflected in the state's pledge to train specialized personnel in all fields, increase the number of intellectuals and 'create conditions to give full scope to their role in socialist modernization'.[20]

Finally, expanded workers' rights were foreshadowed in the provisions that 'state enterprises practice democratic management through congresses of workers and staff and in other ways', and that 'collective economic organizations practice democratic management . . . with the entire body of their workers electing or removing their management personnel and deciding on major issues concerning operation and management'.[21]

Despite the apparent continuity of major rights and the expansion of others, the 1982 Constitution contained an important subtext which implicitly qualified traditional Marxist economic and social rights in important respects. It also deleted or excluded rights which normally formed part of the socio-economic infrastructure of market economies. These errors of omission and commission served to undermine Peng Zhen's broad undertaking that under the 1982 Constitution, 'the citizens of our country have the right to work and rest, the right to receive education, the right to receive material assistance in disability, and enjoy such welfare as social insurance, social assistance, and free medical care'.[22]

For instance, the wide-ranging educational rights provided by the state in Articles 19, 20, 23, and 46 were qualified by the devolution of responsibility for implementation of rights implicit in the new provision in Article 19 that 'the state encourages the collective economic organizations, state enterprises, and other social forces to set up educational institutions of various types in accordance with the law'. Devolution of responsibility for health delivery was also suggested in the state's encouragement, in Article 2, of the establishment of medical and health facilities by the rural economic collectives, state enterprises and undertakings, and neighbourhood organizations. The universal access of citizens to health, education, and social security, particularly in retirement, was also brought into question by the new provisions in Article 49 that 'parents have the duty to rear and educate their minor children, and children who have come of age have the duty to support and assist their parents'.

While qualifying by implication the state's responsibility for providing traditionally guaranteed or traditionally implemented rights (since in the past non-state employees of collective enterprises had enjoyed access to economic and social rights also not formally guaranteed under the earlier constitutions), at the same time the 1982 Constitution omitted any reference to two rights normally associated with industrializing and market-oriented economies. The right to strike, guaranteed under the 1975 and 1978 Constitutions, was dropped. Even more significantly, there was no move to introduce a right to unemployment relief to non-state workers, despite the implicit acceptance of the existence of unemployment. The only relief offered was material assistance to those who had lost the physical ability to work (*sangshi laodong de nengli*) or vocational training to youth awaiting employment (*daiye qingnian*).[23]

Substantive Economic, Social, and Cultural Rights

The most significant structural change relevant to economic and social rights in the modernization decade was a function of the rationalization of the production process — a radical change from the Maoist period when the economic goals of increased production were pursued, not altogether successfully as we have seen, in conjunction with the socio-economic goal of full employment.[24] It was also a function of the expansion of different forms of ownership systems. In the rural sector, where the initial reforms were the most successful, this rationalization was expressed in the virtual decollectivization of agricultural production. Through the 'household responsibility system', responsibility for agricultural production was transferred from the collective to the individual farming household, while administrative functions, public health, education, security, and civil affairs, were moved from the commune to township and village governments, often the same geographic entity. Collective plots were assigned to the most efficient individual peasants to farm, and more specialized crops produced.

These changes released redundant labour to work in collective rural industrial enterprises and allowed the hiring of labour for agricultural production. They also allowed peasants the right, formerly denied them, to work in urban industrial enterprises. Thus, by the summer of 1985 it was estimated that specialized households in rural China employed ten to fifteen million people and collective rural industry employed sixty million more. By the year 2000 the 85 per cent of the rural labour force engaged in agricultural production was expected to decline to about 30 per cent.[25] The redistribution of land created a kind of enclosure system which led to widescale movement of the rural labour surplus from the land to townships and, in many cases, to the large cities.[26] In the language of rights, many of China's peasants thus exchanged their previous source of subsistence, or right to work on the land, for another economic right, the right to choose their employment and for the civil right of movement. On the other hand, most urban state workers and staff (*zhigong*) maintained their job security, while foregoing the right to choose employment.

In the industrial sector, the most significant structural changes had their source in a package of regulations introduced in July 1986 which comprised regulations for the implementation of the labour contract system and for the dismissal of workers by state-owned enterprises, as well as for 'State-owned Enterprise Workers' Wait-for-Employment Insurance'. These regulations affected the 134 million state-employed workers and staff (*zhigong*), who comprised over one-quarter of the total labour force of around 500 million. In the short term, however, these attempts were undermined for a number of reasons, which included the difficulty of introducing the essential structural changes — price reform, enterprise autonomy, and the ability to declare enterprises bankrupt.[27] Nevertheless, the introduction of new incentive systems, the process of wage adjustment, and the gradual introduction of the contract system began slowly to change the face of economic and social rights in the urban enterprises. The introduction of the contract system was crucial to these changes, since it introduced into the state workplace new insecurities of tenure and entailed for those under contract a loss of social rights, in the shape of a loss of access to social welfare and social security, as well as other benefits. For this reason, its universal adoption was strongly resisted by incumbent state workers, who succeeded in amending its original purpose so that eventually the scheme was extended only to new workers who had joined the workplace after 1986.[28] Nevertheless, the economic right to work, unchallenged in constitutional theory, was progressively undermined by market mechanisms. Although the 'iron rice bowl' was not smashed, its surface became marked with hairline cracks in the shape of redundancy, unemployment, large wage differentials, and inflation.

Since social rights in post-1949 China flowed from the right to work, and were thus determined by economic rights, any change in the structure of economic rights had an automatic impact on the provision of social rights. In the modernization era, moreover, the switch in the basis of wage allocation from the graded wage system to a 'floating' wage system linking incomes and social benefits of workers with the quality of management and economic performance of the enterprise, gave this dependence of social rights on economic rights a peculiarly modern twist.[29]

Nevertheless, as already suggested, for those employed in the state sector before the contract system for new workers was introduced, the informal reality of their access to social rights was not as devastating as the formal logic of the structural economic changes might suggest. Despite the absence of a right of collective bargaining in the industrial sector, for the first time in decades, as Andrew Walder has effectively demonstrated, workers were able to influence managers directly to achieve increased income.[30] One reason for this was suggested by Xi Zhongsheng of the State Commission for Restructuring the Economy, who stated in May 1989 that, despite massive redundancies in industry, 'due to the lack of a sound labour market and unemployment insurance system', only 10 per cent of those redundant had actually been laid off.[31]

In other words, precisely because of the absence of a safety net for the unemployed, dismissal or leaving one's job, though formally countenanced, was not considered a feasible option by either management or workers. Despite the absence of the rights of collective bargaining and of democracy in the workplace, the state workers, through expressions of dissatisfaction such as the conscious withdrawal of efficiency, could effectively influence management. For these informal reasons, Chinese managers were uniquely, and paradoxically, in view of the vast unemployment problem, dependent on their labour force.[32] And because the factory manager was at once the manager of an economic enterprise and the leader of a socio-economic and political community, worker pressure produced a number of results.[33] First, it distorted the original purpose of the bonus system and wage reform to enhance industrial efficiency, so that these institutions functioned instead as a means of egalitarian redistribution to inflate the wages of workers.[34] Thus, for the elite group of state workers, the 'iron rice bowl' was maintained. Secondly, worker pressure ensured that the management and the existing workforce were bound together in an effort to oppose such structural by-products of the industrial reforms as the relocation of the funding and adminis- tration of welfare, social security, and unemployment compensa- tion, from the work unit to local governments or other external instrumentalities.[35]

And yet, the new system of management responsibility for profit and loss meant that, in the interests of economic efficiency, the social security functions of the enterprise or unit needed to be relocated elsewhere.[36] A 1985 World Bank report warned that 'it will be increasingly difficult to reconcile the need for greater enterprise independence and efficiency with the present role of enterprises as providers of social welfare benefits and lifetime employment'.[37] In fact, such a change was held to be a prerequis- ite for the establishment of a genuine labour market which would promote industrial efficiency and allow the dissatisfied to leave and managers to dismiss the unproductive.[38]

However, the argument for the need to shift welfare, social security, and unemployment compensation outside the work unit to some central or external location where it would be also avail- able to those outside the state workforce, went far beyond the need for industrial efficiency. It was crucial to the issue of eco- nomic and social rights in China. Even if workers in state enter- prises were protected from the consequences of redundancy, the appearance in the modernization decade of a serious unemploy- ment problem in China meant that a potentially enormous sec- tion of the population was without any social insurance coverage, as well as deprived of the right to work. The continued identification of economic and social rights with the workplace, and the con- tinued dependence of social rights on the right to work meant that a multi-layered class system of workers was now emerging. At the head of this hierarchy were those workers and staff in state enterprises and collectives employed before 1986, who enjoyed differing degrees of wages, bonuses, and welfare protection. That degree of coverage was now determined not only by the type of ownership and by the position of the enterprise within the hierarchy of provincial, district, and county levels, as it had been previously, but also by the quality of the enterprise's performance. The next category of workers were some twelve million contract workers, who enjoyed some social security and welfare benefits, but who were vulnerable to dismissal at the end of their contract. They were followed by workers in the Special Economic Zones (SEZs) who enjoyed higher wages and security benefits but no employment security. The final category consisted of workers in private enterprises who had no old age pension or medical insurance unless they were privately insured, and peasant and temporary migrant workers and the unemployed who were equally unprotected.[39] Complicating this stratification was the practice of moonlighting, whereby non-state workers took more than one job to substitute for their low wages or lack of social security.

In the countryside, the move away from the collective meant the loss of collective sources for social security funding which had not by 1989 been replaced by any universal social services scheme. In terms of economic and social rights, two classes of peasants were created, those from wealthy villages who could afford to finance their own services and those from poor villages who could not.[40] The basic urban/rural dichotomy which had existed under Mao was thus further intensified.

It was precisely collective endeavour rather than state intervention which had allowed egalitarianism to be maintained in pre-modernization China.[41] Under Mao, China's official social security system had consisted of two main categories. The first was social welfare provisions and labour insurance which covered the majority of state and collective workers in the cities and their dependants. The second was social relief which, as in other countries, helped those who were either denied a means of a basic living or who had met with disasters.[42] Within the first category, state welfare policy consistently favoured the urban resident and the 'proletariat' over the rural resident and employees of co-operatives or collectives.[43] The rest of the population not included in these two categories was covered not by the state, but by the supportive functions of co-operative and collective groups, by neighbourhood committees in the cities and collective funds in the countryside.

The loss of the collectively funded social security system entailed in rural decollectivization thus effectively deprived the majority of China's population — its peasantry — of its economic and social rights, minimal as they may have been. The growth of the entrepreneurial and private sector of the economy brought gainful employment to some of those disinherited by the rationalization of rural production: but it did not increase the number of those protected by social security. By 1989 all that remained of the redistributive mechanism were those aspects which the state had always shouldered — the labour insurance and social welfare of state workers and staff, and the provision of social relief to the destitute or handicapped, which, because of China's constitutional guarantee of the right to work, was not extended to the unemployed. In other words, what was left in the modernization decade was the provision of social welfare and unemployment insurance to state workers in the event of redundancy and 'job waiting' (*dai ye*), and the government's functions of replacing lost capabilities to work (*sangshi laodong de nengli*). The loss of co-operative social security mechanisms for non-state workers was not offset by institutions replacing the loss of the opportunity to work (*shiye*).

The result of this switch in social philosophy without a corresponding switch in social mechanisms was a series of negative developments in the area of social security. As has been shown, under Article 45 of the 1982 Constitution, which extended 'the right to material assistance from the state and society when they are old, ill, or disabled' from 'working people' to 'citizens', the provision of social rights was formally universalized. But this formal extension of access to social rights simply served to disguise a number of negative developments in the area of social security and social welfare which during the 1980s led to a severe diminution of social and economic rights and which widened the gap between the constitutional guarantees and the reality of those provisions. These were:

(a) the commodification of social welfare;[44]
(b) the increase of the rural–urban gap in the provision of social services;[45]
(c) the devolution of responsibility for social welfare and social security to lower administrative levels, to the family, or to the individual; and
(d) the lack of a comprehensive unemployment insurance system.

The formal universalization of rights proclaimed by Article 45 of the 1982 Constitution was not, therefore, accompanied in the short term by the development of new structures to institutionalize those rights. On the contrary, the 1980s witnessed a pronounced deterioration of the existing welfare system. Deborah Davis has pointed out that in the shift from a planned socialist economy to a 'marketised' one, when the leadership changes to profit maximization criteria for allocating state resources, non-profit institutions such as schools and hospitals are at a distinct disadvantage because of their non-competitive quality.[46] The result of this development in China was on the one hand a loss of services and, on the other, an attempt to make these services commercially viable, thereby increasing the costs. Studies of China's social conditions in 1988 revealed that by the late 1980s state and local funding for hospitals and medical services had decreased. The 90 per cent of China's population outside the state-employed sector lacking free medical services faced huge medical bills, while the privileges of the remaining 10 per cent were being eroded. In rural areas, access to education and medical care became more dependent on family income. Poor rural areas were consequently experiencing primary school closures and declining student numbers. In housing, the need to raise funds to ease the housing shortage prompted measures such as rent increases which favoured the wealthy and adversely affected the interests of the average urban family.[47]

Education in this period was crucially affected. There was a real decline in the numbers of children enrolled in school, a decrease in the numbers remaining in school at each level of education below university and a major increase at tertiary level.[48] Despite the increase in public expenditure on education from 6.3 per cent of the budget in 1977 to more than 10 per cent a decade later, the school system had adjusted its target from one of universal senior middle school education to the more modest goal of elimination of illiteracy among youth, reduction of the 40 per cent drop-out rate in primary school, and the realization of compulsory universal primary education by 1990.[49] The main obstacle to the latter goal was the demand for child labour created in both rural and urban sectors by the economic reforms. The modernization decade also saw a widening of the traditional urban–rural gap in the provision of educational services, partly as a result of 1984 state regulations devolving financial responsibility for rural education to the level of the *xiang* (township).[50] This widening gap was also the result of the development of a multi-track educational system, involving the identification of elite keypoint schools to be directly funded by the central government. Non-urban children, or four-fifths of China's school age children, were excluded from keypoint schools and redirected towards vocational training.[51] The higher costs to rural parents of keeping a child in secondary school meant, moreover, that 'to the extent that post-secondary education becomes the basic requirement for political and economic leadership in the future, rural born citizens will be prohibited from participating in leadership roles more extensively than virtually in any decade since 1949'.[52]

In the area of health care, the diminution of health services was not so consistent.[53] There was an expansion of medical facilities and the number of hospitals and hospital beds increased, as did research and health delivery for many of the diseases character- istic of more affluent societies. But while the availability of tech- nologically sophisticated health services increased, accessibility of the more basic services decreased. Thus, for instance, it was estim- ated that in the early 1980s state subsidies per capita for health expenditures were about ten times as much for the urban sector (26 yuan) as for the rural sector (3 yuan).[54] The new official view was that the state's responsibility was to provide basic preventive services, although even these diminished in rural areas, whereas curative health services should be paid for.[55] The urban–rural gap in access to health services widened. The shortage of medical ser- vices and medicine in the countryside, which had always been a problem, was exacerbated. As of June 1989, barefoot doctors no longer supplied basic free medical care. Between 1978 and 1986, 3.7 million barefoot doctors, rural midwives, and rural medical workers left their jobs.[56] The collectively funded medical services only existed in more prosperous villages. Village health services now depended on money provided on a voluntary or compulsory basis by villagers. In the case of impoverished villages, this source was often not dependable. Thus in the 1970s, 85 per cent of rural residents had some type of insurance, but by 1987 it had fallen to 9 per cent; and private practitioners were becoming the most common source of primary health care.[57] Hospital costs for the peasants had increased, together with the price of medicine. There was increasing pressure on new hospitals to be 'collectively' owned and run and for hospitals to be self-financing.[58]

Even around big cities like Beijing, there was reported to have been an exodus back to the city of 70 per cent of the medical col- lege graduates assigned to work in the capital's suburban hospi- tals over the previous few years. In Beijing itself, according to a May 1989 report by the Beijing Bureau of Public Health, only 10 to 20 per cent of Beijing hospital income was being underwritten by the government. The remaining income had to be self-generated. The retail price of medicine had also soared from 60 to 80 per cent. In response to these dual pressures the hospitals had started to offer special medical services at higher prices. The inadequacy of medical services in terms of the numbers of beds and doctors per patient in Beijing (4.3 beds per 1,000 population) meant that by the middle of the decade 30 per cent of hospital fatalities consisted of patients who had died in hospital waiting rooms. Private practices had been introduced to relieve this pressure.[59] Even in urban state enterprises, the new contract workers — reportedly comprising all state employees employed since October 1986 — were obliged to make personal contributions along with the enterprise for their health insurance.[60]

Housing also proved to be a problem in the modernization decade. Despite a construction boom from 1979 to 1981 involving a public housing investment of 30.2 billion yuan, an extreme housing shortage remained.[61] Inequality of access to housing also increased in this period. This was due on the one hand to unequal state investment for housing in three types of ownership systems and on the other to the new policy of commercialization of housing provision.[62] The state had invested far more heavily in housing for state-owned enterprises than for collective-owned enterprises or for private housing. In 1982 per capita housing investment in the first category was almost five times more than for collective-owned enterprises.[63] Moreover, rents for the housing of state and collective-owned enterprises were heavily subsidized. This form of subsidized housing added another source of inequality of access to socio-economic rights, extending further privileges to workers in state enterprises who already enjoyed greater income, welfare facilities, and job security. Since rent subsidies were distributed not in terms of need but on a square metre basis, inequalities of distribution were also built into the provisions of the state enterprises themselves.[64] Between state enterprises, unlike the pre-reform period where differentiation was on the basis of the position of an enterprise in the administrative hierarchy, there was more housing for those employees of highly profitable firms with a greater accumulation of funds.[65] The official sanctioning of the sale of housing had thus not relieved the housing problem but meant that those underprivileged workers who did not enjoy subsidized housing were forced into the market-place to buy houses. The majority of households buying new housing had a per capita income below the national average. This created a new disparity between two major groups of urban dwellers — those for whom housing was a matter of right and those who had to finance their own housing.[66]

The deterioration in the provision of social services, and the devolution of financial responsibility for their delivery did not, however, remove from the state the enormous costs for the provision of its traditional responsibilities — the outlay of social security benefits for state-employed workers and staff and the provision of social relief for the destitute and disabled. These costs were a hangover of the pre-modernization use of social security as a redistributive mechanism, in combination with new problems created by the modernization decade. Since wages in Maoist China had been kept low, retirement benefits had been fixed at a high percentage of the wages received; pensions for state enterprise workers were set at 60 to 100 per cent of their last wage.[67] Thus, as wages increased during the 1980s, retirement benefits increased in absolute terms. Estimates were made that by 1990, retirees would constitute 14 per cent of the country's work-force and pensions would reach 20 billion yuan a year. By the year 2,000 it was expected that as many as 40 million workers would be retired on pensions totalling 40 billion yuan.[68] As of 1987, 19.6 million individuals received 23.8 billion yuan.[69] For this reason, both the Sixth Five-Year Plan and the Seventh Five-Year Plan for Economic and Social Development prefigured the gradual transfer of state responsibility for retirement benefits to the collective units, the family, and the individual.[70] After 1986, the pensions of the majority of new state workers employed on contract were partly based on personal contributions. Increasingly, municipalities and counties created shared pension funds spreading the costs among units.[71] By the late 1980s, the traditional retirement insurance scheme for state enterprises based on individual enterprise provision of labour insurance benefits, including retirement pensions, co-existed in most cities and counties with a reformed system where finances were pooled among non-state enterprises in a locality. Nevertheless, the increase of the numbers of retirees after 1978 meant that, while in 1978 pensions absorbed 2.8 per cent of the wage bill, by 1985 they took 10.6 per cent.[72] In contrast, efforts to introduce rural pensions for those who were not state employees had faltered.[73]

By the mid 1980s, the rapid growth in the number of retired elderly and the anticipated growth in their medical care was seen as a major financial burden on the state. And yet the pension income was decreasing in relation to the income of the employed, and was being eroded by inflation.[74] Consequently, the government sought to reduce its financial burden. It introduced co-payments into medical benefits programmes, attempted to solve the issue of uneven pension burden, and targeted selected segments of the elderly population, the politically powerful, and the childless for special services. Finally, it spread the cost burden onto families, and encouraged the elderly to be resources rather than liabilities.[75]

Another cost to the state, and one which also accentuated the differences between the rural and urban population, was the practice of subsidizing urban services and state enterprises. State subsidization of one-fourth to one-third of state enterprises which operated at a loss led to yearly budget deficits after 1984.[76] Price subsidies to urban consumers increased after 1978 and particularly after 1986. These not only absorbed about one-third of the national budget, but they were most heavily utilized in the major cities where they were least necessary.[77] Thus, between 1979 and 1983, the state spent over 50 billion yuan in subsidies for food grain and edible oil, equal to over 12 per cent of the total wage bill for urban state workers. Additional subsidies lowered the cost of cotton, meat, eggs, sugar, vegetables, and coal to the urban populace.[78]

On the other hand, the disappearance of the collective sector in the countryside highlighted the state's responsibility for social relief and, in particular, its undertaking to support the 20 per cent of the rural population living in extreme poverty. Between 1980 and 1987 subsidies ensuring the 'five guarantees' (*wu bao*) for the old and infirm with no children to support them, for poor families, and the elderly in the countryside increased up to 2.3 times to 768 million yuan. In addition the state was reportedly responsible for 40 million disabled servicemen and families of 'revolutionary martyrs', for an estimated 20 million handicapped people, and for 100 million victims of natural disasters.[79] From 1984 to 1987, China spent one-quarter of its total relief funds in aiding poor families and victims of natural disasters, and in 1987, in an effort to encourage self-sufficiency, it increased the amount of funds for the poor from 271 million yuan at the beginning of the year to 873 million yuan at the end of the year.[80] In 1986 the State Council set up a group responsible for the economic development of China's poorer areas. It proposed that by 1990 the majority of inhabitants of these areas would be self-sufficient in food and clothing. To this end the state allocated 8.7 billion yuan for economic development projects and relief funds.[81]

Subsistence maintenance was thus an important official means of both increasing the lowest incomes and attempting to narrow income differentials between rural and urban residents. It meshed with the new social policy of replacing indirect gain sharing with direct gain sharing. However, it failed to compensate for the growing rural–urban inequalities of access to economic and social rights or for the increasing income differentiation occurring between and within rural sectors, and between rural and urban sectors in the latter half of the modernization decade.[82]

Research suggests that in the late 1980s there was a partial reversal of a favorable trend in the urban–rural income gap which had occurred in the early 1980s. For most of the 1980s there was a general trend of a worsening inter-provincial income disparity; and in the first half of the 1980s there was a definite unfavourable trend in the income distribution at the household level in the rural areas, whereas the household-level inequality in the cities was much smaller than its rural counterparts.[83] The World Bank also noted in the mid-1980s that while the policy of national uniform wages had resulted in extremely small income differentials in urban areas, large differentials in average incomes remained between urban and rural areas, especially in poorer regions. Thus, for instance, in Jiangsu the ratio of urban to rural per capita income was 1.9, in Gansu 3.7, and in Dingxi county in Gansu, over 1.5. Moreover, these urban–rural income gaps reflected real differences in living standards. Thus the average urban household owned 1.3 bicycles, 2.1 watches, 1.2 radios, and 0.4 televisions, while the average rural household owned 0.5 bicycles, 0.6 watches, 0.8 radios, and 0.06 televisions.[84] In addition, in terms of absolute poverty, it has been estimated that the rural poverty rate, after declining sharply in the early 1980s, rose again after 1984 or 1985. Thus, in 1988 the rural poverty rate was 13 per cent, or 107 million people.[85] Such inequitable conditions gave rise, on the one hand, to popular complaints about excessive egalitarianism among state employees, and on the other, to dissatisfaction about inequality of opportunities and resultant differentials in income distribution between different ownership systems and different forms of employment, as well as to criticism of the inequality between regions.[86]

The most dramatic source of inequality between Chinese citizens, however, was unemployment. As of June 1989, China's unemployment rate was estimated to be rising from 2 per cent in 1988 to 3.5 per cent.[87] In July 1988 twenty million people, or 20 per cent of the total state-employed workforce, were estimated to be redundant. In addition were those declared redundant by private enterprises, some six million young people in cities and townships entering the labour force every year, and the rural unemployed.

Statistics compiled in 1989 suggest that rural migrants in search of jobs helped comprise some fifty million Chinese 'on the move'. Thus, one in twenty of China's people were outside the family planning programme and subject to no-one's jurisdiction.[88] This new labour mobility was made possible in 1983 when the State Council granted peasants a temporary resident's certificate to start a business in a small town. It was later encouraged by a national directive issued in October 1985 by the National People's Congress, which facilitated the drift of rural people to small market towns. A trend began away from the strict enforcement of the *hukou* system towards a more flexible system whereby peasants were granted temporary *hukou* to work in cities or allowed the use of resident identity cards (*jumin shenfenzheng*) to live and work temporarily in the area of their choice. Since this identity card did not replace the *hukou* in providing access to social services, however, these 'floating' people were deprived of access to urban services. Despite the government's attempt to restrict such migration to small towns, huge numbers flooded into major Chinese cities. Thus, in March 1989, more than one million workers from Sichuan, Hunan, and Henan poured into Guangzhou looking for jobs.[89] In the same month, it was estimated that 'since the adoption of the responsibility system and leasing out of land to individuals', 180 million farm labourers had become redundant and another 200 million would probably find themselves jobless in the coming decade.[90] *Jingji ribao* also estimated that China would have 240 million to 260 million surplus labourers by the year 2,000, most of them in the rural areas.[91]

The greater freedom of movement which was allowed to relieve the pressures of redundancy illustrated perfectly the essential conflict between the right of movement and the right to work discussed earlier. Not only did unemployment constitute a great economic and social problem, it was also a problem with clear socio-political implications for China's large cities. Similarly, the growth of small townships to accommodate rural enterprises presaged great social changes in the countryside, with the potential development of conflict between peasants, many of them immigrants from poorer provinces, working on the land, and those earning twice as much, or more, in township enterprises.[92]

Towards this problem of real and incipient unemployment the government had, before June 1989, adopted a variety of responses. Since 1986, as observed, an unemployment insurance system had covered only workers and staff in state-owned enterprises and contract workers in government organizations. Those who had worked over five years qualified for 60–75 per cent of their monthly standard salary for twelve months and 50 per cent for another year; those who had worked less qualified for 60–75 per cent for a year only. Efforts were made to retrain redundant state workers and relocate them. Redundant workers in non-state enterprises, however, had no insurance coverage or superannuation unless they could afford private insurance.[93]

As to those outside the state system, a number of different policies, reflecting a variety of philosophies, had been devised. The *laissez-faire* solution of finding or creating one's own employment, either through the labour bureaux set up in the modernization decade to replace the centralized system of job allocation, or through private initiative, was obviously seen as the first priority. For surplus rural labour, migration to the cities was discouraged. The rural unemployed were in preference channelled into small town construction work and enterprises, industry and service industry work in villages and towns, although millions still found their way into the big cities.[94] Failing employment, the neo-traditional solution was invoked. In 1986, the Minister for Civil Affairs, Cui Naifu, pointed out that 'because the concept of the family remains strong among the Chinese people, there is no need to shift insurance functions from the family to society. Responsibility for supporting old people should be shouldered by the family'.[95] This statement was reinforced by the new obligation outlined in the 1982 Constitution that 'parents have the duty to rear and educate their minor children, and children who have come of age have the duty to support and assist their parents'.[96] The family role in social security was promoted, not only to care for the old but to support the unemployed youth. This expedient simply compounded poverty.

The long term and most important solution, however, was seen as structural change which would reflect the transition from the command economy to a 'reformed' command economy with market characteristics. Thus, the Seventh Five-Year Plan called for research and experimentation in, and gradual implementation of, a social security system for individual urban and rural workers, although any national insurance system could not exceed financial capacities. It also called for the devolution of total state responsibility for social security to a system combining the resources of the state, enterprises, and the individual.[97] Within the economic research institutions proposals were made to 'change the ineffective insurance system, siphon off part of consumption, and establish social security funds'.[98] More importantly, it was suggested that employment be separated from welfare and job security, thus severing the traditional nexus between employment and the social security system. The proposed replacement of employment security with unemployment compensation was seen as 'a breakthrough point in reform of the whole employment system'.[99] But as of June 1989, this breakthrough had not occurred.

In early 1989, Liu Guoguang, Vice-President of the Chinese Academy of Social Sciences, captured the dilemma underlying these different solutions:

For several reasons China has proceeded with economic reform in a piecemeal fashion, so at present the old and new systems co-exist alongside each other . . . However, this blending of two systems has undoubtedly generated a series of thorny problems . . . with neither the old mandatory system nor the new market system effectively dominating the distribution of resources, the defects of both systems have been magnified.[100]

Thus, in the decade before June 1989, China was caught between two economic systems, rejecting the nexus between social security and guaranteed employment established under the command economy, but not having yet erected the safety net provided in most *laissez-faire* economies, which protects citizens from the 'fallout' factor. Added to these structural problems in 1988–9 were short-term social and economic problems. In 1988, the sharp price rises, officially estimated at 18.5 per cent, but by other sources as fluctuating between 20 per cent and 30 per cent, had effectively undermined the improved living standards which, until 1987, had served in China to cushion and disguise the slow erosion of social and economic rights.[101] As of 1987, the 10–11 per cent GNP increase in real terms over the previous three years had far outweighed a 7.3 per cent inflation rate over the years 1986 to 1987. The trickle-down effect had indeed resulted in an improved general standard of living, estimated by the State Statistical Bureau as having achieved an average net income per capita gain for peasants of 246 per cent (from 133.6 yuan to 462.6 yuan) over the 1978–87 period, and, allowing for price increases, 85.7 per cent better for urban households over the same period.[102]

Even in the two previous years of moderate price rises, however, the real effects of inflation had been severe, because of the high food component of the price index.[103] In 1987, for instance, when the retail price index rose only 7.2 per cent, the price of all food increased 10.1 per cent, and the price of meat, poultry, and eggs rose 16.5 per cent.[104] When in the first quarter of 1988 the national retail price index rose another 11 per cent, the price of non-staple foods went up by 24.2 per cent, with a rise of 48.7 per cent in the price of fresh vegetables.[105] The high inflation rate in 1988 thus exacerbated an already serious situation by transforming the 22.2 per cent increase in nominal per capita income over the previous year to an actual rate of increase in real income of 1.2 per cent. More significantly, it led inevitably to a redistribution of income, so that a sampling survey in thirteen cities revealed that the income of 34.9 per cent of all families had actually decreased purely because of price rises.[106]

In this way, the fall in real living standards served to expose the defects of a dual economic system in which the old machinery of socio-economic security had yet to be replaced by coherent mechanisms reflecting the new social and economic circumstances. More importantly, it served to highlight the yawning gap which existed between the social and economic rights guaranteed under the 1982 Constitution and required under the ICESCR, and those rights which could be exercised in reality. The formal provisions of the 1982 Constitution in some cases outstripped the reality of economic and social rights, and in other cases lagged behind it. Not only did the Constitution fail to mesh with reality, but the normal Marxist priority of economic and social rights, which it still formally upheld, partially at least, was in fact overturned by events.

Thus, by June 1989, China was a country not only in need of a new constitution and new laws giving legislative support to the civil and political freedoms already being exercised in society. It also required a restructuring of the institutional base of the social system to accord with new socio-economic constitutional guarantees, as well as a new, specific guarantee of unemployment relief which reflected the new socio-economic circumstances. The tensions created by these wide divergences between promise and reality were to spill out in a dramatic and unprecedented fashion in the April–June 1989 demonstrations.

6 The Critique of China's Human Rights Before June 1989

ONE of the criticisms frequently levelled at the international human rights regime concerns the arbitrariness and selectivity of its choice of targets. Future generations will find it difficult to comprehend the contrast between the international focus in the 1980s on the condition of human rights in the Soviet Union, and the relative neglect of an arguably worse condition of rights in China. Even if it could not be expected that the diminution of China's economic and social rights would be of concern to a foreign world intent on encouraging the opening up of China's economy to foreign trade, the failure of governments to hold China to account for civil and political rights abuses constituted a logical *non sequitur* with their other human rights policies. Although at an unofficial level concern about China's human rights began to grow, in the scholarly world Roberta Cohen was almost alone in calling attention to China's 'exemption from international accountability' in its human rights practice.[1] One obvious *raison d'état* for this selective treatment was that in the 1980s China, unlike the Soviet Union, was not considered a strategic threat, but rather, a bulwark helping to contain that threat. Moreover, China's developing trade potential gave it an increasingly positive image within the international community.

Yet there were other, more subtle reasons for China's exemption. During the Maoist era, and particularly the Cultural Revolution, China's civil rights abuses were frequently the target of diffuse, politically motivated attacks by Western governments. However, China's isolation, partly imposed, partly self-imposed, meant not only that concrete information about these abuses was difficult to obtain, but that China itself was rendered inaccessible to sanctions, which paradoxically could only have been effective had it been linked with the international community through membership of the United Nations and of international economic agencies. Also, the very stringency of social controls imposed under Mao, with the exception of the Cultural Revolution period, inhibited the development of a tradition of semi-formal dissent which was facilitated in the Soviet Union by a more open political environment and a more pluralist society.

In the modernization decade, on the other hand, other considerations came into play. China began to open to the outside world: but foreign governments were unwilling to blight the fragile flower of *glasnost* by any unwelcome criticism, and so resorted to a cultural relativist position which granted China exemption from normal human rights standards on the basis of its long, enclosed civilization, and its different view of human rights. Moreover, as has been argued above, in the decade after 1979, China had made considerable informal progress in improving the condition of the freedoms of thought, speech, association, and assembly. Thus, in the eyes of public policy makers, objection to the limited extension of those rights seemed grudging and inappropriate, and many observers, particularly foreign governments, took refuge in the expectation that it would be just a matter of time before the improvements in the informal situation of civil and political rights in China would penetrate the formal legal apparatus of rights, particularly in view of the leadership's pledge to institute the rule of law.[2]

Despite this almost universal international myopia, a limited critique of China's human rights record did emerge in the pre-1989 era, internally from students and intellectuals, and externally from, in particular, Amnesty International and the World Bank. The critique had two focuses. The first of these was civil and political rights. In the 1970s and 1980s, Chinese students and intellectuals worked primarily for the expansion of the civil rights of freedom of speech, press, and assembly formally guaranteed them under the constitution, as well as of the political right to influence the choice of leaders and the direction of policy. In their view, the pursuit of these rights was paramount and, as Xu Wenli pointed out in 1980, the 'problem of freedom of thought is more serious than that of physical attacks on people'. On the other hand, since the late 1970s, Amnesty International, and to a lesser extent other International Non-Governmental Organizations, stressed, in China as elsewhere, the protection of the civil rights of immunity. Amnesty also emphasized the importance of proper legal, judicial, and penal conditions for the protection of those rights.

The second focus was on economic, social, and cultural rights, and originated in reports by the World Bank and international development agencies. As part of its brief to give the Chinese government economic, financial, and developmental advice in the early years of the modernization programme, the World Bank published numerous assessments of China's economic and developmental policies which evaluated favourably the achievements of the Mao era, and suggested future social and economic policies which could, on the one hand, promote the economic reform programme and, on the other, shield the citizens from its destructive impact on their economic, social, and cultural rights. The Bank also published specific reports on China's education and health care system which contained numerous recommendations for the restructuring of China's social welfare system.

The Chinese Critique

Earlier chapters have sought to convey the mainstream political, economic, and cultural developments affecting the condition of human rights in China. Change in China's situation was not, however, simply the delayed outcome of alterations in its external and institutional environment. It was also a function of the active mediation of dissenting individuals, normally intellectuals, who sought to achieve convergence between the changing economic and social environment and the essentially conservative and resilient institutions of the Chinese state. Although in most cases these dissenters were not initially successful in changing China's political system, their efforts often paved the way for subsequent political developments.

Political dissent within China fluctuated throughout the twentieth century between relative autonomy from and relative dependence on the state, in direct correlation with the latitude allowed to society at large. Throughout this fluctuating process, a thin line of traditional scholarly remonstrance and retribution continued, sometimes shaping and merging with expressions of public protest, sometimes emerging as the only form of dissent. Even under more liberal, permissive political regimes, however, the underlying premise of both rulers and ruled was the need, and right, of the state to control and manage citizen participation.[3] Among the critics and would-be reformers, the common themes were the expansion of the civil rights of freedom of speech and of the press, and the protection of the civil rights of immunity, so that the common goals of economic and political reform could be realized.[4]

The delicate relationship which existed between the government and its critics, and the effective role of students, leading intellectuals, and writers, working separately or in combination as an informal political pressure group, were part of a discrete tradition of political critique in Chinese history. As we have seen, it was the duty of the literati in imperial China to speak out as the conscience of the government if it departed from Confucian ideals. Chinese intellectuals served simultaneously as ideological spokesmen, servants of the state, and moral critics of the ruler.[5] Censorship was institutionalized in the form of the censorial system, under which censors were required to criticize both the court and the officials.[6] Unsubstantiated charges, on the other hand, could lead to dismissal, the punishment of relatives, and even death. Charges were usually couched in terms of dereliction of duty, but this category ranged from bad temper, to faulty compiling work, to corruption and factionalism, the last two malpractices sometimes incurring the death penalty.[7]

In practice, the majority of Chinese literati, being also power holders, remained loyal to the government, but a minority of individuals, particularly if they worked together with political factions, were able to influence the ideas and policies of the incumbent dynasty.[8] For instance, in the late Ming period, literati cliques formed around academies and extended their rivalry into the bureaucracy. Scholars associated with the Donglin Academy in Wuxi justified their political activity by calling it a Confucian crusade to eliminate corruption at court. They attempted to control appointments and to remove their enemies from office. Factional lines were hardened and a wave of purges further weakened the regime. As a result, in the Qing dynasty both factions among officials and the formation of political associations outside of office were discouraged.[9]

In late imperial China, civic activity, as opposed to the activity of individual intellectuals or of a political faction, grew in strength through the mediation of corporate groups including guilds, clans, neighbourhood associations, and secret societies. In the late Qing and early Republican period, 'professional associations' (fatuan), chambers of commerce, and bankers' and lawyers' associations, served both to extend state power and to represent social interests.[10] The clientelist and corporatist nature of the relations between such organizations and the state was a reflection of the 'vertical' nature of Chinese politics. Even in cases of major political upheaval, in particular the May 4 Movement of 1919 and the May 30 Movement of 1925, which provided a horizontal dimension to

Chinese politics in the form of extensive popular participation, vertical forms were maintained.[11] Thus, although the May 30 Movement at its height drew over 100,000 citizens to Tiananmen Square, they came representing over 150 groups, proclaiming themselves by their banners to be student unions, workers' organizations, or guilds.[12] In such cases of popular mobilization, which threatened to undermine the vertical links facilitating group co-optation, the limits on the resort to coercion by governments and parties 'were more often the result of political stalemate — a rough sort of pluralism by default — than of acceptance of constitutional rules of the game'.[13]

The more open political condition of pre-1949 China was both a function of the enlarged private economic sphere and of a *laissez-faire* political system which allowed many normal governmental functions such as welfare to be undertaken by private organizations. Under the new communist government in 1949, however, the state gradually absorbed the private economic sphere and, together with the collective, resumed responsibility for welfare and other functions. Moreover, in the process of extending the ambit of state control, 'the group itself — a team of peasants, workers on the factory floor, a class of students — became an administered, if not administrative, unit.'[14] Under such conditions, the pendulum of dissent swung heavily in the direction of state dependence and vertical manipulation. Not only was political participation, designed to further leadership goals, mobilized from above in the form of mass campaigns, but political dissent had also to be directed and encouraged from above.[15] Thus, during the Hundred Flowers Movement in 1956, intellectuals were initially reluctant to accept the leaders' invitation to 'let a hundred flowers bloom; let a hundred schools of thought contend'; and their reluctance was shown to have been justified when they and their criticisms subsequently became the target of the Anti-Rightist Campaign of 1957.

The Cultural Revolution proved to be the turning point in the history of dissent, and of civil and political rights, in post-1949 China. Launched from above, as a mass, horizontal movement to undermine the entrenched vertical and horizontal structures of Party and bureaucratic power, and to reanimate lost revolutionary ideals of mass participation and leadership responsibility to the masses, it had significant unintended consequences. Using ideology to attack both structures and individuals, in the process it

not only erected new structures to be inhabited by new bureaucrats, but also devalued the coinage of the ideology. The disappearance of the old structures, which had included a working,
if imperfect, legal system, simply 'crippled the state's institutional
infrastructure while training society in the art of covert resistance'.[16] By encouraging mass political participation which became
spontaneous in that it became too powerful to control, and by the
tactic of either merging large social groups such as students and
workers, or setting them against each other, the Cultural Revolution
strengthened the horizontal reach of society over the vertical control of the state.[17] The potential of horizontal mass movements to
undermine the Party's authority was epitomized by the establishment in February 1967 of the Shanghai Commune, based on the
principles of the Paris Commune of 1871, and involving direct
popular political participation.[18] A horizontal linkage of revolutionary social groups to overturn power holders in the Party and
bureaucracy was authorized by Mao, and the official *People's
Daily* declared 'the integration of revolutionary intellectuals with
worker–peasant masses an objective law'.[19]

Although the Shanghai Commune was soon vetoed by Mao,
the Party's legitimacy was severely weakened by the conduct of
the Cultural Revolution and by its damaging revelations of leadership disunity. In delegitimizing the Party, the Cultural Revolution
opened the way for new political ideas. Those citizens who were
not completely alienated by the spectacle of its violent factional
warfare, and by unavoidable personal involvement in grass-roots
struggle sessions that, in the name of ideas, pitted Chinese against
Chinese, reserved for themselves the right to find a way of giving true content to its ideals. The forms that they discovered, however, were not those that had been anticipated from above.

A major legacy handed down by the Cultural Revolution to its
successors was the firm conviction that the freedoms of speech,
expression, press, assembly, association, and political participation
which it had temporarily allowed Chinese citizens, were arbitrary,
and indeed, invalid rights, if not firmly institutionalized in a
complex set of legal guarantees and structural forms. A second
legacy was the temporary submergence of the normal vertical hierarchy of interests, exhibited in conflict within the elite, under a
larger and more crucial horizontal cleavage between leaders and
led.[20] Already in the Cultural Revolution a daring essay, 'Whither
China', written by Yang Xiaokai of the ultra-left Shengwulian Red

Guard group in Hunan, had exposed the problem of 'a class of red capitalists' which had emerged in China.[21] This 'class' had arrogated unto itself special privileges and high salaries through its monopoly of control, rather than ownership, of the means of production. For this reason, its claim to leadership was in question.

The small voice in the wilderness which 'Whither China?' represented, was given greater resonance by the two dissenting movements which succeeded the Cultural Revolution, both led by young intellectuals with working-class experience, the Li Yizhe Movement (1974–79) and the Democracy Wall Movement (1978–80). These movements called for two main reforms — the establishment of a system of socialist democracy which would truly reflect Marxist principles and eliminate the new system of a privileged political elite, and the establishment of a legal system which would institutionalize these principles. These twin ideals were incorporated in a manifesto written in 1974 by four former Rebel Red Guards, combining forces under the name of Li Yizhe. Adopting the form of the 'big character poster' (*dazibao*) commonly used in the Cultural Revolution, 'On Socialist Democracy and the Legal System' was put up in the streets of Guangzhou. Under the guise of opposing 'the Lin Biao system', it attacked the current ills of Chinese socialism, and the failure of the civil rights guaranteed in the constitution to be allowed in practice. It also exposed the failure of the masses to grasp people's democracy after the Cultural Revolution, and the existence of a 'new bourgeois class' of leaders exploiting privilege and engaging in corruption.

Among other things, Li Yizhe called for the establishment of a legal system to protect 'all the democratic rights rightfully belonging to the masses'; the limitation of special privileges; the enactment of a guarantee of the 'masses' right of revolutionary supervision over the Party's and country's various levels of leadership', as well as the punishment of 'the "mandarins" who have committed monstrous crimes'.[22] They also called for freedom of speech, press, and association: 'The people want democracy; they demand a socialist legal system; and they demand the revolutionary rights and the human rights which protect the masses of the people'.[23]

The Li Yizhe members, comprising Li Zhengtian, Wang Xizhe, Guo Hongzhi, and Chen Yiyang, were a discrete educated group, whose views were only allowed to be circulated because they coincided with the needs of their local political patrons, one of whom was Zhao Ziyang.[24] When in late 1974 they attracted the unfavourable attention of Beijing, however, they were arrested, and were not fully rehabilitated until February 1979. Once again, dissent was allowed from the top, and curtailed from the top. And although Li Yizhe was a group with strong horizontal ties, which sought to articulate the interests of the broad mass of Chinese citizens, it was also part of the vertical structure of the educated elite, and hence ultimately subject to the control of that elite.

A more ominous sign of the potential of China's citizens to link up into a horizontal movement of dissent threatening the Party's monopoly of control was the Tiananmen incident of early April 1976. On the surface, the incident, which occured during the traditional Qingming festival (of the dead), was the result of a popular surge of affection in memory of Premier Zhou Enlai, who had died on 8 January. In reality it was a spontaneous, or semi-spontaneous, gesture of defiance to China's radical leaders, who had not only attempted to subdue the popular mourning for Zhou in January, but had launched an open attack on the equally moderate leader, Deng Xiaoping, soon after Zhou's death.[25] The removal by the authorities of the wreaths, poems, and posters placed by the crowds at the Monument to the People's Heroes in Tiananmen Square was the signal for a violent confrontation between the people and the police on April 5, a confrontation which ended in a number of arrests. It also resulted in the removal of Deng Xiaoping, accused of having incited the Tiananmen violence, from his positions of Party and state power.[26] The significance of this incident was the evidence it provided of the latent but ultimate power of public opinion in China during periods of political crisis and change.[27]

This eruption of popular feeling was soon controlled. Less amenable to physical constraints were the ideas started by the Cultural Revolution and picked up by the Li Yizhe group. They emerged once again in the Democracy Wall Movement of 1978–80. This movement was a product of the adoption of more liberal economic and political policies after the death of Mao and the fall of the radical leadership in 1976, and particularly after the Third Plenum of the Eleventh Central Committee in December 1978.[28] It also had an important connection with the Tiananmen incident, in that it began soon after the original verdict on the incident was reversed, and after some of the original

demonstrators were released from prison.[29] Once again, this movement was to survive only as long as it served the purpose of a
faction of China's leadership. Pro-reform leader Deng Xiaoping,
once again rehabilitated, needed to strengthen his policies against
those of the 'centrist faction' led by Hua Guofeng, and to this
end was prepared to use the democratic impulses of Chinese intellectuals and the spontaneous popular forces they generated. This
movement was similar to the Li Yizhe and succeeding movements
in that, unlike the Cultural Revolution which had mobilized popular support for the forces on the left, it was the political forces
to the right of the dominant leadership faction who turned to the
people for support.

The Democracy Wall Movement began on 25 November 1978,
when crowds gathered to discuss political posters on a large wall
at Xidan, near Tiananmen Square. The three purposes of discussion, which was carried on into the succeeding months, were to
put into practice 'the freedom of assembly and expression' guaranteed by the Constitution; to demand socialist mass democracy
and realize the principles of the Paris Commune under conditions
of stability and unity; and to sweep away obstacles to the realization of the Four Modernizations.[30]

Noteworthy in the context of human rights in this period was
a 'Nineteen Point Declaration' by an organization called the China
Human Rights League, and a poster which was the beginning of
the famous Democracy Manifesto by Wei Jingsheng, 'The Fifth
Modernization'. The Human Rights League, headed by Ren Wanding
and established in Beijing on 1 January 1979, claimed its descent
from the Tiananmen incident which, it insisted, was also 'a human
rights movement'. It demanded, among other things, freedom of
thought and speech; practical safeguards for the constitutional
right to assess and criticize Party and state leaders; 'sufficient
autonomy' for national minorities; general elections of state and
local leaders; open sessions of the National People's Congress; a
transition from state ownership of the means of production to
'social ownership'; the 'realization of the Marxist doctrine that a
socialist society is one in which everyone can develop freely'; freedom of movement, including foreign travel; freedom of information; state guarantees of basic food rations for peasants, and the
elimination of slum quarters and the phenomenon of begging;
and abolition of the secret police system.[31] Moreover, it called for
the citizens' right of supervision over the state's ownership and

distribution of the surplus value of the people's labour, so that it could never again be seized by the tricksters of a 'feudal kind of socialism', Lin Biao and the Gang of Four; and it requested the right to discuss the regulation of the rate and volume of tax, and of the rate and volume of industrial profits handed over to the higher authorities.[32] The Human Rights League thus put equal emphasis on civil, political, and economic rights.

In his 'Fifth Modernization', Wei Jingsheng argued that the four forms of economic modernization sought by Deng Xiaoping were not achievable without a fifth modernization — democracy. His twin goals were 'the realization of human rights' and 'the kind of democracy based on the co-operation of all the people', supported by a 'kind of rule of law which was conducive to the realization of equal rights'.[33] As he put it:

True democracy means the holding of power by the labouring masses . . . It means the right of the people to choose their own representatives to work according to their will and in their interests . . . Furthermore, the people must also have the power to replace their representatives any time so that these representatives cannot go on deceiving others in the name of the people.[34]

Another leader of the Democracy Wall Movement, like Wei Jingsheng an educated worker, was Wang Xizhe, who was one of the original members of the Li Yizhe group. Wang, a more orthodox Marxist than Wei, worked mainly to promote the civil and political rights of 'the labouring people' of China, although he was also concerned about their social and economic rights. Like Wei, he looked to the rule of law to achieve this goal, but, unlike Wei, he anticipated the ultimate goal of communism as a 'beautiful future'. His most controversial thesis was that the proletariat of China, now educated and fully self-conscious, had by the mid-1970s demonstrated that it was equipped to take over from the Chinese Communist Party the role of leadership of the state.[35]

Although Wang's ideas have been given less prominence than Wei Jingsheng's, he had a developed sense of the potential for socialist democracy in China. He anticipated three possible scenarios for political reform: reform under Party leadership; under the leadership of intellectuals; or under the leadership of young workers and students.[36] Although the democratic urge among the popular groups was stronger, he believed that all three groups were alike in wanting the separation of Party and government, direct popular political participation, and freedom of the press and of publication.[37] The main difference he distinguished between the Party reformers and the other two groups was that the groups formed by the people were prepared to accept Party leadership, but could not accept a one party dictatorship.[38] He believed that a multi-party system was not inconsistent with Marxism. If the Communist Party wanted to maintain its position as vanguard of the proletariat, he felt it had to accept supervision from other parties, or the problem of bureaucratism would become insoluble.[39]

With the advent of the Democracy Wall, a host of publications expressing dissent appeared, such as *April Fifth Forum*, *Today*, *Fertile Ground*, *Masses' Reference News*, *Exploration* and *Beijing Spring*, along with such organizations as the Enlightenment Society and the China Human Rights League. The editor of *April Fifth Forum* was another well known activist, Xu Wenli, who, like Wei Jingsheng and Wang Xizhe, was later arrested and given a fifteen year prison sentence. Xu made some important statements on the need for an expansion of China's civil rights, and for the protection of civil rights of immunity.[40] He was also concerned with the economic right to work:

The vague and ambiguous articles of the penal code dealing with counter-revolutionary activities should be amended. The administrative ordinances that permit the Public Security Bureau to exercise judicial powers should be abolished. The freedoms to speak, assemble, associate, publish, march, demonstrate and strike, which citizens have on paper, should be guaranteed in practice.

The focal point of all reforms should be human liberation, and the respect for human values and human rights. The free development of each individual is the basis for all social progress. Military-style authoritarianism must be replaced by moral suasion; all government must act strictly within the law. Administrative units should no longer have control of dossiers on individuals ... Employment agencies should be set up, and staff should be allocated on the basis not of central allocation but of job advertisements, exams and proper selection methods, with the signing of short or long-term contracts. Provision should be made for job allocation in case of unemployment. Restrictions on residence permits should be progressively relaxed so as to eventually guarantee freedom of resettlement.[41]

The magazine *Enlightenment* also published a searching critique of the condition of human rights in China.[42] In an article, 'Democracy and Rule by Law', it stated the issue simply:

The people need democracy. People need to be ruled under law. Democracy allows people to speak out and participate in governing the nation. The rule of law protects and guards the right to speak out and the right to rule. If the former is lost, the law will have nothing to protect. If the latter is lost, democracy will not have any basis.[43]

Another article, 'On Human Rights', called for voting rights, freedom of speech, freedom to demonstrate, and the freedoms of publication, of belief, and of association, in that order.[44]

The importance and significance of the Democracy Wall Movement for Chinese politics is that, in retrospect, it represented the crucial moment when Chinese leaders could have moved towards genuine political reform within the existing socialist system. The active members of the different organizations were mostly in their twenties and early thirties, being either former Red Guards or younger people whose political views were shaped by the Tiananmen incident.[45] Despite their youth, they had a wide experience of Chinese society. They had either travelled around China during the Cultural Revolution, or had spent long periods in the countryside. Some had also spent time in prison. Although well educated and extremely well read, they were not members of the elite intelligentsia. They were not writers, professors, or researchers, but workers, clerks, or teachers who had a close understanding of, and sympathy with, workers, peasants, and the underprivileged. Moreover, unlike many other educated Chinese, they had a close understanding of Marxism and were fired by their reading and wide experience to achieve reform and change for the mass of Chinese people on the basis of a proper interpretation, not of Leninism, which they associated with all the ills of Stalinism, but of Marxism. Although their views were not identical, and although it is popularly believed that thinkers like Wei Jingsheng represented a more liberal stream of thought which anticipated the eventual abolition of the Communist Party, a close reading of their writings reveals more similarities than differences; and all were concerned to find solutions that corresponded with the needs of the lower socio-economic stratum of Chinese society.[46]

The potential of the Democracy Wall Movement to mobilize a broad base of support which could challenge the Communist Party's vanguard position was exemplified by the link established by Fu Yuehua, a thirty-two-year-old unemployed woman from Beijing, with thousands of peasant petitioners from different parts of China, who had journeyed to seek redress from Beijing authorities for 'wrongs' inflicted by local cadres. On 8 January 1979, the anniversary of Zhou Enlai's death, Fu joined a peasant demonstration against 'hunger and oppression'. Her arrest ten days later served to underline the alarm with which the authorities viewed an alliance between the activists of the Democracy Wall Movement and the members of a potentially revolutionary social class on issues that linked economic and civil rights.[47]

The crucial moment for reform of China's existing political system passed. Although China's leaders subsequently co-opted the Li Yizhe slogan of 'socialist democracy and a socialist legal system', it was a slogan bereft of radical content. In March 1980, Deng Xiaoping, who had earlier expressed support for the Democracy Wall, criticized the movement and laid down the 'four basic principles', which established that no exercise of democracy could contradict the socialist road, the proletarian dictatorship, Communist Party leadership, and Marxism-Leninism-Mao Zedong thought.[48] These principles were later incorporated into the 1982 Constitution. In 1979 and 1980, many of the leaders of the Democracy Movement and the editors of the unofficial magazines were arrested and imprisoned.

Although in the following decade the Democracy Wall Movement as such faded from view, the themes it had raised, such as the need for civil and political rights to match China's economic reform, and its criticism of the existence of a privileged political elite and of corruption, continued as implicit, and sometimes explicit, themes in the discourse that marked the complex political manoeuvres between 'conservative' (or 'hardline') and 'reformist' leaders. Over the years, the movement for political reform and ideological relaxation fluctuated in response to the changing fortunes of the economic reform programme.[49] 'Conservative', or orthodox Marxist, opponents of the scope of economic reform, like Chen Yun, Hu Qiaomu, Deng Liqun, and Peng Zhen, exploited any apparent failure in the reform itself, or any obvious systemic flaws laid bare during the process of that reform, such as the practice of the 'feudal remnants' of corruption, nepotism, bureaucratism, bribery, and exploitation of '*guanxi*' (personal connections), to force a return to more orthodox political practices and curb free political discussion, as well as to put limits on the scope of economic reform. Their efforts, however, never succeeded in reversing the move towards openness within the society. On the contrary, each effort seemed to have the effect of taking 'one step backwards, and two steps forward'.

At the same time, the character of political dissent, and of political dissenters, changed. Gradually during the 1980s, in response to the liberalization of the overall political climate, and the official tolerance of a wider range of freedoms and political and economic ideas, dissent began to spread upwards into the intellectual elite. Government recognition of the need for the co-operation of intellectuals in the modernization process was reflected in the setting up of numerous research institutes to debate issues and give advice to government. This semi-institutionalization of the right to have new ideas, and to promote them, was reflected in a government-supported theory conference attended by intellectuals, held under the chairmanship of Hu Yaobang, from mid-January until early April 1979. For the first time at a formal gathering Mao Zedong thought was criticized, and demands made for fundamental reform of the Leninist system of democratic centralism.[50] Moreover, as a result of having their importance recognized, intellectuals as a group began to nurse specific grievances, such as the failure of the government to match their new status with a comparable wage rise, or to increase spending on education.[51] Intellectuals were also encouraged and emboldened to speak up as a result of Deng Xiaoping's move to rehabilitate those persecuted in the 1957 Anti-Rightist Movement and the Cultural Revolution. By 1980 more than 400,000 had had their labels removed; and of the 1,000 or so intellectuals of the Chinese Academy of Science who had suffered in these periods, 800 had been rehabilitated by 1979.[52]

This mass rehabilitation strengthened and universalized the belief in the legitimacy of the critique of the Cultural Revolution, and more generally, in the legitimacy of dissent. It also strengthened the claim for proper legal institutions to underwrite the political system, since the reversal of verdicts on the Cultural Revolution 'raised questions about a political system that could not correct itself until the death of its leader'.[53] While political leaders openly debated the degree to which the political and social ideas of the West should be allowed, or were necessary, to accompany the introduction of Western technology and market economics, the burden of political dissent was in turn assumed by members of the student body, by a number of leading and influential intellectuals, and by some literary figures. As the responsibility for a political critique, often with the open endorsement of elements of the leadership, passed into the hands of a new group of people with closer ties to the leaders, and enjoying fewer connections with working people, the ideas which were espoused became correspondingly more elitist. Somewhat paradoxically in view of the deepening of social cleavages, the horizontal nature of earlier dissenting movements regressed back into a more vertical structure.

The dissenting intellectuals in the immediate pre-1989 period have been described as 'a continuation of the literati in modern guise'.[54] Although advocating democracy, unlike the dissenters in the Democracy Wall Movement who supported universal political participation, they believed it could only be practised by an educated elite. As Merle Goldman has pointed out, there was nothing 'democratic' about the rational, scientific, or technological outlook that this elite advocated. On the contrary, its ideas were reminiscent of the traditional literati's elitism and emphasis on meritocracy.[55] Accordingly, political dissent became less threatening to the Party, and through the 1980s dissent, if resented, was tolerated. Dissenting intellectuals in this period included Su Shaozhi, Yan Jiaqi, Wang Ruowang, Liu Binyan, and Fang Lizhi who, enjoying a high intellectual and social status, empowered their ideas with equivalent, if not superior, authority to that of the Party leaders.[56] They were seen as potent influences upon dissenting students, if not upon disadvantaged social groups.

If the intellectuals were needed by government to suggest policy alternatives, they frequently pursued issues beyond the normal limits of self-censorship. Liao Gailong, for instance, although commonly regarded as a leading representative of the reformers, criticized Leninist political theories which 'emphasized the aspect of violent suppression [by] the dictatorship of the proletariat, and neglected the democratic aspect'. Lenin, he claimed, did this 'to such a degree that he said the proletarian dictatorship was an iron dictatorship not bound by any laws', thus negating any notion of socialist legality.[57] In August 1980, Wang Ruoshui, deputy editor-in-chief of the People's Daily, argued that there was a problem of 'high and mighty' officials at all levels of leadership, and that this was a consequence of the ideological and political alienation caused by the Party's dominant position.[58] In spring 1983, a debate on humanism pursued this issue of alienation, which represented a continuation, in another guise, of the theme of leadership abuse of power first raised in the Cultural Revolution. Su Shaozhi, director of the Institute of Marxism-Leninism and Mao Zedong Thought, argued that Marxism had been treated in a dogmatic fashion, and that 'only by creatively developing Marxism in the process of studying and finding answers to all sorts of problems which have been raised in the contemporary world can we truly uphold Marxism'.[59] At the same time Zhou Yang, former deputy-director of the CCP Propaganda Department, argued that 'Marxism contains humanism.' However, he said:

Because democracy and the legal system were unsound, the servants of the people were able at times to misuse the power bestowed on them by the people, and to become masters of the people. This is alienation in the political domain . . . As for ideological alienation, the best example is the cult of the individual, which was similar in some respects to the religious alienation criticized by Feuerbach . . . Only if you recognise that there exists alienation can you overcome it . . . It is entirely possible for us to overcome alienation by working through the socialist system itself.[60]

Predictably, these ideas provoked a bitter reaction from Wang Zhen, president of the Party school, and precipitated the nation-wide Anti-Spiritual Pollution Campaign. Although the political pendulum eventually swung back towards the reformers, rising food prices and an increase in corruption soon triggered a second assault by the hardliners, who accused reformers of undermining the institutional integrity and solidarity of the Party.[61] Following an open confrontation between Deng Xiaoping and orthodox Marxist Chen Yun at the Party's Congress of delegates in September 1985, Deng argued the need for more extensive reform, declaring that without changes in the political system, economic reform could not proceed.

In line with this new liberalism, intellectuals agitated for more freedom and democracy, and a plethora of articles appeared discussing the ideas of Western political and economic thinkers.[62] Yan Jiaqi, director of the Institute of Political Science under the Chinese Academy of Social Sciences, called for the participation of all citizens in political activities, the adoption of a system of checks and balances to guard against mistakes in political leadership, and strong legislative and judicial oversight of administration.[63] In order to overcome the problem of the overconcentration of political power at the top, he advocated a four way separation of powers — the horizontal and vertical separation of state power, the separation of power between government and social organizations, and citizen political participation.[64] On the thirtieth anniversary of the launching of the Hundred Flowers

Movement by Mao, Wang Ruoshui published 'The Double Hundred Policy and Civil Rights', reaffirming his belief in humanism, and the legal scholar Yu Haocheng published 'The Double Hundred Policy and Legal Guarantees', calling for concrete legal guarantees of the constitutional rights to freedom of speech, research, and creation.[65] In response to such calls, the more orthodox faction of leaders rallied in an effort to pressure the Sixth Plenum of the Twelfth Party Central Committee in September 1986 to adopt a resolution reinforcing 'spiritual civilization', instead of endorsing political reforms.

This reaction by the hardliners prompted a riposte from the reformers. In late November and December 1986, student demonstrations took place in ten major Chinese cities, calling for enhanced civil rights and 'democracy'. Charged with instigating the students' actions and spreading 'bourgeois liberalization', three leading intellectuals, Fang Lizhi, Liu Binyan, and Wang Ruowang, were expelled from the Party and a further group of a dozen were blacklisted.[66] Under criticism for his indecision in the handling of the students, as well as for policy matters, General Party Secretary Hu Yaobang stepped down from his position on 16 January, while still retaining his Politburo seat. Replacing Hu as Acting General Secretary as well as Premier, Zhao Ziyang became General Secretary at the Seventh National People's Congress which met in April 1988. Li Peng, former Premier Zhou Enlai's adopted son, succeeded Zhao as Premier.

By early 1989, a further development in the movement of dissent began to test the limits of tolerance of China's leadership. China's intellectuals attempted to link their cause with that of the first democracy movement. They also began to organize political activities publicly, and to start their own journals, such as *New Enlightenment* and *The Thinker*. In February 1989, Fang Lizhi sent an open letter to Deng Xiaoping requesting a general amnesty for political prisoners to celebrate the fortieth anniversary of the Chinese People's Republic in October 1989. He mentioned particularly the case of Wei Jingsheng. In mid-February, citing what they called a world-wide trend towards increasing respect for human rights, thirty-three prominent intellectuals signed a letter to the Central Committee of the Chinese Communist Party and to senior officials of the National People's Congress requesting an amnesty for political prisoners.[67] The signatories included famous intellectuals, a poet, and a playwright. And a mid-March petition presented to the government by forty-two scientists called for greater democracy, freedom of the press, of speech and publication, increased spending on education, and the release of political prisoners.[68]

These calls for a political amnesty were officially rejected on 6 March 1989, when the *Beijing ribao* reported the minutes of a talk between the Beijing Higher People's Court and the voters of the first branch school of Beijing University. The grounds for rejection were firstly that, since amnesties could only be granted to political prisoners, any call for amnesty was groundless in terms of the law, because now in China there 'were only criminal offenders and no political prisoners'. Secondly, it was asserted that, since the promulgation of its first constitution China had revoked amnesty, because amnesty absolved the convicted person from guilt, while only a special pardon pardoned one who was guilty. It would thus be detrimental to society if amnesties were granted to all criminal offenders.[69]

Like China's students, China's intellectuals agreed on the need for an expansion of civil and political rights, but differed as to the specific political mechanisms. Critics of the regime such as Su Shaozhi, Liu Binyan, Wu Zuguang, Wang Ruowang, and Wang Ruoshui demanded political liberalization and reform, while supporting the general tenets of socialism. Their views could be summed up in Liu Binyan's words, 'there can't be socialism without democracy'.[70] Within that consensus, Liu Binyan stressed the importance of press freedom and inner Party reform, based on political criticism, or 'a second kind of loyalty', and Wang Ruowang emphasized the importance of inner Party reform and the separation of the Party, and not just the state, from the enterprises.[71] Liu Binyan believed that the problem did not lie with socialism, but with its practitioners, Stalin, Mao, and Pol Pot, who 'ignored Marx's basic tenet that socialism presupposes a high level of material development'. The need for political as well as economic reform in China was, he said in January 1989, first suggested by Deng Xiaoping but was defeated by resistance within the Party:

Senior officials refused to give up their positions and privileges. They are not concerned with socialism: they are concerned only with their own interests and that of their children and grandchildren. I think real *glasnost*, or openness, will gradually come about, not because conservatives want it, but because the people will force them to accept it.[72]

The kind of political change advocated by Liu did not encompass a multi-party system. As he observed:

> Before 1957, the question of multiple parties was actually raised in China, but for the near future I don't think it's possible to have multiple parties.
>   China is a very special country. There is no other country with such a long 'feudal' history, two thousand times the length of European medieval times. Furthermore, in the forty years since the revolution the Party has not allowed opposition parties or tolerated people with different political ideas. It has not allowed non-political ideologies to spread.
>   As a result, it is even more difficult for a political society or organisation to appear in China than in the Soviet Union or Eastern Europe. Unless social chaos and popular pressure develop to the degree that they render the Party utterly powerless, a new opposition is not likely to appear. The more realistic possibility is the evolution of pluralism within the Party.[73]

Fang Lizhi, on the other hand, espoused a more individualistic interpretation of civil and political rights, and considered that socialism was no longer the answer to China's problems. He believed that Chinese intellectuals, the 'brain workers', should be the carriers of political liberalization and change and, like Wei Jingsheng, that economic development was impossible without political change, or 'democracy'. In the long term Fang looked to the establishment of a multi-party system in which intellectuals and businessmen could form one pressure group. In the short term, however, he stressed the transfer of real civil rights to the Chinese people, as well as the removal of political controls exerted by the Party. Human rights were the prerequisite of democracy, for democracy could not be pursued by undemocratic means.[74] As he said in late April 1987:

> In China the Party wants not only to manage politics. It wants to control everything, including people's lifestyles and thinking. Today, factories are being run by managers, but the real power still lies in the hands of Party cadres. Peasants enjoy a free market system, but the cadres tell them: 'You still need our rubber stamp and for that you still have to buy us'. And here lies the root of the new corruption. In order to create a true economic democracy in China, one ought to abolish political controls. And that is exactly what the Party fears most.[75]

Writing in February 1989, Fang summed up the issues most commonly discussed in China:

(1) Guarantee of human rights. Most importantly, freedom of speech, freedom of the press, and freedom of assembly. Also, release of Wei Jingsheng and all political prisoners.

(2) Establishment of a free economic system. Gradual implementation of economic reforms that will include reforms in property rights.

(3) Support for education. Abandonment of the 'ignorant masses' policy; provision of the needed and entirely feasible education that would be commensurate with China's economic level.

(4) Supervision of public officeholders. Use of open *glasnost*-style means to root out corruption.

(5) An end to China's state of civil war; promotion of peace in the Taiwan straits. The mainland side to call for mutual renunciation of force as a means of settling differences. A transition from mutual hostility toward peaceful competition.

(6) Establishment of rule by law. Opposition to rule by individuals, whether directly or in disguised form — as when Party documents or policies override the laws of the nation.

(7) Revision of the constitution. Deletion of all language that relies on the principle of 'class struggle' to support dictatorship. Drafting of a Chinese constitution that provides for political democracy and economic freedom (sic).[76]

Despite a more elitist concept of 'human rights', and despite the fact that the dissenters of the 1980s foresook the concern with economic and social rights which had animated the first democracy movement, it is important to note that neither Fang Lizhi nor Yan Jiaqi conformed in this period with the Western view of human rights as something inherent and inalienable.[77] Their ideas remained within the ambit of the collectivist notions of Chinese tradition, and they saw rights as closely associated with duties and with the characteristics of national culture.[78]

The External Critique

China's Civil Rights

Until the late 1970s, there was no serious, systematic attempt by governments, human rights organizations, or even the United Nations, to call China to account for its human rights abuses. As Roberta Cohen observes, it was the Chinese people, through their own public revelations about the Cultural Revolution, who drew attention to the importance of an issue that had been obscured by a conspiracy of silence. In much the same way, it was the demonstrators in Tiananmen Square in April–May 1989 who exposed the comfortable fiction that the Chinese people were content with economic and social rights alone, and were prepared to remain politically passive. In the mid to late 1970s, details on human rights conditions in China were provided by the Chinese Human Rights Society, formed in the United States in 1975, and by the Society for the Protection of East Asian Human Rights (SPEAHR): but these were not lobbying or pressure groups.[79]

In the late 1970s, however, the revelations about the Cultural Revolution, the gradual opening up of Chinese society through trade and joint business ventures, and the exit to foreign universities of tens of thousands of Chinese students, served to draw aside the veil of internationally professed ignorance. At the end of 1978 the Carter administration issued the first public statement on human rights made by a Western government.[80] In the same year, Amnesty International issued its first major report on China, *Political Imprisonment in the People's Republic of China*. The subsequent international publicity accorded to the Democracy Wall Movement in 1978 and 1979, and the moving public spectacle of the incandescent features of Wei Jingsheng, head shaven and neck exposed, arguing his own defence at his trial, wrought indelible images on the collective international consciousness.

From these images, it was difficult to retreat. In 1980, the first US congressional report on human rights in China was contained in the series, *Country Reports on Human Rights Practices for 1979*. Journals such as *Index on Censorship*, *Freedom Appeals*, *Freedom at Issue*, and *Speahrhead*, made available in translation information on the Democracy Wall Movement and its activists, as well as prison memoirs.[81] Expatriate Chinese took up the cause of Chinese prisoners of conscience. In 1982, 132 Chinese academics studying in the US and Canada sent a letter to the PRC protesting the secret trial and fourteen year sentence of Wang Xizhe, and calling for public trials for all Chinese arrested for connection with unofficial journals.[82] In December 1982, the first issue of *China Spring*, founded by a Chinese graduate in the United States to support the development of democracy in China, carried an open letter to the people of China urging support for democracy, freedom, and human rights.[83] In Hong Kong, the two major universities set up groups to support human rights in China, and two groups of human rights activists, the Resource Centre for the Chinese Democratic Movement and the Hong Kong

Association for Solidarity with the Chinese Democratic Movement, were established.

Apart from isolated interventions by the Paris-based Fédération Internationale des Droits de l'Homme ('International Federation for the Rights of Man'), by Freedom House, and by the Minority Rights Group in London, however, the only International Non-Governmental Organization (INGO) to take concerted action on China at this time was Amnesty International,[84] although in high-level, bilateral exchanges, a few governments began to make representations to the Chinese government on human rights, to some effect.[85]

Amnesty International, after initial hesitation, developed a sustained and systematic programme to deal with human rights abuses in China, concentrating mainly on the protection of civil rights of immunity. It monitored the nature of Chinese legislation and the structure of the legal, judicial, and penal systems which gave rise to such abuses. It also documented the treatment and condition of detainees and prisoners, particularly prisoners of conscience. Amnesty International's concerns included the arrest and imprisonment of prisoners of conscience, inadequate trial procedures, and the extensive use of the death penalty, as well as the prolonged detention without trial of people arrested on political grounds.[86] It was also concerned with torture and other ill-treatment of criminal suspects and prisoners in China.[87] These concerns were first raised in its 1978 Report, and in its 1984 Report, *China, Violations of Human Rights: Prisoners of Conscience and the Death Penalty in the People's Republic of China*. In March 1987, Amnesty submitted a Memorandum to the Chinese government on recommended safeguards against torture and other ill-treatment of prisoners, and in July issued a report, *China: Torture and Ill-Treatment of Prisoners*.[88] This report noted that in early 1987 the Chinese official press had indicated that China had readjusted its policy on the issue of human rights so that it was now participating in the international human rights movement in a 'more active and spontaneous way'. It also noted that discussions had started in China on legal-structural reforms to take place in the next five years, and that in December 1986, China had signed the UN Convention against Torture and Other Cruel, Inhuman or Degrading Treatment or Punishment.[89] Despite these advances, it observed that no fundamental changes had yet been made in legislation to lessen the risk of detainees being subjected to torture, or to ensure that investigations of alleged abuses were carried out rigorously and impartially.[90] Abuses included severe beatings, use of electric batons and tight handcuffs, suspension from a pole by the arms for long periods of time, sustained periods of solitary confinement, sleep deprivation, and 24-hour interrogation.

Amnesty called for the introduction of a number of safeguards into the Chinese legal system: limits on incommunicado detention; separation of authority over detention and investigation; safeguards during interrogation and custody; review of administrative detention, of citizens' power of arrest and of the powers of informal security units to reduce the number of arbitrary or illegal detentions; prompt investigations of all complaints and reports of torture by independent and impartial bodies not involved in the process of arrest, detention, or investigation; prosecution of alleged torturers; the establishment of training procedures for all officials involved in the process of arrest, interrogation, or the administration of justice; and the introduction of medical safeguards to ensure that detainees were examined by independent, fully-qualified medical practitioners immediately upon arrest and at regular intervals thereafter.[91] Finally, it called for the review of legislation and procedures aimed at preventing, investigating, or punishing acts of torture.[92]

In January 1989 Amnesty published a report, *People's Republic of China: The Death Penalty in China*, which stated:

The death penalty is used extensively in China. Amnesty International has documented over 1,500 executions since 1983 but believes the true figure to be far higher. The number of crimes punishable by death has increased substantially during the past decade. Prisoners have been executed for stealing bicycles, for 'molesting women', for hanging a banner with a 'counter revolutionary' slogan from a hotel window and for plotting to set up 'subversive' organizations. Trial procedures do not conform to international standards for fair trial. Procedural safeguards have been curtailed; verdicts may be decided before trial and there is no effective protection of the right to defence. Cases of death sentences imposed on innocent people have been publicised in the Chinese press. Prisoners are often publicly humiliated by being paraded in public and taken to mass sentencing rallies to have their crimes denounced before being taken away to be executed by pistol shot.[93]

In this report, Amnesty noted that since 1980 China had substantially increased the number of offences punishable by death to over thirty.

Apart from criticizing judicial procedures of appeal and review as being 'largely a formality', Amnesty regretted the fact that the requirement in the Criminal Procedure Law that all death sentences be automatically reviewed and approved by the Supreme People's Court had been abandoned in recent years. Most prisoners sentenced to death, it charged, were executed shortly after the sentence had been upheld in appeal and were not given the opportunity to seek pardon or commutation of sentence. Those sentenced to death were often taken before execution to mass sentencing rallies attended by thousands of people, which 'serve to educate the masses'.[94]

In an April 1989 report, *People's Republic of China: The Death Penalty Debate*, Amnesty foreshadowed that in 1989 it would call on the Chinese government to stop all executions, commute all outstanding death sentences, and consider abolishing the death penalty in law. In line with international standards, it called for the establishment of all facilities for a fair trial before an independent and impartial tribunal, for the cessation of all cruel, inhuman, and degrading treatment of prisoners, for the right of the accused to seek pardon or commutation of death sentence, and for an undertaking that the scope of the death penalty should be limited to 'the most serious crimes'.[95]

Soon after the crushing of the Tiananmen Square demonstrations by sections of the People's Liberation Army (PLA), Amnesty International issued an Urgent Action appeal calling on the Chinese government to prevent further killings and halt the use of lethal force. It expressed concern that 'large-scale arbitrary arrests may be carried out and that those detained, particularly those suspected of active participation in the recent demonstrations, face the risk of torture or other ill-treatment'.[96] The realization of these fears was reflected in the 30 August Amnesty report, which documented not only the human rights abuses of the early June period, but also those which occurred from June to August.[97]

Apart from monitoring the nature of China's legal, judicial, and penal systems, Amnesty documented the treatment and condition of prisoners of conscience in China, who, since 1979, had comprised religious prisoners, Tibetan nationals, supporters of the Democracy Movement, students and workers arrested following demonstrations, and officials arrested on political grounds. Certain proven leading dissidents were adopted by the organization as cases whose condition and treatment were regularly monitored, and whose plight was represented to the Chinese government.

In May 1987, Amnesty followed up its 1984 report on prisoners of conscience with a report on dissenters still imprisoned because of activities connected with the Democracy Wall Movement and the 1986 student demonstrations.[98] It reported that Dai Zhen, Fu Shenqi, Fu Yuehua, Liu Liping, Liu Nianchun, Ren Wanding (re-arrested June 1989), Tao Sen, and Yang Zaixing had been released. On the other hand, Chen Erjin, Geng Qichang, Guo Shuzhang, Liu De, Liu Qing, Liu Shanqing, Wang Xizhe, Wei Jingsheng, Xu Shuiliang, Xue Deyun, and Xu Wenli were still in prison.[99] Notable among these cases was Xu Wenli, former editor of the *April Fifth Forum*, who was able to smuggle out of China a graphic account of his arrest, pre-trial detention, and court hearing. His report, 'My Self Defence', described the conditions of his detention in K Block of Banbuqiao detention centre during the period of interrogation:

Audio-surveillance equipment was installed in the cell. There was a one-way visual-surveillance peephole in the door, and a black curtain was draped across . . . Although they would not use violence against me, within the prison buildings the sounds of beatings and cursing, and the sound of electrical assaults being carried out, were commonplace. Some people had been swallowed up by this place for a good few years already. The limitation on the pre-trial detention period was basically quite ineffectual here. Some people had already assumed an obviously broken-down demeanour, and I greatly feared being consumed by the place, being dragged down and broken. For my wife and child's sake, I must on no account break down here.[100]

In June 1982 Xu was given a sentence of 15 years' imprisonment. Between September 1982 and late 1985, he was held in solitary confinement in a cell measuring six square metres. After several months solitary confinement in a strict regime cell in 1986, he returned to a normal prison regime.[101] Despite this, his condition was known to have deteriorated. As Jay Mathews reported in August 1989: 'Xu Wenli, a gentle, thoughtful electrician and former editor of an independent Chinese magazine, has been in prison in Beijing since 1981. His hair has turned white. His nerves are shot. He is unable to do much more than weep on those rare occasions he is allowed to see his wife and daughter . . .'[102]

Another political prisoner, Liu Qing, who was accused of having smuggled to the outside world the transcript of Wei Jingsheng's trial, wrote a 196 page testimony in which he reported that after his arrest in November 1979 he was held for five months in solitary confinement in a cold and wet cell, and that he developed rheumatism and lost his eyesight and his hair. In April 1980 he was moved to a large shared cell but was beaten for refusing the warder's order to walk with his hands below his stomach. He wrote:

When I was brought back to the cell my body was covered with blue and purple bruises from the beating. I had been forced to wear a gas mask that made it very hard for me to breathe, and I was restricted with handcuffs that cut into my flesh.[103]

Liu was reported to have been sentenced to seven years imprisonment in late 1982 at the same time as his brother, Liu Nianchun (later released), was tried and sentenced.

One of the most important activists of the 1978–80 Democracy Wall Movement, Wang Xizhe, was arrested on 20 April 1981, tried on 28 May 1982 and sentenced to fourteen years imprisonment with four-and-a-half years suspension of political rights. All information of his trial, according to Amnesty International, indicated that he was accused only of activities involving the 'non-violent exercise of fundamental human rights'. No news had been received of him since his trial.

Of Wei Jingsheng, author of 'The Fifth Modernization', Amnesty reported:

Following his trial, Wei Jingsheng was reported to have been held for several years in solitary confinement in the detention centre adjacent to Beijing Prison No. 1. According to a former prisoner who was held in the Banbuqiao detention centre adjacent to the prison during 1980 and 1981, Wei Jingsheng was then detained in isolation in cell No. 11 of Section 2 — a block reserved for 'major criminals'. He reported that Wei Jingsheng went on a hunger-strike once during that period, and that in April 1981 he was suddenly moved from his cell because he was constantly 'making trouble' and it was feared that his rebellious spirit would influence the other prisoners.

Wei Jingsheng is reported to have been held in solitary since his trial. In the past four years there have been persistent reports that his mental health had deteriorated as a result of his conditions of detention. In 1984, he was reported to have been transferred twice to a hospital needing treatment of schizophrenia. Amnesty International launched several appeals expressing concern about his health but the authorities have not responded.[105]

A subsequent report suggested that Wei Jingsheng had been moved to Qinghai province. He was said to have lost his teeth and hair. A report in 1988 that he had died was subsequently denied by the Chinese Ministry of Justice.[106]

Economic, Social, and Cultural Rights

The condition of China's economic, social, and cultural rights was not a focus of Amnesty International's concerns. It was, however, a concern of international economic and developmental institutions which had an important role in advising China on its developmental programmes for the modernization decade. Apart from organizations like the UN Development Programme, whose primary focus was the issue of development and poverty, the World Bank, while placing a priority on structural economic adjustment, was simultaneously concerned with the social impact of its assistance programmes. Since 1987, moreover, the Bank's operational guidelines required President's reports supporting structural adjustment loans (SALs) to 'pay particular attention to . . . an analysis of the short-term impact of the adjustment program on the urban and rural poor, and measures proposed to alleviate negative effects'.[107] The Bank's investigatory country missions therefore combined economic policy proposals with recommendations on social welfare and social security policies which emphasized the interdependence of economic development and social justice.

China's entry into the World Bank in 1980 resulted in a series of Bank missions in late 1980 to examine different sectors of the Chinese economy and to make a broad analysis of the achievements and shortcomings of thirty years of socialist economic development.[108] In 1983 the Bank published a major report of its findings, *China: Socialist Economic Development*. A second major study of the Chinese economy, the outcome of a second mission in 1983, was published in 1985.[109] Although these reports were not couched in terms of a formal critique, the positive assessments of the social developmental achievements under the Maoist era by functional specialists provided official and professional endorsement of the earlier evaluations by a number of China scholars. Somewhat paradoxically, in view of the Bank's reputation in the 1960s and 1970s for conservative economic policies, the warnings by Bank experts about the social consequences of the economic restructuring process, and their recommendations in favour of redistributive policies in education, welfare, and social security, placed them in a position which was well left of centre in relation to Chinese policies on economic reform.

The 1985 report was particularly important in that it was written half-way through the modernization decade, at the end of a period of extraordinary rural growth, and thus was able to test the strengths and weaknesses of the Chinese economic reforms. It provided a broad survey of the social problems which had resulted, or which it was anticipated would result from the economic reforms, together with recommendations for their solution. Its underlying assumption was the inextricable link between economic development and social redistribution, between efficiency and equity.[110] It addressed two important questions:

Do China's social policy instruments still meet the social and equity objectives of a modernising society rapidly approaching middle income levels? And are they compatible with the other changes that are taking place in the economic and social system? Unwillingness to confront the possible social consequences of economic reform has been a critical flaw in many East European attempts. *The result is often an incorrect impression that reform must entail the abandonment of social concerns. This risk exists in China also, perhaps to an even greater degree than in other socialist countries, because income distribution and economic security are being met in unusual ways,* and particularly because social instruments are so entangled with economic instruments.[111]

Apart from recommending such policies as the greater use of market regulation to stimulate innovation and efficiency, and stronger planning combining indirect and direct economic controls, the 1985 report called for the 'modification and extension of social institutions and policies to maintain the fairness in distribution that is fundamental to socialism, despite the greater inequality and instability that market regulation and indirect controls would tend to cause'.[112] It stated:

China has been outstandingly successful in reducing extreme poverty. Although there is substantial income inequality between urban and rural areas and among different rural localities, the hunger, disease, high birth and infant death rates, general illiteracy, and constant fear of distribution and starvation that haunt very poor people have been more or less banished.[113]

However, it warned, 'economic reforms and greater technological dynamism could increase income disparities, while economically desirable changes in the price, wage, and employment systems could make it more difficult to use these things as instruments of social policy. Demographic trends, and major changes in the pattern of disease, will also pose new problems'.[114]

Accordingly, the report suggested alternative policies to the ones being adopted by the Chinese government in the areas of social security, of housing and social services, of population control and health delivery, and in the problem areas of poverty and income disparities. Because, it suggested, under the new reforms prices and wages would be increasingly governed by economic considerations, it would be difficult to use them to guarantee minimum urban living standards.

This problem, together with the anticipated increase in unemployment levels, made it essential for China to introduce a comprehensive social security system that was 'effective, affordable and workable for a lower middle income country'. Two approaches were suggested: a state run insurance scheme financed primarily by compulsory wage-related contributions from workers and their employers, which could provide old-age pensions, unemployment benefits, sickness and maternity benefits to contributors, together with non-contributory income supplements to very poor households: or the concentration of resources on non-contributory income supplements to low-income households, partly financed from taxes on high incomes. In urban areas there could be a uniform scheme, including the self-employed as well as state and collective employees. In rural areas, the state should encourage collective and local development of contributory pension and insurance schemes. The urgency of establishing such social security schemes was underlined by the increase of the aged cohort, from the current 5 per cent of the population to a future estimated 20 per cent.

Similarly, the report suggested the transfer of the responsibilities of housing, education, and health services away from the work unit. This would involve some privatization of housing, giving households responsibility for their own homes, through individual ownership and housing co-operatives. On the other hand, because the introduction of the production responsibility system had 'adversely affected social services in rural areas', the report required 'increased central and provincial government support of rural social services'. Although in prosperous rural areas these services could be obtained through 'self-reliance', in poor areas a large proportion of the costs should be state financed.

In the health sector, the challenge facing China was to deal with a 'second health care revolution' resulting from the changes in the nature of China's health problems, from those typical of low-income countries to a pattern evinced in high-income countries where the leading causes of death were heart disease and cancer. These problems, the report suggested, should be solved by 'prevention' strategies rather than through 'endlessly costly investments in medical technologies of limited efficacy'. Such preventive strategies were outlined in another World Bank report, *China: The Health Sector*.[115]

In both the health and education sectors, the main 1985 report advised that the state should take more financial responsibility and should avoid privatization of services.[116] While in urban areas this responsibility should be shifted from work units to government at various levels, in the rural areas it should be undertaken by the state. This was because in rural areas, 'economic trends by themselves may not sufficiently narrow rural–urban income disparities, and because poorer areas are likely to fall further behind other parts of the country'.[117]

In relation to the problem of rural poverty, the World Bank suggested that it was unlikely that China's agricultural productivity would grow fast enough to narrow the large agricultural–non-agricultural earnings gap (even in proportionate terms) until the twenty-first century. To resolve the problem of rural poverty, it suggested measures such as direct income supplements to broad categories of farm households, increased government expenditure, financed by taxation of non-agricultural gains, in the development of agricultural and other rural infrastructure, improvements in agricultural research and extension services, and support to rural social services. It also suggested subsidies to rural participants in social security schemes.[118]

World Bank recommendations thus focused, on the one hand, on the importance of decentralizing certain areas of economic activity and of maintaining centralized control over macro-economic planning, and on the other, of centralizing the majority of social security and social welfare services which had previously been administered in the state sector by the work unit and, in the non-state and rural sector, both administered and financed by the collective.

The findings of the 1985 report on the rural sector were paralleled by those in Annex 2 of the report, *China: Agriculture to the*

Year 2000, which also focused on the issue of income and geographic differentials. It found that recent rural reforms had significantly narrowed the average urban/rural income differentials, although 'in real terms it remains large, partially because the government pays for as much as one half of the cost of non-commodity expenditures in urban areas (rent, water and power, schooling, child care, transportation, etc.), and urban residents receive additional consumption benefits through their employers'.[119] However, during the same period, interpersonal income differentials in the rural areas 'almost certainly increased, with official support'. While taxation offered an instrument to control these differentials, the Chinese government had paid less attention to geographical and inter-regional income disparities. Relative poverty remained characteristic of much of the north-west and parts of the north and south-west (which were also areas populated by large numbers of minority peoples). Similar geographic income differentials existed within provinces. To slow the growth of these differentials, the report suggested that the government should invest in infrastructure and support services and in the improvement of the transportation system. It also suggested the supply of external sources of food grains to these areas at minimum cost. On the other hand, it suggested that 'subsidies to more prosperous areas implicit in present government policies might well be removed'.[120]

Following up this concern about poverty in outlying provinces, in 1988 the World Bank published a further report, *China: Growth and Development in Gansu Province*, which dealt with problems symptomatic of all other impoverished geographical regions in China. The Gansu report concluded that 'neither collectives nor households in most rural areas of Gansu have resources to finance a minimum level of social services'.[121] This was implicit criticism of the current system of funding health and education services through self-financing, which had led to a situation where expenditure on these items as a percentage of GDP was low relative to other countries. In rural education, the report suggested that 'whether or not there are any formal changes in the responsibilities of the government for rural education, a further shift in the financing from collectives and individuals to government is clearly warranted'.

The World Bank country-based reports thus formed the most influential and authoritative critiques of the condition of China's economic, social, and cultural rights in the modernization decade before 1989, as well as providing responsible prescriptions for future change. Backing up the findings of these reports were Bank reports on specific themes, and findings of the UN Development Programme. Thus, the World Bank's Development Report for 1990, *Poverty*, which, *inter alia*, covered the conditions of Chinese development for the modernization decade 1979–89, identified not only the continuation of China's economic restructuring, but also continued favourable distribution of income as indispensable conditions for China's projected 6.8 per cent growth rate of GDP in the 1990s:

The projected drop in the number of poor . . . depends on maintaining the favourable distribution of income that has marked China's development. An erosion of the agricultural terms of trade or a failure of lagging regions to join in growth could compromise China's overall progress, especially in rural areas. At the same time, greater reliance on market forces and decentralisation could further undermine the community level system of health care and social security. *The challenge that China faces is to encourage gains in efficiency through market reforms while maintaining or replacing social safety nets threatened by reform.* If external conditions are unfavourable and internal reforms are not implemented, annual growth is unlikely to exceed 5 per cent in the 1990s. This would leave China with 90 million poor by 2,000. A fall in the real incomes of the rural poor (caused, for instance, by a shift in relative prices) could easily boost this number to more than 100 million.[122]

A similar position was adopted by the UN Development Programme in its Human Development Report. Using the three key indicators of life expectancy, literacy, and basic income (or purchasing-power-adjusted real GDP per capita figures), it ranked China 66 out of 130 countries in the Human Development Index (HDI) for 1987, 44 places higher than its GNP per capita rank, which was 22.[123] A close examination of the basis for China's favourable HDI rating, however, reveals that it was largely due to the socio-economic development policies adopted in the era *preceding* economic reform. The report's findings aptly summarized the general critique by international financial and development agencies of China's economic and social rights in the decade prior to June 1989:

China dramatically improved its human condition through extensive, well-structured, across-the-board . . . interventions (with some targeting) during a period of arguably moderate growth, roughly 1960–78. But even with good subsequent growth, reduction in the coverage of . . . policies (has) led to a stagnation or, by some accounts, even a reversal of these trends . . .

The post 1978 reforms undoubtedly increased the production incentives, as reflected in accelerated growth but they appear also to have hurt, probably unintentionally, the variables that contribute directly and indirectly to human development, slowing the earlier rate of progress. *There is no rationale for neglecting social development in a period of accelerated economic growth.*[124]

7 The 1989 Chinese Democracy Movement and Human Rights: April 1989–January 1990

Patiently endured so long as it seemed beyond redress, a grievance comes to appear intolerable once the possibility of removing it crosses men's minds.

Alexis de Tocqueville

On the eve of the 1989 Democracy Movement, despite China's overall economic growth, Chinese citizens were clearly suffering an objective deprivation of human rights. These causes of discontent were not, however, in themselves sufficient to account for a major, if peaceful, civilian uprising throughout the country. Such causes were only significant because they coincided with other more subjective conditions.

In line with de Tocqueville, David Landes has observed that 'students of revolution have long noted that trouble comes not from the depths of misery but from the appetite that grows with better eating'.[1] This observation is a restatement of the theory of relative deprivation, first articulated as a social theory by W.G. Runciman and Ted Gurr.[2] Consistent with this theory, and with the objective condition of civil, political, economic, and social rights in China outlined in preceding chapters, the popular demonstrations which arose throughout China's cities from April to May 1989 were the outcome of a revolution of rising expectations in the arena of civil and political rights, and of a combination of rising expectations and relative deprivation in the area of social and economic rights.[3] The 1989 Democracy Movement was the ultimate point of collision between the old structures of Maoist rights and the new rights of the modernization decade. Unlike most other post-1949 movements, it was a spontaneous mass uprising, reminiscent of the May 4 Movement, expressing a plethora of discontents, which incorporated men and women from all social classes and occupations. Its tragic culmination was to draw China irrevocably into the arena of international human rights scrutiny.

The popular uprising of April–June 1989 is now a given which is fed into the mental computers of China scholars and which has provided them with a new perspective on the deep-rooted political, economic, and social problems of contemporary China. The danger is that, as in the past, every new revelation and every new reference point may be accepted by scholars as the final word on the subject, as the *point final*, as the end of Chinese history.[4] For that reason, it is important to examine the sources of discontent, real and perceived, behind the 1989 Democracy Movement. Only then can a judgement be made as to whether the present stability in China reflects a real, or only an apparent, adjustment by citizens to the current condition of their rights.

Origins

The 1989 Democracy Movement was a dramatic explosion of mass grievances which brought to the political surface the profound anxieties and exaggerated popular expectations triggered by the modernization era. As Runciman has observed: 'Most people's lives are governed more by the resentment of narrow inequalities, the cultivation of modest ambition . . . Yet there are times and places at which the resentment of inequality rises to a level where it not merely corresponds with the facts of inequality but even overreaches them'. The key to this precise moment is seen by Runciman and Gurr as the phenomenon of relative deprivation, a concept of psychology which is given a collective social dimension.

Relative deprivation is defined by Runciman as a sense of deprivation borne of perceptions of inequality in class, status, or power when compared with a 'comparative' or 'normative' reference group. While Runciman uses the theory as it pertains to feelings of inequality in inter-personal or inter-group relations, Gurr utilizes it to explain revolutions. For Gurr, relative deprivation is a condition of disequilibrium resulting from the gap between collective value expectations and collective value capabilities. It exhibits three main patterns: 'decremental' deprivation, where value expectations are constant but capabilities are seen to decline; 'aspirational' deprivation, where capabilities remain static and expectations intensify; and 'progressive' deprivation, marked by a substantial and simultaneous increase in expectations and a decrease in capabilities.[5] Although not utilizing the precise Weberian terminology adopted by Runciman, that is, of class, status, and power, Gurr nevertheless utilizes the same category of value distinctions, between 'welfare' values (well-being and self-realization), 'interpersonal' values (status, community, and ideational values), and 'power' (participation and security).[6]

Relative deprivation only triggers revolutionary change when there is a confluence of a number of factors — the existence of objective sources of deprivation, a subjective sense of grievance, and a perception of the possibility of change. Relative deprivation is both a vertical and a horizontal concept. That is, it occurs with reference to time, felt in relation to the loss of some value or values enjoyed in the past or to some inconsistency between expectations and present capabilities, and to space, or 'reference groups', with whom the deprived group compares itself. While normally this reference group is situated close to the condition of the class, status, and power of the referring group, in situations characterized by a loss of societal norms — the condition of *anomie* referred to by Durkheim — there is a 'danger of confusion and violence precisely because people do not know where to look for their reference groups, whether comparative or normative, and thereby become prone to exaggerated hopes and fears'.[7] Relative deprivation has led to collective violence, or collective action, in cases where 'citizens felt sharply deprived with respect to their most deeply valued goals, had individually and collectively exhausted the constructive means open to them to attain these goals, and lacked any non-violent opportunity to act on their anger'.[8]

The relevance of this theory to Chinese conditions may be apparent but as a 'grand' theory it is not without its critics. Some have reservations about the application of concepts of individual psychology to the social arena; others have objected that the theory is too all-inclusive.[9] Still others complain that it is just another way of describing what it was intended to explain. What the theory does offer in terms of explanation, however, is located in the word 'relative'; expectations or disappointments are not necessarily objectively based, but relative to time and to space. This relativity is particularly significant in a socialist context where egalitarianism is, or has recently been, the prevailing ethos. Explanatory power also lies in the idea that deprivation is as much a function of hope as it is of disappointment, that is, it is as much the result of a reasonable expectation of change as of verifiable, empirical circumstances. As such, it is based as much on perceptions of reality as on the reality itself. To apply the theory to China, one must therefore not only isolate the objective sources of grievance which have been analysed in earlier chapters, but chart popular perceptions in China about these circumstances, and about the possibility of change.

That Chinese society in the modernization decade experienced the most profound changes is not in doubt. That these changes were of 'kind' rather than 'degree' has already been argued.[10] There is no doubt that the profound changes in the arena of politics, the economy, and social structures were destructive of the common norms which served to legitimate Party rule.[11] Dissatisfaction with the results of these changes was indicated in numerous opinion polls taken during the decade.[12] Stanley Rosen has pointed out the double-edged nature of opinion polling in China. Increasingly in the 1980s China's leadership recognized that, in the absence of the normal political channels available in liberal democracies, policies for coping with the social impact of economic reform could only be formulated by obtaining some kind of feedback through public opinion polls. On the other hand, once the polling process was established as an important part of policy making, 'the public pulse required constant monitoring, and public demand for the tangible benefits of reform grew faster than the available supply'.[13] In other words, polling was not only a means of recording dissatisfaction, but in itself fed the expectations of the citizens. Polling thus had a similar effect to the 'cahiers de doléances' ('lists of grievances') which were drawn up on the eve of the French Revolution and which similarly raised expectations of reforms. One of the reasons for this effect in China was the authoritative status of the body which conducted the majority of polls in the 1980s. The Chinese Economic System Reform Research Institute (CESRRI) was founded by Zhao Ziyang, under the direct authority of the State Council, as a think-tank to provide the leaders with advice on economic reform, and to conduct extensive surveys on public opinion. The widespread media publicity given to the pro-reform findings of the early CESRRI surveys triggered heightened, and often unrealistic, expectations of the improved living standards which reform could deliver to the urban people.[14]

During the 1980s, polls were carried out by official, private, and semi-private organizations.[15] A focal point of resentment was the unequal distribution of new wealth, a fact particularly disturbing for pensioners, and urban fixed-salary earners, including academics, whose salaries were low and who did not enjoy bonuses. The widespread perception that top officials and their children, Party members, and local cadres were, through various corrupt practices, receiving a disproportionate share of new wealth, only exacerbated the sense of inequality produced by inflation.[16] For instance, a poll conducted among 12,000 workers (36 per cent manual, 64 per cent non-manual) in sixteen cities in August 1988 by the Institute of Sociology of the Chinese Academy of Social Sciences and the State Statistical Bureau, revealed that 94 per cent of the interviewees felt that prices were rising too rapidly, 64.1 per cent believed that further price rises would be more likely to lead to social unrest, and 35.3 per cent that the ever widening income gaps would have the same effect. Of the respondents, 46 per cent claimed that embezzlement and bribe-taking by government employees were the biggest social problem and 61 per cent felt that officials often took advantage of their position and power by disregarding the law. Likewise, 63 per cent of those polled believed that the worst political problem was improper deeds committed by Party members.[17] A poll of 435 Beijing residents conducted in 1988 also singled out the abuse of power by Party members and officials for personal gain as the most troublesome issue of the year. The polls found that the enforcement of the law, the curbing of rampant abuses of power, and the stabilization of prices were considered by people to be the best ways to promote China's reforms.[18]

The most interesting and informative polls, however, were those conducted by the CESRRI, not only because they were followed up over time, but because they revealed a simultaneous sense of popular discontent and of rising expectations. Fourteen longitudinal surveys conducted by CESRRI between 1984 and 1986 suggested three stages in the evolution of popular attitudes.[19] The first stage followed the adoption of urban reforms by the October 1984 Party Plenum, and was characterized by an enthusiastic popular response. The second stage, which focused on the issue of price reform in 1985, was marked by increasing popular dissatisfaction, particularly over commodity price rises, coupled with widespread optimism that popular aspirations for higher incomes were justified.[20] The third stage was similarly marked by both dissatisfaction and expectations. Sources of dissatisfaction included rising prices, nepotism, wage inequities, and abuse of official power for personal gain, while hopes extended not only to rising incomes but to a variety of political, social, and economic issues.[21]

These issues were not expressed in the specific terms of

economic and social rights, since Chinese citizens were more closely acquainted with their duties than with their rights. But the deterioration of living standards, including such unfamiliar experiences as unemployment, lack of social security and social welfare benefits, and the rising cost of medicine, was felt strongly. The problem of 'upward emulation', constantly referred to as a social problem in the 1985 CESRRI report, was reflected in the finding that although enterprise cadres regarded their work as important, fully 78 per cent of those interviewed would choose to leave their management work, mainly for the government bureaucracy, because they felt caught between the demands of the workers and the demands of the state. This sense of dilemma had sharpened as reform increased managerial power and, thus, the workers' expectations of what the managers could provide.[22]

The most powerful source of discontent, however, was inequality of opportunity. This was most clearly reflected in a February 1986 survey which indicated that only 29.3 per cent of the people felt that reform offered opportunities to all.[23] A growing perception of inequality was reflected in subsequent polls from 1986 to 1988.[24] On the other hand, a July 1985 poll revealed that 79.8 per cent of respondents preferred 'living a stable life at the expense of earning less', while only 18.6 per cent would choose 'living a life full of challenge, but with a bigger opportunity to earn more'.[25] The polls thus demonstrated that not only was there excessive anxiety about what had been lost as a result of the reforms, both in relation to time and to other groups, but that there were excessive expectations of, and anxieties about, the future. These excessive responses, coupled with the wide range of 'reference groups' to which the discontented compared their lot, was suggestive of a profound sense of *anomie*. Although there was increasing disparity between groups as regards aspirations and attitude to reform, the tendency was to compare one's lot not just with the closest 'reference group', but even with the elite stratum of Party officials, at least in the sense that this stratum was seen as a 'normative' reference group.[26] In this sense, socialism was still used as a yardstick by which citizens measured their conditions. On the other hand, the 'comparative' reference groups to which citizens often compared their lot, the *getihu* (entrepreneurs) and pop stars, were a reflection of the extent to which modernization had changed Chinese values. Because of this dual value system, the issue of corruption, which was the source of much discontent in the polls, and which was the one issue uniting all social groups in the 1989 Democracy Movement, is of greatest interest.

The public issue of corruption was particularly powerful because it was at once a symptom of popular deprivation and of popular expectations. It represented the clash between old and new values. Although it has been argued that the clientelist legacy of China's feudal and patrimonial society survived the Maoist state, the form of clientelism involved generally fell more into the category of 'integrative corruption', that is, of forms that 'link people and groups into lasting networks of exchange and shared interest'.[27] Needless to say, this form of clientelism also took the form of a political and administrative corruption that involved the abuse of power and status: but these were ends in themselves, and only indirectly related to the pursuit of economic gain. For integral to the legitimating ideology of the Chinese Communist Party were redistributional goals and notions of egalitarianism, self-sacrifice, serving the people, honesty, and a Spartan, simple lifestyle. Popular resistance to the many forms of economic corruption which emerged at the interstices between the command economy and the market economy in the modernization decade only achieves perspective when seen against these earlier Maoist norms of equality and personal abstinence. Corruption within the Party itself was an even greater source of resentment, as it symbolized the abuse of power by an elite whose status and claim to rule was vested in the very norms it was in the process of dissolving. The phenomenon of corruption, moreover, symbolized the rejection of such values as the economic and social rights which were still constitutionally guaranteed. On the other hand, the new values of the modernization decade were reflected in the fact that the main popular objection to rampant official corruption was not that it represented a denial of the values of equal distribution, but that it represented a denial of equal opportunity — the equal opportunity to taste the fruits of economic reform.

Economic reform allowed the already existing forms of political and administrative clientelism to be expanded into economic avenues. This expansion was encouraged by numerous developments — the new support for profit making, competition and consumer spending, the removal of central controls and the new emphasis on the expansion of the economy at the expense of other goals.[28] In urban China this economic corruption took a predominantly 'disintegrative form', resembling what has been termed 'crisis corruption'. This was characterized by a situation in which 'private parties ... so thoroughly penetrated the public realm that most public goods and services (were) up for sale', and in which there was 'an extraordinary influx of illicit resources from without'.[29] In urban areas, economic corruption was encouraged by the freedom given state enterprises to contract among themselves, set prices, and engage in profit-making activities. Individual cadres or entire state organizations bought scarce commodities at low state prices and resold them at inflated prices. Power abuse for personal gain, excessive price rises, bribery, graft, and nepotism were rife.[30] In rural areas, apart from such problems as nepotism and cronyism, the key administrative and decision-making locus of the cadre made him open to bribery in matters of treatment of specialized households, the determination of contracts, the securing of loans, foreign currency, technology, and scarce raw materials.[31] Jean Oi has concluded that: 'The reforms clearly have made peasants more vulnerable as *individuals* to a *wider variety* of arbitrary or discriminatory behaviour by officials and petty clerks than during the Maoist period'.[32]

By the beginning of 1989, the sense of a loss of societal norms, of *anomie* reflected in popular attitudes to corruption, was also manifested in the overall political environment. A general and diffuse feeling of crisis was suggested in the nationwide debate as to whether China's political system should incline towards 'democracy' or towards 'new authoritarianism', a concept derived essentially from the politico-economic systems of the Capitalist Development States (CDS) in Asia, or the 'four little dragons'.[33] In March 1989, Louise do Rosario observed prophetically:

The Party is in disarray. It has been confronted by problems from all sides — complex economic problems, unrest in Tibet, widespread corruption, deterioration of public order, restless youth and increasingly vocal intellectuals. It has no experience in handling the newly emerging pluralistic society, while its old controls have been ineffective.

In economics, its administrative orders to slow down overheated growth are ignored by localities. In ideological control, it cannot muster enough support and determination to conduct a purge of dissident intellectuals. In Party matters, it fails to police its own members against corruption. To many Chinese, the present disorder is reminiscent of troubled times when a ruling dynasty declines.[34]

This sense of crisis was reflected in the powerful and emotive six-part documentary, 'River Elegy' *(Heshang)*, televised throughout China in the last quarter of 1988. Using the history and character of China's Yellow River as a metaphor for the history and fate of China, the documentary concluded that China was approaching a historical crossroads, where the traditional culture was giving way before the forces of modernization. In the face of this crisis, China's people had the potential to create a new society based on new principles and institutions:

Reform on a deeper level means a major transformation of the civilisation — a painful and arduous process that may require the sacrifice of this generation and of several generations to come. We are standing at the crossroads: either we let an ancient civilization fall never to rise again, or we help it to acquire the mechanisms for a new life. Whatever we do, there is no way that any of us can shirk our historical responsibility.[35]

At the same time, a reasonable expectation of the possibility of political change was exhibited both in the polls and in the political behaviour of intellectuals. A July 1987 poll prepared by a private research organization in China asked the question, 'Do you think that China needs to carry out a reform of the political system?' A positive response was received from cadres (80.41 per cent), intellectuals (78.89 per cent), workers (57.39 per cent), farmers (53.17 per cent), and hired labour (44.82 per cent positive, 28.45 per cent negative).[36] A survey on political reform by the Public Opinion Research Institute at the Chinese People's University in the summer of 1987 involved a random selection of 1,240 Beijing residents.[37] The sample differentiated itself into five groups of political attitudes, namely the 'emulators', the 'optimists', the 'spectators', 'radicals' and, 'outliers'. The 'emulators' and the 'optimists', comprising 47 per cent of those interviewed, had a strong feeling of political efficacy (defined as the citizens' feeling of the capacity and desire to influence political life), and the 'spectators', or 29 per cent of the sample, had a more modest sense of political efficacy. In addition, while the emulators (or 34 per cent of the sample) supported the official agenda for political reform (separating Party and government functions and simplifying the administration), others chose as the most urgent political issues the ensuring of press freedom, citizens' civil liberties, and the reform of the electoral system.

An expectation of change was also reflected in the behaviour of intellectuals who, particularly in the year leading up to June 1989, demanded greater political powers, greater mobility, more information, and higher wages. Even their action in calling for an amnesty for prisoners of conscience was an indication of their confidence in the reality and prospect of greater freedom of speech. Political confidence was also indicated by the number of strikes held by workers in the modernization decade, despite the fact that the right to strike was no longer guaranteed by the constitution. The result of these expectations, in the urban areas at least, was 'a profound shift in the traditional relationship between strong Leninist states and their weak, captive societies'.[38]

At the same time, this reasonable expectation of political change was a predominantly urban phenomenon. It was not shared by the majority of China's citizens, the peasantry. The objectively based and the subjectively perceived grievances of China's peasants matched those of urban citizens, and have been amply documented.[39] They lacked, however, both a strong class consciousness and an institutionalized base from which to press their claims. Although the post-1949 events had politicized them at least to some extent, in the absence of institutional mechanisms or urban centres facilitating peasant mobilization, peasant grievances before 1989 were expressed mainly in sporadic and diffuse acts of violence, and in physical conflict between and within villages.[40] The existence within a village of different types of wealth meant that, unlike the city, comparative groups tended to be local ones. Reports of internecine rural conflict emphasized the loss of community norms, the confusion of pre-modernization norms with current norms, uncertainty about what constituted illegal entrepreneurial activity, loss of cadre authority, and the inability of the legal system to substitute for the loss of consensual norms or official authority within rural areas. The new mobility of redundant peasant labour and the communications revolution, moreover, increased the relevance of more extensive comparative reference groups in the future, and thus the likelihood of aggravated grievances.

However, if before 1989 all the conditions of a state of relative deprivation were not met in rural China, they were more than satisfied by the conditions in the cities. There, relative economic deprivation was acutely felt in relation to the past; at the same time, both the opinion polls and observable behaviour suggested rising expectations (or what Gurr would call 'aspirational deprivation'), both about economic values (or economic and social rights) and political power (or civil and political rights). This overall condition of simultaneous expectation and dissatisfaction could, moreover, be said to correspond to Gurr's notion of 'progressive deprivation'.[41]

The theory of relative deprivation does not, of course, provide a sufficient explanation for why an uprising or a revolution occurs at a particular point in time. The Chalmers Johnson theory of revolution, which is not inconsistent with the Runciman–Gurr model, serves to bridge the gap. It sees revolution as the combined product of 'multiple (social, political and economic) dysfunction', of elite intransigence and of 'accelerators of dysfunction'.[42] The preceding chapters have documented the objective sources of dysfunction, as well as the circumstantial factors such as price reform which, in instituting inflation rates of an unacceptable level, acted as the 'accelerators of dysfunction' leading to mass protest. The immediate precipitant of the April uprising, however, was the death of a known political moderate, ousted Party leader, Hu Yaobang, on 15 April. A potent influence on the course of the movement proved to be the arrival of Soviet President Gorbachev in Beijing a month later for talks with Chinese leaders.[43]

The Events of April–June 1989 and their Aftermath

A huge literature, in Chinese, English, German, and French, now exists which documents the precise events of the Democracy Movement and interprets their meaning and significance.[44] It is not the intention here to add to what already amounts to a very adequate coverage. The concern rather is to examine the relevance of the movement to human rights in China. As a generalization, it could be said that the very strength of the April–May movement, which lay in its spontaneous, peaceful, and mass character, was at once the source of its weakness. Although it quickly developed organizational capacity, unlike the earlier Democracy Wall Movement, it lacked a coherent philosophy and a focused political programme which could provide it with future continuity. Although it exuded the moral strength and conviction which was the only weapon at the disposal of those without arms, that moral strength only had a temporary effectiveness in deterring armed attack, and in the end was submerged by the rolling of the tanks.

For these reasons, the 1989 demonstrations had the character of a general protest movement, rather than of a revolution, whose ultimate political goals were not clearly defined. In a general sense, political reform appeared as one mechanism enabling citizens to tackle the problem of official corruption, as well as to influence the choice of leaders and of policies. As an editor of a youth magazine observed in May:

China needs a Gorbachev ... we had a little one, Hu Yaobang, but he was purged by the conservative old men. We lead the Soviet Union in economic reform, they lead us in political and intellectual reform.[45]

Political reforms, in the view of the students who led the movement, necessitated the prior expansion of the freedoms of speech and the press. Consequently, although the demands of students changed in response to leadership tactics in May and June, throughout the period they persisted in stressing the need for enhanced civil and political rights. Thus, students interviewed by *The New York Times* emphasized the need for elections to choose leaders, an independent judiciary, and a legal system willing to punish officials as well as ordinary people, and supervision over government through the press.[46] At no time were there reports of students calling openly for the overthrow of the Communist Party or for the introduction of a two-party or multi-party system. The main political aims seemed to be to achieve the citizens' right to influence the choice of leaders and of policies through the medium of open elections and a free press.

The 1989 demonstrations were not, of course, limited to the student group, or to Beijing itself. At the high points of the movement, on 4 May, the seventieth anniversary of the May 4 Movement, and in the period 15–20 May after the arrival in China of Soviet President Gorbachev, the demonstrations spread to all major cities in China. In Beijing, they were attended by intellectuals, museum workers, factory workers, entrepreneurs (*getihu*), journalists, employees of state ministries, auto mechanics, railroad employees, work units from the People's Liberation Army, from the Foreign Ministry, Central People's Broadcasting, *People's Daily*, Communist Party Central Committee Cadre School, and employees from the Chinese Academy of Social Sciences.[47] They were also joined by students from all over China who travelled to Beijing to show their support. Interestingly, despite the unprecedented horizontal nature of this movement, like the May 4 Movement in 1919 and the May 30 Movement in 1925, it also maintained a vertical character — the various occupational groups remained distinct within the crowd under their work unit banners.

Workers were an important component of the demonstrations. Although manifestly lacking an organized base, they took part in the 4 May and subsequent demonstrations as individuals. During the 17 May and succeeding demonstrations in Beijing, however, workers held banners indicating that they represented, among other organizations, the Beijing Petrochemical Company, the Capital Hospital, the Beijing Workers' Union, the All China Federation of Trade Unions, the No. 1 Machine Tool Factory, Capital Iron and Steel, the Beijing Electric Utilities Company, the Ministry of Railways, and the Beijing Municipal Institute of Labour Protection.[48] On 19 May, in the first open attempt by workers to set up an autonomous organization outside the official All China Federation of Trade Unions, a group of young and middle-aged workers announced the establishment of the Beijing Workers' Autonomous Federation (*Beijingshi gongren zizhi lianhehui*) and called for a general strike in Beijing to support the students and protect them from violence.

The new Federation claimed to represent more than forty industries and over 100,000 employees.[49] Its concerns included the wide wage discrepancy between the workers and plant managers, the lack of workplace democracy, the lack of genuine worker representation in the policy-making process, poor labour protection and working conditions, and the deterioration of workers' living standards in recent years.[50] Workers also set up a 'Dare to Die Corps' as protection for the students, and established a camp near Tiananmen Square which was reported to have later borne the brunt of the military attack.[51] The proposed Beijing-wide strike, however, although supported by the students, never materialized.

This failure to strike was no doubt due in part to an organized government campaign, in Beijing as elsewhere, to discourage workers from joining the demonstrations, a campaign which included threats of bonus cancellations and, in Beijing, a visit by Premier Li Peng to the Capital Iron and Steel Works factory to mobilize support for the government. As the case of Fu Yuehua in the earlier Democracy Wall Movement had demonstrated, the government's abiding fear was the possibility of a horizontal linkage being established between intellectuals and workers. The failure of the workers to link effectively in Solidarity fashion with students in 1989 may be ascribed to a mixture of reasons: lower expectations among workers, the existence of the quota system, the vulnerability of workers' organizations to government sanctions, and the elitism of the student movement. It may also have been due to the conflicting aims of the different interest groups. Moreover, the absence of a developed civil society which could provide mechanisms for the expression of divergent social interests was another difference betweeen China and Eastern Europe. The claim that the lack of unity could also have been due to the fact that the workers' standard of living had been rising faster than that of other social groups would, however, appear to have little statistical basis, in view of the heavy impact of inflation on the workers' real wages.[52]

The crucial moment in the history of human rights in China proved to be the declaration of martial law in Beijing on 20 May, with its precedent in the earlier martial law declaration in Tibet.[53] In one of history's great ironies, on the eve of this declaration, in an important speech to Party, government, and army cadres in Beijing, Premier Li Peng conceded the validity of student demands:

It must be stressed that even under such circumstances [the imposition of martial law] we should still persist in protecting the patriotism of the students, make a clear distinction between them and the very, very few people who created the turmoil, and we will not penalize students for their radical words and actions in the student movement. Moreover, dialogue will continue in an active way through various channels, in different forms and at different levels between the party and the government on one hand and the students and people from other walks of life on the other, including dialogue with those students who have taken part in parades, demonstrations, class boycotts, and hunger strikes, so as to take full heed of opinions from all fields. We will not only give clear-cut answers to the reasonable demands raised by them, but will also pay close attention to and earnestly accept their reasonable criticisms and suggestions, such as punishing profiteering officials, getting rid of corruption, and overcoming bureaucratism as well as promoting democracy, developing education and so forth, so as earnestly to improve the work of the party and the government.[54]

Despite this speech, no open government concessions were made which satisfied the students. On 29 and 30 April the All-China Student Federation and the Beijing Autonomous Students' Association met with senior government leaders, and on 18 May four of the five members of the Politburo Standing Committee, Zhao Ziyang, Li Peng, Qiao Shi, and Hu Qili paid a visit to students who had collapsed during a hunger strike.[55] Later that day, representatives of the hunger strikers had a meeting with Li

Peng at which the now famous exchange between Wu'er Kaixi and Li Peng occurred. However, while hardline leaders believed they had answered some student demands, the students felt that no meaningful concessions had been made. A number decided to extend for a few weeks their occupation of the Square. After two weeks of uncertainty, intense political activity, protracted behind-the-scenes bargaining, and official threats to the dwindling number of student demonstrators, on the night of 3–4 June the military assault on Tiananmen Square and surrounding areas began.

Following the military action, which was extended over a week in the full glare of world-wide publicity, Chinese authorities sought to round up the leaders of the movement and began a hunt for twenty-one chief 'counter-revolutionary' suspects and seven leading intellectuals. At the same time, state radio and television appealed to members of the Chinese public to inform on those suspected of having had dealings or sympathies with the student protesters. At a street committee level and at a work unit level, Chinese citizens and workers were required to account for their attitudes and actions (*biaotai*) during the period of demonstrations in Tiananmen Square.

As a result of the nationwide activities of Public Security officials and their civilian informers, by the end of June the number of those arrested throughout China stood at an official Amnesty International estimate of 'at least hundreds', and at an informal estimate of 1,800.[56] Television footage showed many of those arrested with shaven heads, being held in the humiliating jet plane position with their arms behind their backs and their heads between their knees; many had been severely beaten. Those arrested included students, workers who had tried to form an independent trade union, a leader of the China Youth Democratic Party, a previously arrested member of the Democracy Movement of 1978–80, Ren Wanding, a well known literary critic, leading intellectuals, professors, a self-employed worker, a peasant, a radio announcer, and a reporter.[57]

By 13 June, in the effort to track down suspects, the Chinese military had issued shoot-to-kill orders and had sealed the country's borders.[58] New regulations announced by the Public Security Ministry stated: 'All organizations engaged in counter-revolution and social turmoil are abolished. Independent student and worker associations must immediately cease their activities and leaders must turn themselves in'. The new rules prohibited offering assistance to the leaders of these unofficial groups and called on anyone with weapons or counter-revolutionary leaflets to turn them in or face strict punishment. Anyone who blocked traffic or attacked officers of the Communist Party or the mass media would be arrested, and troops could use force 'to disperse people gathering together to cause chaos'. The police were authorized to use their weapons against rioters and those who resisted arrest, as well as to protect themselves. The Ministry also stated: 'Every citizen should search for criminals and report them'.[59] Freedom of movement was also inhibited throughout the country and administrative obstacles impeded the efforts of some Chinese to leave the country.

The variety of civil rights abuses in China listed by Amnesty International from June until the end of August included the confirmed arrest of 4,000 people, although unofficial figures estimated 30,000 and above; arbitrary detention or imprisonment of many Chinese, under regulations for administrative detention; formal arrests of people for the peaceful exercise of their basic human rights, charged with taking part in a counter-revolutionary group or with disseminating counter-revolutionary propaganda; torture and ill treatment of detainees; summary trials not conforming to international standards for a fair trial; and summary executions, since many of those arrested had been charged with offences punishable by death and local courts had been instructed to expedite their trials. Of those reportedly executed for offences related to the protests, the Amnesty report listed three from Shanghai, thirty-five from Beijing, two from Chengdu, seventeen from Jinan, and two from Wuhan. It cited the Hong Kong paper *Ming pao*'s report that 400 from Beijing had been executed.[60]

Other sources, however, and in particular the *Washington Post*, contained estimates of up to 10,000 detained or arrested by early July. In mid to late July, 771 people were estimated arrested in the city of Taiyuan, 3,000 in Jiangsu province, and 4,000 in Hunan province.[61] The Chinese practice of merging the statistics of political prisoners and common criminals, thereby establishing guilt by association, complicated the task of estimating the precise numbers of arrests on political grounds. A further complication was that the initial direct and overt repression of dissent by the Chinese government had, in response to international protests, been replaced by a covert form, so that news of arrests was no longer obtainable from open TV broadcasts and news reports but, at the most, from radio reports and word of mouth.

Aside from the continuing judicial and extra-judicial activity at the formal level, there was a persistent and widespread denial of civil rights in the form of 'a general environment of white terror', characterized, as one observer put it, by:

the careful orchestration of media campaigns to rewrite the historical record of events and impose the official version, by sheer force of repetition, on the public memory: the swift and severe treatment of some individuals to serve as a warning to others who might contemplate resistance to authority; the methodical, routinised investigation of the activities this past spring of any who took an active leadership role; the imposition, in schools and work-places, of ideological indoctrination sessions to bring all into at least lip service to the new orthodoxy on socialist democracy, bourgeois liberalisation, reform and opening to the outside, and the counter-revolutionary rebellion suppressed by the PLA.[62]

At the level of the ordinary citizen, freedom of speech and thought was undermined by the organized interrogation of residents in their streets and workers in their units as well as by the Public Security Ministry's 12 June order for citizens to inform on each other. Special attention was paid to educational institutions, with a policy that those teachers who were worried about the turmoil should be re-educated, and that those who contradicted the 'four basic principles' should be dismissed. Chinese first year tertiary students were required to spend one-third of their time doing military training, one-third in political education classes which involved self-criticism and reporting on others, and one-third in studying foreign languages. Students about to graduate from university were required to submit a satisfactory self-examination about their political attitudes before they could receive their diplomas. Freedom of the press was jeopardized by the dismissal of numerous newspaper editors and journalists, including the editor-in-chief of the *People's Daily* and the editor of the *Guangming Daily*; by the sealing of all published and unpublished material in newspaper offices for investigation by censors; and by the nationwide censorship drive which resulted by early August in the closure of 2,300 sales points, the suspension of 2,000 publication units, and the confiscation of more than 2.66 million copies of books and more than 8.72 million 'illegal' publications. Freedom of association was undermined by the crushing of the autonomous organizations set up in April and May all over China, including eleven in Shanghai and six in Beijing (the Federation of Intellectual Circles, Beijing College Students' Autonomous Federation, Beijing Workers' Dare to Die Squad, Beijing Workers' Pickets and the Beijing Workers' Autonomous Federation). Finally, freedom of assembly was almost negated by the new draft law on demonstrations, according to which people across units, professions, and in different geographical locations could not demonstrate together.[63]

The general repression was organized in four stages:
(1) the study of documents and the leaders' speeches;
(2) self-criticism (*ziwo jiancha*) and reporting on others (*jianju jiefa*);
(3) the procuring of evidence and checking (*quzheng shencha*); and
(4) the organizational phase (*zuzhi chuli*) of meting out punishments.

On 21 August, an address by new Party General Secretary Jiang Zemin to a conference of the heads of organizational departments brought a new focus in the campaign on the examination of the political errors of party members and of senior cadres: 'Towards the majority of young students we must be more lenient, because after all they are young and politically immature', he stated, 'but towards the cadres we must be strict, and of the cadres, strictest towards leading cadres'.[64] A Central Committee document published in *Zhengming*, 'On the Purge of the Nineteen Types of People', itemized ten kinds of people who were liable to investigation (*qingcha*) and severe punishment and nine kinds who were vulnerable to a lesser degree of punishment (*qingli*) including loss of a job or position, demotion or other kinds of political discrimination. The latter constituted:

(1) Those who have communicated with the planners and organizers of the counter-revolutionary rebellion;
(2) Those who communicated with foreigners of a suspicious nature, or with people of a suspicious nature from beyond the border of the People's Republic of China, in the period of disorder and rebellion;
(3) Those who joined illegal organizations;
(4) Those who supported the disorder and the rebellion, or opposed the Party and socialism by their speech and behaviour;
(5) Those who spread large numbers of political rumours;
(6) Those who took part in mob attacks on major departments of the Party and government, who surrounded troops of the People's

Liberation Army and who built street barricades and blocked communications;

(7) Those who provided substantial financial aid and practical assistance to the disorders and rebellions;

(8) Those who leaked state secrets; and

(9) Those who gave other cause for suspicion and require to be investigated and dealt with.[65]

The all inclusive nature of the ninth category suggested a certain arbitrariness in the choice of targets which was further underlined by the fact that in such campaigns a quota system for targeting people was often introduced into work units. The choice of targets in this case was on the basis of 'least innocence' rather than guilt *per se*, and often external facts, such as the experience of having studied abroad, were sufficient to tip the balance.[66] The scope for arbitrary targeting of persons on the basis of personal animosity, a problem in past campaigns, was also increased by the broad ambit of the ninth category. Even if under this category a person was not immediately punished, his record would remain in his personal dossier (*dang'an*) for possible use against him at a future date.

Following the celebration of the fortieth anniversary of the founding of the People's Republic of China on 1 October 1989, an intensification and extension of the purge began. While it was originally intended by 1 October 1989 to clear (*jietuo*) the ordinary people who had passively taken part in, but not organized, the demonstrations, for some reason this clearance was delayed. Moreover, in mid-October the Beijing Municipal Party Committee headquarters announced that its members should re-register and that those deemed 'hostile and anti-Party' elements would be purged.

At the same time, the surface condition of martial law in Beijing was partially altered after National Day. On 6 September, Premier Li Peng had ruled out an immediate end to martial law in Beijing, declaring that the authorities' fight against subversion and infiltration would take a long time. On 31 October, however, in an odd contrast to the intensification of the purge, government sources stated that the struggle against counter-revolution had succeeded and that Beijing, after being 'basically closed' could return to normality and stability. Consequently, Notice 17 from martial law headquarters announced that troops would leave the streets and the square. At the same time it was stated that the troops would continue, along with police, to patrol several Beijing suburbs, particularly those in the north-west with universities situated in them, and that in the centre of the city the troops would be replaced by armed police. Finally, on 10 January 1990, Premier Li Peng announced the lifting of martial law, but stressed that the Party had not softened its opposition to 'attempts to subvert the socialist system'.[67] In this way the post-National Day purge was characterized by a dual policy of tightening and external loosening of controls, corresponding with the Chinese concept of *'nei jin wai song'* ('internal tightening, external loosening'). 'Internal tightening' proceeded along the dual track of inner-Party purge and the continued investigation of the ordinary citizen at the work unit and street committee level.

Domestic and International Repercussions

The impact of the June events and their aftermath on the condition of Chinese citizens' civil rights was, at one level, self-evident. In general terms, it was clear that the declaration of martial law in Beijing on 20 May, and its brutal enforcement on 3–4 June and in succeeding weeks, marked an abrupt break in the informal evolution of civil and political rights which had been occurring in China over the modernization decade. The abuse of civil rights entailed by martial law and the June crackdown was matched by the continuing state of deprivation in the area of economic and social rights. June 4 thus brought to a nadir the overall condition of China's human rights. It also brought a qualitative change in the relations between leaders and led. The establishment of autonomous unions by students and workers throughout China represented an assertion of political sovereignty by the people, and, in its broad, horizontal reach represented 'an unprecedented expression of Chinese society's separation from the omnipotent state'.[68] Moreover, the disproportionate resort to force by the government served to further discredit and delegitimize both the leadership and the Party. On the one hand, the peaceful demonstrations of April to June revealed the latent political and social grievances of the people, with their strong moral content. It also revealed latent popular power, all the more effective for having been peacefully wielded. The high moral ground was thus imperceptibly transferred from the leadership to the people.

In international terms, the most dramatic result of the June

1989 events was to draw China inexorably into the international arena of human rights obligation. The process of the internationalization of China's human rights movement, slowly beginning in the 1980s, became irreversible as a result of the 4 June events.[69] In the end, it was not the international community but the citizens of China, who, in their peaceful protests, confronted the world with the indisputable fact that they wanted civil and political as well as economic and social rights. The way the demonstrators were treated, moreover, provided proof that the government of China was prepared to waive the citizens' most basic civil rights of immunity in its bid to deny their claims. The events of 4 June and succeeding weeks became international property as they entered the living rooms of the world. The method of communication made it clear that Chinese citizens were looking to the outside world to assist in a number of ways, not least by raising a non-distorting mirror to those events, and reflecting them internationally.

Information on, and estimates of, the variety of civil rights abuses was provided for the international community in a series of reports prepared by International Non-Government Organizations (INGOs), Amnesty International, Asia Watch, and the International League for Human Rights. In line with Amnesty International, the International League for Human Rights listed the following abuses: the unrestrained use of lethal weapons against unarmed civilians making legitimate requests for political and social change; the killing of large numbers of civilians; the continuing campaign of repression; the arbitrary arrest and detention of many thousands involved in non-violent action; the torture and ill treatment of detainees; the failure of Chinese trial procedures to accord with accepted international standards; the occurrence of expedited capital sentences and executions and of extra-legal executions and secret trials; the suppression of student groups and workers organizations, thereby violating freedom of association and assembly; and the violation of the freedoms of expression, of the press, and of access to information.[70] In addition, on 19 June 1989 the International Confederation of Free Trade Unions (ICFTU) presented a complaint to the ILO (International Labour Organization) Governing Body Freedom of Association Committee against the government of China, alleging the violation of trade union rights.[71]

To what extent these civil rights abuses were justified under a condition of martial law was a question also subjected to scrutiny by a number of international human rights organizations. Judgements by Amnesty International and other INGOs extended the boundaries of the human rights critique. According to Amnesty, not only was the June action in violation of the standard of civil rights laid out in the UNDHR but it represented a violation of the United Nations own regulations, the 'Code of Conduct for Law Enforcement Officials'. The killing of unarmed civilians in Beijing was classified by Amnesty as 'extrajudicial execution' — deliberate killings by government forces acting outside the limits of the law. This was in violation of Article 3 of the Code which established that the use of force by law enforcement officials should be 'exceptional', and should not be used when it was 'disproportional to the legitimate objective to be achieved'.[72] The International League for Human Rights judged that the Chinese government had violated a number of rights from which international law permitted no derogation, *even in a time of national emergency threatening the life of the nation*: the right to life and the right not to be subjected to torture or other cruel, inhuman or degrading treatment or punishment. Other rights violated, which, the League acknowledged, international law did permit to be restricted in some extraordinary circumstances, that is, which were derogable, included the right not to be subjected to arbitrary arrest and detention; the rights to freedom of peaceful assembly and association; the right to a fair and public trial by an independent and impartial tribunal, and the right of an accused person to be presumed innocent and to be provided with the guarantees necessary for his defence. They also included the right to freedom of opinion and expression and the freedom to seek, receive, and impart information and ideas.[73]

On the other hand, most of the latter category of rights listed by the International League for Human Rights were included among the international standards of *non-derogable* human rights established in the Paris Minimum Standards of Human Rights Norms in a State of Emergency. The Paris Minimum Standards, which were adopted and disseminated by the International Law Association (ILA) in 1984, have a general acceptance and status among European nations.[74] The list of sixteen non-derogable rights which they identified were the right to legal personality; freedom from slavery or servitude; freedom from discrimination; the right to life; the right to liberty; freedom from torture; the right to a fair trial;

freedom of thought, conscience, and religion; freedom from prison for inability to fulfil a contractual obligation; rights of minorities; rights of the family; the right to a name; rights of the child; the right to nationality; the right to participate in government; and the right to remedy.

In Section A of the Paris Minimum Standards, the 'Declaration, Duration, and Control of an Emergency', the articles most relevant to China were Article 2: 'The constitution of every state shall define the procedure for declaring a state of emergency; whenever the executive authority is competent to declare a state of emergency, such official declaration shall always be subject to confirmation by the legislature, within the shortest possible time'; and Article 3 (a) 'The declaration of a state of emergency shall never exceed the period strictly required to restore normal conditions'; and 3 (d) 'Every extension of the period of emergency shall be subject to the prior approval of the legislature'. The most relevant article in Section B, 'Emergency Powers and the Protection of Individual', was Article 3. Clause (a) required that 'the fundamental functions of the legislature shall remain intact despite the relative expansion of the authority of the executive'; and Clause (c) that 'the guarantees of the independence of the judiciary and of the legal profession shall remain intact'.

However, whether adopting the standards laid down by the Paris Minimum Standards, or the minimum definition laid down by the International League for Human Rights, it is clear that the suppression of the Democracy Movement undermined the basic facets of the right to life, including freedom from torture and mistreatment, which were established in the early pages of this book as a standard that had universal consensus and was part of customary law. To reiterate B. G. Ramcharan's position: even for those nations like China which had not signed or ratified the international covenants, the UN Charter represented a binding legal obligation for all states, and the International Covenants and the Universal Declaration of Human Rights represented 'minimal standards of conduct for all peoples and all nations'.[75] Moreover, apart from China's obligations under the Charter and the Universal Declaration of Human Rights, it also had obligations through its membership of the UN Commission on Human Rights and through its adherence to such relevant treaties as the Convention against Genocide and the Convention against Torture and Other Forms of Cruel and Degrading Treatment. Chinese official awareness of these obligations was indicated in the attempt to portray the movement not as a peaceful expression of popular grievances, but as an attempt by 'a small handful of people' to subvert the Chinese state. It was also indirectly reflected in the publication of a book soon afer June seeking to justify violent government intervention on the basis of claims that the Democracy Movement had violated different aspects of Chinese laws and the constitution. It made no attempt to vindicate government actions in terms of international legal standards of human rights.[76]

The response of the international community to the televised and documented evidence of civil rights abuses in China was immediate. Apart from condemnation by individual governments, concerted action was taken in multilateral forums. While no significant diplomatic relations with China were broken, a range of economic and technology transfer agreements and future arrangements, crucial to Beijing, were placed on hold.[77] In a human rights context, perhaps the most significant reactions were the Group of Seven Statement and the resolution of the sub-commission under the UN Human Rights Commission. The 15 July joint 'Declaration on China' by the Group of Seven announced that the repression in China had led each to suspend bilateral ministerial and high-level contacts, to suspend arms trade with China, request the postponement of new loans to China by the World Bank, and to extend the stay of Chinese students in their respective countries. It urged Chinese authorities to 'create conditions which would avoid their isolation and provide for a return to co-operation based upon the resumption of movement towards political and economic reforms and openness'.[78] The resolution of 29 August by the UN Sub-Commission on the Prevention of Discrimination and the Protection of Minorities, the panel of human rights experts under the UN Human Rights Commission, was carried by fifteen votes to nine. It stated:

The Sub-Commission on the Prevention of Discrimination and the Protection of Minorities:
Concerned about the events which took place recently in China and about their consequences in the field of human rights
Requests the Secretary-General to transmit to the Commission on Human Rights information provided by the Government of China and by other reliable sources

<u>Makes an Appeal</u> for clemency, in particular in favour of persons deprived of their liberty as a result of the above mentioned events.[79]

This resolution was reported to be the first time the human rights record of one of the permanent members of the UN Security Council had been considered in any UN human rights organization.[80] Subsequently, in response to a complaint by the International Confederation of Trade Unions (ICFTU), China was further taken to task by the ILO Committee on Freedom of Association and asked to supply detailed information on the allegations, particularly in respect of the treatment of leaders and members of the various Workers' Autonomous Federations.[81]

A second effect of 4 June on China's human rights movement was that it intensified the vertical and horizontal expansion of democratic ideals which had taken place within and without China over the previous decade. As already argued, vertical movement had occurred within China as a result of the gradual development over the previous decade of an elite group of dissenters, like Fang Lizhi, Yan Jiaqi, Wang Ruowang, and Su Shaozhi, who, as Stanley Rosen has pointed out, were 'internationalized' dissenters, readily recognizable by the world community. Dissent over the condition of civil and political rights from within China had, since the early 1980s, risen like cream to the top, paralleling the movement of dissent in 1957. More importantly, it had become horizontally dispersed outside China's borders. The global pressure for civil and political rights from many of the 80,000 Chinese students who had studied abroad over the previous decade, and in particular, from the members of the China Alliance for Democracy (CAD) in the United States, had given rise to a kind of diaspora of ideas. The Chinese government action of 4 June, by persuading foreign governments to allow Chinese students to stay longer on foreign soil, was instrumental in freezing that diaspora in place. It was also instrumental in bringing about the institutionalization, in international form, of Chinese demands for democracy and human rights. The establishment in Paris on 23–4 September 1989 of the Federation for a Democratic China (FDC), headed by expatriate political scientist Yan Jiaqi, and with the express aim of promoting human rights in China, provided Chinese intellectuals and students with an important international focal point for the dissemination of political ideas which were forbidden in China, a fact reflected in angry Chinese government condemnations of that body.[82]

This newly articulated concern about China's policies, both from within the international community and among expatriate Chinese organizations, marked a new era in which human rights had finally become part and parcel of China's relations with the rest of the world.

8 Human Rights in Post-Tiananmen China

Internal Developments

The focusing of world attention on the condition of China's human rights, or at least on the condition of its civil rights, and the imposition of sanctions, or threats of sanctions, were to have a considerable impact. So too were domestic political imperatives. In post-Tiananmen China, regime legitimacy and ideological consensus, already undermined by the Cultural Revolution and by the corruption of the 1980s, have been further weakened, while the main unifying national symbol, fear of chaos, has been at best a negative one. Although the regime has continued by a confusing variety of means to attempt to reconstruct its legitimacy, its chief hope of doing so is through successful performance of its economic goals, or by 'performance' legitimation. In the event that this effort fails, what will be left are the negative forms of legal control and coercion. But the dangers of coercion have been pinpointed by Gurr:

The most fundamental human responses to the use of force is counter-force. Force threatens and angers men, especially if they believe it to be illicit or unjust. Threatened, they try to defend themselves; angered they want to retaliate . . . If a regime responds to the threat or use of force with greater force, the effect is likely to be an intensification of resistance . . . There are only two inherent limitations on the escalating spiral of force and counter-force: the depletion of either group's resources for coercion, or the attainment by one of the capacity for genocidal victory over its opponents. There are societal and psychological limitations as well, but they require tacit bonds between opponents: the acceptance by one of the ultimate authority of the other, submission to arbitration by a neutral authority, recognition of mutual interest that makes bargaining possible, perception that acquiescence will be less harmful than risking certain annihilation.[1]

In China, the June action provoked extreme anger among the citizenry, particularly in view of its perceived injustice, and resulted in sporadic acts of violence. Continued coercion was symbolized by the failure to lift the state of martial law in Beijing until January 1990. Although gradually a tacit 'bond' has been established between the government and its citizens, in the form of a popular recognition that acquiescence is less harmful than continued resistance, the resentment this acquiescence engendered, although latent, could always resurface. The Chinese government has recognized this problem, and has thus found it expedient not only to stress positive performance goals, but to develop other more acceptable negative means to induce popular compliance to its will. But precisely because of the need to continue economic reform, political stability has been perpetually at risk.[2] This has been so, not only because economic reform altered existing social and economic structures but because it exacerbated the possibilities of official corruption, and thus of public perceptions of relative deprivation. For this reason, the 'tacit bond' has had to be continually renegotiated.[3]

The post-June period can be divided into three main, if overlapping phases, wherein the regime has sought to balance the dual requirements of 'reform and stability' by adopting positive means to obtain popular support, and a gradual alteration in the form of negative sanctions. The regime has made more concessions to ensure stability, and more efforts to modify its own behaviour. And it has moved from a policy of applying sanctions through instruments of blunt coercion to the adoption of more acceptable legal channels to maintain social control. In general, the goods offered or promised by the leadership to the public represent attempts to remedy the problems of relative deprivation through 'inequality substitution', that is, through the renewed attack on corruption, efforts to improve relative standards of living and control inflation, the expansion of economic and social rights, and moves to close 'unfair' income gaps. These measures have been accompanied by some degree of 'political reform' in exchange for political stability and legitimation.[4] While not loosening controls over the formal civil liberties which have a direct bearing on politics — the freedoms of speech, press, religion, assembly, and association — the government has again begun to concede the citizen more personal space in terms of dress, habits, and popular culture.

The first phase, extending roughly from June to December 1989, saw continuing coercion in the form of arbitrary arrests, summary executions, forced interrogation, and the maintenance of martial law in Beijing. This coercion was accompanied by emotionally charged propaganda which manipulated nationalism, historical

fears of foreign influence, national destabilization, and disintegration, as well as concerns about a return to the chaos of the
Cultural Revolution.[5] The political line adopted was a reversion
to more orthodox policies, which re-emphasized the primacy of
economic and social, as opposed to civil and political, rights. This
priority reflected the ideology and general constituency of the new
Jiang Zemin–Li Peng leadership, which drew its support from
a coalition of central planning institutions, from heavy industry
and its related bureaucracies, financial interest groups, the propaganda apparatus, sections of the military, and an unknown
proportion of the peasantry.[6] It also reflected the concern of the
leadership to win over workers and ordinary citizens who had
become disenchanted by inflation, corruption, and the loss of
economic and social rights, and whose presence in the student
demonstrations had transformed an elite protest into a mass
movement.[7] Finally, the leadership sought to woo the 'swinging
voter', including undecided elements of the urban population,
those parts of the military whose loyalties had not been determined, and a mass of peasants who, although politically inert
during the April–May demonstrations, were known to have
substantial economic grievances.[8]

The new policies were clearly designed to outflank the intellectuals and students. They combined ideological and political
propaganda with recentralizing economic policies which stressed
planning, the strengthening of state-owned enterprises and constraints on small, collective, and private enterprises. There were
also pledges to control inflation and corruption and to give priority to agriculture. Social policies sought the expansion of a
national labour insurance system to meet the needs of all employees working under different systems of ownership, and the
Ministry of Public Health announced plans for a rural primary
health care programme to help meet the 'national target of providing every Chinese with health care by the year 2,000'.[9] The
practice of stimulating production through consumption was dis-
carded in favour of a policy justifying rule on the basis of public
ownership and the provision of material and cultural needs. There
was a renewed emphasis on distribution according to work and
on the prevention of an excessive wealth gap and 'unjust' distribution, although 'egalitarianism in distribution' was attacked and
the notion of 'some people becoming prosperous' maintained.[10]
On the other hand, curbs on further civilian political activity were

devised in the form of firm controls over educational and media institutions, the constricting new law on demonstrations and the deepening and extension of the purge, which ensured universal if temporary compliance from the urban population.

By December 1989, however, a number of developments, in parallel with the ongoing jockeying for power at the elite level, had created pressures for a readjustment to this renewed and almost exclusive emphasis on social and economic rights. The efforts to base claims to mass legitimacy on achievement in areas of social and economic welfare were stymied by the parlous state of the Chinese economy and the need to maintain an anti-inflationary austerity programme. Ambitious social programmes became difficult to implement and unemployment increased.[11] Furthermore, international repudiation of the June massacre and the ensuing economic sanctions severely limited China's room for economic manoeuvre. The speed and scope of political reform in Eastern Europe, moreover, although initially discounted by the Chinese leadership, had an inevitable impact on Chinese domestic opinion and on the regime's political options. The combination of these internal economic limitations and external political pressures was decisive in producing a somewhat more liberal attitude to political reform.[12] This second phase was also marked by the end of martial law in Beijing in January 1990, and a shift away from overt coercion to the increased use of the legal system as a more acceptable and orthodox means of achieving 'stability'.[13]

Thus, on 12 December 1989, Premier Li Peng ushered in a new phase by calling for the reform of China's political structure to be carried out simultaneously with reforms of the economy, at the same time stressing that political restructuring should aid the country's stability and prosperity and not cause social disturbances.[14] In his Report on the Work of the Government submitted to the third session of the Seventh National People's Congress in Beijing, Li said that political restructuring involved continued efforts to perfect the system of people's congresses, to pursue multi-party co-operation and establish and improve the procedures and systems for democratic decision making and supervision.[15] On 11 June 1990, Jiang Zemin also stated that 'political structural reform should keep pace and co-ordinate with economic structural reform and the two should promote each other'.[16]

These statements reflected a realization of the need to return to pre-Tiananmen legitimizing processes, whereby the Party was impelled to claim 'less dramatic political virtues as well as potential economic virtues'.[17] The content of this political reform, however, closely resembled the old idea of 'mass line' and appeared to depend on the enhanced contact between Party members, the leadership elite, and the people, with communication proceeding downwards rather than in the opposite direction. Its close resemblance to a corporatist system of political organization was reflected in the restrictive provisions of the law on the organization of urban residents' committees and a similar law on rural residents' committees. Also significant were the regulations on the registration of social organizations issued at the end of October 1989, and the 21 December 1989 circular calling for CCP leadership over mass organizations as 'bridges and ties for the Party to link with the people as well as important pillars of state power'.[18]

The dual face of legislation promulgated allegedly to protect specific civil rights was particularly well illustrated in the case of the Law on Assemblies, Parades, and Demonstrations of the PRC (*Zhonghua renmin gongheguo jihui youxing shiwei fa*) of 31 October 1989.[19] In fact, it has been argued that, apart from vestigial concessions to principles of freedom of expression and due process, this law reflected a preoccupation with stability as a value above all else, and 'merely equip[ped] the state with better mechanisms of prior restraint, accompanied by improved justificatory language'.[20] The use of rules and guidelines to incorporate elements of society potentially outside the reach of Party and state were also reflected in the much acclaimed document, 'Guidelines of the Central Committee of the Communist Party of China for Upholding and Improving the System of Multi-Party Co-operation and Political Consultation under the Leadership of the Communist Party of China'.[21]

In the final analysis, whether or not real content could be put into these renewed calls for political reform depended on whether the controls on the exercise of citizens' civil rights were loosened. That is, the question remained whether the current purpose of political reform, focused as it was on 'improving socialist democracy and the socialist legal system' was, in fact, as Jiang Zemin claimed, 'to ensure effectively that the people enjoy status and rights as citizens of the country'. There were some signs that controls were being eased. Yet the lifting of martial law in Beijing in January 1990 and the reported release of 881 political prisoners appeared to have been more closely related to achieving the removal of international economic sanctions than to any liberalization of domestic policy. Pressure was still maintained on the media, with the continuing censorship of publications and the press. The publication of the Code of Collegiate Student Behaviour and of the Regulations on the Management of College Students served to reinforce control over educational institutions. There were also calls for the expansion of the judiciary, in view of the doubling of China's crime rate in 1989, and another wave of executions of criminals took place.[22] Amnesty International recorded more than 960 death sentences, including at least 750 executions as part of the anti-crime campaign, the highest since 1983, although it also recorded 'unconfirmed allegations that up to 12,000 death sentences were pronounced between July and September' of 1990.[23]

In social policy, continued attention was paid to problems of rising unemployment, a product of the 1989 austerity compaign designed to reduce inflation, with the *Economic Daily* reporting that the urban 'job waiting' rate might exceed 4 per cent in 1990, and rise further in 1991. In 1990, urban job hunters were expected to exceed ten million, of whom 3.78 million had been laid off in 1989. The country was reported to have more than 300 million rural labourers, with only 180 million needed for farming, and over 120 million surplus farmers having to look for jobs. There were calls from the Ministry of Personnel and the Minister for Labour for a national labour insurance system, and especially an unemployment pension system, along with reports that in 1989 three million rural enterprises had been closed and 20,000 projects postponed or cancelled.[24]

Suggestions as to the means of resolving the unemployment crisis included the renewed expansion of village and township enterprises, lower wages and increased employment for workers, and a dual and 'flexible' employment system differentiating between different kinds of enterprises, with large enterprises operating on the basis of production efficiency and small enterprises adopting labour intensive methods. Draft labour laws were planned for 1990 and, in view of the lowering of the inflation rate by early 1990 (reported at around 6 per cent) and the easing of credit, reinvestment in rural industries began, with an anticipated expansion rate of 15 per cent in 1990. At the same time, measures were undertaken to stop the mass exodus of surplus rural labour, with 1.3 million rural workers being sent back from cities in 1989 and plans for the return of another 900,000 in 1990. One of the main means of facilitating the absorption of surplus labour into the economy was the labour service network, with 3,000 sub-agencies throughout the country. Its functions, however, included not only the allocation of jobs for unemployed urban workers but the return of unemployed rural workers to the countryside.[25]

In parallel with continued work on the expansion of a primary health care system in China, the government announced plans to set up a timetable for providing basic education for the whole population and for eliminating illiteracy among young people and adults. Despite its austerity policy, the government pledged a very considerable increase in its annual budget for 1990 to education, an area which was now accorded top priority. It also increased state wages and subsidies, attempting to resolve the housing problem and pay off government IOUs to the peasants. Finally, it put renewed emphasis on poverty relief, claiming to have fed and clothed 70 per cent of poor farmers since the commencement of the five-year plan to relieve rural poverty (defined as 200 yuan or less annual income) by 1990. For 1990, the government pledged a further 4,000 yuan in grants, low interest loans, and materials to poor regions.[26]

The third stage in the development of human rights after Tiananmen pinpointed the delicate manoeuvring required to maintain a balance between 'reform' and 'stability'. It began in the first quarter of 1991, with the release of the 'Proposals for the Drawing up of the Ten-Year Programme and the Eighth Five-Year Plan for National and Economic Social Development', and the announcement by Duan Muzheng, Vice-President of China's Supreme People's Court, on 2 April 1991, that the adjudication of criminals involved in the anti-government riots in 1989 was basically completed.[27] It coincided with a period of upturn in the Chinese economy, and the reassertion of control over the problem of inflation.[28] Finally, it reached its full expression with the call by Deng Xiaoping in January 1992 to further expand economic reform.

This new phase was formally inaugurated in a statement by Premier Li Peng who claimed that 'through the efforts of all people, political and social stability now prevails in our country and the most difficult period is over . . . One of the most important experiences is that we must properly handle the relationship between development, reform, and stability. In a given time, we gave first priority to stability: now with political, economic, and social stability and with unity in thinking, we may make a little more effort to carry out reforms'.[29] He thus not only acknowledged the tension between stability and reform, but the government's tactic of pursuing these goals not simultaneously, but seriatim. He strongly implied that, despite the existence of the Bankruptcy Law, the process of rationalization of labour in enterprises had been obstructed by fears of instability. In view of the new situation of stability, 'the enterprises cannot simply support people without work to do'. Therefore, having handled the problem of funds for a social insurance system for the aged, he maintained, the next move was to consider the question of 'a mechanism in connection with employment for job seekers'.[30] Housing and medical reforms were also necessary.

Li Peng's words, however, should be seen as a statement of intent. Not only was there still disagreement within the leadership over the necessary degree of economic restructuring, but there also appeared to be uncertainty as to the best means of ensuring the consensual goal of expanding economic and social rights. We have seen that in 1985 the World Bank had advised China to 'encourage gains in efficiency through market reforms while maintaining or replacing social safety nets threatened by reform'. There was still, however, uncertainty within the leadership as to whether to pursue its common goal by maintaining existing social safety nets or by replacing them. Despite a large budget deficit, there were fears of short term political instability if subsidies for basic food commodities and failed enterprises were removed. Equally, the leadership was wary of alienating state workers by taking the administration of social welfare services and social security out of the work unit, as the World Bank advised. Nevertheless, at the level of articulated policy, Li Peng's statement was similar in its priorities to one made in March 1991 by Chen Jinhua, Minister in Charge of the State Commission for Restructuring the Economy. According to Chen, further structural reform in the economy was premised on two related reforms. The first was enterprise reform, which required a second round of contracts, the second was reform in housing, social labour insurance, unemployment insurance, and medical services.[31]

The Outline of the Ten-Year Programme and the Eighth Five-Year Plan and the State Council's 'Major Economic Restructuring Points for 1991' clarified and gave shape to these undertakings.[32]

The State Council report called for pilot studies of old-age insurance in provinces and cities and, in well-to-do rural areas, pilot schemes for old-age insurance funded mainly by individual payments and supplemented by collective subsidies. It also called for the expansion of pilot job-waiting (*daiye*) insurance schemes, by expanding the insurance to cover all workers in enterprises under total state ownership, and a gradual establishment of job-waiting insurance in enterprises under all other kinds of ownership.[33] As in the case of projected housing reforms, the basic assumption underlying these reforms was the principle of joint burden-sharing between state, enterprise, and individual. Such pilot schemes, which were basically aimed at easing the social security responsibilities of the work unit, would then open the way for the rationalization of labour within enterprises, and the further reform of the wage system. Within enterprises, efforts would be made to 'reduce distribution in kind'. Instead, welfare allowances would be incorporated into wages, in conjunction with reform in prices, housing, and medical insurance, and in line with a reduction in subsidies.[34]

The clearest statement of the policies to realize the priorities of reform in the housing system, social insurance (*shehui baoxian*), and health systems was provided by Chen Jinhua.[35] His analysis built on earlier calls for the development of a social security system by Gao Shangquan, Vice-Minister of the same Commission, and, in particular, on Meng Wanhe's more daring assertion of the need for a broader unemployment insurance system, both of which emphasized the importance of such reforms for social stability and the promotion of labour mobility.[36] Chen proposed a number of changes in the area of housing policy, including raising rents for public housing, encouraging state workers to buy public housing, and establishing housing foundations and investment systems in which the state, work enterprises, and individuals shared construction costs.[37] He also criticized the current system of old age, medical, unemployed (*dai ye*), and accident insurance cover. In relation to the old age pension, he suggested the promotion of the system, already in operation in different parts of China, whereby the individual and the enterprise made a joint contribution. He envisaged that the individual's rate of contribution would be increased with the development of the economy. The collective enterprises in cities and townships would establish an integrated two-layer pension system consisting of both a unified pool system and individual savings funds. Privately-run enterprises would combine individual contributions with the individual savings fund and a mutual aid fund. Peasants and workers in rural enterprises would rely mainly on self-insurance, with supplementary subsidies from the collective. Insurance for those awaiting work, on the other hand, should, in line with the reform in the labour system, gradually be extended from state enterprises to enterprises of other systems of ownership, while responsibility for the payment of funds would gradually be shifted from the enterprise alone to combined payment by enterprise and individual. Similarly, reform of the health system would be funded by a fixed ratio of payment between state, enterprise, and individual.

In the case of the unified pool system, public funds were raised from contributions by the state, enterprises, and individuals, and managed and distributed by the social insurance agencies operating under the Labour Departments responsible for the different groups. The individual savings system likewise involved individual schemes set up by the People's Insurance Company of China.[38] It is to be noted that in his policy statement, Chen Jinhua continued to use the old term for the unemployed, *daiye*, which meant the youthful unemployed, or former state workers awaiting work. On the other hand, Gao Shangquan and Meng Wanhe both used the term which unambiguously embraced the larger categories of those who had lost work (*shiye*), and thus implied, and in Meng's case advocated, the eventual establishment of a universal unemployment insurance scheme. This position was also in line with a World Bank proposal that China move gradually towards a three-tiered pension system covering all unemployed and retiring urban workers.[39] The urgency of these measures was highlighted by the estimate in the Outline of the Ten-Year Programme that in the next five years jobs would have to be provided for thirty-two million people in cities and towns, and that efforts would have to be made in this period to keep down the unemployment rate to a level below 3.5 per cent.[40]

In the area of health, the Outline of the Ten-Year Programme advocated that new policies in medical and health care should be focused on the establishment of three-level co-operative health networks in rural areas, and the construction of health facilities in the old revolutionary base areas, in minority nationality areas, frontier areas, and poor areas.[41] A programme, sponsored by the National Patriotic Health Campaign under the State Council, was planned to be promulgated in the form of a legal document in late 1991.[42] A 'National Programme for Health Development and Reform in China', jointly drafted by the Ministry of Public Health and the State Administration of Traditional Chinese Medicine, was designed to adapt principles from the early 1950s to the changed economic and social conditions of the country. These principles were to serve workers, peasants, and the military; to stress preventive health care; to integrate Western and traditional medicine; and to link health work with mass campaigns.[43] Emphasis on preventive work was necessitated by the fact that, although the incidence of epidemic diseases had declined from 544 per 100,000 in 1985 to 244 per 100,000 by the end of 1990, new cases of typhoid, cholera, and dysentery were being reported, over 100,000 people carried hepatitis B, 446 HIV positive cases had been found, and over 50 per cent of children under five were reportedly exposed to anaemia by malnutrition.[44]

Despite achievements in the medical field, which had resulted in an increase in the number of hospitals, hospital beds, and professional health staff, and despite the receipt over the previous five years of grants for health assistance from international organizations totalling $78.5 million, a number of serious problems in health delivery were reported in the Chinese press during 1991.[45] The Ministry of Public Health reported 'a widening gap between the medical facilities available in the country's urban areas and those in the rural areas'. Urban residents, accounting for about 20 per cent of the total Chinese population, now took up over 50 per cent of hospital beds and over 50 per cent of doctors, and about 14 per cent of villages did not have any kind of medical establishment.[46] Only 20 per cent of the rural population enjoyed the basic health care offered by rural co-operative health care services.[47] Surveys indicated that 92.5 per cent of the students who graduated from medical institutes between 1985 and 1987 found jobs in cities. Of those assigned to jobs below county level, about 22 per cent had since moved to cities or had been transferred to other jobs.[48]

In addition, 16,466 collectively owned and privately owned clinics and hospitals were closed throughout China during 1990 because they were unlicensed or had been overcharging patients.[49] The parlous condition of rural services contrasted with the massive medical bills for the free medical services covering state employees, the vast majority of whom lived in urban areas.[50] Consequently, the State Council issued a nationwide circular calling for a comprehensive preventive medical care system to be set up at county, township, and village level. A report by five relevant ministries and commissions praised the old rural co-operative health system.[51] And a new programme was initiated to train 800,000 rural youth in higher and secondary medical institutes. The Minister for Health, Chen Minzhang, appealed to local governments to increase their budgets for medical education, and to improve welfare aid for rural medical staff.[52]

In contrast with the clear-cut policy guidelines established in the area of economic, social, and cultural rights in the third phase, the condition of civil rights in 1991 presented an ambiguous and even schizophrenic picture. In view of the official assertion that adjudication of the 'criminals' involved in the 1989 Democracy Movement was basically complete, and social stability restored, this ambiguity was surprising. In January 1991, more than thirty leaders of the pro-democracy movement, including leading dissidents Chen Ziming, Wang Juntao, Wang Dan, Ren Wanding, and Bao Zunxin, were brought to trial in Beijing on charges of 'counter-revolution'. Most were sentenced to prison terms ranging from two to thirteen years, although seven, including Liu Xiaobo, were released without punishment.[53] In terms of formal legal procedures, the trials complied with the letter of the law: they were open, and defendants were allowed to exercise the rights of defence and of appeal. However, numerous issues such as the speed of the trials, the limited opportunities afforded defendants to prepare a defence, the denial of the defendants' right of appointing their own defence counsel, the failure of prosecutors to reply to or refute their defences, and the exclusion of independent observers, entailed questions of 'justice, fairness and due process' which were raised by INGOs and academic legal specialists alike.[54] Moreover, while some important pro-democracy activists, like Han Dongfang, leader of the Beijing Workers' Autonomous Union, and Li Jinjin, its legal adviser, were released, others, like Yang Zhou, accused of establishing Shanghai's first 'China Human Rights Issue Research Society', Fu Shenqi of the Democracy Wall Movement, and Liu Xianbin, were reported to have been arrested during 1991.[55] In addition, by mid-June, among the thousands of Tibetan nationalists detained without trial for months at a time since 1987, at least 200 were known to be still held in Lhasa.[56]

Apart from the procedural problems associated with the January

trials, prisoners of conscience and common criminals ha~
chance of getting fair treatment than they had before 1989. Polit.
interference in the courtroom was especially pronounced during
the crackdown on crime in 1990, when Chinese officials were told
that death sentences should be meted out 'without pity' and cases
should be handled 'rapidly'.[57] The mounting crime rate in this
period, which doubtless contributed to the speed of such trials,
suggested that the condition of civil rights of immunity would
deteriorate before it improved. Between January 1988 and March
1991, it was reported, China's procuratorate departments had
arrested almost 1.9 million criminal suspects and referred 1.78
million of them to the people's courts.[58] In a report to the fourth
session of the Seventh NPC, Ren Jianxin, President of the Supreme
People's Court, stated that 457,500 cases had been concluded in
1990, an increase of 17.4 per cent over 1989. Among those convicted, 36.99 per cent had been sentenced to more than five years,
life imprisonment, death, or death with reprieve, and 61.44 per
cent had been given a prison term of less than five years or detention and surveillance. 88,000 economic cases were handled, 14 per
cent more than in 1989, and cases of 'drug abuse and obscenity'
had registered a 42 per cent increase.[59] The continuing battle
against corruption saw procuratorial organs handle 94,600 cases
of embezzlement and bribery. Yet there was a widespread belief
in the community that the law only caught up with petty corruption,
and that the important cases were not prosecuted. Nevertheless,
Chief Procurator Liu Fuzhi claimed that citizens' personal rights
were being protected. In 1990, procuratorial offices had allegedly
turned down requests for thousands of arrest warrants and investigated 3,509 cases of unlawful detention, 472 cases of alleged
interrogation under torture, and 461 cases of trumped-up charges.[60]

Apart from resort to the courts, mechanisms for social control
included the reported establishment of a Central Commission for
Overall Control of Public Security to supplement the activities of
the Ministry of Public Security and the Ministry of National
Security, and handle 'highly confidential security cases'.[61] A 'Code
of Professional Ethics for Chinese Journalists' was adopted at the
First Plenum of the Fourth Council of the All China Journalists'
Association on 19 January 1991, which required journalists to
'keep to dialectical materialism and proceed from the fundamental interests of the people'.[62] On 14 March, 'Provisional Regulations on Press Management' were promulgated.[63] The Party and

relevant government departments issued guidelines for literature
and art which promised writers and artists 'broad freedom in subject matters, themes, forms, methods, styles, schools, and so forth',
but simultaneously declared the artist 'duty-bound to provide society with wholesome and beneficial mental products'.[64] A campaign
was announced to encourage the youth to take part in a type of
neighbourhood watch to foster political stability, and over two
million college students were sent to the countryside and factories
during the six week summer vacation.[65] Some twenty members of
staff of the only 'ministerial level' newspaper, the *People's Daily*,
were reportedly disciplined and punished in April for 'commit-
ting political mistakes' during the 1989 student movement.[66]

Curbs on freedom of publication were accompanied by more
severe restraints on freedom of religion. In the two years after
June 1989, lay and ordained members of the Catholic and Protestant
churches and Tibetan Buddhists were detained and imprisoned.
New regulations on religion reduced the scope of legal religious
activities in various areas, including those where Islam was practised, for instance, by prohibiting worship outside authorized places
of worship.[67] During the second and third phases which have been
delineated, particular government attention was paid to outlying
minority areas and provinces in China, as political instability, irre-
dentism, and demands for ethnic self-determination in Eastern
Europe and the former Soviet Union increased. At the same time
as attempts were made to restrict the enjoyment of civil rights,
the Vice-Chairman of the NPC's Standing Committee, Peng Chong,
pledged to step up work on six categories of law, the third category of which was for 'protecting the basic rights of citizens',
including a publications law, a press law, an assembly law, a trade
union law, an appeal law, a national indemnity law, laws for protecting women and minors, laws protecting the rights of minorities, and laws related to the improvement of the people's congress
system, such as a supervision law and a law on people's congress
deputies.[68]

During 1991, at a formal level, civil rights of expression, particularly as they had an implication for politics, and civil rights of
immunity were still heavily circumscribed. Where supporting legislation existed, it was overwhelmingly used as a means of social
control. At an informal level, however, the efforts to enforce this
control appeared increasingly inappropriate, arbitrary, and piecemeal.[69] To the question, where was repression and where was

resistance, there was no consistent or firm answer: no sooner had the locus been pinpointed than it moved.[70] Nor was it possible to discover a consistent guideline as to what kind of activities and thoughts were officially proscribed. The bottom line appeared to be simply that Chinese citizens could not openly question Marxism or the Chinese Communist Party. Intellectual debate continued, although within parameters somewhat more restricted than before Tiananmen. Discussions on neo-conservatism, if not of liberal democracy or Marxist humanism, were even allowed by the leadership. Moreover, the open debate on human rights in scholarly journals, briefly interrupted in 1989, now expanded.

In this culturally flexible and yet dangerous environment, a 'nearly absurd' situation developed on the literary scene, which was at once repressive and lax.[71] At the level of popular culture, the pop star Cui Jian continued his concerts outside Beijing, and discos thrived; pop music blared from radios, television intermingled the domestic fifty-part series of *Ke Wang* ('Longing') with Hong Kong movies; in urban areas, styles and colours of dress were more exotic than those generally found in Hong Kong; and mildly pornographic magazines were freely available. The easy accessibility of high-frequency radios enabled Chinese citizens to listen to the BBC, and to the Voice of America when it was not jammed; Fujian residents routinely watched Taiwanese television and those in Guangzhou watched Hong Kong television. Among the general populace a conspiracy of silence reigned, in which the unspoken rule was that one could inform to protect oneself but not to hurt one's neighbour; there even appeared to be a collective agreement as to what should and should not be said. The general consensus seemed much the same as in Hong Kong — to wait patiently for the future and to try to prosper in the interim.

The dilemma for the Chinese government was that, if it were to avoid the inevitable confrontation which would result from continued resort to coercion as a means of social control, some personal space had to be allowed the populace at large, and the discontented intellectuals in particular. The 'tacit bond' between government and people involved an acceptance by the government of the need to allow that space in exchange for popular acquiescence. A parallel, semi-independent society was necessary to strengthen the legitimacy of the state, yet at the same time it had the potential to subvert the state. In the government's dialogue with society, it tried to co-opt that space, but the space was continually moving beyond official reach. In the government's favour, particularly after inflation had been controlled and the economy had begun its recovery, was the fact that there was no major issue which could serve as an accelerator to ignite the still smouldering embers of popular perceptions of relative deprivation. The government's dilemma, on the other hand, was that now within the Chinese world political boundaries still existed but, precisely because of government policies, social and cultural boundaries had dissolved. The regime now had to cope with a pan-Chinese society whose horizons also escaped the reach of the state.[72] A reorientation of the Chinese world had occurred, away from the situation of the 1980s where Beijing was the centre of culture, and the rest of China the periphery. Now Beijing competed, as the first among equals, with the other centres of Taiwan and Hong Kong. Chinese writers published in Hong Kong and Taiwan, and were paid in US dollars. Rock and roll had become a pan-Chinese activity. The bourgeois culture so abhorred by Chinese leaders could be imported invisibly across borders wearing a Chinese face.

By late 1991, the application of controls became so inconsistent and contradictory that it was clear that a power struggle at the elite level was being conducted through the medium of civil rights. This struggle was accentuated by the approaching Eighth Party Plenum scheduled for early December. In the cultural field, there was an official policy to carry out rectification while at the same time encouraging cultural growth. Conflicting messages included the call to journalists by Propaganda Minister Li Ruihuan to 'liberate their thoughts, stick to the facts and make new contributions to modern times', and the reported plans of the reformist wing of the Party to revamp the propaganda establishment by replacing leftist ideologues.[73] Former Minister of Culture Wang Meng also sought to assert his civil rights by resort to the judicial process in a libel suit against *Wenyi bao*, details of which were then published in a gesture of press independence by Shanghai's *Dushu zhoubao*.[74] On the other hand, an official report called for the tightening of censorship over the arts and the press to combat rising teenage delinquency.[75] Public Security Minister Tao Siju called for heightened police vigilance and predicted considerable 'intertwining and collusion among foreign-based infiltrators, domestic advocates of liberalization, as well as ordinary criminals'.[76] And Justice Minister Cai Cheng reiterated that Chinese law must be

at the service of the class struggle and that there was no question of 'the law being supreme'.[77]

In this third post-Tiananmen phase, no blueprint for the institutionalization of political rights was put forward to give meaning to the pledges of political restructuring in the earlier phase.
Unlike earlier phases in which developments in the former socialist world constituted a source of political pressure, the increasingly disturbing economic, social, and political fall-out from the
political changes in Eastern Europe and the Soviet Union provided China's leaders with confirmation that their emphasis on
economic rather than political reform reflected the proper priorities. The ritualism and formalism characteristic of Chinese public
life was nowhere as evident as in the political domain. At the elite
level of policy formation, Jiang Zemin repeated the essential aims
of political restructuring: to perfect the system of people's congresses, enabling the people to exercise state power; to strengthen
legal and work supervision of the people's congresses; to improve
the electoral system; and to carry out activities of the Communist
Party 'within the framework of the Constitution and the law'.
These essentially conservative aims of reform within the existing
system were, however, immediately contradicted by his simultaneous insistence that 'the propositions of the Party should be
turned into the will of the state through legal procedures. The
leadership of the Communist Party over the people's congress
should be strengthened'.[78]

It was clear that the limits of political restructuring were set at
the point at which its utilitarian function of legitimizing Party rule
and enhancing the efficiency of the state apparatus began to be
overshadowed by its negative impact on the Party. Party supremacy was seen as the only meaningful safeguard against the dangers of 'peaceful evolution' and bourgeois liberalization, and was
to be achieved through a combination of spiritual and institutional
means.[79] Exhortations in favour of a return to Marxist-Leninist
principles were accompanied by a revival of interest in Mao Zedong
thought and by a celebration of Mao's life and achievements in
both print and film media. 'Party building' was seen as the institutional means to safeguard Party supremacy: but such normative
and structural goals contrasted in bizarre fashion with the realities of normlessness and corruption within the Party, with reports
of large-scale withdrawal from Party membership, and with the
reported findings of the Party's Organization Department in May

1991 that 'sound and comparatively sound' party cells numbered one million, 'just so-so' party cells numbered 2.4 million, and poor and rather poor party cells numbered 600,000.[80]

Within the context of these restrictive political assumptions, it was clear that the main mechanism for the strengthening of popular supervision over the political process was still seen to be the traditional method of attitudinal change on the part of the ruling elite, by changes in working style, rather than a goal to be achieved through institutional means. The main institutional changes which were sought were increased legislation and the continued streamlining of the bureaucracy, both of which were primarily aimed at improving administrative and economic efficiency and, in the former case, at enhancing political stability.

The other institutional areas in which achievement was hailed demonstrated the inherent ritualism of the political process. Claims by Peng Chong, Vice-Chairman of the NPC Standing Committee, that the elections at county and township levels for the local people's congresses held at the end of 1990 marked a great event in China's political democracy appeared to have been justified in numerical terms.[81] Thus, in Beijing's Haidian district, a student deputy said that in his ward at Qinghua the voters nominated fifty-eight candidates, of whom ten were later elected. These ten then broadcast speeches, and voters elected two candidates, one of whom was then elected by secret ballot to be candidate.[82] But the third stage of the nominating process, the 'consultation' and 'fermentation' stage, still allowed numerous opportunities for the Party leadership to exert its will.[83] And the lack of universalized procedures for nomination, as well as the origins of the nominating procedure in political study groups, made the 'democratic' nature of the elections a relative rather than a substantive improvement over past electoral practices.[84] Members of the Chinese People's Political Consultative Conference (CPPCC) also hailed the government's new receptiveness to its proposals issuing from the fourth session of its Seventh National Committee. Of the 1,915 proposals put forward by the CPPCC covering a wide range of areas in the economy, culture, education, science and technology, 563 had been incorporated into government decrees, 1,129 were under careful study, and 213 remained for reference.[85]

In the NPC itself, it was reported that delegates had made numerous alterations to Premier Li Peng's Work Report, yet the changes listed were of minimal policy significance.[86] This resort to numbers, to claims of the quantitative rather than qualitative content of political change, was itself symbolic, as was the co-option of terminology, the use of political terms such as 'popular supervision' to describe an inappropriate reality. This was a process with antecedents in the adoption by the Deng regime of the political terminology used by the disgraced dissenters of the Democracy Wall Movement.

The one area in which structural reform was meaningfully implemented in support of civil/political rights was administrative. The Law of the People's Republic of China Governing Administrative Litigation (*Zhonghua renmin gongheguo xingzheng susong fa*) which came into effect on 1 October 1990, formally invested Chinese citizens with the legal right to bring lawsuits against government officials and theoretically brought administrative organizations under legal scrutiny. However, apart from the complications already noted, the problem with such legislation was that many Chinese citizens were unfamiliar with the new law or were fettered by the long-standing idea of 'people not suing officials'. One official commentator, for instance, stated in 1990 that there had been a series of difficulties in the course of setting up the administrative procedural system, which included the fact that:

Certain administrative organs refuse to respond to charges or enforce the court's verdict, with some even interfering with the verdict of the courts . . . Some judicial personnel are intimidated by the official being sued and cannot handle the cases with impartiality. With the implementation of the Administrative Procedure Law, the problems cited above are not likely to disappear immediately, while new problems are bound to crop up.[87]

Moreover, as in the case of the law on demonstrations, it was clear that this law was meant as much to protect the authorities and bureaucrats, and their work, as to protect the citizens. Thus, in response to the objection by family planning workers that the new law would inhibit their work, the *Chinese Population Newspaper* indicated that, where previously family planning authority rested simply on orders from a supervisor, now family planning workers would have recourse to the law to clarify their powers. If, for instance, violators of a family planning regulation refused to pay a fine, the family planning workers could now take them to court and sue them for breach of regulations.[88] However, despite all its complexities, the potential of this new law for protecting citizens' civil rights was considerable, and it has been welcomed as a positive development towards a rule of law.

Another form of popular supervision was the offence-reporting system, introduced in June 1988 and backed up in 1991 with protective legislation. Although another obvious means of extending the watchfulness of neighbourhood committees to the supervision of crime and corruption, it allowed some popular protection against bureaucratic corruption and the abuse of power.[89] These supervisory mechanisms bore a close similarity to the traditional popular rights of complaint against officials.

Despite such positive developments, which had some potential to protect citizens' rights, few of the prerequisites for effective, as opposed to ritualistic, participatory politics within the present Chinese political system had developed by the end of 1991. The concepts of popular sovereignty, free (or freer) speech, a free (or freer) press, the rule of law equally applicable to both Party and state, and the institutional separation of powers, all theoretically possible under a one party system, had yet to be unambiguously reflected in laws, other than the formal guarantees of the constitution, in institutions, or, equally importantly, in leadership consciousness. The political situation had not reached the ideal expressed by one Chinese constitutional lawyer:

There are some rights . . . which are inherent in a system of democracy, whether it is capitalist or socialist. So long as there is free election based upon public opinion, it is always possible to compel the Government not to overstep the boundaries of its powers, for there is a minority who would give attention to any abuse, and to persuade the electorate to oppose those abuses. And if the government is not responsive, it may be turned out. There will be no democracy if minority opinions cannot be expressed, or if people cannot meet together to discuss their opinions and their actions, or if those who think alike cannot associate for mutual support and for the propagation of their common ideas. Yet these ideas are vulnerable and they are most likely to be subject to attack. Therefore the fundamental liberty is not only of free election but also of limitation of government powers.[90]

In the third post-Tiananmen phase, therefore, China's leadership was grappling with the problem of the management of its human rights policies. The goal of expanding economic and social rights in order to preserve the political stability necessary for the continued pursuit of economic reform was a consensual one. The dilemma was whether to achieve this goal by maintaining or by replacing the existing social welfare and social security structures. Replacement of structures, if the most logical and the most beneficial to popular welfare in the long term, could, in the short term, temporarily destabilize the living standards of the urban work-force, and risk reviving popular consciousness of relative deprivation with its grave political consequences. On the other hand, the policy of maintaining the existing system was undermined by the fact that the prevailing structures were either collapsing, or due to collapse, under the weight of economic reform. It was clear that if these structures were maintained, the rationalization of labour and similar policies which were part of the logic of the economic restructuring process, could not proceed. For these reasons, the leadership began to move reluctantly towards the option of replacing the social safety nets while deepening economic reform. At the same time, the open leadership disagreement about the amount of civil, rather than political, freedom which could be allowed, a problem exacerbated both by domestic and international pressures, reflected uncertainty as to how to best negotiate this new phase, while maintaining the delicate balance between political stability and economic reform.

International Pressures and the Chinese Government Response

The most significant effect of the crackdown on the Democracy Movement in June 1989 was without doubt the mobilization of international pressure. This took the form of both symbolic and economic sanctions, and aimed to improve the condition of China's civil rights, in particular, the civil rights of immunity. A year later these pressures reaped their reward. After months of virulent counter-attacks against the international community, based on the continued re-assertion of the principles of sovereignty and non-interference in another country's internal affairs, the Chinese government indicated its readiness to become a serious participant in the international debate. Apart from international economic sanctions, external pressures which influenced China included the continuing debate in the United States on China's eligibility to enjoy Most Favoured Nation status, criticism by the UN Human Rights Commission and the International Labour Organization, Chinese dissident activity abroad, and the stepping up of the critique by International Non-Governmental Organizations. The clearest symbol of China's realization of the need to wrestle with the human rights issues raised at an international level was the State Council's publication in October 1991 of a White Paper on Human Rights, translated into English in November.

Powerful international moral pressure was exerted on China through criticisms of the June crackdown by the UN Human Rights Commission, the Human Rights Sub-Commission and the International Labour Organization. These were of particular significance in view of China's permanent membership of the UN Security Council. A report transmitted by the UN Secretary General to the UN Commission on Human Rights at its forty-sixth session from February to March 1990 contained reports by Amnesty International, the International Commission of Health Professionals for Health and Human Rights, and the International League for Human Rights, in consultation with the UN Economic and Social Council.[91] Following on action initiated by the Human Rights Sub-Commission, a draft resolution, called the 'Situation in China', with eighteen co-sponsors (twelve EEC countries, the US, Japan, Sweden, Norway, Canada, and Australia) was put before the Human Rights Commission at its forty-sixth session.[92] It expressed concern at allegations of violations of human rights in China and endorsed the appeal of the Human Rights Sub-Commission for clemency towards persons deprived of liberty as a result of the events of June. While welcoming the decision of the Chinese government in January 1990 to lift martial law in Beijing and release 573 detained persons, it urged the government to take additional measures along the same lines to ensure full observance of human rights. Finally, it requested the Secretary-General to submit further information on human rights in China to the forty-seventh session of the Commission.[93]

The Chinese delegation rejected the draft resolution on the grounds that the demonstrations in Beijing were an 'anti-government rebellion aimed at overthrowing the government of China', whose response was 'totally different in nature from "violation of human rights"'. It insisted that 'the Chinese government has always abided by the principles and purposes of the UN Charter, committed itself to the respect and protection of human rights and

fundamental freedoms, and actively involved itself in, and supported, the United Nations in its work in the field of human rights'.
After intense lobbying, the 'Situation in China' draft resolution
was defeated in the Human Rights Commission by an oral 'no
action' motion. This was proposed by the Pakistani delegate, who
claimed that the situation in China was an internal matter which
was not appropriate for the Commission on Human Rights to consider; and it was passed on 6 March 1990 by a simple majority of
17–15 with 11 abstentions. In favour of the motion, apart from
China, were socialist, African, and South Asian countries unwilling to censure China — the USSR, Yugoslavia, Ukraine, Pakistan,
India, Bangladesh, Sri Lanka, Somalia, Iraq, Cyprus, and five
African states.

This setback, did not, however, prove a permanent one. On 23
August 1991, the UN Human Rights Sub-Commission passed a
further resolution expressing 'concern' at 'continuing reports of
violations of fundamental human rights and freedoms which threat-
en the distinct cultural, religious, and national identity of the
Tibetan people'. Although China's Ambassador to the UN, Fan
Guoxiang, announced that China considered the resolution 'null
and void' and that it was not binding on China, the issue was
passed to the UN Commission on Human Rights, for its meeting
in March 1992.[94]

Furthermore, pursuant to the 13 November 1989 report on
China by the ILO Governing Body Freedom of Association Committee, on 27 February 1990 the ILO Governing Body approved
the Committee's mid-February recommendations on the situation
in China. These included the expression of 'deep concern at the
seriousness of the allegations in this case which include deaths,
detentions and ill-treatment of Workers' Autonomous Federation
(WAF) leaders and activities', and requested that the Chinese
government supply detailed information on the nature and objectives of labour re-education measures imposed on trade unionists,
on the killing of leaders of the WAF during the attack on Tiananmen
Square, on the sentences passed on nine workers from Changchun,
and on the arrest of leaders and members of the WAF set up in
Beijing and elsewhere. The Committee also 'deplored' the fact
that the basic principle of the right of workers to establish organizations of their own choosing and independent of any political
party had not been respected in China's case. It further drew the
Chinese government's attention to the fact that 'if the conditions

for granting registration of a trade union are tantamount to obtaining prior permission from the public authorities, this would undeniably constitute an infringement of the principles of freedom of association'.[95] At its meeting in May 1990, the ILO committee adjourned the examination of the ICFTU complaint and urged the Chinese government to provide the previously requested information as soon as possible.[96] On 11 October 1990, more than a year after the original request, the Chinese government partially acceded to the requests, and, while protesting that the committee's conclusions represented unwarranted interference in its internal affairs, supplied the outcomes of proceedings against 91 workers.[97]

Further moral pressure was exerted on China by the award of the Nobel Peace Prize to the Dalai Lama. In April 1991 the International Press Institute, the leading international organization devoted to press freedom, also called on the Chinese government to respect the liberty and freedom of expression of Chinese journalists. The Institute recorded its 'sorrow at the inability of any journalists from the People's Republic of China to join its discussions on press freedom in Asia'. It also expressed regret at the imprisoning of Chinese journalists after Tiananmen, and urged the Chinese government to end its suppression of debate and free expression.[98]

The Western sanctions package combined not only moral condemnation of the June massacre and the subsequent repression, but also limited economic sanctions, including an embargo on military sales to China and the suspension of new loans, particularly from the World Bank and other international institutions. These sanctions remained in place for about a year: but by June 1991 most economic sanctions had been lifted. Gradually, China resumed its privileged position in relation to World Bank loans and as recipient of economic aid and technology transfers from the developed world.[99] One potential economic sanction remained, however, which was arguably more effective than any of the earlier measures. Its implementation depended upon the outcome of the continuing debate within the United States over China's eligibility to enjoy Most Favoured Nation trading status, a privilege China had enjoyed since 1980, but which was required to be renewed every twelve months.[100] On 23 July 1991, the US Senate approved legislation that would require China to improve human rights, reduce arms sales, and modify its trade policy in order to retain special export rights to the American market the following year.

The Senate vote was 55–44, far short of the two-thirds majority required to override a presidential veto. However, on 26 November 1991, the US House of Representatives passed by 409 votes to 21 a bill setting conditions to be applied when China's MFN status came up for renewal in June 1992. Apart from requirements on unfair trade practices and arms proliferation, the conditions were that China release demonstrators imprisoned in the 1989 Tiananmen Square massacre and that it make significant progress in human rights. Thus, the China MFN debate in the US Congress hung over Chinese authorities as a cloud threatening to mar its economic development and placing pressure on its human rights policies.[101]

Apart from the MFN question, the gradual diminution of economic sanctions on China was offset by an increase in international moral sanctions. Multilateral economic sanctions were gradually replaced by bilateral moral pressures on a government-to-government basis. This process began in December 1990 with the visit to Beijing by Richard Schifter, US Assistant Secretary of State, who raised questions of human rights with the Chinese government. This precedent was followed by a number of other visitors to China in the following year, including Britain's Prime Minister, John Major, in September and US Secretary of State, James Baker, in November. But the most significant form of moral pressure stemmed from Beijing's own initiative. Its invitations to Australian and French human rights delegations to visit China represented an important precedent, whereby China officially conceded, in total contrast to earlier vehement protestations, that international groups had the right to monitor its human rights situation.[102]

Despite some public scepticism among liberal thinkers both within and outside China as to the value of such governmental delegations, both the Australian and French delegations produced constructive reports which gave crucial international publicity to the situation in China and also obtained new information on the workings of China's legal system.[103] The report of the Australian delegation criticised many aspects of the Chinese legal system, such as the lack of 'judicial independence', Party interference in judicial decisions, the failure to make public many laws and guidelines, and the lack of effective time limits for detention and trial. It expressed concern about the practice of administrative detention, reports of mistreatment of prisoners and the 'frequent, and often inconsistent, use of the death penalty'. It considered that 'the prosecution of so-called counter-revolutionary crimes' amounted to 'an infringement of basic freedoms as set out in the Universal Declaration of Human Rights'. It also found that the freedoms of assembly, peaceful association, and the press guaranteed under the Chinese constitutions were not in fact respected, and deplored the total monitoring of the individual through personal dossiers, household registration, and the ID card, as well as through the street committee and its security organization, and the security section in the factory. It reserved its most stinging criticism for the condition of civil, political, economic, and social rights in Tibet, where 'martial law . . . continues to exist in all but name'. Apart from observing the lack of religious freedom, and of other civil, as well as political rights, it reported Tibetan complaints of a lack of justice, a lack of access to education and employment, as well as of a restriction on freedom of movement. Despite these criticisms, the Report emphasized the positive achievements made in legal reforms in the modernization era. Its basically constructive and cautiously optimistic tone ensured that such criticism was palatable to Chinese officials, and provided the basis for a continuing exchange of views and visits between the two governments.

The Australian Report was complemented in October 1991 by the Report of the Mission of French Jurists, *Justice Repressive et Droits de l'Homme en République Populaire de Chine* ('Repressive Justice and the Rights of Man in the People's Republic of China'). Concentrating on the formal legal apparatus underpinning civil rights, the report endorsed some of the Australian conclusions, and in other respects extended the inquiry. Like the Australian report, the French report was criticial of the invasive Party role in the legal system, decrying the lack of independence of judges and of lawyers. Institutional causes of dependence included, in the case of judges, the overriding powers of the political and judicial committees (*zhengfa weiyuanhui*), the dependence of judges on a strong internal hierarchy, and their submission to the authority of the Public Security organs. In the case of lawyers, independence was undermined by the requirement of an annual application for licences to practice, the lack of confidentiality in relations with clients, and the harassment of lawyers who interpreted the right to defence as the right to plead the client's innocence. The report was critical of the 'opaque' situation in regard to legal detention; it suggested that the official Chinese numbers of prisons and prisoners, the same supplied to the Australian delegation, constituted an underestimation; and it reported a practically unchanged penal system, despite the transfer of responsibility for the administration of penal affairs to the Chinese Ministry of Justice. It was particularly critical, however, of the extra-legal process of administrative detention, dominated by the Public Security organs, which involved sentences whose numbers, estimated at between two to four million, might well exceed the numbers of those imprisoned under legal procedures.

The effects of the events of June 1989, according to the delegation, were that they impeded the most ambitious reforms of the Chinese judicial system: a press law was no longer under consideration, and any text aiming at enlarging or providing improved guarantees for the rights of the citizen was immured by numerous political obstacles — the role of the Communist Party, administrative obstacles, and the pre-eminence of the Public Security organs. Moreover, in texts on counter-revolutionary crimes, as in practice, there was hardly any distinction observed between counter-revolutionary statements, counter-revolutionary acts, or the preparation of counter-revolutionary acts.

The French delegation recognized the progress which had been made in China's attitude towards human rights, reflected in the lifting of martial law, in the release since 1991 of 950 people arrested for their involvement in the Democracy Movement, in the attitude of Chinese officials that it was 'natural' and 'normal' that foreigners should take an interest in China's human rights, and in the fact that this interest was 'no longer systematically considered as interference'. Nevertheless, in view of the above constraints, and in view of the failure to apply the Administrative Litigation Law which 'could allow the judicial control of detentions of this type and more broadly, the control of the activities of the Public Security', the delegation concluded that it could 'only note with regret that the conditions of a truly constructive dialogue are not currently in place'.

Another significant source of pressure on China was the expatriate Chinese dissidents whose numbers had been swollen by the June 1989 events. The total number of mainland Chinese scholars, students, and other nationals scattered around the world since June 1989 has been estimated to be about 100,000.[104] The establishment of the Federation for a Democratic China (FDC) was followed by a joint conference with the US-based China Alliance for Democracy (CAD) in Chicago in July 1989.[105] The main difference between the two bodies was that the various groups within the CAD were in favour of 'reform outside the system'; they opposed the primacy of the Party and intended to wrest power from it. The primary aim of the FDC, on the other hand, was not to overturn the CCP, but to require it to share power with other parties.[106] Within the United States, intellectuals in exile split into two rival 'academic' camps, the 'Chicago School', including most literary theoreticians, preferring scholastic research to direct political involvement, and the 'Princeton School', preferring more political activity, including Su Xiaokang, Yuan Zhiming, Su Wei, Fang Lizhi, Li Shuxian, Liu Binyan, and student leader Chai Ling.[107] Another group, 'the Contemporary China Research Centre' inaugurated at Stanford University by a former senior policy adviser to the Chinese government, Chen Yizi, began a survey of reforms in the Soviet Union and Eastern Europe.

Efforts to use the period of exile to integrate democratic ideas and practices from the West with Chinese realities were, however, handicapped by numerous problems, including factionalism, the continued concentration by exiles on the debates raging in China before June 1989 on 'peaceful evolution' and 'new authoritarianism', and uncertainty on the part of the dissident organizations themselves as to their future role in a new, democratic China. Other problems were reflected in the intellectuals' self-critiques. Yuan Zhiming, for instance, pointed out that 'we never wanted to be standard-bearers: we did our level best to keep out of it'. Liu Binyan pointed to the moral failure of Chinese intellectuals, to their naïve belief in wise rulers, and to their inability to take independent action. And Xu Jilin criticized the utilitarian nature which had characterized China's political quest since the May 4 Movement: since 'this (cultural) reassessment was in itself inspired by a mood of political utilitarianism rather than a quest for knowledge, all cultural debates have invariably been tinged with an ideological hue and marked by a desire for immediate results'.

If the role of the exiled dissidents in the future government of China was problematic, however, the significance of their role for human rights in China was not. Apart from their important function in conveying news about the situation in China to foreign governments and INGOs, they also constituted an important pressure group on the United States Congress during debate over

MFN status. Their activities as a pressure group became particularly significant when bilateral government-to-government contacts began to replace multilateral economic sanctions as the main source of external pressure on China. For example, in November 1991 the FDC sent US Secretary of State James Baker an open letter urging him to insist on the following during his visit to China:

(a) the release of all pro-democracy activists presently in Chinese prisons including those not known by the international community;

(b) the granting of amnesty to all political prisoners; and

(c) permission for the return to China of those political dissidents currently in exile and the guarantee of their safety and freedom.[108]

Perhaps the most effective pressure was, however, exerted on China by the continuing activities and reports of INGOs, whose strength lay precisely in the fact that they were seen as neutral and above political pressures, and who could absorb and communicate all the information which other groups garnered.[109] Between 1990 and 1991, Amnesty International and Asia Watch published a number of influential reports on the condition of China's human rights and maintained pressure on UN human rights organs and on the US Congress.[110]

The Chinese response to all these pressures took a number of forms. External pressures clearly prompted a number of much publicized releases of prisoners of conscience detained after June 1989, and lighter sentencing for those undergoing trials in January 1991. They also gave rise to invitations to foreign human rights delegations and created a sense of obligation within China to respond to some of the accusations, and to formulate a more sophisticated theoretical response than hitherto.

The dilemma created by external pressures for China was reflected in a review of a book on human rights published in 1991:

The question of human rights is one of the most complex and hotly debated of all issues in the international arena. It seems that all major political incidents in the modern world are intimately linked with human rights. It is also an issue of considerable political significance with China, and one of great sensitivity. The international bourgeoisie has been able for far too long to carry on as though they have some monopoly over human rights ... We are therefore faced with the urgent task of coming to grips with the theory of this issue and educating the broad masses of cadres and people, in particular young students, how to utilise a Marxist perspective to achieve a thorough and correct understanding of human rights.[111]

The urgency of this new undertaking was reflected in the gathering of over thirty scholars and experts in June 1991 to discuss the topic, 'The history and present situation of human rights', from political, legal, and philosophical viewpoints. Those present included scholars from the Centre for International Studies under the State Council and from Beijing University.[112] In the last quarter of 1991, two academic missions on human rights visited the United States and had talks with senior officials from the Department of State and with members of Congress. Preparations also began for the establishment of the first Centre of Human Rights Studies in China. At the same time, a change in the human rights stance of the Chinese leadership was suggested by a new official emphasis on the 'right to subsistence' (*shengcun quan*), which bolstered the earlier arguments about state sovereignty and non-interference in internal affairs. Thus Premier Li Peng informed former US President Jimmy Carter in April 1991 that, without the people's right to subsistence and the country's right of independence, there would be no human rights.[113] The right to life in an economic sense was thus counterposed against the right to life in a civil rights sense.

The 'right to subsistence' was also a central theme in the White Paper on Human Rights released by China's State Council in October 1991. Another more familiar argument was that each country's human rights conditions were circumscribed by its historical, social, economic, and cultural conditions, and that human rights evolved as a cumulative process which reflected the stage of historical development. The time-honoured sovereignty argument was now, however, expressed in a marginally weaker sense: 'The argument that the principle of non-interference in internal affairs does not apply to the issue of human rights is, in essence, a demand that sovereign states give up their state sovereignty in the field of human rights, a demand that is contrary to international law.'[114]

Apart from such familiar arguments, the White Paper contained some important innovations. Although it has been seen by some as just another sophisticated weapon to answer Western criticism, it was more than a refutation of the bourgeois conception of human rights.[115] In the first place, it established a new hierarchy of rights. The 'right to subsistence' was identified as a basic right and analysed in the manner of Henry Shue as 'the most important of all rights, without which the other rights are out of the question'. In one sense, the right to subsistence as defined in the Paper should more properly have been officially translated as the right to existence or life, as it also encompassed the historical notion of the Chinese people's right to physical security in the face of imperialist aggression. On the other hand, in relation to the post-1949 era, it referred solely to subsistence, in the sense of 'the right to eat one's fill and dress warmly'. The right to subsistence thus effectively established the priority of a lowest common denominator of economic, social, and cultural rights. This new theoretical development could be interpreted on the one hand as the downgrading of socio-economic redistributive goals and on the other as an assertion of the continuity of non-Western priorities. The section on the right to subsistence, however, was followed by a section entitled, 'The Chinese People Have Gained Extensive Political Rights'. Under this heading, both civil and political rights were included. The White Paper thus formally amended the normal Marxist hierarchy of rights emphasizing economic, social, and cultural rights as a whole, and not just rights to subsistence, over civil and political rights. It also identified the three salient characteristics of Chinese human rights as 'extensiveness, equality, and authenticity'. It thus in a quaintly anachronistic way resuscitated norms and qualities associated with the pre-modernization era. For the 'extensiveness' of access to economic, social, and cultural rights which it cited, was a feature not of the modernization decade but of Maoist China. Equality, however, was not conceptualized in the sense it was used in Maoist China, but rather in the liberal democratic sense of an equality of rights.

The White Paper presented a curious *mélange* of Maoist norms, new and old priorities of rights, and guarantees of rights which either no longer existed in substance or were already on the point of being formally abandoned. It placed particular stress on judicial guarantees of human rights, including prisoners' rights, and on the right to work. It stressed the social security benefits guaranteed to 'every worker', emphasizing financial subsidies and the rapid increase of workers' wages. At the same time it neglected to refer to the proposed reforms of housing, subsidies, and wages referred to above, which would substantially undermine those 'rights'. Nor was there any reference to existing plans to provide unemployment insurance schemes. Other emphases were on the freedom of religious belief, the rights of minorities, and the issue of family planning. Particular stress was laid on the rights of the disabled, although it was admitted that the employment rate of the handicapped was only 50.19 per cent. There was little reference to education, to the programme for caring for the poor, or to the massive problems of retirement and unemployment insurance.

In its overall structure, with the exception of the stress on the right to subsistence and on the issue of sovereignty, the White Paper concentrated more on the human rights issues stressed in Western critiques than on China's own human rights priorities. The achievements it claimed in economic and social rights were more descriptive of the Maoist past than of the real economic and social issues with which China was currently grappling.

Under the heading of political rights, the Paper claimed that 'since the very day of its founding, the Communist Party of China has been holding high the banner of democracy and human rights'. The people's congresses were seen as the means 'to guarantee that the people are the real masters of the country with the right to run the country's economic and social affairs'. The value of the electoral system was claimed to be that more candidates were posted than deputies elected, that upwards of 90 per cent of voters participated in elections, and that those elected were 'broadly representative' of all social strata. The claim of the National People's Congress to 'represent the people's common will' was based on its 'full airing of opinion' before adopting major policy decisions. Party leadership, on the other hand, was 'mainly an ideological and political leadership' and was 'the result of historical choice'. However, the Paper claimed, 'the Party does not take the place of the government in the state's leadership system'. Furthermore, 'the Party conducts its activities within the framework of the Constitution and the law and has no right to transcend the Constitution and the law'.

Workers' congresses were seen as the main form of democratic management through which workers participated in decision-making. In contrast, the function of trade unions since 1979 was seen to have been a predominantly welfare one. Apart from the improvement of the system of workers' congresses, the achievements of trade unions were listed as the establishment of various workers' schools, the mobilization of workers to overfulfil state plans, the guarantee of workers' welfare and the establishment of committees to deal with labour disputes. Of 18,573 labour disputes in 1990, only 932 cases were reported to have been settled through arbitration, about 6 per cent of the total decided cases. The lack of industrial rights reflected in this Chinese assessment was later underlined by the US Human Rights Reports of 1991, which noted that the Chinese government neither allowed independent trade unions nor collective bargaining and that, although the ACFTU was increasingly concerned about protecting workers' basic living standards, it 'generally acts simply as a channel for workers' complaints to the management of individual enterprises and municipal labour bureaus, or as a channel for passing CCP demands and propaganda to workers'.[116]

A wide range of 'political rights' was enumerated as being the preserve of the citizen, such as the freedoms of speech, the press, assembly, association, procession, and demonstration. It was claimed that 'there is no news censorship in China', and that only one-fifth of the newspapers and magazines were 'run by Party and state organizations'. It was claimed that there were 2,000 associations in China in 1990, including societies, research institutes, foundations, federations, and clubs. It was also claimed that, 'to guarantee the people's democratic rights and other lawful rights and interests', China was improving its legal system. Apart from major laws and administrative laws and regulations, numerous local laws and administrative rules had been formulated, 'of which more than 1,000 were about human rights'. These claims were reported to have been viewed cynically by the majority of Chinese intellectuals, but at the same time the potential of the document to serve as an authoritative basis for their own claims to civil rights was realized.

In the matter of civil rights of immunity, the White Paper asserted the accused's rights of defence and appeal. Cases should be tried publicly 'except those involving state secrets or individual privacy or involving minors'. Furthermore, 'with no other evidence except the confession of the accused as a basis, the accused cannot be pronounced guilty or sentenced'. The extortion of confessions by torture was prohibited, and 472 cases which involved such abuses were filed for investigation in 1990. Moreover, in the same year, China's procuratorial organs put forward suggestions for the correction of illegal practice in 3,200 cases of lawsuit procedures and judicial activities. Interestingly, the Paper claimed that if a person took exception to an administrative decision on

226   CHINA AND HUMAN RIGHTS

education through labour, he or she could appeal to the administrative committee or lodge a complaint with the People's Court in accordance with the Law of Administrative Litigation. Yet on this question, the *Report of the Australian Human Rights Delegation to China* stated that 'it appeared that there had been no cases of *laojiao* detention being challenged (under the administrative procedure law); moreover, this possibility seemed not to have been considered by officials or defence lawyers'.

On the question of the death penalty, the White Paper stated that 'China, like most countries in the world, maintains capital punishment, but imposes stringent restrictive regulations on the use of this extreme measure'. Finally, maintaining that there were 'no "political prisoners" in China', it asserted that 'in China, ideas alone, in the absence of action which violates the law, do not constitute a crime; nobody will be sentenced to punishment merely because he holds dissenting political views'. On the contrary, it argued, the 'kinds of criminal acts that endanger state security', those acts which come under the rubric of 'counter-revolutionary crime', 'are punishable in any country'. Although it did not provide statistics of the number of prisoners indicted for 'counter-revolutionary crimes', the White Paper estimated that there were 680 prisons and reform through labour (*laodong gaizao*) institutions in China, holding 1.1 million prisoners. These figures, which were questioned in the report by the French human rights delegation, were identical to those supplied to its Australian counterpart, which was also informed that there were 160,000 people undergoing re-education through labour (*laojiao*) in 200 special centres.[117]

The White Paper devoted considerable space to the subject of freedom of religious belief, asserting that people were not arrested 'only because of their religious beliefs'. As in the case of prisoners of conscience, actual crimes had to be associated with these beliefs, including disruption of public order, interference with the health of others or with the state's educational system, criminal activities, or acts of subversion against the state. Considerable space was also devoted to documenting the guarantee of minority rights, along with copious statistics. The distance which still had to be traversed was, however, suggested in the concluding paragraph:

The disparity between the minority regions and the inland and coastal areas arose and developed over a long historical period. For more than

40 years since the People's Republic of China was founded, the Chinese government has made positive achievements in its effort to narrow the gap, promote social development and bring about a change for the better in the backward minority areas.[118]

The White Paper's claims also set into bold relief an article published in the official Xinhua news agency in May 1991 which took issue with the notion that the right to self-determination could apply to the Tibetan people. This right, the article stated, applied only to 'the right of the oppressed nations and people to cast off the rule of imperialism and colonialism and to fight for independence'. Any attempt to disrupt a nation's unity and break its territorial integrity was 'against the goals and principles of the UN Charter'.[119]

The White Paper's optimistic account of its minorities policies was later implicitly challenged by the US State Department's human rights report for 1991:

In practice ... discrimination based on ethnic origin persists. The concept of a largely homogeneous Chinese people pervades the general thinking of the Han ethnic majority ... Most minority groups reside in areas they have traditionally inhabited, with standards of living often well below the national average. Government economic development policies have had some success in raising living standards but have at the same time disrupted traditional patterns of living.

The Communist Party's avowed policy of increasing minority representation in the Government and the CCP has resulted in members of minority groups accounting for 15 per cent of the deputies in the NPC. ... Ethnic minorities are effectively shut out of all but a few positions of real political and decision-making power. Some minorities resent Han officials holding key positions in minority autonomous regions. Ethnic minorities in Tibet, Xinjiang, and elsewhere have demonstrated against Han Chinese authority, and the underlying causes of unrest continue to fester. While martial law in Lhasa, Tibet's capital, was lifted in 1990, foreign visitors to Tibet in 1991 observed that there was still a pervasive armed police and military presence there. Reports reaching the West in 1991 suggested the existence of smoldering ethnic tension in Inner Mongolia. Central authorities have made it clear that they will not tolerate opposition to Beijing's rule in minority regions.[120]

Economic, social, and cultural rights were seen in the White Paper as extensions of the people's basic right of subsistence, which existed within restrictive parameters. These were that 'although China has basically solved the problem of food and clothing, its economy is still at a fairly low level, its standard of living falls considerably short of that in developed countries, and the pressure of a huge population and relative per capita paucity of resources will continue to restrict the socio-economic development and the improvement of people's lives'. Within these physical constraints, the Paper made the large claim of guaranteeing 'the basic necessities of every worker and his family'. It further claimed that:

Although Chinese workers have relatively low monetary wages, they enjoy a large amount of subsidies, including financial subsidies for housing, children's attendance at nursery and school and staple and non-staple foods, as well as social insurance such as medical treatment, industrial injury and retirement pension and many other welfare items, which are not counted in the wages. Statistics indicate that urban residents in China pay only 3–5 per cent of their living expenses for housing, communication and medical treatment.

The Report claimed that 1990 statistics showed that the average consumption level per capita of urban residents had increased from 149 yuan in 1952 to 1,442 yuan, an inflation-adjusted increase of 3.8 times. The only acknowledgement of the vast changes which had taken place, or were planned to take place, in the structure of social security and social welfare in the intervening post-Mao decade was encapsulated in the following sentence: 'Since China carried out reforms in 1979, past payment measures have been modified'.

The contemporary provision of medical services was also overstated: 'China provides free medical service in the urban state institutions and undertakings and co-operative medical service in most rural areas'. On the other hand, the level of unemployment was understated: in 1990, the Paper claimed, the urban and rural unemployment rate stood at only 2.5 per cent. It also distorted the real income gaps between rural and urban areas and within rural areas by taking a large percentage of urban dwellers in the top quintile (20 per cent), and comparing it with the bottom quintile, and universalizing the result. Thus, it claimed, China is 'one of the nations that register the lowest income gap in the world' because 20 per cent of urban dwellers with the highest disposable incomes earned only 2.5 times as much as the 20 per cent with the lowest incomes. In fact, it has been shown that in 1988 the income of the top quintile of the combined rural and urban population was 7.3 times that of the bottom quintile, while the corresponding quintile ratio for rural and urban populations was 5.9 and 3.2 respectively. It has also been estimated that by 1988 overall inequality in China appeared greater than in Taiwan in 1978 and perhaps greater than in South Korea, and possibly as high as in some of the more egalitarian south and south-east Asian countries.[121] By 1990, it was unlikely that this trend had been reversed.

A significant aspect of the White Paper was section ten, which contained a full and detailed summary of China's international human rights activities, and traced China's respect for human rights back to the Bandung Declaration of April 1955, and to a speech by Premier Zhou Enlai in May of the same year. Apart from China's support for the Declaration of the Right to Development, and its signature and ratification of seven UN human rights conventions relating to civil rights, the Paper cited China's 'active part in drafting and formulating international legal instruments on human rights within the UN', including the Convention against Torture and Other Cruel, Inhuman or Degrading Treatment or Punishment and the Declaration on the Protection of Rights of Persons Belonging to National, Ethnic, Religious, and Linguistic Minorities. While reiterating arguments on sovereignty and self-determination, the White Paper concluded:

China is ready to work with the international community in a continued and unremitting effort to build a just and reasonable new order of international relations and to realise the purpose of the United Nations to uphold and promote human rights and fundamental freedoms.

The White Paper was a dramatic declaration of the Chinese Government's intent to engage the international community in a debate over the condition of China's human rights. In the process, it showed it was prepared to accept the language of human rights and to make some concessions over priorities, as well as to admit to the justice of part of the international critique. At the same time it introduced a new right, 'the right to subsistence', which, although asserting the importance of economic, social, and cultural rights, also served to modify their application. It also made some claims about the condition of its rights which have been shown in the earlier part of this chapter to be either incorrect or no longer accurate. Some of these claims had also already been contradicted by the findings of Asia Watch, Amnesty International, and by the Report of the Australian Human Rights Delegation. Nevertheless, the White Paper was a significant document, a milestone in the history of China's human rights, not least because it was published in its entirety over succeeding days in the *People's Daily*, the country's most authoritative newspaper. As has been observed, it could thus be used as an authoritative basis on which citizens could challenge the government's human rights policies. If as a document it showed that China still had a long way to go on human rights, it also showed that China had already travelled some distance from its position in the early days of communist rule. The pressure of the international critique, and of its own domestic policies, had thus eventually forced a response which reached throughout the length and breadth of China, and was not contained merely within the international arena. It was one hopeful sign that the official, international position of China on human rights could no longer be compartmentalized, and that foreign pressure and pressures from within might, slowly but surely, have their impact on the actual condition of China's human rights.

Conclusion

> The existence of consciousness creates conflict . . . it is at those points at
> which the implicit consensus breaks down and needs articulation that
> social change occurs.
>
> Roberto Unger, *Law in Modern Society*

At the outset, this study supported the argument for the establishment of a basic right which incorporated both the civil and
political rights emphasized by Western liberal democracies and
the economic, social, and cultural rights endorsed by developing
and socialist states like China. The right to life, consisting of the
economic right to subsistence (the right to adequate food, clothing, shelter, and minimal health care) and the civil right to physical security (the right not to be subjected to murder, torture, or
other physical abuse) was seen as fulfilling this function. It provided a minimum standard of rights which enjoyed customary and
universal acceptance by the international community. The publication in October 1991 of China's White Paper, *Human Rights in
China*, has brought the argument full circle. In this document one
facet of the notion of the right to life, the right to subsistence,
was given priority. The White Paper thereby implicitly counterposed the right to subsistence, the economic aspect of the right
to life, against the civil aspect of the right to life. Yet it also sought
to defend China's record in civil and political rights. It thus indicated, on the one hand, convergence with the Western discourse
on human rights, and, on the other, divergence in favour of the
non-Western discourse. This balancing act indicated the profound
changes which, it has been argued, have occurred to the structure
and hierarchy of China's civil, political, economic, social, and cultural rights in the modernization period, themselves the outgrowth
of economic reform. These changes have been illustrated by the
comparisons which have been made between the requirements of
the International Bill of Rights, China's changing constitutional
provision of rights, and the informal and substantive rights which
Chinese people have actually been able to enjoy since 1949.

The Constitutions of 1954, 1975, and 1978 were in general con-
gruent with a rigidly controlled society characterized by an un-
mistakable Marxist 'trade-off' of civil and political rights for
economic, social, and cultural rights. The effective absence of civil

and political rights in the Mao era, despite their nominal guarantee in the constitutions, was thus in conflict with many requirements of the International Covenant on Civil and Political Rights.
The provisions of the 1982 Constitution, on the other hand, while
attempting to uphold the normal Marxist priorities, were in fact
out of step with the informal and substantive reality of all rights
in China, at least until June 1989. The effective cancellation by
laws and other constitutional articles of the civil and, to a lesser
extent, political rights contained in the Constitution contrasted
dramatically with citizens' increased access before June to greater
freedoms of movement, of speech, press, publication, association,
and assembly, and of the right to more personal space. This was
the case, even though at the beginning of this period the activists
of the Democracy Wall Movement received severe prison sentences, and even though civil rights of immunity were increasingly
circumscribed, particularly during anti-crime campaigns. The informal and substantive condition of civil and political freedoms
in this pre-June period, while not therefore conforming in many
respects with the requirements of the ICCPR, nevertheless came
closer than ever before to the spirit of many of its articles. The
expanded civil rights of expression were not, however, anchored
in any enabling legislation and were therefore vulnerable, as in
the Maoist era, to arbitrary cancellation at the leaders' whim. At
the formal international level, in contrast, the Chinese government gradually began to be drawn into activities related to human
rights and to sporadically support moves in the United Nations
to monitor the condition of human rights in other countries. Its
firm position on sovereignty and non-intervention was thus modified
in practice, while its conception of human rights was expanded to
encompass a notion of civil and political rights.

At the same time, the economic, social, and cultural rights which
Chinese citizens could actually enjoy in the modernization decade
diminished, so that the substantive condition of these rights contrasted dramatically with provisions of the 1982 Constitution, particularly in view of the fact that the constitution's extension of
many economic and social rights from 'working people' to 'citizens' nominally universalized access to them. The rights that could
be enjoyed thus also diverged from requirements of the International
Covenant on Economic, Social, and Cultural Rights. At the source
of this reversal was a switch in social philosophy during the modernization decade which was not matched by a corresponding

change in social welfare structures. Thus, divergence between the rigid norms embodied in the constitutions and laws and reflected in supporting institutions, and the changing informal condition of rights, demonstrated the degree to which actual social, political, and economic conditions had altered in China in the moderniza- tion decade, and was itself a symptom of the deep-seated social and political disturbances and the conditions of relative depriva- tion in living standards and in political and civil freedoms which produced and empowered the 1989 Democracy Movement.

The Chinese government's suppression of the Democracy Move- ment entailed the abuse of the basic human right to life, as well as of the freedoms of speech, assembly, association, freedom from arbitrary arrest and imprisonment, and freedom from torture, itself part of the right to physical security. It also entailed a further loss of legitimacy for the government, and the transfer of moral power to the people, whose expression of legitimate grievances in a non- violent form required a response more adequate than short-term violence. The political focus thus shifted from the people's grievances, which were implicitly acknowledged by the leadership, to the gov- ernment and its response. The challenge for the government was to respond to the people's grievances without undermining the process of economic reform. Moreover, because of the need to continue with reform, political stability was continually at risk. Therefore, a process of implicit 'renegotiation' began between the leaders and people, in which the government was obliged first to attempt to expand economic and social rights, then to resume the rhetoric of political reform and, finally, to concede some personal freedoms which did not impinge on politically sensitive areas. It also moved away from openly coercive instruments of social con- trol to the more socially acceptable use of the mechanism of the law, and of popular grass-roots mediation through neighbourhood and street committees. It sought to incorporate and neutralize alternative political viewpoints through the encouragement of 'multi-party' co-operation, expanding its own power and legitim- acy through a corporatist form of politics.

The problem was that the government was attempting to impose these solutions on a changed social and political reality, in which the old structures of economic and social rights, and in particu- lar the right to work, had broken down under the weight of eco- nomic reform. The government was confronted by the spread of poverty throughout China, and by its own diminishing share of total revenues, with the resulting loss of control over distributional decisions.[1] It is now clear that, in terms of social control the government is faced with the loss of the consensual value system and a condition of normlessness or *anomie* and lack of respect for authority which hinder the attempt to utilize *Gemeinschaft* practices of mediation and conciliation. At the same time, the government's use of the law primarily as an instrument of social control means that, as of old, the law can not be used as a vehicle for wresting people's rights from an adversarial state, even though it is no longer being used as a means whereby one class obtains control over other classes. While during 1991 some members of the intellectual elite made an effort to employ the law to protect their civil rights or to appeal administrative decisions and practices, the ordinary citizen is not only ignorant of the laws that exist, but perceives 'rule by law' as a state instrument of which he himself is the object. At a time of rising urban self-consciousness, the growth of a middle class influenced by the communications revolution, pressures from within the labour movement to obtain greater worker participation, and rising material and political expectations, neither coercion nor rule by law offer adequate mechanisms for ensuring social stability or social consensus.[2] Nor do they prove satisfactory vehicles for social control in the countryside, where grievances arising from a sense of relative deprivation are being resolved through physical conflict among peasants within and between villages, and where law as an instrument of coercion is incapable of replacing the respect for authority and the cohesive community value system which have been lost.

    Thus, the enduring characteristics which translated themselves from imperial times into the socialist era, the right to subsistence and an unequalized and marginalized bureaucratic legal system coexisting with traditional *Gemeinschaft* practices of mediation and conciliation, have both proved vulnerable in the reform era. Moreover, the form of the *Gesellschaft* system of law that was introduced after 1979 maintained the essentially patrimonial content of law as an instrument of the state, and was marked neither by the separation of powers, nor by autonomy and accessibility. The fact that in its White Paper on Human Rights the Chinese government affirmed the priority of subsistence rights, and then proceeded to make questionable claims about civil and political rights in China, may not, on the other hand, be such an irony if viewed simply as an expression of government aims and intent, rather than of government achievements. This, after all, was often the form which official pronouncements took in the Maoist era — programmatic aims were frequently projected as concrete achievements, and were commonly misunderstood as such by the world outside.

In the post-June 1989 era, it is clear that the Chinese government faces major dilemmas in the areas of both civil/political and economic/social/cultural rights. The almost single-minded pursuit of economic modernization has given way to a more complex effort to balance 'reform' and 'stability'. Given the close correlation which existed between economic reform and political instability in the pre-June period, and in view of the government's decision to continue with economic reform, it has been under pressure to improve general living standards by either maintaining, or replacing, existing social and economic institutions. But the partial destruction of the collective and the 'iron rice bowl', which had defined access to, financed, and distributed social services, meant that these services could no longer be maintained through such institutions. The World Bank's advice to China to institute a social security and social welfare system which would maintain general living standards in a reform era therefore necessitated the replacement of existing structures. Necessary changes included the abandonment of the practice of subsidizing prices of basic commodities in urban areas in order to proceed with further price reform, and the transfer of the social welfare and social security system out of the work unit, in order to facilitate the enforcement of the contract system and the rationalization of labour in urban enterprises. Both procedures have the potential to aggravate worker discontent and revive widespread perceptions of relative deprivation. The crucial issue has thus been the timing of the introduction of new social security and welfare schemes, so that a viable structure can be well in place before the economic reforms take full effect. Even then, the ability of the government to effect these reforms in the time planned is problematic, given the tendency of authorities at the local level to evade or deflect instructions from the centre, and given the workers' informal influence on enterprise decision making. More importantly, there is a crucial contradiction between the need for increased state intervention to underwrite and finance social reforms, particularly at a time of reduced central government revenue, and the simultaneous requirement to limit state intervention in order to ensure the unfettered expansion of the market.

A similar dilemma faces the government in its management of civil and political rights. The problem is not just one of what degree of civil rights to allow citizens, of what degree of press freedom, or of freedoms of speech, association, and assembly, to extend at any given time. Nor is it simply a matter of more laws and institutions. More fundamentally, the issue strikes at the uses and concept of the law itself. It is clear that the use of the law to protect citizens' rights requires the development of the autonomy of the legal system — the separation of the judiciary from the legislative and executive arms of government. Such a development, however, threatens the position of the Party as final arbiter, a function which has hitherto remained unchallenged, despite the post-1978 development of a substantial legal framework and legal institutions. In other words, in order to retain power, the Party has to be prepared to relinquish some. In addition, what is needed to guarantee the protection of citizens' rights is, in Max Weber's words, a change in the 'consensual understandings' which underlie the application and formulation of legal rules.[3]

To a certain extent the pressure for change in these 'consensual understandings' is a function of the outcome of the modernization process itself. Relevant structural outgrowths of China's reform include the increasing pluralism and differentiation of the society which is spawning a plethora of different interest groups and factions. They also include the communications revolution which serves to inform and integrate a growing middle class with rising political aspirations, as well as to alert it to the profound changes occurring in the former socialist world. Finally, they involve the growing familiarity with Western notions of law which is an inevitable function of the increasing contacts between China and the West through trade, technology transfer, educational exchanges, and personal channels.

On the other hand, we have seen that these developments in China have not to date altered the patrimonial uses of the law. As Weber has observed:

the mere *change of external conditions* is neither sufficient nor necessary to explain the changes in 'consensual understandings'. The really decisive element has always been *a new line of conduct* which then results either in a change of the meaning of the existing rules of law or in the creation of new rules of law.[4]

In China's case, this new line of conduct would appear first to require conscious attitudinal changes involving leadership recognition that to mediate the tension between reform and stability, a more effective, modern, and humane system of law has to be developed, whatever the threat to Party power. Such a change in attitudes can only occur as a result of the acknowledgement, at both elite and grass-roots level, that it is not only necessary, but crucial. The sense of urgency will be driven less by normative considerations than by the realization that the development of a system of law with rational-legal content is essential in order to avoid social disorder. Popular legal education about the distinction between the rule *of* law and rule *by* law will also be required to change citizens' perceptions.

Secondly, the new line of conduct involves the conscious imposition of legal change from above. This would include specific legislation for the protection of people's rights as well as structural change underwriting the separation of powers and the autonomy of the legal system, which, according to Weber, are a precondition of change.[5] These processes are all cumulative: unlike the expansion of economic, social, and cultural rights, whose essence is *timing* and which may be bestowed from above, the development of a legal consciousness in its best sense, and of appropriate legal and political institutions, requires *time*, and must grow from below, as well as be promoted from above. Time, however, is something that the Chinese people may not be prepared to vouchsafe their leaders. And enhanced power may not be something that China's current leaders are prepared to bestow upon their people.

In the final analysis, the continuation of the socialist system in China would appear to hinge, if not on the Western-style democratization of the political system, then on its liberalization. It will depend not on a retreat to neo-conservatism but on the leadership's ability to develop the characteristics of socialism with a human face, in line with the proposals originally advanced by dissenters in the first democracy movement of 1978–80. It will also depend on the government realizing that in the present era human rights are seen by the world's citizens as involving a mix of rights

— of civil and political, as well as economic, social, and cultural rights. In the wake of the political, economic, and social disruption attending the sudden collapse of communism in Eastern Europe and the former Soviet Union, the message to statesmen is that the management of human rights entails a balance, not a trade-off. The trade-off of economic, social, and cultural rights for civil and political rights is no more politically acceptable than is the reverse. The Chinese government's acknowledgement of this reality would be indicated by its acceptance that the basic right to life, which transcends state boundaries and political cultures, is both an economic and a civil right. In today's China, the economic right to life can no longer be counterposed against the civil right to life. For the right to subsistence and the right to physical security are but two sides of a single coin.

Chapter Notes

Notes to Preface

1. M. Agosin, 'Untitled', (transl. C. Kostopulus-Cooperman) *Human Rights Quarterly* 13 (August 1991) No. 3, 426.

Notes to Introduction

1. A. Kent, 'Waiting for Rights: China's Human Rights and China's Constitutions, 1949–1989', *Human Rights Quarterly*, 13 (May 1991), No. 2, 201.
2. R. Cohen, 'People's Republic of China: the Human Rights Exception', *Human Rights Quarterly, 9* (November 1987), No. 4, 448–549.
3. *Report of the Australian Human Rights Delegation to China*, 14–26 July 1991 (Canberra, Department of Foreign Affairs, September 1991).
4. See discussion of the issues in R. Wacks (ed.), *Civil Liberties in Hong Kong: Some Preliminary Observations* (Hong Kong, Oxford University Press, 1988; J.M.M. Chan, *Renquan zai Xianggang* ('Human Rights in Hong Kong') (Hong Kong, Wide Angle Press Ltd, 1990); and E. Lau, 'Future Fears', *Far Eastern Economic Review* (20 April 1989), 2.
5. The system of romanization used for Chinese characters in this work is the official Chinese *pinyin* system, except in the case of the name of the Nationalist Party, Kuomintang, and in the case of titles of Western books using the earlier Wade-Giles system.

Notes to Chapter 1

1. B.G. Ramcharan, 'Strategies for the International Protection of Human Rights in the 1990s', *Human Rights Quarterly* 13 (May 1991), No. 2, 155–6.
2. Human Rights Questions: Human Rights Situations and Reports of Special Rapporteurs and Representatives, 'Situation in Myanmar', UNGA Agenda item 98 (c), UN Doc. A/C. 3/46/L.43 (25 November 1991).
3. H. Bull, 'Human Rights and World Politics', in R. Pettmann (ed.), *Moral Claims in World Affairs* (Canberra, Australian National University Press, 1979), 79.
4. R.J. Vincent, *Human Rights and International Relations* (Cambridge, Cambridge University Press, 1986), 14.
5. Ibid. 8.
6. H. Shue, *Basic Rights: Subsistence, Affluence, and U.S. Foreign Policy* (Princeton, Princeton University Press, 1980) 52–3.
7. Bull, 'Human Rights', 79–81.
8. Vincent, *Human Rights*, 11.
9. Cited in J. Starke, 'Human Rights and International Law', in E. Kamenka and A.E.S. Tay (eds), *Human Rights* (London, Edward Arnold, 1978), 122.
10. The chronological development here referred to is not the classical model of human rights expounded by T.H. Marshall and R.P. Claude, among others,

which allots different human rights to different centuries, and to different European countries. According to this model, the liberal idea of civil rights forbidding interference with the individual is an eighteenth-century phenomenon, political and civil rights requiring legal accommodation to demands for equal rights of civic participation belong to the nineteenth century, and economic and social claims to the twentieth century. See T.H. Marshall, 'Freedom as a Factor in Social Development', in T.H. Marshall, *The Right to Welfare and Other Essays* (London, Heinemann, 1981), 157–75; and R.P. Claude, 'The Classical Model of Human Rights Development', in R.P. Claude (ed.), *Comparative Human Rights* (Baltimore, The Johns Hopkins University Press, 1976), 41–2. The model adopted here is based on the timing of the introduction of different rights into United Nations human rights instruments. It is the model which many Chinese human rights analysts combine with an historical discussion of the evolution of the concept of natural 'bourgeois' rights. One particularly interesting variant is Xu Bing's model of human rights development, divided into six stages: the development (1) from a hazy consciousness to a clear-cut theory; (2) from a theory to a political declaration; (3) from a political declaration to its incorporation into law; (4) from a human rights movement representing a minority of countries to one representing the world community; (5) from a capitalist slogan to a proletarian slogan; and (6) from domestic legal norms to international legal norms. See 'Renquan lilun de chansheng he lishi fazhan' ('The Origins and Historical Development of the Theory of Human Rights'), *Faxue yanjiu* ('Legal Studies') (1989) No. 3, 1–3.

11. P. Bailey, *Human Rights: Australia in an International Context* (Sydney, Butterworths, 1990), 1.

12. Ibid. 16.

13. E. Kamenka, 'Human Rights, Peoples' Rights', in J. Crawford (ed.), *The Rights of Peoples* (Oxford, Clarendon Press, 1988), 137.

14. Universal Declaration of Human Rights and International Covenant on Civil and Political Rights in *United Nations, Human Rights: A Compilation of International Instruments of the United Nations* (New York, United Nations, 1973), 1–3, 7–15. See also L. Henkin in R.R. Edwards, L. Henkin, and A.J. Nathan, *Human Rights in Contemporary China* (New York, Columbia University Press, 1986), 25–6.

15. See, for instance, I.D. Duchacek, *Rights and Liberties in the World Today: Constitutional Promise and Reality* (California, Clio Press, 1973).

16. Article 25, International Covenant on Civil and Political Rights, in *United Nations, Human Rights*, 11.

17. Article 25(1), Universal Declaration of Human Rights, in *United Nations, Human Rights*, 2–3.

18. Ibid. Articles 23–4.

19. P. Sieghart, cited in J. Crawford, 'The Rights of Peoples: "Peoples" or "Governments"?', in Crawford (ed.), *The Rights of Peoples*, 56–7.

20. Antonio Cassese, 'The Self-determination of Peoples', in L. Henkin (ed.), *The International Bill of Rights* (New York, Columbia University Press, 1981), 92–3, 109; and Vincent, *Human Rights*, 80.

21. Government of the Netherlands, *Human Rights and Foreign Policy* (The Hague, 1979), cited in P. Alston, 'Some Notes on the Concept of the Right to Development', in Daniel Prémont (ed.), *Essays on the Concept of a 'Right to Live'* (Brusselles, Bruylant 1988), 82.

22. Kamenka, 'Human Rights', 137–8.

23. Ibid. 137. See also discussion on tension between different kinds of rights in J. Barbalet, *Citizenship: Rights, Struggle and Class Inequality* (Milton Keynes, Open University Press, 1988), 2–28.

24. Bailey, *Human Rights*, 13–14. R.P. Claude distinguishes between the civil rights which protect freedom by forbidding interference with the individual, and

the positive civil and political rights, correlative with government protection and enforcement. See Claude, 'The Classical Model', 41.

25. Bailey, *Human Rights*, 20.

26. Peter Schneider, 'Social Rights and the Concept of Human Rights', in D.D. Raphael (ed.), *Political Theory and the Rights of Man* (London, Macmillan, 1967), 81. Chinese writers have also commented on this phenomenon of politicization, claiming not only that human rights have provided a 'pretext' for capitalist countries to attack the socialist system, but that they were used in the early eighties as a weapon in the struggle for 'hegemony' between the United States and the Soviet Union. See Shen Baoxiang, Wang Chengquan, and Li Zerui, 'Guanyu guoji lingyu de renquan wenti' ('On the Question of Human Rights in the International Arena'), *Hongqi* ('Red Flag') (1982) No. 8, 47. See also Liu Fengming, 'Renquan ji qi guoji shishi' ('Human Rights Law and its International Implementation', *Zhongguo fazhi bao* ('Chinese Legal System News'), 18 July 1984, 4.

27. W. Hayden, 'Human Rights: the Practical and Moral Imperative', Address to the Australian Parliamentary Group of Amnesty International in Canberra, 28 May 1987, 3.

28. For a discussion of these differences, see M. McDougal, H. Lasswell, and Lung-chu Chen, *Human Rights and World Public Order* (Yale, Yale University Press, 1980), 76–9; C.B. MacPherson, 'Problems of Human Rights in the Late 20th Century', in C. B. MacPherson, *The Rise and Fall of Economic Justice and Other Essays* (Oxford, Oxford University Press, 1985), 22–34; and I.F. Stone, 'The Rights of Gorbachev', *The New York Review of Books*, XXXVI, No. 2, 16 Feb. 1989, 3–7.

29. A. Tay, 'Marxism, Socialism and Human Rights', in Kamenka and Tay (eds.), *Human Rights*, 107.

30. Vincent, *Human Rights*, 76.

31. Alston, 'Some Notes', 78.

32. Marshall, 'Freedom as a Factor', 169; Claude (ed.), *Comparative Human Rights*, 43–6; and A. Kent, 'China: Human Rights or Social and Economic Rights?', in J. Girling (ed.), *Human Rights in the Asia-Pacific Region* (Canberra, Department of International Relations, Australian National University, 1991), 7–15.

33. Marshall, 'Freedom as a Factor', 169–70; Macpherson, 'Problems of Human Rights', 27. In the case of China, Simon Leys denies that in the Mao era there was any effective trade-off of civil and political rights for economic and social rights. See S. Leys, 'Les Droits de l'Homme en Chine' ('The Rights of Man in China') in S. Leys, *La Forêt en Feu: Essais sur la Culture et la Politique Chinoises* ('The Forest on Fire: Essays on Chinese Culture and Politics') (Paris, Hermann, 1983), 113–15.

34. Shue, *Basic Rights*, Ch. 3; Vincent, *Human Rights*, 89.

35. J. Girling, 'Introduction', *Human Rights*, 1–6. For a concise statement of this problem, see Marshall, 'Freedom as a Factor', 169.

36. J. Donnelly, 'Human Rights and Development: Complementary or Competing Concerns?', *World Politics*, 36 (1984), No. 2, 255–83.

37. M. Cranston, *What Are Human Rights?* (London, The Bodley Head, 1973), 7.

38. D. Lane, 'Human Rights under State Socialism', in R.P. Claude and B.H. Weston (eds.), *Human Rights in the World Community: Issues and Action* (Philadelphia, University of Pennsylvania Press, 1989), 124.

39. I. Kovacs, 'General Problems of Rights', in I. Szabo et al., *Socialist Concept of Human Rights* (Budapest, Hungarian Academy of Sciences, 1966), 11.

40. Ibid. 12.

41. Tay, 'Marxism, Socialism', 107.

42. I. Szabo, 'Fundamental Questions Concerning the Theory and History of Citizens' Rights', in *Socialist Concept*, 37.

43. Ibid. 74.

44. Hao Ru, 'Renquan de lishi he xianzhuang', ('The History and Present Condition of Human Rights'), *Renmin ribao* ('People's Daily'), 13 April 1982, 5.

45. Szabo, 'Fundamental Questions', 76–7.

46. Tay, 'Marxism, Socialism', 108–09.

47. Ibid.

48. Vincent, *Human Rights*, 31. See also J.P. Cabestan, 'L'État de la Legislation Chinoise en Matière de Droits de l'Homme et l'Organisation Judiciaire de la Chine Populaire au Regard des Normes Internationales' ('The Condition of Chinese Legislation as Regards the Rights of Man and the Judicial Organisation of People's China in Relation to International Norms'), in L. Koch-Miramond, J.-P. Cabestan, F. Aubin, Y. Chevrier (eds.), *La Chine et les Droits de l'Homme* ('China and the Rights of Man') (Paris, l'Harmattan, Amnesty International, 1991), 84.

49. Ibid. 19–27.

50. G.W. Shepherd, 'Transnational Development of Human Rights: The Third World Crucible', in V.P. Nanda, R. Scaritt, G.W. Shepherd (eds.), *Global Human Rights: Public Policies, Comparative Measures, and NGO Strategies* (Colorado, Westview Press, 1980), 215.

51. For instance, Kamenka argues that the solution is to accept the priority of first generation rights and to treat all rights as involving balance, care, and complexity, Kamenka, 'Human Rights, People's Rights', 139. A. Pollis and P. Schwab argue the need for a 're-evaluation' of human rights, A. Pollis, P. Schwab (eds.), *Human Rights: Cultural and Ideological Perspectives*, (New York, Praeger, 1980), 1.

52. Shue, *Basic Rights*, 26. See also S. Harris, 'Human Rights and Australia's Foreign Policy', in Girling (ed.), *Human Rights*, 94.

53. Shue, *Basic Rights*, 20.

54. Vincent, *Human Rights*, 125.

55. Shue, *Basic Rights*, 19.

56. Ibid. 90. See also J. Kleinig, 'Human Rights, Legal Rights and Social Change', in Kamenka and Tay (eds.), *Human Rights*, 36–7.

57. Cited in Shepherd, 'Transnational Development', 215.

58. See Prémont (ed.), *Essays on the Concept of a 'Right to Live'*.

59. O. Veyrat, ' Du "Droit de Vivre" comme Concept Educatif dans l'Enseignment des Droits de l'Homme' ('On "the Right to Life" as an Educational Concept in Teaching about the Rights of Man'), in Prémont, *Essays*, 57.

60. T.C. van Boven, 'The Need to Stop Deliberate Violations of the Right to Life', in Prémont, *Essays*, 286.

61. M.L. Balanda, 'Le Droit de Vivre' ('The Right to Life'), in Prémont, *Essays*, 32–5.

62. Y. Khushalani, 'Right to Live', in Prémont, *Essays*, 283.

63. For elementary rules, see H.L.A. Hart, *The Concept of Law* (Oxford, Clarendon Press, 1961).

64. Bull, 'Human Rights', 90.

65. Shue, *Basic Rights*, 27–8.

66. L. Henkin, *The Age of Rights* (New York, Columbia University Press, 1990), 21.

67. D. Prémont, 'Le Droit à la Vie, Plus Petit Dénominateur Commun entre les Droits de l'Homme, La Paix et le Développement' ('The Right to Life, Lowest Common Denominator in the Rights of Man, Peace and Development'), in Prémont, *Essays*, 294.

68. See Cranston, *What are Human Rights?*, 68.

69. Xu Wenli, Feb. 1980, cited in G. Barmé and J. Minford (eds.), *Seeds of Fire: Chinese Voices of Conscience* (New York, Hill and Wang, 1988), 304–5.

70. Zhao Ziyang, 'Advance along the Road of Socialism with Chinese

Characteristics', Report Delivered to the 13th National Congress of the CCP, 25 October 1987, *Beijing Review*, 30 (9 Nov. 1987), No. 45, XXII.

71. D. Shelton, 'State Responsibility for Aiding and Abetting Flagrant Violations of Human Rights', in Prémont, *Essays*, 221.

72. For an argument against cultural relativism see A. Tay, 'China and Legal Pluralism', *Bulletin of the Australian Society of Legal Philosophy, 8* (December 1984), No. 31, 23–43.

73. See, for instance, J. Hsiung (ed.), *Human Rights in East Asia: a Cultural Perspective* (New York, Paragon, 1985), 3–28.

74. Vincent, *Human Rights*, 53. For Vincent's cultural relativism argument, summarized below, see also 54.

75. Ibid. 52–3.

76. See, for instance, A.J. Nathan, 'The Place of Values in Cross-Cultural Studies: The Example of Democracy and China', in P.A. Cohen and M. Goldman, *Ideas Across Cultures: Essays on Chinese Thought in Honour of Benjamin I. Schwartz* (Cambridge, Harvard University Press, 1990), 293–314; and Nathan, 'Is There a Universal Concept of Human Rights?' *Human Rights Tribune*, 11 (April 1991), No. 2, 4–7.

77. J. Crawford, 'The Rights of Peoples: Some Conclusions', in Crawford (ed.), *The Rights of Peoples*, 168–71.

78. J. Donnelly, *Universal Human Rights in Theory and Practice* (Ithaca, Cornell University Press, 1989), 148.

79. A. Cassese, 'Political Self-Determination — Old Concepts and New Developments', cited in Kamenka, 'Human Rights', 136.

80. G. Klintworth, *'The Right to Intervene' in the Domestic Affairs of States*, Working Paper 243 (Canberra, Strategic and Defence Studies Centre, Australian National University, 1991), 2.

81. Henkin, *The Age of Rights*, 56.

82. Ibid. 53.

83. See, for instance, the ambiguities in an article in the official journal, *Beijing Review*: 'China has no objection to the United Nations expressing concern in a proper way over consistent and large-scale human rights violations in a given country, but it opposes the interference in other countries' internal affairs under the pretext of defending human rights'. See Ma Jun, 'Human Rights: China's Perspective', *Beijing Review*, 31 (28 November 1988), No. 48, 8.

84. Henkin, *The Age of Rights*, 25.

85. Ibid. 21.

86. Part ll, Article 2, *United Nations, Human Rights*, 8.

87. Article 2 (1), ibid.

88. B.G. Ramcharan, *The Concept and Present Status of International Protection of Human Rights: Forty Years after the Universal Declaration* (Dordrecht, Martinus Nijhoff, 1989), 58–9.

89. Henkin, *The Age of Rights*, 22.

90. See also I. Russell, 'Australian Human Rights Policy from Evatt to Evans' in P. Van Ness and I. Russell, *Australia's Human Rights Diplomacy* (Canberra, Australian Foreign Policy Publishing Programme, Australian National University and Allen and Unwin, 1992 forthcoming).

91. R. Falk, *Human Rights and State Sovereignty* (New York, Holmes and Meier, 1981), 33; and Vincent, *Human Rights*, 99.

92. J. Starke, 'Human Rights and International Law', in Kamenka and Tay (eds.), *Human Rights*, 125.

93. Klintworth, *'The Right to Intervene'*, 8.

94. See Henkin, *The Age of Rights*, 22–4; Donnelly, *Universal Human Rights*, 213–18.

95. Ibid. 218–20.
96. Ibid. 126–7.
97. Crawford, 'The Rights of Peoples: Some Conclusions' in Crawford (ed.), *The Rights of Peoples*, 162. A similar argument may be found in Wang Delu and Jiang Shihe (eds.), *Renquan xuanyan* ('Declarations of Human Rights') (Beijing, *Qiushi* chubanshe, April 1989), 4–5. They point out that the development of human rights from a concept mainly serving the capitalist class to a term embracing the 'common interests of all mankind' meant that 'no political system in the world, whatever its ideology, could publicly oppose the concept of human rights'.
98. Henkin, *The Age of Rights*, 17.
99. J.C. Strouse and R.P. Claude, 'Empirical Comparative Rights Research — Some Preliminary Tests of Development Hypotheses', in Claude (ed.), *Comparative Human Rights*, 51.
100. Ibid.
101. For distinction drawn between 'moral', 'positive', and 'empirical' rights, see Bull, 'Human Rights', 79–81; between 'instrumentation' and 'compliance' in legal rights, see J. Seymour, 'Human Rights and the Law in the People's Republic of China', in V.C. Falkenheim and I.J. Kim (eds.), *Chinese Politics from Mao to Deng* (New York, Paragon, 1989), 272–3; for distinction between the 'theory' and 'practice' of rights, see Vincent, *Human Rights*, 2–4; for between 'nominal' and 'substantive' rights, see A.J. Nathan, 'Is There a Universal Concept?', No. 2, 4–7; and for between 'formal' and 'informal' rights, see A. Kent, *Human Rights in the People's Republic of China: National and International Dimensions* (Canberra, Peace Research Centre, Australian National University, 1990).
102. See Claude (ed.), *Comparative Human Rights*, 51.
103. This approach has been adopted in the path-breaking work of R.R. Edwards, L. Henkin, and A.J. Nathan, *Human Rights in Contemporary China* (New York, Columbia University Press, 1986): but here the emphasis is more on the comparison between national and international norms via comparisons with Chinese constitutions, and less on the charting of the informal exercise of those rights. It is also adopted in J. Seymour, 'Human Rights and the Law', 271–297. See also A. Kent, 'Waiting for Rights: China's Human Rights and China's Constitutions', *Human Rights Quarterly* 13 (1991), No. 2, 170–20. China's acceptance of international law as part of PRC law is demonstrated in A.H.Y. Chen, *An Introduction to the Legal System of the People's Republic of China* (Singapore, Butterworths Asia, 1992), 103.
104. Y. Ghai, 'The Rule of Law in Africa: Reflections on the Limits of Constitutionalism', Conference Papers, Ninth Commonwealth Law Conference, Auckland, May 1990, 495–9.
105. W. Safran, 'Civil Liberties in Democracies: Constitutional Norms, Practices, and Problems of Comparison', in Nanda, Scaritt and Shepherd (eds.), *Global Human Rights*, 196.

Notes to Chapter 2

1. M. Dutton, *Policing and Punishment in China: From Patriarchy to 'the People'* (Cambridge, Cambridge University Press, 1992, forthcoming), 350.
2. J.C. Hsiung (ed.), *Human Rights in East Asia: A Cultural Perspective* (New York, Paragon House, 1985), 13; Fei Xiaotong, *China's Gentry: Essays in Rural–Urban Relations* (Chicago, University of Chicago Press, 1953), 77–9; V. Shue, *The Reach of the State: Sketches of the Chinese Body Politic* (Stanford, Stanford University Press, 1988), 89; and citation of Tang Tsou in M. Goldman, 'China's Sprouts of Democracy', *Ethics and International Affairs*, 4 (1990), 72.

3. B. Schwartz, 'On Attitudes towards Law in China' reprinted in J. Cohen, *The Criminal Process in the People's Republic of China, 1949–1963: An Introduction* (Cambridge, Harvard University Press, 1968), 63. See also F. Aubin, 'Traditions Chinoises, et Droits de l'Homme' ('Chinese Traditions, and the Rights of Man') in L. Koch-Miramond, J.-P. Cabestan, F. Aubin, and F. Chevrier, *La Chine et Les Droits de l'Homme* ('China and the Rights of Man') (Paris, l'Harmattan, 1991), 17–19.

4. Schwartz, 'On Attitudes towards Law', 64.

5. R.M. Unger, *Law in Modern Society: Toward a Criticism of Social Theory* (The Free Press, New York, 1976), 94.

6. The modern words for power and rights are different characters but are also homophones. See debate on *quanli* ('rights') and *quanli* ('power') in Zhang Chunjin, *Renquan lun* ('On Human Rights') (Tianjin, Renmin chubanshe, 1988), 66–7.

7. Wang Gungwu, *Power, Rights and Duties in Chinese History: the 40th George Ernest Morrison Lecture in Ethnology*, (Canberra, Australian National University, 1979), 6–7.

8. Schwartz, 'On Attitudes towards Law', 65.

9. A.E.S. Tay and E. Kamenka, 'Elevating Law in the People's Republic of China', *Bulletin of the Australian Society of Legal Philosophy*, 9 (March 1985) No. 32, 69.

10. Dutton, *Policing and Punishment*, 25.

11. See Unger, *Law in Modern Society*, 98; Aubin, 'Traditions Chinoises', 19–34; and Schwartz, 'On Attitudes towards the Law', 67.

12. Ibid.

13. Unger, *Law in Modern Society*, 102.

14. Ibid. 103.

15. Ibid. 104.

16. D. Bodde and C. Morris, *Law in Imperial China* (Cambridge, Harvard University Press, 1967), 50–1.

17. Dutton, *Policing and Punishment*, 88.

18. A.H.Y. Chen, 'Civil Liberties in China: Some Preliminary Observations', in R. Wacks (ed.), *Civil Liberties in Hong Kong* (Hong Kong, Oxford University Press, 1988), 109. Cf. T.E. Greiff, 'The Principle of Human Rights in Nationalist China: John C.H. Wu and the Ideological Origins of the 1946 Constitution', *The China Quarterly* (September 1985), No. 103, 450.

19. See J.F. Copper, F. Michael, and Yuan-li Wu, *Human Rights in Post-Mao China* (Boulder, Westview Press, 1985), 11–12.

20. Goldman, 'China's Sprouts', 72.

21. Chen, 'Civil Liberties', 108–9; and Aubin, 'Les Traditions Chinoises', 19–34.

22. Cited in H. Shue, *Basic Rights: Subsistence, Affluence, and U.S. Foreign Policy* (Princeton, Princeton University Press, 1980), 28.

23. Cited ibid.

24. J.P. Brady, *Justice and Politics in People's China: Legal Order or Continuing Revolution?* (London, Academic Press, 1982), 32.

25. Ibid.

26. L. Pye, *The Mandarin and the Cadre: China's Political Cultures* (Ann Arbor, Center for Chinese Studies, University of Michigan, 1988), 39.

27. Ibid. 40–1.

28. Ibid. 42.

29. A.J. Nathan, *Chinese Democracy* (New York, Alfred A. Knopf, 1985), X–XI; and Chen, 'Civil Liberties', 100–10.

30. Nathan, *Chinese Democracy*, 51.

31. A.J. Nathan, 'Sources of Chinese Human Rights Thinking', in R.R. Edwards, L. Henkin, and A.J. Nathan, *Human Rights in Contemporary China* (New York, Columbia University Press, 1986), 149.

246   NOTES TO PAGES 38–43

32. Ibid. 148.
33. B. Schwartz, *In Search of Wealth and Power: Yen Fu and the West* (Cambridge, Harvard University Press, 1964), 136, 141; and Nathan, 'Sources', 155–7.
34. Wang Gungwu, *Power, Rights and Duties*, 16.
35. Ibid. 18
36. Ibid. 17.
37. Ibid.
38. J.B. Grieder, *Hu Shih and the Chinese Renaissance: Liberalism in the Chinese Revolution, 1917–1937* (Cambridge, Harvard University Press, 1970), 330.
39. For analysis of this question, see D.C. Price, 'Constitutional Alternatives and Democracy in the Revolution of 1911', in P.A. Cohen and M. Goldman, *Ideas across Cultures: Essays on Chinese Thought in Honor of Benjamin I. Schwartz* (Cambridge, Harvard University Press, 1990), 224–60.
40. Ibid. 238.
41. Ibid. 260.
42. Yang Kai, *Human Rights in China: History, Disputes and Regional Influence*, NPCSD Working Paper No. 9 (Ontario, York University, February 1992), 4.
43. Chen, 'Civil Liberties', 111, citing E.C.Y. Tseng, 'Democratic and Authoritarian Elements in Twentieth-Century Chinese Political Thought', unpublished Ph.D thesis, New York University, 1968, 103, 114.
44. Nathan, *Chinese Democracy*, xii.
45. C. Tan, *Chinese Political Thought in the Twentieth Century* (New York, Doubleday and Co., 1971), 227.
46. Hu Shi, 'Renquan yu yuefa' ('Human Rights and the Provisional Constitution'), *Xinyue* ('Crescent Moon'), April 1929, cited in Tan, 227.
47. Hu Shi, 'Women shenma shihou cai keyou xianfa?' ('When Will We Have a Constitution?'), *Xinyue* ('Crescent Moon'), June 1929, cited in Tan, 227.
48. Chen, 'Civil Liberties in China', 137, f.26.
49. T. Narramore, *Luo Longji and Chinese Liberalism, 1928–32* (Canberra, Department of Far Eastern History, Australian National University, 1985), Papers on Far Eastern History 32, 174.
50. Ibid.
51. Ibid. 172.
52. Ibid. 170.
53. Luo Longji, 'Lun renquan' ('On Human Rights'), in Hu Shi and others, *Renquan lunji* ('Collected Essays on Human Rights') (Shanghai, *Xinyue* Shudian, 1930), 60–73.
54. Ibid. 66–7.
55. Zhou Jingwen (ed.), *Renquan yundong zhuan lunji* ('Selected Essays on the Human Rights Movement') (Hong Kong, *Shidai piping* ('Modern Critique'), 1941), reprint.
56. Qin Yingjun, 'Renquanpai zhengzhi sixiang qianxi' ('A Brief Analysis of the Political Thought of the Human Rights School'), *Shixue yuekan* ('Historical Studies Monthly') in *Fuyin baokan ziliao* (Reprinted Material from Newspapers and Periodicals), K4, Zhongguo xiandai shi ('Contemporary Chinese History'), 1 (1987), 67.
57. Ibid.
58. Gong Yongkang, Liu Wenzhu, Sun Youcai, 'Qianlun renquanpai de zhengzhi sixiang' ('A Brief Discussion of the Political Thought of the Human Rights School'), *Liaoning shifan daxue xuebao* ('Academic Journal of Liaoning University'), in *Fuyin baokan ziliao*, K4, Modern Chinese History, 2 (1987), 28. See also Liu Jianqing, 'Renquanpai lunlue' ('A Brief Discussion of the Human Rights School'), *Fuyin baokan*, 5 (1987), 77–82.
59. For the nominal rights in the Kuomintang constitution of 1946, see Greiff, 'The Principle of Human Rights', 445–8.

60. Chien Ssu, 1960, translated in J.A. Cohen and Hungdah Chiu, *People's China and International Law, A Documentary Study*, Vol. 1 (Princeton, Princeton University Press, 1974), 609.

61. Ibid. 607.

62. See A. Chen, 'Civil Liberties', 113–15.

63. Mao Zedong, 'Introductory Remarks to *The Communist*', 14 Oct 1939, *Selected Works of Mao Tse-tung* (London, Lawrence and Wishart, 1954), 3, 57.

64. Mao Zedong, 'On New Democracy', 28 Jan. 1940, *Selected Works*, 3, 120–1.

65. For discussion of these terms and Mao's theory of the state, see S. Schram, 'Decentralisation in a Unitary State: Theory and Practice 1940–1984' in S. Schram (ed.), *The Scope of State Power in China* (Hong Kong, The Chinese University Press, 1985), 90–2.

66. Cited in ibid. 90.

67. Mao Tse-tung, 'On the Correct Handling of Contradictions Among the People'. 27 February 1957, *Selected Works of Mao Tse-tung*, V (Beijing, Foreign Languages Press, 1977).

68. Subsequent post-Maoist rationalizations of the Maoist position on human rights have offered a number of explanations for this early view:

(a) After 1949 the people had become masters of the country, so that a human rights problem no longer existed;

(b) human rights were seen as a slogan of the bourgeoisie;

(c) the extreme leftism of the revolution brought contempt for, and abuse of, basic human rights; and

(d) the doctrine of human rights was at that time restricted to the narrow interpretation of civil and political rights, and only later developed its socio-economic and developmental aspects.

See Xu Bing, 'Renquan lilun de chansheng he lishi fazhan' ('The Creation and Historical Development of Human Rights') *Faxue yanjiu* ('Legal Studies'), 1; and see Wang Delu and Jiang Shihe (eds.), *Renquan xuanyan* ('Declarations of Human Rights') (Beijing, *Qiushi* Chubanshe, 1989), 4.

69. 1978 Constitution, Art. 44, in *Peking Review* 21 (17 March 1978), No. 11, 13.

70. L. Henkin, 'The Human Rights Idea in Contemporary China: A Comparative Perspective', in Edwards, Henkin, and Nathan, *Human Rights*, 32. Although the Chinese constitutions contain no prohibition of torture, it is prohibited by law. See J. Seymour, 'Human Rights and the Law in the People's Republic of China', in V.C. Falkenheim and I.J. Kim (eds.), *Chinese Politics from Mao to Deng* (New York, Paragon House, 1989), 295–6, f. 42.

71. A. Tay, 'Communist Visions, Communist Realities and the Role of Law', *Bulletin of the Australian Society of Legal Philosophy*, 13 (December 1989), No. 51, 240.

72. 1982 Constitution, Art. 51, 4 Dec. 1982, *Beijing Review*, 25 (27 Dec. 1982), No. 52, 18.

73. Schwartz, 'On Attitudes towards Law', 70.

74. R.M. Pfeffer, 'Crime and Punishment: China and the United States,' in J.A. Cohen (ed.), *Contemporary Chinese Law: Research Problems and Perspectives* (Cambridge, Harvard University Press, 1970), 261.

75. A. Tay, 'China and Legal Pluralism', *Bulletin of the Australian Society of Legal Philosophy*, 8 (Dec. 1984), No. 31, 33.

76. Shao-chuan Leng and Hungdah Chiu, *Criminal Justice in Post-Mao China: Analysis and Documents* (Albany, State University of New York Press, 1985), 7.

77. A.T. Turk, 'Political Deviance and Popular Justice in China: Lessons for the West', in R.J. Troyer, J.P. Clark, and D.G. Rojek (eds.), *Social Control in the People's Republic of China* (New York, Praeger, 1989), 41.

78. 'China', *Country Reports on Human Rights Practices for 1988*, Reports

Submitted to the Committee on Foreign Relations, U.S. Senate, and Committee on Foreign Affairs, U.S. House of Representatives, by the Department of State, (Washington D.C., U.S. Government Printing Office, 1989), 167.

79. Kong Meng, 'A Criticism of the Theories of Bourgeois International Law Concerning the Subjects of International Law and Recognition of States', *Studies in International Problems* (1960) No. 2, 44–51, cited in Cohen and Chiu, *People's China and International Law*, 98. On the state as basic unit of international law, see J. Crawford, 'The Rights of Peoples: "Peoples" or "Governments"?', in J. Crawford (ed.), *The Rights of Peoples* (Oxford, Clarendon Press, 1988), 55–6; and Hungdah Chiu, 'The Nature of International Law and the Problem of a Universal System', in Shao-chuan Leng and Hundah Chiu (eds.), *Law in Chinese Foreign Policy: Communist China and Selected Problems of International Law* (New York, Oceana Press, 1972), 1–33.

80. See also S. Ogden, 'The Approach of the Chinese Communists to the Study of International Law, State Sovereignty and the International System', *The China Quarterly* (June 1977), No. 70, 327.

Notes to Chapter 3

1. J.A. Cohen, 'China's Changing Constitution', *The China Quarterly* (December 1978), No. 76, 798. See also T.E. Greiff, 'The Principle of Human Rights in Nationalist China: John C.H. Wu and the Ideological Origins of the 1946 Constitution', *The China Quarterly* (September 1985), No. 103, 441–61.

2. A.J. Nathan, 'Political Rights in Chinese Constitutions' in R.R. Edwards, L. Henkin, and A. Nathan, *Human Rights in Contemporary China* (New York, Columbia University Press, 1986), 103.

3. This is the relationship described by Cohen, 'China's Changing Constitution', 839.

4. See also A. Kent, 'Waiting for Rights: China's Human Rights and China's Constitutions, 1949–1989', *Human Rights Quarterly* 13 (May 1991), No. 2, 182.

5. For discussion of impact of class on Chinese society, see R.C. Kraus, *Class Conflict in Chinese Socialism* (New York, Columbia University Press, 1981).

6. See M. Goldman, 'China's Sprouts of Democracy', *Ethics and International Affairs* 4 (1990), 86–7.

7. M. Dutton, *Policing and Punishment in China: From Patriarchy to the People* (Cambridge, Cambridge University Press, 1992 (forthcoming)), 219.

8. *Important Documents of the First Plenary Session of the Chinese People's Political Consultative Conference* (Peking, Foreign Languages Press, 1948), 1–20, cited in F. Michael, 'Law: A Tool of Power', in Yuan-li Wu et al., *Human Rights in the People's Republic of China* (Boulder, Westview Press, 1988), 36.

9. Shao-chuan Leng with Hungdah Chiu, *Criminal Justice in Post-Mao China: Analysis and Documents* (Albany, State University of New York, 1985), 11–13 and 177–86; and Nathan, 'Political Rights', 104.

10. Translated in Leng and Chiu, *Criminal Justice*, 183.

11. Translated in J.A. Cohen, *The Criminal Process in the People's Republic of China, 1949–1963: An Introduction* (Cambridge, Harvard University Press, 1968), 301.

12. For analyses of the 1954 Constitution, see ibid; Cohen, 'China's Changing Constitution', 798–802; and Leng and Chiu, *Criminal Justice*, 13–15.

13. See Preamble and Art. 1, 1954 Constitution, in T.H.E. Chen, *The Chinese Communist Regime: Documents and Commentary* (New York, Pall Mall Press, 1967), 75–7.

14. Ibid. 90–1.
15. Li Guangcan, *Woguo gongmin di jiben quanli he yiwu* ('The Fundamental Rights and Duties of the Citizens of Our Country') (Beijing, People's Press, 1956), 7–8, cited in Leng and Chiu, *Criminal Justice*, 15.
16. ICESCR Art. 2.2; see also ICCPR Art. 2.1.
17. See, for instance, yearly reports of Department of State, 'China', *Country Reports on Human Rights Practices*, Reports to the Committee on Foreign Affairs, House of Representatives and the Committee on Foreign Relations, US Senate (Washington DC, US Printing Office); in particular, Reports for 1991, February 1992, 827–9. See also D. Norbu, *Red Star over Tibet* (London, Collins, 1974).
18. Cohen, 'China's Changing Constitution', 839.
19. Ibid. 829–31.
20. 1975 Constitution, Art. 12, *Peking Review* 18 (24 Jan. 1975), No. 4, 15.
21. As in 1954 Constitution, Arts. 10, 90, and 97.
22. As in ibid. Arts. 76, 85 and 89. See also Nathan, 'Political Rights', 111–12; and Cohen, 'China's Changing Constitution', 802–5.
23. As in 1954 Constitution. Art. 78; and 1975 Constitution, Art. 25.
24. Ibid.
25. For above political rights, see ibid. Arts. 2, 3, and 13.
26. 1978 Constitution, *Peking Review* 21 (17 March 1978), No. 11, Arts. 1 and 2. See also Cohen, 'China's Changing Constitution', 827–36; and Nathan, 'Political Rights', 112–15.
27. 1978 Constitution, Arts. 41 and 43.
28. Ibid. Arts. 15–17; and Art. 21.
29. Nathan, 'Political Rights', 114.
30. Cohen, *The Criminal Process*, 50–1.
31. Ibid. This is an excellent source for the structure and functioning of China's judicial and penal system in the Maoist era.
32. See Leng and Chiu, *Criminal Justice*, 21. The main legal documents relevant to these institutions were (1) the 1954, 1975, and 1978 Constitutions; (2) the Organic Law of the People's Courts, Sept. 1954; (3) the Organic Law for the People's Procuratorate, Sept. 1954; (4) the Act for Punishment of Counter-revolution, 1951; (5) the Provisional Act on Guarding State Secrets, 1951 (republished in 1980); (6) Measures for the Control of Counter-revolutionaries, 1952; (6) the Act of Reform through Labour, 1954; (7) the Provisional Measures for Dealing with the Release of Reform through Labour Criminals at the Expiration of their Term of Imprisonment and for Placing them and Getting Employment, 1954; (8) the Arrest and Detention Act, 1954; (9) the Decision of the Standing Committee of the National People's Congress Relating to Control of Counter-revolutionaries in All Cases Being Decided upon by Judgement of a People's Court, 1956; (10) the Decision of the State Council Relating to Problems of Rehabilitation through Labour, 1957; and (11) the Security Administration Punishment Act, 1957. See Amnesty International, *Political Imprisonment in the People's Republic of China* (London, Amnesty International, 1978), 2.
33. Cohen, *The Criminal Process*, 48.
34. Leng and Chiu, *Criminal Justice*, 14; Amnesty International, *Political Imprisonment*, 37; and Leng Shao-chuan, *Justice in Communist China: A Survey of the Judicial System of the Chinese People's Republic* (New York, Oceana Publications, Inc., 1967), 106.
35. Ibid. 84–6.
36. Ibid. 122. For detailed analysis of the structure and role of legal institutions, see A.H.Y. Chen, *An Introduction to the Legal System of the People's Republic of China* (Singapore, Butterworths Asia, 1992), 104–51.
37. J.-P. Cabestan, 'L'État de la Législation Chinoise en Matière de Droits de l'Homme et l'Organization Judiciaire de la Chine Populaire au Regard des Normes

Internationales' ('The State of Chinese Legislation in Relation to the Rights of Man and Judicial Organization Relating to International Norms'), L. Koch-Miramond, J.-P. Cabestan, F. Aubin, Y. Chevrier (eds.), *La Chine et les Droits de l'Homme* ('China and the Rights of Man') (Paris, l'Harmattan, Amnesty International, 1991), 88.

38. Leng, *Justice in China*, 125; Cohen, *The Criminal Process*, 19–20; F. Schurmann, *Ideology and Organization in Communist China* (Berkeley, University of California Press, 1968), 368–80; and J.P. Clark, 'Conflict Management outside the Courtrooms of China', in R.J. Troyer, J.P. Clark and D.G. Rojek (eds.), *Social Control in the People's Republic of China* (New York, Praeger, 1991), 62–7.

39. Cohen, *The Criminal Process*, 19.

40. Dutton, *Policing and Punishment*, 200–10; and Zhang Qingwu (ed.), *Hukou dengji changshi* ('Basic Information on Household Registration') (Beijing, Falu chubanshe, 1983), 1–21, 52–68; and for regulations, 75–88.

41. Dutton, *Policing and Punishment*, 211.

42. J.P. Béja, 'Une Société sous Surveillance' ('A Society under Surveillance'), in Koch-Miramond, Cabestan, Aubin, and Chevrier (eds.), *La Chine*, 127–32.

43. See Leng and Chiu, *Criminal Justice*, 25–6; Amnesty International, *Political Imprisonment*, 58–9; and Hungdah Chiu, 'China's Changing Criminal Justice System', *Current History* 87 (Sept. 1988), No. 53, 270–1.

44. See text in Cohen, *The Criminal Process*, 249–50.

45. Amnesty International, *Political Imprisonment*, 58.

46. Ibid. 84.

47. Ibid. 86–94.

48. Ibid. 86. For personal accounts of the different forms and conditions of imprisonment, see Bao Ruowang and R. Chelminski, *Prisoner of Mao* (New York, Coward, McCann, and Geogohan, 1973); A. and A. Rickett, *Prisoners of Liberation* (New York, Doubleday, 1973); Lai Ying, *The Thirty-sixth Way: A Personal Account of Imprisonment and Escape from Red China* (London, Constable and Co., 1970); and Yang Xiguang, *Captive Spirits* (forthcoming). For secondary sources, see M.K. Whyte, 'Corrective Labor Camps in China', *Asian Survey*, XIII (March 1973), No. 3, 253–69; Whyte, 'Corrective Labor Camp Inmates and Political Rituals', in M.K. Whyte, *Small Groups and Political Rituals in China* (Berkeley, University of California Press, 1974), 189–92; *Livre Blanc sur le Travail Forcé dans la Republique Populaire de Chine* ('White Paper on Forced Labour in the People's Republic of China'), Commission Internationale contre le Régime Concentrationnaire (Paris, Centre International d'Édition et de Documentation, 1958), 2 Vols.; and Hongda H. Wu, *Laogai — The Chinese Gulag*. Transl. T. Slingerland (Boulder, Westview Press, 1992).

49. Amnesty International, *Political Imprisonment*, 91.

50. Wei Jingsheng, 'Q1-A, Twentieth Century Bastille', translated in G. Barmé and J. Minford, *Seeds of Fire: Chinese Voices of Conscience* (New York, Hill and Wang, 1988), 279–89.

51. Amnesty International, *Political Imprisonment*, 95–101.

52. Act of the People's Republic of China for Punishment of Counter-revolutionaries, 1951, Art. 2, transl. Leng and Chiu, *Criminal Justice*, 177.

53. Amnesty International, *Political Imprisonment*, 14.

54. Mao Zedong, 'On the Correct Handling of Contradictions among the People', 27 February 1957, *Selected Works of Mao Tse-tung*, V (Beijing, Foreign Languages Press, 1977), 385.

55. Amnesty International, *Political Imprisonment*, 13.

56. Cohen, *The Criminal Process*, 9–18; Leng and Chiu, *Criminal Justice*, 10–28; and Shao-chuan Leng, *Justice in Communist China*, 45–74.

57. F.C. Teiwes, *Politics and Purges in China: Rectification and the Decline of Party Norms, 1950–1965* (New York, M.E. Sharpe, 1979), 105–383; Leng, *Justice*

in Communist China, 29–44; and P. Moody, *Opposition and Dissent in Contemporary China* (California, Hoover Institute, 1977).

58. See R. MacFarquhar, *The Hundred Flowers* (London, Stevens, 1960); and Mu Fusheng, *The Wilting of the Hundred Flowers: Free Thought in China Today* (London, Heinemann, 1962).

59. Leng and Chiu, *Criminal Justice*, 27.

60. Michael Weisskopf, 'Ex-Inmate Recalls Life in China's Gulag', *The Washington Post*, 12 February 1982, A1, A4–45, cited Leng and Chiu, *Criminal Justice*, 27.

61. Zhou Enlai, 'Report to the National People's Congress, June 1957', cited Amnesty International, *Political Imprisonment*, 29.

62. Norbu, *Red Star over Tibet*, 160–72.

63. See accounts in Hua Linshan, *Les Années Rouges* ('The Red Years') (Paris, Éditions du Seuil, 1987); Gao Yuan, *Born Red: A Chronicle of the Cultural Revolution* (Stanford, Stanford University Press, 1987); A. Thurston, *Enemies of the People: The Ordeal of the Intellectuals in China's Great Cultural Revolution* (Cambridge, Harvard University Press, 1988); Hong Yung Lee, *The Politics of the Cultural Revolution: A Case Study* (Berkeley, University of California Press, 1978); Nien Cheng, *Life and Death in Shanghai* (London, Grafton Books, 1986); N. Hunter, *Shanghai Journal: An Eyewitness Account of the Cultural Revolution* (Boston, Beacon Press, 1969); and A.E. Kent, *Indictment without Trial: the Case of Liu Shao-ch'i* (Canberra, Department of International Relations, Australian National University, 1969). See also 'Twenty Years On: Four Views of the Cultural Revolution', *The China Quarterly* (December 1986), No. 108, 597–651.

64. Amnesty International, *Political Imprisonment*, 20.

65. *A Great Trial in Chinese History* (Beijing, New World Press, 1981), 20–1; 173–84, cited in Leng and Chiu, *Criminal Justice*, 32, f.72.

66. Jin Jitong, 'Reverse Unjust and Wrong Verdicts', *Chinese Encyclopedia Yearbook*, 1981, 189, cited in Leng and Chiu, *Criminal Justice*, 40.

67. J.R. Townsend, *Political Participation in Communist China* (Berkeley, University of California Press, 1967), 199.

68. See, for instance, A. Kent, 'Red and Expert: The Revolution in Education at Shanghai Teachers' University, 1975–76', *The China Quarterly* (June 1981), No. 86, 304–21; and A. Kent, 'Grass Roots Politics in Shanghai Teachers' University, 1975–1976', in S.A. FitzGerald and P. Hewitt (eds.), *China in the Seventies: Australian Perspectives* (Canberra, Contemporary China Centre, Australian National University, 1980) 73–99.

69. R.R. Edwards, 'Civil and Social Rights: Theory and Practice in Chinese Law Today', in Edwards, Henkin, and Nathan, *Human Rights*, 67.

70. 1954 Constitution, Preamble.

71. Ibid. Chapt. 1, Art. 19.

72. For concept of citizenship in Western society, see T. Marshall, *Citizenship and Social Class and Other Essays* (Cambridge, Cambridge University Press, 1950); and J. Barbalet, *Citizenship: Rights, Struggle and Class Inequality* (Milton Keynes, Open University Press, 1988).

73. Huang Xiaojing and Yang Xiao, 'From Iron Ricebowls to Labour Markets: Reforming the Social Security System', in Bruce Reynolds (ed.), *Reform in China: Challenges and Choices — A Summary and Analysis of the CESRRI Survey Prepared by the Staff of the Chinese Economic System Reform Research Institute* (New York, M.E. Sharpe, 1987), 148.

74. Universal Declaration of Human Rights, Art. 25 (1): 'Everyone has the right to a standard of living adequate for the health and well-being of himself and of his family, including food, clothing, housing, and medical care and necessary social services, and the right to security in the event of unemployment, sickness, disability, widowhood, old age or other lack of livelihood in circumstances beyond his control'.

75. 1954 Constitution, Art. 91, 1978 Constitution, Art. 48.

76. 1975 Constitution, Art. 9.

77. 1954 Constitution, Arts. 94–5, 1978 Constitution, Art. 52.

78. 1975 Constitution, Art. 12.

79. The strike by a foreign teacher at Shanghai Teacher's University in late 1975 was seen by Chinese colleagues as a justified, if unorthodox, procedure, because of the guarantee of the right to strike in the 1975 Constitution.

80. 1975 Constitution, Art. 27.

81. 1954 Constitution, Arts. 92–3, 1978 Constitution, Arts. 49–50.

82. 1978 Constitution, Art. 50.

83. On equality of poverty, see D.S.G. Goodman, 'Communism in East Asia: the Production Imperative, Legitimacy and Reform', in Goodman (ed.), *Communism and Reform in East Asia* (London, Frank Cass, 1988), 4. Even in the Maoist era, the 'relativity' of this 'equality' of distribution has been emphasised by Deborah Davis, who points out that 'keeping social services as a government monopoly and allocating them by job status also meant that the quality of service varied by the rank of the job, not by the price or cost of the service'; D. Davis, 'Chinese Social Welfare: Policies and Outcomes', *The China Quarterly* (September 1989), No. 119, 579.

84. S.C. Thomas, 'Social and Economic Rights Performance in Developing Countries: The People's Republic of China in Comparative Perspective, *Policy Studies Journal* 15 (September 1986), No. 1, 92, estimate on the basis of the PQLI figures supplied in J.W. Sewell, R.E. Feinberg, and V. Kallab, *US Foreign Policy and the Third World*, Overseas Development Council, U.S. Third World Policy Perspectives, No. 3 (New Brunswick, Transaction Books, 1985).

85. State Statistical Bureau, 'Changes in the Life-style of Urban Residents', Decade of Reform, VIII, *Beijing Review* 31 (14 Nov. 1988), No. 46, 26.

86. See, for instance, M. Oksenberg, 'On Learning from China', in M. Oksenberg (ed.), *China's Developmental Experience* (New York, Praeger, 1973), 2.

87. G. White, 'Chinese Development Strategy after Mao', in G. White, R. Murray, and C. White (eds.), *Revolutionary Socialist Development in the Third World* (Sussex, Harvester Press, 1983), 155.

88. A.P. Liu, 'How Can We Evaluate Communist China's Political System Performance', *Issues and Studies*, 23 (February 1987), No. 2, 82–121; R.H. Myers, 'How Can We Evaluate Communist China's Economic Development Performance', in ibid. 122–51.

89. Liu, 'How Can We Evaluate', 101.

90. Ibid. 115–16.

91. G. White, 'The New Economic Paradigm: Towards Market Socialism', in R. Benewick and P. Wingrove (eds.), *Reforming the Revolution: China in Transition* (London, Macmillan Education, 1988), 82.

92. M. Huang, 'Human Rights in a Revolutionary Society: The Case of the People's Republic of China', in A. Pollis and P. Schwab, *Human Rights: Cultural and Ideological Perspectives* (New York, Praeger, 1980), 67.

93. R.F. Dernberger, 'The Chinese Search for the Path of Self-Sustained Growth in the 1980s: An Assessment' in *China under the Four Modernisations*, Part 1, Selected Papers Submitted to the Joint Economic Committee of the U.S. Congress (Washington D.C., U.S. Government Printing Office, 13 August 1982), 21, 24; cf. A Chinese estimate of the increase in peasant income between 1954–78 as 70 yuan: see Du Runsheng, 'Prosperity to Some, to Most, Then to All', 20 December 1985, in Du Runsheng, *Many People, Little Land: China's Rural Economic Reform* (Beijing, Foreign Languages Press, 1989), 193.

94. Ibid. 193. By 1984, according to Du, that gap had jumped to 2.6 times.

95. Oksenberg, 'On Learning from China', 10–11.

96. Ibid. 7.

97. Ibid. 8.

98. See Chapter 6; and *China under the Four Modernisations*, Parts 1 and 2.

99. See ICESCR, Art. 7; 1978 Constitution, Art. 49, 44.

100. cf. Liu on Lardy.

101. See Leung Wing-Yue, *Smashing the Iron Rice Pot: Workers and Unions in China's Market Socialism* (Hong Kong, Asia Monitor Resource Center, 1988), 17–36.

102. See, for instance, interview with Ma Chunku, All-China Federation of Trade Unions, 'How Do Chinese Trade Unions Function?', *Peking Review* 21 (8 December 1978), No. 49, 5–7.

103. See ICESCR, Art. 9, 12; 1978 Constitution, Art. 50.

104. J.P. Emerson, 'The Labour Force of China, 1957–80', in *The Four Modernisations*, Part 1, 236.

105. A.G. Walder, 'Organised Dependence and Cultures of Authority in Chinese Industry' *The Journal of Asian Studies* 63 (November 1983), No. 1, 53–4.

106. V.W Sidel, 'Medicine and Public Health', in Oksenberg, *China's Developmental Experience*, 110–20; J. Horn, *Away with All Pests: An English Surgeon in People's China* (London, Hamlyn, 1969); and D.M. Lampton, 'Performance and the Chinese Political System: A Preliminary Assessment of Education and Health Policies', *The China Quarterly* (September 1978), No. 75, 509–39.

107. See World Bank, *China: Socialist Economic Development*, 111, 'The Social Sectors: Population, Health, Nutrition, and Education', (Washington D.C., The World Bank, 1981), 7.

108. Ibid. 8.

109. L. Orleans, 'China's Urban Population: Concepts, Conglomerations, and Concerns' in *China under the Four Modernisations*, Part 1, 293.

110. World Bank, *China: Socialist Economic Development*, 111, 7.

111. Ibid. 135.

112. Kent, 'Red and Expert', 316.

113. World Bank, *China: Socialist Economic Development*, 111, 134.

114. M.K. Whyte, 'Inequality and Stratification in China', *The China Quarterly* (December 1975), No. 64, 685.

115. Ibid. 687.

116. Ibid. 688.

117. A.G. Walder, 'Some Ironies of the Maoist Legacy in Industry', in M. Selden, V. Lippit (eds.), *The Transition to Socialism in China* (New York, M.E. Sharpe, 1982), 226, 231–32.

118. Emerson, 'The Labor Force', 236.

119. Whyte, 'Inequality and Stratification', 695.

120. World Bank, *China: Socialist Economic Development*, The Main Report, cited in Thomas, 'Social and Economic Rights', 95.

Notes to Chapter 4

1. A.G. Walder, 'Wage Reform and the Web of Factory Interests', *The China Quarterly* (March 1987), No. 109, 38.

2. A. Wedell-Wedellsborg, 'Literature in the Post-Mao Years', in R. Benewick and P. Wingrove (eds.), *Reforming the Revolution: China in Transition* (London, Macmillan Education, 1988), 194.

3. This point has been made by Bill Brugger in 'Ideology, Legitimacy and

Marxist Theory in Contemporary China', in J.Y.S. Cheng (ed.), *China: Modernization in the 1980s* (Hong Kong, The Chinese University Press, 1989), 10.

4. The informal sphere in contemporary China is effectively delineated in P. Link, R. Madsen, and P. Pickowicz (eds.), *Unofficial China: Popular Culture and Thought in the People's Republic* (Boulder, Westview Press, 1989). See also A. Kent, 'Red and Expert: The Revolution in Education at Shanghai Teachers' University, 1975–76', *The China Quarterly* (June 1981), No. 86, 304–21; and F. Lewins, 'Everyday Culture as Institutional Culture: The Case of Chinese Intellectuals,' unpublished paper, 1992.

5. See Walder, 'Wage Reform'; and 'Factory and Manager in an Era of Reform', *The China Quarterly* (June 1989), No. 118, 249–53.

6. Ibid.

7. Xue Muqiao, 'Adjust the National Economy and Promote Overall Balance', *Jingji yanjiu* ('Economic Research') (20 February 1981) No. 2, 27, cited in R. Dernberger, 'The Chinese Search for the Path of Self-sustained Growth in the 1980s: An Assessment', in *China under the Four Modernizations*, Selected Papers Submitted to the Joint Economic Committee, Congress of the United States (Washington D.C., US Government Printing Office, 1982). Pt. 1, 28.

8. G. White, 'The New Economic Paradigm: Towards Market Socialism', in Benewick and Wingrove (eds.), *Reforming the Revolution*, 84.

9. M. Lockett, 'The Urban Economy', in Benewick and Wingrove (eds.), *Reforming the Revolution*, 112.

10. Xue Muqiao, *China's Socialist Economy* (Beijing, Foreign Languages Press, 1986), 10.

11. Liu Guoguang, Liang Wensen and others, *China's Economy in 2000* (Beijing, New World Press, 1987), 20–1. See also Ma Hong, *New Strategy for China's Economy* (Beijing, New World Press, 1983), 26–7.

12. See Communique in *Peking Review* 21 (29 December 1978), No. 52; and A.H.Y. Chen, 'Civil Liberties in China: Some Preliminary Observations', in R. Wacks (ed.), *Civil Liberties in Hong Kong* (Hong Kong, Oxford University Press, 1988), 120.

13. G. Young, 'Party Reforms', in Cheng (ed.), *China: Modernization*, 66.

14. The former were articulated in Su Shaozhi and Feng Lanrui, 'Wuchanjieji qude zhengquan hou de shehui fazhan jieduan wenti' ('The Question of the Stages of Social Development after the Seizure of Power by the Proletariat') *Jingji yanjiu* ('Economic Research'), (1979), No. 5 14–19; the latter by Zhao Ziyang, 'Advance along the Road of Socialism with Chinese Characteristics', Report Delivered to the 13th National Congress of the Communist Party of China on 25 October 1987', *Beijing Review*, 30 (9 November 1987), No. 45, *iii–vi*. See also Brugger, 'Ideology, Legitimacy', 6–7.

15. J. Cheng, 'Whither China's Reform?', in Cheng (ed.), *China: Modernization*, 654.

16. Liu Guoguang, Liang Wensen and others, *China's Economy*, 310.

17. Ibid.

18. Xue Muqiao, *China's Socialist Economy*, 92.

19. For consequences of modernization policy, see G. White, 'Towards Market Socialism', 85–90.

20. T. Saich, 'Modernization and Participation in the People's Republic of China', in Cheng (ed.). *China: Modernization*, 42.

21. For Deng Xiaoping's promise to move towards 'socialist democracy' and 'socialist legality', see 'Dang he guojia lingdao zhidu de gaige' ('Reform of the Leadership System of our Party and State'), in *Deng Xiaoping wenxuan* ('The Selected Works of Deng Xiaoping') (Beijing, Renmin chubanshe, 1983), 282.

22. R. Lowenthal, 'On Established Communist Party Regimes', *Studies in Comparative Communism* 7 (Winter 1974), No. 4.

23. Hu Sheng, 'On the Revision of the Constitution', *Beijing Review* 25 (3 May 1982), No. 18, 15.

24. For analyses of the 1982 Constitution, see Chen, 'Civil Liberties in China', 120–4; R.R. Edwards, L. Henkin, and A. Nathan, *Human Rights in Contemporary China* (New York, Columbia University Press, 1986); Shao-chuan Leng and Hungdah Chiu, *Criminal Justice in Post-Mao China: Analysis and Documents* (Albany, State University of New York Press, 1985), 40–4; T. Saich, 'The Fourth Constitution of the People's Republic of China', *Review of Socialist Law* 9 (1983), No. 2, 113–24; *Zhonghua renmin gongheguo xianfa lunwenji* ('Collected Essays on the Constitution of the Chinese People's Republic') (Hong Kong, Xianggang zhongwen daxue, 1990); and Byron S.J. Weng (ed.), 'Studies on the Constitutional Law of the People's Republic of China', *Chinese Law and Government XVI* (Summer–Fall 1983), Nos. 2–3, 3–192. See also Hu Sheng, 'On the Revision', 15; Peng Zhen, 'Explanations on the Draft of the Revised Constitution of the People's Republic of China, 22 April 1982', *Beijing Review* 25 (10 May 1982), No. 19, 18–26; and 'Report on the Draft of the Revised Constitution of the People's Republic of China', *Beijing Review* 25 (13 Dec. 1982), No. 50, 9–11. For Chinese analysis of specific rights guaranteed under the 1982 Constitution, see *Gongmin shouce* ('Citizen's Handbook') (Beijing, Huayi chubanshe, 1988), 60–145; and Wu Jialin (ed.), *Xianfaxue* ('Constitutional Studies') (Beijing, Qunzhong chubanshe, 1983), 364–97.

25. These aims were outlined by Peng Zhen, the vice-chairman of the constitutional revision committee, in introducing the new constitution. See Peng Zhen, 'Explanations on the Draft', 18–26; Edwards, Henkin, and Nathan, *Human Rights*, 115.

26. 1982 Constitution, Article 33.

27. Article 39.

28. Articles 37 and 38.

29. Article 41.

30. Articles 126, 131.

31. Hu Sheng, 'On the Revision', 17.

32. Article 40.

33. Article 36.

34. For an excellent discussion of China's population policy, see Australian International Development Assistance Bureau, *Recent Population Policy in China*, Sector Report No. 4, prepared by Terence Hull (Canberra, 1991).

35. Article 41.

36. Article 51.

37. Article 28.

38. M. Oksenberg and R. Bush, 'China's Political Evolution: 1972–82', 1–19, cited in B.L. McCormick, *Political Reform in Post-Mao China: Democracy and Bureaucracy in a Leninist State* (Berkeley, University of California Press, 1990), 2.

39. Saich, 'The Fourth Constitution', 113.

40. Ibid. 115–17.

41. Articles 79–84; Articles 93–4; and Leng and Chiu, *Criminal Justice*, 41–2.

42. Articles 74 and 75.

43. Article 3, 1982 Constitution; Article 21, 1978 Constitution.

44. Article 97.

45. Articles 112–22.

46. Articles 66–7; Article 95. See also Hu Sheng, 'On the Revision', 17.

47. Articles 99–110.

48. Article 111.

49. Nathan, 'Political Rights', 119.

50. Ibid. 120.

51. Leng, 43.

52. Chen, 'Civil Liberties in China', 123.

53. Chen Chumao (ed.), *Shehuizhuyi fazhi tonglun* ('A General Survey of the Socialist Legal System') (Nanjing, Nanjing daxue chubanshe, 1986), 16.

54. Leng and Chiu, *Criminal Justice*, 46.

55. See also E. Epstein, 'China's Legal Reforms', in Kuan Hsin-chi and M. Brosseau, *China Review* (Hong Kong, The Chinese University Press, 1991), 92–3.

56. See *Minfa yuanli* ('Basic Principles of Civil Law') (Beijing, Falu chubanshe, 1986) 37, and W.C. Jones (ed.), *Basic Principles of Civil Law in China* (New York, M.E. Sharpe, 1989), 37. In contrast, see list in E. Epstein, which omits the category of 'freedom', and therefore claims that 'personal rights are comparable to social and economic rights rather than political rights'. See Epstein, 'China's Legal Reforms', 9.26–9.27. In fact, freedom is a civil right (in Chinese usage, a 'political' right), while the 'right to life', as discussed, is both a civil and an economic right.

57. J. Cohen, 'Law and Leadership in China', *Far Eastern Economic Review* (13 July 1989), 23.

58. Chen, 'Civil Liberties in China', 123.

59. See Wu Jialin (ed), *Xianfaxue*, 380–1.

60. See *The Criminal Law and Criminal Procedure Law of China* (Beijing, Foreign Languages Press, 1984), 217–51.

61. Ibid. 246–7.

62. Ibid. 226–8; 218.

63. See Amnesty International, 'The Death Penalty in China', January 1989, ASA 17/01/89, 3–13; on the uses of the law, F. Michael, 'Law: A Tool of Power', in Yuan-li Wu et al., *Human Rights in the People's Republic of China* (Boulder, Westview, 1988), 50–3.

64. Amnesty International, 'The Death Penalty', 1–4.

65. Ibid. 5–7.

66. Leng and Chiu, *Criminal Justice*, 46.

67. Criminal Law and Criminal Procedure Law, 37–9.

68. On the failure of the legal system to uphold civil rights, see J. Seymour, 'Human Rights and the Law in the People's Republic of China', in V.C. Falkenheim and I.J. Kim (eds.) *Chinese Politics from Mao to Deng* (New York, Paragon, 1989), 271–97.

69. Amnesty International, *China, Violations of Human Rights: Prisoners of Conscience and the Death Penalty in the People's Republic of China'* (London, Amnesty International Publications, 1984), 9–10.

70. Ibid. 56–9.

71. Cited in the *Report of the Australian Human Rights Delegation to China, 14–26 July 1991* (Canberra, Department of Foreign Affairs, September 1991), 26.

72. Ibid. 20–35. This Report contains a detailed description of the functions of these different organs.

73. Ibid. 29–32.

74. Ibid. 32–3. For both *laogai* and *laojiao* systems, see Hongdah H. Wu, *Laogai — The Chinese Gulag*, Transl. T. Slingerland (Boulder, Westview Press, 1992).

75. R.R. Edwards, 'Civil and Social Rights: Theory and Practice in Chinese Law Today', in Edwards, Henkin, and Nathan, *Human Rights*, 63.

76. McCormick, *Political Reform*, 114.

77. See Lawasia and Tibet Information Network, *Defying the Dragon: China and Human Rights in Tibet* (Manila, Lawasia Human Rights Committee, 1991), 21. For information on the Chinese suppression of the 1956–7 rebellion in eastern Tibet, during which 87,000 Tibetans were reportedly killed, see ibid. 1; see also B. Martin, *Tibet: the Current Situation and its Background*, Current Issues

Paper, No. 8 (Canberra, Legislative Research Service, Parliament of Australia, 1987).

78. Lawasia and T.I.N., *Defying the Dragon*, 47. For official Chinese position on human rights in Tibet just prior to the declaration of martial law in Tibet, see 'Tibet: Human Rights and Religion', *Beijing Review* 32 (27 February 1989), 24–7.

79. For problems in implementation, see Seymour, 'Human Rights and the Law', 237–70.

80. McCormick, *Political Reform*, 135.

81. Ibid. 133.

82. P. Link, 'Hand-copied Entertainment Fiction from the Cultural Revolution', in Link, Madsen, Pickowicz (eds.), *Unofficial China*, 17–36. See also G. Barmé and J. Minford (eds.), *Seeds of Fire: Chinese Voices of Conscience* (New York, Hill and Wang 1988); and H.F. Siu and Z. Stern, (eds.), *Mao's Harvest: Voices from China's New Generation* (Oxford, Oxford University Press, 1983).

83. P.P. Pickowicz, 'Popular Cinema and Political Thought in Post-Mao China: Reflections on Official Pronouncements, Film, and the Film Audience', in Link, Madsen, and Pickowicz (eds.), *Unofficial China*, 40.

84. See also H. Harding, *China's Second Revolution: Reform after Mao* (Washington D.C., The Brookings Institution, 1987), 174–8.

85. Liu Peng, Zheng Lansun, *Xin guannian — guannian biange mianmian guan* ('New Concepts — Every Aspect of the Change in Concepts'), (Beijing, Zhonguo xinqiao chubanshe gongsi, 1989), 1–218. The authors underlined the importance of a change of concepts to the successful carrying out of the 10 years of reform, and pinpointed the failure to change old concepts as an important cause of any failures in the reform. See also T.B. Gold, 'After Comradeship: Personal Relations in China since the Cultural Revolution', *The China Quarterly* (December 1985), No. 104, 657–75.

86. K. Hartford, 'The Political Economy behind Beijing Spring', in T. Saich (ed.), *The Chinese People's Movement: Perspectives on Spring 1989* (New York, M.E. Sharpe, 1990), 50–82.

87. Hou Meixian, (ed.), *Zhenxi ni de quanli: gongmin falu quanli guwen,* ('Value your Rights — Advice on the Legal Rights of the Citizen') (Jingji guanli chubanshe, Beijing, 1987). At the same time, the legal and constitutional restraints on the exercise of civil rights in a socialist system were acknowledged, and the inseparability of the rights and duties of socialist 'citizens' emphasized, 11–12. See also *Gongmin shouce ('The Citizen's Handbook')*, (Beijing, Huayi chubanshe 1988); for rights, 60–145; for duties, 147–74.

88. A. Nathan, *Chinese Democracy* (New York, Alfred A. Knopf, 1985), 195–6.

89. Deng Xiaoping, 'Dang he guojia lingdao di gaige' ('The Reform of Party and State Leadership'), August 1980, *Deng Xiaoping wenxuan, (The Selected Works of Deng Xiaoping)*, (Beijing, Beijing renmin chubanshe), 1983, 134. For his call on 30 October 1979 for the development of socialist democracy and a socialist legal system, see Li Zhongji, Xu Yaoxin and Wei Li (eds.), *Shehui zhuyi gaige de shi* ('A History of Socialist Reform') (Beijing, Qiushi chubanshe, 1988), 566.

90. Zhao Ziyang, 'Advance along the Road'. For assessments of the implementation of these policies, see J.P. Burns, 'China's Governance: Political Reform in a Turbulent Environment', *The China Quarterly* (September 1989), No. 119, 481–518; and You Ji, 'Politics of China's Post-Mao Reforms: From the CCP's 13th Party Congress to the Dawn of Beijing Students' Demonstrations', MA thesis (Canberra, Australian National University, August 1989).

91. Zhao Ziyang,' Advance along the Road', *xx*.

92. 'Senate Committee on Foreign Relations and House Committee on Foreign Affairs, 'China', *Country Reports on Human Rights Practices for 1988*, 101st Congress, 1st session (1989), 771.

93. Zhao Ziyang, 'Advance along the Road', xx.

94. For instance, the *Beijing Review* cites 14 surveys on popular attitudes to reform. *Beijing Review* 30 (29 June 1987), 22. Surveys include an August 1989 poll co-sponsored by the Institute of Sociology, CASS and the State Statistical Bureau, reported in *Liaowang and China Daily*, 11 February 1989; '1987 Survey of the Political Psychology of Citizens in China', *Inside China Mainland* 11 (May 1989), No. 5, issue No. 125, 1-3; public opinion surveys in Bruce Reynolds (ed.), *Reform in China*, 147-87; and Min Qi, *Zhongguo zhengzhi wenhua: minzhu zhengzhi nanchan di shehui xinli yinsu* ('Chinese Political Culture: Social Psychology and the Birthpangs of Democratic Politics') (Yunnan, Yunnan renmin chubanshe, February 1989).

95. L. Dittmer, 'China in 1988: The Continuing Dilemma of Socialist Reform', *Asian Survey* XXIX (January 1989), No. 1, 16.

96. Ibid. 16.

97. *Beijing Review* 32 (17 April 1989), No. 16, 5.

98. *China Daily*, 7 April 1989.

99. Burns, 'China's Governance', 510-11. See also M.D. Swaine, 'China Faces the 1990s: A System in Crisis', *Problems of Communism XXXIX* (May–June 1990), 20-7.

100. McCormick, *Political Reform*, 142.

101. Burns, 'China's Governance', 511-16. For a contrary view, see Li Zhongjie, Xu Yaoxin and Wei Li (eds.), *Shehuizhuyi gaige shi* ('A History of Socialist Reform') (Beijing, Chunqiu chubaushe, 1988) 565-77.

102. You Ji, 'Politics of China's Post-Mao Reforms', 208.

103. See, for example, H.K. Jacobson and M. Oksenberg, *China's Participation in the IMF, World Bank and Gatt: Toward a Global Economic Order* (Ann Arbor, University of Michigan Press, 1990).

104. See Guowuyuan xinwen bangongshi, *Zhongguo de renquan zhuangkuang* (Beijing, Zhongyang wenxian chubanshe, October 1991), 65-6. In English translation, Information Office of the State Council of the People's Republic, *Human Rights in China* (November 1991), 57; and Chapter 2.

105. See S. Kim, *China, the United Nations and World Order* (Princeton, Princeton University Press, 1979), 485; and J.F. Copper, 'Defining Human Rights', in Yuan-li Wu et al., *Human Rights in the People's Republic of China* (Boulder, Westview Press, 1988), 15.

106. Based on my analysis of China's voting patterns recorded in the UNGA *Resolutions and Decisions Adopted by the General Assembly, Press Releases* GA/4548-7814, 1971-1988, 26th-43rd session, UN, New York. See also R. Cohen, 'People's Republic of China: The Human Rights Exception', *Human Rights Quarterly* 9 (November 1987), No. 4, 537-8.

107. *Peking Review* 20 (11 March 1977), No. 11, 23-4.

108. See UNGA Resolutions, Press Releases GA/4598-6546, 1971-1981, 26th-36th sessions.

109. Cohen, 'People's Republic of China', 537.

110. 1986 Press release GA/7272, 40th session, 13 December 1985, res. 40/114, 461-3. It reaffirmed that 'all human rights are indivisible and interdependent and that the promotion and protection of one category of rights can never exempt or excuse States from the promotion and protection of the other rights' and stated that 'the full realization of civil and political rights is inseparably linked with the enjoyment of economic, social and cultural rights'.

111. See Commission on Human Rights, Report on the 45th Session (30 January-10 March 1989), Economic and Social Council, Official Records 1989, Supplement 2, E/1989/20, E/CN.4/1989/86. For the resolution on Chile, see 'Situation of Human Rights and Fundamental Freedoms in Chile', 1989/62, 144-6; for the

decision on Burma, see 1989/112, 178; on civil and political rights resolutions, in order, see 1989/31, 90–1; 1989/24, 78–80; 1989/32, 92–3; 1989/38, 106; 1989/39, 107; 1989/56, 136; 1989/51, 126; 1989/64, 148–9.

112. Guowuyuan xinwen bangongshi, *Zhongguo de renquan zhuangkuang*, 65–6; Information Office of the State Council of the People's Republic, *Human Rights in China*, 57–8.

113. Ibid.

114. Ibid. 58–9.

115. See Li Haibo, 'China Applauds Human Rights', *Beijing Review* 31 (19–25 December 1988), No. 51, 5–6.

116. Cohen, 'The People's Republic of China', 538–89. See also G. Chan, *China and International Organizations: Participation in Non-Governmental Organizations since 1971* (Hong Kong, Oxford University Press, 1989).

117. A. Kent, 'Human Rights in China: the Formal Framework', Briefing to the Ministerial Seminar for the Australian Human Rights Delegation to China, July 1991, unpublished paper, 10.

118. Xiao Weiyun, Luo Haocai, Wu Xieying, 'Makesi zhuyi zenmayang kan "renquan" wenti' ('How Marxism Views the Question of Human Rights') *Hongqi* ('*Red Flag*') (1979), No. 5, 43. For the following citations, see 45–8.

119. Sheng Zuhong, 'Renquan yu fazhi' ('Human Rights and the Legal System'), *Minzhu yu fazhi* ('Democracy and the Legal System') (September 1979), 2, 19–20.

120. See, for instance, *Xianfa zidian* ('Constitutional Dictionary') (Jilin, Jilin chubanshe, 1988), 5; *Faxue zidian* ('A Legal Dictionary') (Shanghai, Cishu chubanshe, 1980), 8–9; Lin Rongnian and Zhang Jinfan, 'Tan renquan wenti' ('A Discussion of the Question of Human Rights') *Xuexi yu tansuo* ('Study and Exploration') (1980), No. 1, 30–7; Wang Delu and Jiang Shihe (eds.), *Renquan xuanyan* ('Declarations of Human Rights') (Beijing, *Qiushi* chubanshe, April 1989), 1–6; and *Jiandan shehui kexue zidian* ('A Concise Dictionary of the Social Sciences') (Shanghai cidian chubanshe, 1982), 17.

121. *Peking Review* 20 (11 March 1977), No. 11, 24.

122. Xu Bing, 'Renquan lilun de chansheng he lishi fazhan', *Faxue yanjiu* ('Legal Studies'), No. 3, 1989, 7–9.

123. Lin Rongnian and Zhang Jinfan 'Tan renquan wenti', 37.

124. Shen Baoxiang, Wang Chengquan, Li Zerui, 'Guanyu guoji lingyu de renquan wenti' ('On the Question of Human Rights in the International Arena'), *Hongqi* ('Red Flag') (1987), No. 8, 47–8.

125. Guo Shan, 'China's Role in Human Rights Field', *Beijing Review* 30 (9 February 1987), Nos. 5–6, 23–4.

126. Ma Jun, 'Human Rights: China's Perspective', *Beijing Review* 31 (28 November 1988), No. 48, 18.

127. Cited in Li Haibo, 'China Applauds Human Rights', 6.

Notes to Chapter 5

1. Liu Guoguang, Liang Wensen, and others, *China's Economy in 2000* (Beijing, New World Press, 1987), 365.

2. cf. Strouse and Claude have stated that 'economic modernization is a type of social change'. See J.C. Strouse and R.P. Claude, 'Empirical Comparative Rights Research: Some Preliminary Tests of Development Hypotheses', in R.P. Claude (ed.), *Comparative Human Rights* (Baltimore, The Johns Hopkins University Press, 1976), 64. In fact, economic modernization can occur in socialist states under socialist conditions without involving social change. See, for instance, G. White, 'Chinese

Development Strategy after Mao' in G. White, R. Murray, and C. White (eds.), *Revolutionary Socialist Development in the Third World* (Sussex, Harvester Press, 1983), 155–92. It is only when the mechanisms promoting economic modernization are altered that social change necessarily occurs.

3. J. Donnelly, 'Human Rights and Development: Complementary or Competing Concerns?', *World Politics, XXXVI* (January 1984), No. 2, 276.

4. Ibid. 256–7.

5. K. Griffin and J. James, *The Transition to Egalitarian Development*, 7, cited in Donnelly, 'Human Rights and Development', 275.

6. Here the formula of Harry Harding, of 'moderate reformers' and 'radical reformers', is used to describe the main leadership factions. The usual dualism of conservatives and reformers is misleading. First, the word 'conservative' is ambiguous as it is suggestive in Western cultures of right wing tendencies, whereas it is used in China to describe those espousing a more orthodox Marxism. At the same time these more orthodox Marxists also espouse reform. See H. Harding, *China's Second Revolution: Reform after Mao* (Washington D.C., The Brookings Institution, 1987), 77–83.

7. Ibid. 2.

8. World Bank, *China, Long-term Development: Issues and Options* (World Bank, Johns Hopkins University Press, 1985), 16.

9. G. White, 'Chinese Development Strategy', 180–1.

10. Ibid. 181.

11. Harding, *China's Second Revolution*, 3–4.

12. Liu Guoguang, Liang Wensen, and others, *China's Economy*, 22.

13. S. Chin, 'The Constitution of China and the Economic Base', in B.S.J. Weng (ed.), Studies on the Constitutional Law of the People's Republic of China, *Chinese Law and Government* XV1 (Summer–Fall 1983), Nos. 2–3, 45–66.

14. 1982 Constitution, Arts. 6–11.

15. Article 13.

16. Articles 46 and 47.

17. Article 48.

18. Article 21.

19. Article 22.

20. Article 23.

21. Articles 16 and 17.

22. Peng Zhen, 'Explanations on the Draft of the Revised Constitution of the People's Republic of China' at the 23rd session of the Fifth National People's Congress Standing Committee on 22 April 1982, *Beijing Review* 25 (10 May 1982), No. 19, 23.

23. 1982 Constitution, Arts. 45 and 42.

24. M. Oksenberg, *China's Developmental Experience* (New York, Praeger, 1973), 7–11.

25. Harding, *China's Second Revolution*, 102.

26. D. Zweig, 'Prosperity and Conflict in Post-Mao Rural China', *The China Quarterly* (March 1986), No. 105, 17.

27. Harding, *China's Second Revolution*, 117.

28. For an excellent discussion of this debate, see G. White, 'The Politics of Economic Reform in Chinese Industry: The Introduction of the Labour Contract System', *The China Quarterly* (September 1987), No. 111, 365–89.

29. I thank Cao Yong for this insight.

30. A. Walder, 'Wage Reform and the Web of Factory Interests', *The China Quarterly* (March 1987), No. 109, 41.

31. *China Daily*, 8 May 1989.

32. A. Walder, 'Factory and Manager in an Era of Reform', *The China Quarterly*

(June 1989), No. 118, 252–3. This informal reality contrasts with the lack of formal democratic management in enterprises. See H.B. Chamberlain, 'Party-Management Relations in Chinese Industries: Some Political Dimensions of Economic Reform', *The China Quarterly* (December 1987), No. 112, 654–58.

33. Walder, 'Factory and Manager', 249.

34. Walder, 'Wage Reform', 33.

35. Walder, 'Factory and Manager', 263.

36. H.K. Jacobson and M. Oksenberg, *China's Participation in the IMF, the World Bank and GATT: Toward a Global Economic Order* (Ann Arbor, University of Michigan Press, 1990), 116.

37. World Bank, *China: Long Term Development*, 16.

38. Walder, 'Factory and Manager', 263.

39. Welfare provisions for these different categories of workers are described in Leung Wing-Yue, *Smashing the Iron Rice Pot: Workers and Unions in China's Market Socialism* (Hong Kong, Asia Monitor Resource Centre, 1988): for state workers, 55–8; for contract workers, 59–62; for SEZs, 138–148; and for peasant and temporary migrant workers, 64–6, 151–4. See also E.B.C. Li and Wai-Tsang Yeung, 'China's Social Welfare in the 1980s', in J.Y.S. Cheng (ed.), *China: Modernization in the 1980s* (Hong Kong, The Chinese University Press, 1989), 595; and Teh-wei Hu, Ming Li, and Shuzhong Shi, 'Analysis of Wages and Bonus Payments among Tianjin Urban Workers', *The China Quarterly* (March 1988), No. 113, 92–3.

40. J. Unger and J. Xiong, 'Life in the Chinese Hinterlands under the Rural Economic Reforms', *Bulletin of Concerned Asian Scholars* 22 (1990), No. 2, 4–17.

41. For philosophy of social welfare, see J. Dixon, *The Chinese Welfare System, 1949–1979* (New York, Praeger, 1981), 3–20; and Li and Yeung, 'China's Social Welfare', 594.

42. N. Chow, 'Modernization and Social Security Reforms in China', *Asian Perspective*, 13 (Fall–Winter 1989), No. 2, 55.

43. D. Davis 'Chinese Social Welfare: Policies and Outcomes', *The China Quarterly* (September 1989), No. 119, 578.

44. This concept was first used by Deborah Davis, ibid. 596.

45. Ibid. 578; and J. R. Taylor, 'Rural Employment Trends and the Legacy of Surplus Labour, 1978–86', *The China Quarterly* (December 1988), No. 116, 753–8.

46. Davis, 'Chinese Social Welfare', 579.

47. A. Chan, 'The Challenge to the Social Fabric', *The Pacific Review 2* (1989), No. 2, 127–8; M. Bastid, 'China's Educational Policies in the 1980s and Economic Development', *The China Quarterly* (June 1984), No. 98, 194, 218; and L. Travers, 'Post-1978 Rural Economic Policy and Peasant Income in China', ibid. 252.

48. Davis, 'Chinese Social Welfare', 581–2.

49. Bastid, 'Chinese Educational Policies', 194. See also L.N.K. Lo, 'Chinese Education in the 1980s: A Survey of Achievements and Problems', in Cheng (ed.), *China*, 554.

50. Davis, 'Chinese Social Welfare', 582.

51. Bastid, 'Chinese Educational Policies', 194.

52. Davis, 'Chinese Social Welfare', 548.

53. Ibid. 586–90.

54. The World Bank, *China: The Health Sector* (World Bank, Washington DC, 1984), 73.

55. S. Hillier, 'Health and Medicine in the 1980s', in R. Benewick and P. Wingrove (ed.), *Reforming the Revolution: China in Transition* (London, Macmillan, 1988), 151; and G. Henderson, 'Increased Inequality in Health Care', in D. Davis and E.F. Vogel (eds.), *Chinese Society on the Eve of Tiananmen: The Impact of Reform* (Cambridge, Harvard University Press, 1990), 264–73. For World Bank

warning against costly investments in sophisticated medical technologies, see Chapter 6.

56. J.R. Taylor, 'Rural Employment Trends', 757.

57. Davis, 'Chinese Social Welfare', 587.

58. Hillier, 'Health and Medicine', 153.

59. *China Daily*, 5 May 1989.

60. Davis, 'Chinese Social Welfare', 588–9.

61. I.H.S. Chow, 'Trends in the Application and Impact of Work Incentives in Chinese Industrial Enterprises', in Cheng (ed.), *China*, 345. 'Billion' is always used to denote a thousand million.

62. Y.S.F. Lee, 'The Urban Housing Problem in China', *The China Quarterly* (September 1988), No. 115, 397–8.

63. Ibid. 398.

64. Ibid. 399.

65. From comments of Cao Yong.

66. Lee, 'The Urban Housing Problem', 406.

67. Chow, 'Modernization', 59.

68. On 1990 retirees, see *China Daily*, 9 May 1989; by the year 2,000, see Huang Xiaojing and Yang Xiao, 'From Iron Ricebowls to Labor Markets: Reforming the Social Security System', in B. Reynolds (ed.), *Reform in China: Challenges and Choices*, A Summary and Analysis of the CESRRI Survey Prepared by the Staff of the Chinese Economic System Reform Research Institute (New York, M.E. Sharpe, 1987), 148–9.

69. Davis, 'Chinese Social Welfare', 593. See also Li and Yeung, 'China's Social Welfare' 604.

70. Ibid. 603.

71. Davis, 'Chinese Social Welfare', 594.

72. D. Davis, 'Unequal Chances, Unequal Outcomes: Pension Reform and Urban Inequality', *The China Quarterly* (June 1988), No. 114, 237.

73. Davis, 'Chinese Social Welfare', 593.

74. C. Ikels, 'New Options for the Elderly', in Davis and Vogel (eds.), *Chinese Society on the Eve of Tiananmen*, 219–20.

75. Ibid. 221–2.

76. Chu-yuan Cheng, *Behind the Tiananmen Massacre: Social, Political and Economic Ferment in China* (Boulder, Westview Press, 1990), 31.

77. Davis, 'Chinese Social Welfare', 593–4.

78. Ma Hong (ed.), *Modern China's Economy and Management* (Beijing, Foreign Languages Press, 1990), 464–5.

79. Bian Jibu, 'Strengthening Social Welfare', *Beijing Review* 32 (30 January 1989), No. 5, 27–8.

80. Ibid. 28.

81. Ibid. 28. See also Li and Yeung, 'China's Social Welfare', 605.

82. See, for instance, M. Blecher, 'The Reorganization of the Countryside', in Benewick and Wingrove (eds.), *Reforming the Revolution*, 100–7; I. Thireau, 'From Equality to Equity: An Exploration of Changing Norms of Distribution in Rural China', *China Information* V (Spring 1991), No. 4, 42–55; Davis, 'Chinese Social Welfare'; Li and Yeung, 'China's Social Welfare', 600–2; Chow, 'Modernization and Social Security Reforms'; D. Zweig, 'Prosperity and Conflict in Post-Mao Rural China', *The China Quarterly* (March 1986), No. 105, 15–18; J. Delman, 'Current Peasant Discontent in China: Background and Political Implications', *China Information* IV (Autumn 1989), No. 2, 42–64; M.C. Bergère, 'Les Retombées Sociales de la Politique de Reforme Economique de Deng Xiaoping, 1978–1986' ('The Social Repercussions of the Politics of Deng Xiaoping's Economic Reform'), *Quaderni di Ricerca*, Instituto di Studi Economico-Sociali Per l'Asia Orientale, 1/1986, 1–26; and Unger and Xiong, 'Life in the Chinese Hinterlands', 4–17.

83. Ma Guonan, 'China's Income Distribution in the 1980s', Paper delivered at

the 'Towards the Year 2000: Socio-economic Trends and Consequences in China Conference', Fremantle, Western Australia, 29–31 January 1992. See also figures in Chong-chor Lau, 'Society: Structure and Problems under Turbulent Change', in Kuan Hsin-chi and M. Brosseau (eds.), *China Review* (Hong Kong, The Chinese University Press, 1991), 17.12–13.

84. World Bank, *China: Long-Term Development Issues*, 87.

85. C. Riskin, 'Rural Poverty in Post-Reform China', Paper prepared for Presentation at the Conference on the Chinese Economy in the Reform Period, The Australian National University, Canberra, 11–14 November 1991, 34.

86. Chong-chor Lau, 'Society', 17.12–13. See also Liu Jianxing, 'Luelun "Shehui fenpei bugong de wenti"' ('On the Question of Unfair Social Distribution'), *Beijing shifan xueyuan xuebao* ('Academic Journal of Beijing Teachers' College'), No. 1, 1991, 76–8.

87. See *Far Eastern Economic Review* (1 June 1989), 16.

88. *People's Daily*, 26 February 1989, *Summary of World Broadcasts* (*SWB*) *FE*/0398/B2/1, 2 March 1989 and *SWB*/*FE*/0518/B2/6, 26 July 1989.

89. *Beijing Review*, 32 (13 March 1989), No. 11, 7.

90. Xinhua, 2 March 1989, in *SWB*/*FE*/0402/B2/3, 7 March 1989.

91. *Jingji ribao* ('Economic Daily'), 2 March 1989, in ibid.

92. See, for instance, H.F. Siu, 'The Politics of Migration in a Market Town', in Davis and Vogel (eds.), *Chinese Society on the Eve of Tiananmen*, 61–82; and D. Davis, 'Urban Job Mobility', in ibid. 85–108. On general problems of unemployment and labour management, see Zhao Likuan and Pan Jinyun, *Laodong jingji yu laodong guanli* ('Labour Economy and Labour Management') (Beijing chubanshe, 1984), 56–92; and Ma Hong, *Modern China's Economy*, 433–62.

93. See Zhang Zeyu, 'Enterprises Optimise Labour Organization', *Beijing Review* 31 (19 December 1988), No. 50, 20.

94. Zhao Dongwan (Minister of Labour and Personnel), 8 August 1987, *Zhongguo nianjian* (*ZGNJ*) ('China Yearbook') (Beijing, *Zhongguo nianjianshe*, 1988), 614.

95. *China Daily*, 13 May 1986.

96. 1982 Constitution, Art. 49.

97. 'Proposal of the CCP Central Committee on the Implementation of the Seventh Five Year Plan', *ZGNJ* (1986), 91.

98. Huang Xiaojing and Yang Xiao, 'From Iron Ricebowls', 149.

99. Ibid. 154 and 159.

100. Liu Guoguang, 'A Sweet and Sour Decade', *Beijing Review* 32 (2 January 1989), No. 1, 21.

101. State Statistical Bureau, 'Changes in the Life-style of Urban Residents', *Beijing Review* 31 (14 November 1988), No. 46, 26–7; and 'Improved Living Standards for Farmers', *Beijing Review* 31 (21 November 1988), No. 47, 25.

102. Ibid.

103. This point is made in Chu-yuan Cheng, *Behind the Tiananmen Square Massacre*, 29.

104. State Statistical Bureau, 'Statistics for 1987 Socio-Economic Development', *People's Daily*, 24 February 1988, cited in ibid. 29.

105. *Beijing Review* 31 (2 May 1988), No. 18, 12, cited in ibid. 29.

106. State Statistical Bureau, 'China's Economy in 1988', *SWB*, *FE*/0401/C1/5–6, 6 March 1989. See also B. Stavis, 'Contradictions in Communist Reform: China before 4 June 1989', *Political Science Quarterly* 105 (1990). No. 1, 40–1.

Notes to Chapter 6

1. R. Cohen, 'People's Republic of China: the Human Rights Exception', *Human Rights Quarterly* 9 (November 1987), No. 4, 451.

2. A. Kent, 'Waiting for Rights: China's Human Rights and China's Constitutions 1949–1989', *Human Rights Quarterly* 13 (May 1991), No. 2, 170.

3. For an excellent discussion of the relationship between the state and 'civil society' in twentieth century China, see D. Strand, 'Protest in Beijing: Civil Society and Public Sphere in China, *Problems of Communism*, XXXIX (May–June 1990), 1–19.

4. A.J. Nathan, 'Political Rights in Chinese Constitutions', in R.R. Edwards, L. Henkin, and A.J. Nathan, *Human Rights in Contemporary China* (New York, Columbia University Press, 1986), 152.

5. M. Goldman, *China's Intellectuals: Advise and Dissent* (Cambridge, Harvard University Press, 1981), Introduction, 3–5. For dissent in China, see also M. Goldman, 'Human Rights in the People's Republic of China', *Daedalus*, Human Rights 112 (Fall 1983), No. 4, 111–38.

6. See, for instance, A.C. Liu, *Chinese Censors and the Alien Emperor, 1644–1660* (Hong Kong, Centre of Asian Studies, University of Hong Kong, 1978).

7. Ibid. 59.

8. Goldman, *China's Intellectuals*.

9. S. Naquin and E.S. Rawski, *Chinese Society in the Eighteenth Century* (New Haven, Yale University Press, 1987), 16.

10. Strand, 'Protest in Beijing', 3–4.

11. For analyses based on the 'vertical'–'horizontal' model of political organization, see ibid; and K.E. Brodsgaard, 'The Democracy Movement in China, 1978–1979: Opposition Movements, Wall Poster Campaigns, and Underground Journals', *Asian Survey* XXI (July 1981), No. 7, 747–74.

12. Strand, 'Protest in Beijing', 7.

13. Ibid.

14. Ibid. 11.

15. For analysis of 'Leninist' systems of political organization, see B.L. McCormick, *Political Reform in Post-Mao China: Democracy and Bureaucracy in a Leninist State* (Berkeley, University of California Press, 1990).

16. Ibid. 57.

17. See account in Hong Yung Lee, 'Mao's Strategy for Revolutionary Change: A Case Study of the Cultural Revolution', *The China Quarterly,* (March 1979), No. 77, 50–73. Many recent Chinese accounts of personal Cultural Revolution experiences have thrown new light on the complex developments of this period, including Liang Heng and J. Shapiro, *Son of the Revolution* (New York, Vintage, 1983); and Gao Yuan, *Born Red: A Chronicle of the Cultural Revolution* (Stanford, Stanford University Press, 1987). The best, however, is Hua Linshan, *Les Années Rouges* ('The Red Years') (Paris, Éditions de Seuil, 1987).

18. A brilliant exposition of this movement is found in N. Hunter, *Shanghai Journal: An Eyewitness Account of the Cultural Revolution* (Boston, Beacon Press, 1969). See also McCormick, *Political Reform*, 37–44; and Brodsgaard, 'The Democracy Movement', 749.

19. *Renmin ribao* ('People's Daily'), 1 Jan. 1967, cited in Hong Yung Lee, *The Politics of the Chinese Cultural Revolution: A Case Study* (Berkeley, University of California Press, 1978), 141.

20. This vertical–horizontal dualism is conceptualized by Brodsgaard, 'The Democracy Movement', 773–4; in retrospect, he could have been less tentative.

21. 'Whither China', *Survey of China Mainland Press* (4 June 1968), No. 4190, 1–18. See also K. Mehnert, *Peking und die Neue Linke: in China und im Ausland* ('Peking and the New Left: At Home and Abroad') (Stuttgart, Deutsche Verlags, 1969), 75, 91; and Brodsgaard, 'The Democracy Movement', 740–50.

22. Translated in A. Chan, S. Rosen, and J. Unger (eds.), *On Socialist Democracy and the Legal System: The Li Yizhe Debates* (New York, M.E. Sharpe, 1985),

31–85. See also S.L. Shirk, 'Human Rights: What about China?', *Foreign Policy* (Winter 1977–8), No. 29, 113–17.

23. Cited in Brodsgaard, 'The Democracy Movement', 755.

24. S. Rosen, 'Guangzhou's Democracy Movement in Cultural Revolution Perspective', *The China Quarterly* (March 1985), No. 101, 26.

25. For interpretation of the 1975–6 period, see A. Kent, 'Grass Roots Politics at Shanghai Teachers' University, 1975–76', in S.A. FitzGerald and P. Hewitt (eds.), *China in the Seventies: Australian Perspectives* (Canberra, Contemporary China Centre, Australian National University, 1980), 73–99. See also A. Kent, 'Red and Expert: The Revolution in Education at Shanghai Teachers' University 1975–76', *The China Quarterly* (June 1981), No. 86, 304–21.

26. Kent, 'Grass Roots Politics', 96.

27. Ibid. 74.

28. This movement, and the post-1976 and early 1980s period, have been well documented by J. Fraser, *The Chinese: Portrait of a People* (Toronto, Collins, 1980); R. Garside, *Coming Alive: China After Mao* (New York, McGraw-Hill, 1981); R. Thwaites, *Real Life China* (Sydney, Collins, 1986); G. Barmé and J. Minford (eds.), *Seeds of Fire: Chinese Voices of Conscience* (New York, Hill and Wang, 1988); H. Siu and Z. Stern (eds.), *Mao's Harvest: Voices from China's New Generation* (Oxford, Oxford University Press, 1983); J. Seymour (ed.), *The Fifth Modernization: China's Human Rights' Movement, 1978–79* (New York, Human Rights Publishing Group, 1980); C. Widor (ed.), *Documents on the Chinese Democratic Movement, 1978-80: Unofficial Magazines and Wallposters* (in Chinese), Vol. 1 (Paris, Éditions de l'École des Hautes Études en Sciences Sociales, 1981); M. Goldman, 'Human Rights', 118–26; and A.J. Nathan, *Chinese Democracy*, (New York, Alfred A. Knopf, 1985).

29. Brodsgaard, 'The Democracy Movement', 758.

30. Nathan, *Chinese Democracy*, 10–11.

31. Documents in Seymour (ed.), *The Fifth Modernization*, 83–6.

32. This requirement is not included in Seymour's translation, but in an original copy of the Human Rights Manifesto, kindly sent me by David Goodman.

33. Seymour (ed.), *The Fifth Modernization*, 69. See also He Baogang, 'Chinese Dissidents' Ideas of Human Rights: A Constructive Critique, *Human Rights Tribune* 11 (November 1991), No. 5, 21–4.

34. Seymour (ed.), *The Fifth Modernization*, 52.

35. Wang Xizhe, 'Strive for the Class Dictatorship of the Proletariat', in Chan, Rosen, and Unger (eds.), *On Socialist Democracy*, 154–6.

36. Wang Huaixue, 'Wang Xizhe fangwenlu' ('Interview with Wang Xizhe'), *Qishi niandai* ('The Seventies') (July 1982), 34.

37. Ibid. 35

38. Ibid.

39. Ibid. 36.

40. See translated extracts in Barmé and Minford (eds.), *Seeds of Fire*, 304–10.

41. Ibid. 305.

42. Translated in Seymour (ed.), *The Fifth Modernization*, 111–27.

43. Ibid. 116.

44. Ibid. 118–25.

45. Ibid. 762–3. Brodsgaard, 'The Democracy Movement', 762–3.

46. Brodsgaard, for example, discerns an inherent dualism in the political alternatives offered by dissenters from the time of the Cultural Revolution, between 'reformers ' and 'abolitionists', 749–67. While serving to distinguish between groups, this dualism seems overdrawn, and disguises their many overlapping features.

47. Brodsgaard, 'The Democracy Movement', 764.

48. Nathan, *Chinese Democracy*, 33.

49. For detailed analyses of the complex political, social, and intellectual developments in this period, see, for instance, Nathan, *Chinese Democracy*; L. Dittmer, 'China in 1988: The Continuing Dilemma of Socialist Reform', *Asian Survey* XXIX (January 1989), No. 1 2–28; O. Schell, *Discos and Democracy: China in the Throes of Reform* (New York, Pantheon Books, 1988); I. Wilson, *Political Reform and the 13th Congress of the Communist Party of China*, Working Paper No. 149 (Canberra, The Strategic and Defence Studies Centre, Australian National University, February 1988); D. Kelly, 'The Emergence of Humanism: Wang Ruoshui and the Critique of Socialist Alienation', in M. Goldman with T. Cheek and C.L. Hamrin (eds.), *China's Intellectuals and the State: in Search of a New Relationship*, Council on East Asian Studies (Cambridge, Harvard University Press, 1987), 159–82; D. Kelly, 'The Chinese Student Movement of December 1986 and its Intellectual Antecedents', *The Australian Journal of Chinese Affairs* (January 1987), No. 1, 127–42; S. Pepper, 'Deng Xiaoping's Political and Economic Reforms and the Chinese Student Protest', *Universities Field Staff International Reports*, No. 30, 1986; B. Stavis, 'Contradictions in Communist Reform: China before 4 June 1989', *Political Science Quarterly* 105 (1990), No. 1, 31–52, and M. Goldman, 'The Zigs and Zags in the Treatment of Intellectuals', *The China Quarterly* (December 1985), No. 104, 709–15.

50. See M. Goldman, 'Hu Yaobang's Intellectual Network and the Theory Conference of 1979', *The China Quarterly* (June 1991), No. 126, 119.

51. For example, see complaint by Li Shuxian, wife of Fang Lizhi, in Chu-yuan Cheng, *Behind the Tiananmen Massacre: Social and Political and Economic Ferment in China* (Boulder, Westview Press, 1990), 87.

52. Ibid. 83.

53. M. Goldman, 'China's Sprouts of Democracy', *Ethics and International Affairs*, 4 (1990), 82.

54. Ibid. 75.

55. Ibid. 75–6.

56. See J. Tong (ed.), 'Between Party and Principle: the Exit and Voice of Fang Lizhi, Liu Binyan and Wang Ruowang', *Chinese Law and Government* 21 (Summer 1988), No. 2; J. Tong (ed.), 'Party Documents on Anti-Bourgeois Liberalisation and Hu Yaobang's Resignation, 1987', *Chinese Law and Government* 21 (Spring 1988), No. 1; and Schell, *Discos and Democracy*, 119–76. See also *Fang Lizhi, Liu Binyan, Wang Ruowang: yanlun zhaibian* ('The Selected Speeches of Fang Lizhi, Liu Binyan and Wang Ruowang') (Hong Kong, Shuguang tushu, 1988).

57. Liao Gailong, 'Lishi de jingyan he women de fazhan daolu' ('Historical Experience and our Road of Development') *Zhonggong yanjiu* 15 (15 September 1981) No. 19, 142–3, cited in S. Schram, 'Economics in Command? Ideology and Policy since the Third Plenum, 1978–1983', *The China Quarterly* (Sept. 1984), No. 99, 426–7.

58. Ibid. 441.

59. Su Shaozhi, 'Lizu dangdai, ba makesizhuyi tuixiang qianjin' ('Let us Take our Stand in this Present Age, and Carry Forward the Development of Marxism'), Beijing (2 March 1983), 3–4, cited in ibid. 435. See also D. Kelly, 'Chinese Intellectuals in the 1989 Democracy Movement', in G. Hicks (ed.), *The Broken Mirror: China after Tiananmen* (Hong Kong, Longman, 1990), 28–9.

60. Zhou Yang, 'Guanyu makesizhuyi de jige lilun wenti de tantao' ('A Discussion of Some Theoretical Questions in Marxism', *Renmin ribao* ('People's Daily) 16 March 1983, 5–6, cited in Schram, 'Economics in Command', 443.

61. Chu-yuan Cheng, *Behind the Tiananmen Massacre*, 54–5.

62. Ibid. 56. See also Kelly, 'The Chinese Student Movement', 135–8.

63. Chu-yuan Cheng, *Behind the Tiananmen Massacre*, 85.

64. Yan Jiaqi, *Wo de sixiang zizhuan* ('My Intellectual Autobiography') (Hong

Kong, Sanlian shudian, 1988), 79. See also Dai Qing, 'Tan zhongguo zhengzhi gaige — fang Yan Jiaqi' ('Discussing China's Political Reform — Interview with Yan Jiaqi'), *Guangming ribao* ('Guangming Daily'), 30 June 1986.

65. Kelly, 'The Chinese Student Movement', 136–7. For Yu's ideas on civil rights, see G. Barmé, 'A Gentle Voice of Reason Pierces the Rhetoric', *Human Rights Tribune* 11 (November 1991), No. 5, 5–6.

66. Kelly, 'The Chinese Student Movement', 129.

67. *The Age*, 18 February 1989.

68. *Far Eastern Economic Review*, 23 March 1989.

69. Reported in Zhongguo tongxunshe, Hong Kong, 7 March 1989, *SWB/FE/0404/B2/4*.

70. See 'The Price China Has Paid: An Interview with Liu Binyan', *The New York Review of Books, XXXV* (19 January 1989), Nos. 21 and 22, 31.

71. Ibid. and translations in Tong (ed.), 'Between Party and Principle'. See also 'Butong zhengjianzhe de piping: Wang Ruowang tan zhengzhi gaige' ('The Criticism of a Political Dissenter: Wang Ruowang Discusses Political Reform'), *Jiushi niandai* ('The Nineties'), December 1988, 65–75.

72. 'The Price China has Paid: An Interview with Liu Binyan', 34.

73. Ibid. 35.

74. Ming Lei, 'Fang Lizhi he Wen Hui, Ming Lei de Duihua' ('Fang Lizhi's Conversation with Wen Hui and Ming Lei'), *Zhengming*, July 1987, 19–20.

75. Barmé and Minford (eds.), *Seeds of Fire*, 334.

76. Fang Lizhi, 'China's Despair and China's Hope', *The New York Review of Books, XXXVI* (2 February 1989), 3–4. See also Fang Lizhi, *Bringing Down the Great Wall: Writings on Science, Culture, and Democracy in China* (New York, Alfred A. Knopf, 1991), 135–88.

77. A.J. Nathan, 'Tiananmen and the Cosmos', *The New Republic*, 29 July 1991, 34–5.

78. Ibid.

79. Cohen, 'People's Republic of China', 469.

80. Ibid. 450.

81. Ibid. 501.

82. Ibid. 498.

83. Ibid.

84. Ibid. 502–3, 509.

85. An outstanding example of the effectiveness of bilateral exchange was the release and rehabilitation of the three authors of the Li Yizhe poster, after intercession on their behalf by French Prime Minister Jacques Chirac. For this and other instances, see Cohen, 'People's Republic of China', 530–3.

86. Amnesty International, 'China: Torture and Ill-treatment of Prisoners', September 1987, ASA 17/07/87, 4.

87. Ibid.

88. Ibid. For more information on political imprisonment and penal conditions in China, see Chapter 3.

89. Amnesty International, 'China: Torture and Ill-treatment of Prisoners', 1–3.

90. Ibid. 44.

91. Ibid. 44–5.

92. Ibid.

93. Amnesty International, 'People's Republic of China: The Death Penalty in China', January 1989, ASA 17/01/89, 1.

94. Ibid. 10.

95. Amnesty International, 'People's Republic of China: The Death Penalty Debate', April 1989, ASA 17/14/89, 14–15.

96. Amnesty International, 'Urgent Action', 9 June 1989.

97. See Amnesty International, 'People's Republic of China: Preliminary Findings on Killings of Unarmed Citizens, Arbitrary Arrests and Summary Executions since 3 June 1989', London (August 1989), ASA 17/60/89.

98. Amnesty International, 'Prisoners of Conscience in the People's Republic of China', June 1987, Appendix I, 1–2; and 14–35.

99. Amnesty International, 'Prisoners of Conscience', Appendix 1, 1–2; and 14–35.

100. Ibid. 33.

101. Amnesty International, 'People's Republic of China: Summary of Amnesty International's Concerns' (January 1987 to April 1988), May 1988, ASA 17/07/1988, 4.

102. J. Mathews, 'Edgar Snow Told You So', *The Washington Monthly*, July/August 1989, 50–4.

103. Amnesty International, 'Prisoners of Conscience', 21.

104. Ibid. 28.

105. Ibid. 30.

106. Amnesty International, 'China: New Information on Prisoners of Conscience', 1987, ASA 17/15/87, 3. For Chinese report on Wei, see *Beijing Review* 32 (1–7 May 1989), No. 18, 25.

107. See H. Ribe and S. Carvalho, *World Bank Treatment of the Social Impact of Adjustment Programs* (Washington DC, World Bank, 1990), 1 and 56–8.

108. See H.K. Jacobson and M. Oksenberg, *China's Participation in the IMF, World Bank, and GATT: Toward a Global Economic Order* (Ann Arbor, University of Michigan Press, 1990), 110.

109. World Bank, *China, Long-Term Development: Issues and Options* (Washington DC, Johns Hopkins University Press, 1985).

110. World Bank, ibid. 123.

111. Ibid. 161. My emphasis.

112. Ibid. 19.

113. Ibid. 16.

114. Ibid. For following details of report, see 17–19.

115. World Bank, *China, The Health Sector* (Washington DC, International Bank for Reconstruction and Development, 1984).

116. See also one of the six annexes to the 1985 report, *China: Issues and Prospects in Education.*

117. World Bank, *China, Long Term Development*, 164 and 91.

118. Ibid. 19.

119. World Bank, *China, Agriculture to the Year* 2000 (Washington DC, International Bank for Reconstruction and Development, 1985), 109–10.

120. Ibid. 110–13.

121. World Bank, *China, Growth and Development in Gansu Province* (Washington DC, International Bank for Reconstruction and Development, 1988), 51. For following details, see 56–61.

122. The World Bank, *World Development Report of 1990: Poverty* (Oxford, Oxford University Press, 1991), 140, my emphasis.

123. United Nations Development Programme (UNDP), *Human Development Report 1990* (Oxford, Oxford University Press, 1991), 128.

124. Ibid. 51–3, my emphasis.

Notes to Chapter 7

1. D. Landes, 'Rethinking Development', *Dialogue* (1991), No. 91, 71.

2. W.G. Runciman, *Relative Deprivation and Social Justice: A Study of Attitudes to Social Inequality in Twentieth-Century England*, (London, Routledge & Kegan

Paul, 1966); T.R. Gurr, *Why Men Rebel* (Princeton, Princeton University Press, 1970); and T.R. Gurr with C. Ruttenberg, *The Conditions of Civil Violence: First Tests of a Causal Model*, (Princeton, Princeton University Press, April 1967).

3. A. Kent, 'Waiting for Rights: China's Human Rights and China's Constitutions, 1949–89', *Human Rights Quarterly* 13 (May 1991), No. 2, 170–201; and 'Human Rights: The Changing Balance Sheet', in D.S.G. Goodman and G. Segal (eds.), *China in the Nineties: Challenges and Choices* (Oxford, Clarendon Press, 1991), 64–86. For expansion of the following argument, see also Kent, 'Living Standards, Relative Deprivation and Political Change in China', in D.S.G. Goodman and B. Hooper (eds.), *China's Quiet Revolution: New Interactions between State and Society* (Hong Kong, Longman-Cheshire, 1993).

4. Carol Lee Hamrin has made similar suggestions.

5. Gurr, *Why Men Rebel*, 46–56.

6. Ibid. 25.

7. Runciman, *Relative Deprivation*, 22.

8. Gurr, *Why Men Rebel*, 92.

9. J.L.S. Girling, *America and the Third World: Revolution and Intervention* (London, Routledge and Kegan, 1980), 93–5.

10. See also R. Baum, 'Epilogue: Communism, Convergence, and China's Political Convulsion', in R. Baum (ed.), *Reform and Reaction in Post-Mao China: the Road to Tiananmen* (London, Routledge, 1991), 341.

11. See, for instance, D.S.G. Goodman, 'Communism in East Asia: The Production Imperative, Legitimacy and Reform', in D.S.G. Goodman (ed.), *Communism and Reform in East Asia* (London, Frank Cass, 1988), 1–8.

12. For instance, the *Beijing Review* cites 14 surveys on popular attitudes to reform, *Beijing Review* 30 (29 June 1987), No. 26, 22. Surveys include an August 1988 poll co-sponsored by the Institute of Sociology, CASS and the State Statistical Bureau, reported in *Liaowang* ('Outlook') and *China Daily*, 11 February 1989; and a 1987 'Survey of the Political Psychology of Citizens in China', reported in *Inside China Mainland* 11 (May 1989), No. 125, 1–3; and in Min Qi, *Zhongguo zhengzhi wenhua: minzhu zhengzhi nanchan de shehui xinli yinsu* ('Chinese Political Culture: Social Psychology and the Birthpangs of Democratic Politics') (Yunnan, Yunnan renmin chubanshe, 1989).

13. S. Rosen, 'The Rise (and Fall) of Public Opinion in Post-Mao China', in R. Baum (ed.), *Reform and Reaction*, 60.

14. Rosen, 'The Rise and Fall', 66.

15. See ibid. 81, f. 27 for distinctions between these categories.

16. L. do Rosario, *Far Eastern Economic Review*, 2 March 1989, 61–2.

17. Ibid.

18. *China Daily*, 11 February 1989.

19. B. Reynolds (ed.), *Reform in China: Challenges and Choices*, A Summary and Analysis of the CESSRI Survey Prepared by the Staff of the Chinese Economic System Reform Research Institute (New York, M.E. Sharpe, 1987). See also extensive report of these surveys in Rosen, 'The Rise and Fall'.

20. Ibid. 67.

21. Ibid.

22. Reynolds (ed.), *Reform in China*, 34.

23. Rosen 'The Rise and Fall', 67.

24. Ibid.

25. Yang Guangsan, Yang Xiaodong, and Xuan Mingdong, 'The Public Response to Price Reform', in Reynolds (ed.), *Reform in China*, 71.

26. For instance, see J.C. Oi, 'Partial Market Reform and Corruption in Rural China' in R. Baum (ed.), *Reform and Reaction*, 156, 161 f. 50.

27. The first point is cogently argued in McCormick, *Political Reform*. This author, however, does not agree that such patrimonial, clientelist forms were necessarily part of the internal logic of Leninist forms of the state. Rather,

patrimonialism and clientelism were the function of the poverty and underdevelopment of the Chinese state, under whatever political regime. For the second point, see C.S. Meaney, citing M. Johnston, 'Market Reform and Disintegrative Corruption in Urban China', in R. Baum (ed.), *Reform and Reaction*, 125.

28. See also McCormick, *Political Reform*, 181.

29. See Meaney citing Johnston in 'Market Reform', 129–32.

30. Ibid. 130–1.

31. Oi, 'Partial Market Reform', 148–156.

32. Ibid. 154.

33. This debate is synthesized in the collection of writings, Liu Jun and Li Lin (eds.), *Xin quanwei zhuyi: dui gaige lilun gangling* ('New Authoritarianism: Towards a Theoretical Programme of Reform') (Beijing, Beijing jingji xueyuan chubanshe, April 1989). For a perceptive analysis of the CDSs, see C. Johnson, 'South Korean Democratisation: The Role of Economic Development', *The Pacific Review* 2 (1989), No. 1, 1–10.

34. do Rosario, *Far Eastern Economic Review*, 2 March 1989, 62.

35. Translated in F. Wakeman, Jr., 'All the Rage in China', *The New York Review of Books*, XXXVI (2 March 1989), No. 3, 19.

36. *Inside China Mainland* 11 (May 1989), No. 5, issue 125, 4.

37. Jianhua Zhu, Xinshu Zhao, and Hairong Li, 'Public Political Consciousness in China', *Asian Survey* XXX (October 1990), No. 10, 992–1006.

38. McCormick, *Political Reform*, 185.

39. See Oi, 'Partial Market Reforms', 143–61; J. Unger and J. Xiong, 'Life in the Hinterlands under the Rural Economic Reforms', *Bulletin of Concerned Asian Scholars* 22 (July 1990), No. 2, 4–17; J. Delman, 'Current Peasant Discontent in China: Background and Political Implications', *China Information* IV (Autumn 1990), No. 2, 42–64; and I. Thireau 'From Equality to Equity: An Exploration of Changing Norms of Distribution in Rural China', *China Information* V (Spring 1991), No. 4, 42–57.

40. D. Zweig, 'Prosperity and Conflict in Post-Mao Rural China', *The China Quarterly* (March 1986) No. 105, 1–18; and Thireau, 'From Equality to Equity'.

41. This condition was also manifested in Tibet, where a wave of protests began after seven years of cultural, economic, and religious liberalization, initiated by the then Communist Party Secretary, Hu Yaobang, in 1980. See Lawasia and the Tibet Information Network, *Defying the Dragon: China and Human Rights in Tibet* (Manila, Lawasia Human Rights Committee, 1991), 1.

42. C. Johnson, *Revolution and the Social System* (Stanford, The Hoover Institution on War, 1964), 12.

43. For chronology and documentation of events, see M. Oksenberg, L. Sullivan, M. Lambert (eds.), *Beijing Spring, 1989: Confrontation and Conflict*, The Basic Documents (New York, M.E. Sharpe, 1990).

44. See Chinese and English publications listed in Helmut Martin, *China's Democracy Movement 1989: A Selected Bibliography of Chinese Source Materials* (Carstenn Herrmann-Pillath, 1990). See also *Lianhe bao* editorial department, *Tiananmen yijiubajiu* ('Tiananmen, 1989')(Taibei, Lianjing chuban shiye gongsi, 1990); Amnesty International, *People's China: Preliminary Findings on Killings of Unarmed Civilians, Arbitrary Arrests and Summary Executions since 3 June 1989* (London, Amnesty International, August 1989), ASA 17/60/89; International League for Human Rights and the Ad Hoc Study Group on Human Rights in China, *Massacre in Beijing: the Events of 3–4 June 1989 and their Aftermath* (New York, December 1989); Han Minzhu (ed.), *Cries for Democracy: Writings and Speeches from the 1989 Democracy Movement* (Princeton, Princeton University Press, 1990); T. Saich (ed.), *The Chinese People's Movement: Perspectives on Spring 1989* (New York, M.E. Sharpe, 1990); J. Unger (ed.), *The Pro-Democracy Protests in China: Reports from the Provinces* (New York, M.E. Sharpe, 1991); L. Pye, 'Tiananmen

and Chinese Political Culture: The Escalation of Confrontation from Moralizing to Revenge', *Asian Survey* XXX (April 1990), No. 4, 331–47; A.G. Walder, 'The Political Sociology of the Beijing Upheaval of 1989', *Problems of Communism* XXXVIII (September 1989), 30–40; A.J. Nathan, 'Chinese Democracy in 1989: Continuity and Change', *Problems of Communism* XXXVIII (September 1989), 16–29; L. Dittmer, 'The Tiananmen Massacre', *Problems of Communism* XXXVI-II (September 1989), 2–15; Luo Qiping, Mai Yanting, Liang Meifen, Li Peper, 'The 1989 Pro-Democracy Movement: Student Organizations and Strategies', *China Information* V (Autumn 1990), No. 2, 30–43; Tianjian Shi, 'The Democratic Movement in China in 1989: Dynamics and Failure', *Asian Survey* XXX (December 1990), No. 12, 1186–1205; and Ta-ling Lee and J.F. Copper, *Failure of Democracy Movement: Human Rights in the People's Republic of China*, 1988/89', Occasional Papers in Contemporary Asian Studies (1991), No. 2.

45. *The Australian*, 16 May 1989.

46. *The New York Times*, 28 April 1989.

47. *The New York Times*, 18 May 1989; and Unger (ed.), *The Pro-Democracy Protests*.

48. See 'Chronology of Events', *Echoes from Tiananmen* (15 June 1989), No. 1, 4.

49. Ibid.

50. Ibid. 13. See also interview of Qiu Wu in W.L. Chong, 'The Chicago Congress: Recent Activities of the Front for a Democratic China', *China Information* IV (Autumn 1989), No. 2, 23–6; and L.R. Sullivan, 'The Emergence of Civil Society in China, Spring 1989', in T. Saich (ed.), *The Chinese People's Movement*, 136–42.

51. *Echoes from Tiananmen* (15 June 1989), No. 1, 13.

52. cf. do Rosario, 'Workers Disunited', *Far Eastern Economic Review* (1 June 1989), 17.

53. 'Martial Law Declared in Peking', Peking Television, 20 May 1989, in *SWB*, FE/0463/B2/1–2, 22 May 1989.

54. Text of video report on 'important speech' delivered by Li Peng, 'on behalf of the Party Central Committee and the State Council' at a meeting of cadres from the Party, government, and army convened by the CCP Central Committee and the State Council on 19 May, in *SWB*, FE/0463/B2/4, 22 May 1989.

55. M. Manion, 'Introduction: Reluctant Duelists: The Logic of the 1989 Protests and Massacre', in Oksenberg, Sullivan, and Lambert (eds.), *Beijing Spring, 1989*, xxvii–xxxi.

56. Amnesty International Australia source, 28 June 1989.

57. Amnesty International, ASA 17/30/89–17/62/89.

58. *The Australian*, 14 June 1989.

59. *The New York Times*, 13 June 1989.

60. Amnesty International, *People's Republic of China: Preliminary Findings*, 43–6.

61. *The Washington Post*, 27 July 1989 cited in K. Hartford, 'China Now, Repression in Full Swing', *China Update* (August 1989), No. 1, 2–3.

62. Hartford, 'China Now', 2–3.

63. On tertiary students, ibid. 2-3; on press dismissals, *SWB*, FE/0535/B2/2, 15 August 1989; on censorship drive, *SWB*, FE/0545/B2/5, 26 August 1989, *SWB*, FE/0569/B2/6–7, 23 September 1989; on autonomous organizations, *SWB*, FE/0538/i, 18 August 1989; and 'The Casualties', *Echoes from Tiananmen* (August 1989), No. 2, 32–43; on draft law on demonstrations, *SWB*, FE/0506/B2/5–6, 12 July 1989. See also International League for Human Rights, *Massacre in Beijing*, 26–49.

64. Jiang Zemin, 'Zai quanguo zuzhi buzhang huiyi shang de jianghua' ('Speech as the Meeting of Heads of China's Organizational Departments'), *Renmin ribao* ('People's Daily'), 21 August 1989.

65. 'Guanyu qingcha shijiu zhong ren de Zhongong Zhongyang wenjian' Party

Central Committee Document on the Purge of the Nineteen Types of People', *Zhengming* (October 1989), No. 10, 12. There were two targets in the campaign, the targets of repression (*daji duixiang*) and the targets of purge (*qingli duixiang*).
66. This distinction has been pointed out by Anne Gunn.
67. *The Australian*, 1 November 1989; and *The Canberra Times*, 12 January 1990.
68. L.R. Sullivan, 'The Emergence of Civil Society', 130.
69. Stanley Rosen's notion of the internationalization of Chinese dissent has here been applied to the Chinese human rights movement in general. See S. Rosen, 'Dissent and Tolerance in Chinese Society', *Current History* 87 (September 1988), No. 530, 261.
70. See, for instance, 'Question of the Violation of Human Rights and Fundamental Freedoms in Any Part of the World, with Particular Reference to Colonial and other Dependent Countries and Territories: Situation in China', Note by the Secretary-General', Commission on Human Rights, Forty-sixth session, Agenda Item 12, E/CN.4/1990/52, 30 January 1990.
71. Governing Body, International Labour Office, *Case No. 1500 (China):* Complaint against the Government of China presented by the International Confederation of Free Trade Unions, 268th Report of the Committee on Freedom of Association (Geneva, November 1989), GB.244/5/6, 668–701.
72. Cited in Amnesty International, *People's Republic of China: Preliminary Findings*, 47–8.
73. International League for Human Rights and the Ad Hoc Study Group on Human Rights in China, *Massacre in Beijing: The Events of 3–4 June 1989 and their Aftermath* (New York, The International League for Human Rights, 1989), 45–6.
74. For history and exegesis of these standards, see S.R. Chowdhury, *Rule of Law in a State of Emergency: The Paris Minimum Standards of Human Rights Norms in a State of Emergency* (London, Pinter Publishers, 1989). For non-derogable rights, 143–261; for Paris Minimum Standards, 11–12 and 89–90.
75. B.G. Ramcharan, *The Concept and Present Status of International Protection of Human Rights: Forty Years after the Universal Declaration* (Dordrecht, Martinus Nijhoff, 1989), 58–9.
76. Beijingshi sifaju fazhi jiaocai jiaoyu bianxiezu ('The Editorial Group for the Compilation of Educational Material on the Legal System, Beijing Judicial Bureau'), *Zhizhi dongluan pingxi fangeming baoluan falu wenti jieda* ('Curbing the Turmoil and Subduing the Counterrevolutionary Rebellion') (Beijing, Beijing chubanshe, August 1989).
77. For analysis of the symbolic and material sanctions, see P. Van Ness, *Analysing the Impact of International Sanctions on China*, Working Paper 1989/4 (Canberra, Department of International Relations, The Australian National University), 2–11.
78. Ibid. 7. See also J. Seymour, *The International Reaction to the 1989 Crackdown in China* (New York, East Asian Institute, Columbia University, February 1990).
79. Reprinted in 'Situation in China', Note by the Secretary-General, 1.
80. Van Ness, *Analysing the Impact*, 14.
81. 'Complaint against the Government of China Presented by the International Confederation of Trade Unions (ICFTU)', Case No. 1500, Committee on Freedom of Association, International Labour Organization, Geneva, 9127 n/v2, 13 November 1989.
82. For the aims of the Federation, which place a priority on human rights, see *Minzhu zhongguo zhenxian xuanyan* ('Manifesto of the Federation for a Democratic China') (Paris, 24 September 1989).

Notes to Chapter 8

1. T.R. Gurr, *Why Men Rebel* (Princeton, Princeton University Press, 1970), 232.

2. See also M. Dutton, *Policing and Punishment in China: From Patriarchy to 'the People'* (Cambridge, Cambridge University Press, 1992, forthcoming), 325–6.

3. This 'tacit bond' is not something new in Chinese communist history. Before 1976 there was an 'implicit social contract' between leaders and led, whereby citizens were guaranteed the rights of subsistence, the right to work and the gradual raising of living standards. Between 1976 and 1989 there was an explicit government undertaking to raise living standards via improved income and direct gain sharing. What was different about the bond established after June 1989 was that it became another implicit social contract, but one which was being continually renegotiated. Moreover, the parameters of renegotiation had expanded to include political and, to a lesser extent, civil rights.

4. The concept of 'inequality substitution' has been suggested by Ma Guonan.

5. Clemens Ostergaard, 'Citizen Groups and a Nascent Civil Society in China: Towards an Understanding of the 1989 Student Demonstrations', *China Information* IV (Autumn 1989), No. 2, 39–41.

6. Cf. Ostergaard, p. 40. See analysis in You Ji, 'Politics of China's Post-Mao Reforms: From the CCP's 13th Party Congress to the Dawn of Beijing Students' Demonstrations' M.A. thesis (Canberra, Australian National University, August 1989), 35.

7. For further details of this first phase, see A. Kent, *Human Rights in the People's Republic of China: National and International Dimensions* (Canberra, Peace Research Centre, The Australian National University, 1990), 67–76.

8. See J. Delman, 'Current Peasant Discontent in China: Background and Political Implications', *China Information* IV (Autumn 1989), No. 2, 42–64; and J. Unger and J. Xiong, 'Life in the Chinese Hinterlands under the Rural Economic Reforms', *Bulletin of Concerned Asian Scholars* 22 (July 1990), No. 3, 4–17.

9. *China Daily (CD)*, 5 August 1989; and *CD*, 11 August 1989.

10. Jiang Zemin, 'Speech at the Meeting in Celebration of the 40th Anniversary of the Founding of the People's Republic of China', 29 September 1989, *Beijing Review* 32 (9 October 1989), No. 41, 18.

11. For instance, 'Beating around the Gooseberry Bush', excerpts from *Xuexi yu yanjiu yuekan* (March 1990), *Inside China Mainland* (June 1990), p. 10; and Chen Te-sheng, 'Mainland China's Economic Reform Policies in the Wake of the Fifth Plenum of the CCP's Thirteenth Central Committee', *Issues and Studies* 26 (March 1990), No. 3, 25–42.

12. See this argument in A. Kent, 'Human Rights: The Changing Balance Sheet', in D.S.G. Goodman and G. Segal (eds.), *China in the Nineties: Crisis Management and Beyond* (Oxford, Clarendon Press, 1991), 64–86.

13. C. Wing-Hung Lo, 'The Trials of Dissidents in the 1989 Democratic Movement: The Limits of Criminal Justice in Deng's China', Paper delivered at the Second Biennial Conference of the Chinese Studies Association of Australia, University of Sydney, 1–4 July 1991, 15, 19.

14. *CD*, 14 December 1989.

15. In *SWB, FE/0720/C2/1–19*, 23 March 1990.

16. 'Jiang Zemin Replies to American Students', *Beijing Review* 33 (25 June 1990), No. 26, 8–12.

17. B.L. McCormick, *Political Reform in Post-Mao China: Democracy and Bureaucracy in a Leninist State* (Berkeley, University of California Press, 1990), 175.

18. *CD*, 1 November 1989, 2 February 1990.

19. *Renmin ribao* ('People's Daily') Overseas Edition, 1 November, 1989.

20. J. Polumbaum, 'In the Name of Stability: Restrictions on the Right of Assembly in the People's Republic of China', *The Australian Journal of Chinese Affairs* (July 1991), No. 26, 63.

21. See *CD*, 9 March 1990; and M.D. Swaine,'China Faces the 1990s: A System in Crisis', *Problems of Communism* XXXIX (May–June 1990), 27–9.

22. For Jiang, *Beijing Review* 33 (25 June 1990), No. 26, 10; political prisoners, *Beijing Review* 33 (18 June 1990), No. 25, 6–7; Code of Collegiate Student Behaviour, *CD*, 25 November 1990; Regulations, *CD*, 10 February 1990; crime rate, ibid.

23. Amnesty International, 'The People's Republic of China: the Death Penalty in 1990' (London, Amnesty International, Februrary 1991), ASA 17/17/91, 1.

24. For urban unemployment rate, *CD*, 28 February 1990 and 19 April 1990; rural labourers, *Workers' Daily* in *CD*, 23 January 1990; calls for unemployment pension system, *CD*, 29 November 1989, 31 January 1990; rural enterprises, *CD*, 6 December 1989.

25. For solutions to unemployment, *CD*, 6 December 1989, 23 January 1990; labour laws, *CD*, 28 November 1990; rural workers' return, *CD*, 20 March 1990; labour service network, *CD*, 20 March 1990.

26. On primary health care, *CD*, 6 February 1990; illiteracy, *CD*, 9 December 1989; education, Xinhua, 21 March 1990, *SWB*, *FE/0719/C2/1*, 22 March 1990; on other measures, Swaine, 'China Faces the 1990s', 32 and *CD*, 21 February 1990; and on poverty relief, *CD*, 21 February, 6 and 16 March 1990.

27. Xinhua, 2 April 1991, *SWB*, *FE/1037/C1/3*.

28. R. Garnaut, 'Economic reform and Internationalisation: China's Experience in International Context', Paper presented at the 19th Pacific Trade and Development Conference, Beijing, 27–30 May 1991.

29. Li Peng, 'Further Deepen Reform, Invigorate Big and Medium-sized Enterprises', *Zhongguo jingji tizhi gaige* ('China's Economic Structural Reform'), No. 5, 1991, *SWB*, *FE/1082/B2/2*, 27 May 1991.

30. Ibid. B2/5.

31. 'Chen Jinhua and Li Lanqing Give Press Conference on the Economy', 30 March 1991, *SWB*, *FE/1035/C1/5*, 2 April 1991.

32. 'Outline of the Ten–Year Programme and the Eighth Five–Year Plan for National Economic and Social Development of the PRC — Approved by the Fourth Session of the 7th National People's Congress on 9 April 1991,' *Renmin ribao*, 16 April 1991, *SWB*, *FE1058/C1/1–29*, 29 April 1991; and 'State Council Approves, Transmits 1991 Major Points Submitted by State Commission for Economic Restructuring', Xinhua 20 June 1991, *SWB*, *FE/1108/C3/1–6*, 26 June 1991.

33. Ibid. C3/5.

34. *SWB*, *FE1058/C1/24*.

35. Chen Jinhua, 'Zhubu jianli shehui zhuyi you jihua shangpin jingji de xin tizhi' ('Gradually Establish a New System of Planned Socialist Commodity Economy'), *Renmin ribao* ('People's Daily'), 11 March 1991, 2.

36. Gao Shangquan, 'Jianli shehui baozhang tixi shi yi xiang poqie renwu' ('The Building up of Social Security System is an Urgent Task'), *Zhongguo jingji tizhi gaige* ('Reform of China's Economic Structure), 1991, 7–10; and Meng Wanhe, 'Guanyu jianli Zhongguo shiye baoxian zhidu de tantao' ('Looking into the Establishment of a System of Unemployment Insurance for China'), *Beijing daxue xuebao* ('Journal of Peking University'), 1990, No. 5, 114–120.

37. Ibid.; and *SWB*, *FE/1103 B2/7*, 20 June 1991.

38. 'Social Insurance: Old Age and Unemployment', *China News Analysis*, (1 June 1991), No. 1436, 3. By the end of 1990, about 220 million Chinese were

claimed to have life insurance coverage. See Han Guojian, 'Life Insurance in China Developing', *Beijing Review* 34 (July 29 1991), No. 30, 20.

39. See Li Hong, 'Pensions System to Change', *CD*, 17 January 1991.

40. *SWB, FE*/1058/C1/29, 29 April 1991.

41. Ibid. C1/27.

42. *CD*, 11 February 1991.

43. *CD*, 20 February 1991.

44. *CD*, 14 February 1991.

45. *CD*, 12 February 1991.

46. *Renmin ribao*, cited in *CD*, 13 July 1991.

47. *Guangming ribao*, cited in ibid.

48. *CD*, 13 February 1991.

49. *CD*, 31 January 1991.

50. *CD*, 24 January 1991.

51. *CD*, 30 January 1991.

52. *CD*, 13 February 1991.

53. See Asia Watch, 'The Beijing Trials: Secret Judicial Procedures and the Exclusion of Foreign Observers', 27 February 1991; and Asia Watch, 'The Case of Wang Juntao', 11 March 1991.

54. See ibid.; Amnesty International, 'The People's Republic of China: Trials and Punishments since 1989', April 1991, ASA 17/34/91, 2–10; and C. Wing-Hung Lo, 'The Trials of Dissidents', 29–38.

55. *Human Rights Tribune*, 11 (June 1991), No. 3, 3.

56. Amnesty International, 'China: Crackdown on Pro-Democracy Activists Continues in Courts and Jails', 4 June 1991, ASA 17/40/91, 2.

57. Ibid.

58. Zhongwen xinwen she, 6 June 1991, *SWB, FE*/1093/B2/4, 8 June 1991.

59. Xinhua, 3 April 1991, *SWB, FE*/1038/C1/2, 5 April 1991.

60. *CD*, 4 April 1991.

61. *Tang tai*, Hong Kong, 15 June 1991, *SWB, FE*/1117/B2/3, 6 July 1991.

62. Text in *Zhongguo jizhe*, 15 May 1991, *SWB, FE*/1117/B2/3, 6 July 1991.

63. Chiang Chen-ch'ang, 'Tighter Restraints on Mainland Press', *Issues and Studies*, 27 (June 1991), No. 6, 7–9.

64. Xinhua, 8 May 1991, *SWB, FE*/1070/B2/5–9, 13 May 1991.

65. Xinhua, 19 July 1991, *SWB, FE*/1132/B2/1, 24 July 1991; and Xinhua, 17 July 1991, *SWB, FE*/1128/B2/6, 19 July 1991. On the other hand, continued student resistance was suggested by a declaration of human rights posted up briefly at Beijing University in November calling for authorities to release all prisoners held for political or religious beliefs or actions. See *Ming pao*, Hong Kong, 16 November 1991.

66. *Ming pao*, Hong Kong, 11 April 1991, *SWB, FE*/1045/B2/1, 13 April 1991.

67. Amnesty International, 'The People's Republic of China: Trials and Punishments since 1989' (April 1991), ASA 17/34/91, 2.

68. Zhongyang renmin guangbuo diantai, 2 April 1991, *SWB, FE*/1038/C1/6–7, 5 April 1991.

69. See, for example, P. Goodspeed, 'The Conflict between Reform and Repression', *World Press Review* (March 1991), 26–8.

70. The following discussion builds on ideas circulating within a Contemporary China Centre discussion group, consisting of Jonathan Unger, Geremie Barmé, Barrett McCormick, David Kelly, Anita Chan, Frank Lewins, and myself. The thoughts of Barrett McCormick and Geremie Barmé have been particularly helpful.

71. G. Barmé, 'An Iron Fist in a Velvet Prison: Literature in Post-June 1989 China', *China News Analysis* (15 September 1991), No. 144, 1.

72. I am indebted to Geremie Barmé for this insight.

73. *South China Morning Post*, 8 and 9 November 1991.
74. Ibid.
75. UPI, 29 October 1991.
76. *South China Morning Post*, 6 November 1991.
77. Ibid. 12 November 1991.
78. Jiang Zemin, 'Building Socialism the Chinese Way', *Beijing Review* 34 (8 July 1991), No. 27, 22.
79. See, for instance, Duan Ruofei, 'Persist in People's Democratic Dictatorship, Oppose, Prevent, "Peaceful Evolution"', *Renmin ribao*, 5 June 1991, *SWB*, *FE*/1095/B2/2–4, 11 June 1991.
80. Cen Shan, 'A CCP Investigation Confirms that Quality of Party Member Officials is Poor', *Zhengming*, Hong Kong, 1 July 1991, *SWB*, *FE*/1124/B2/5, 15 July 1991.
81. Xinhua, 2 April 1991, *SWB*, *FE*/1036/C1/1, 3 April 1991.
82. *CD*, 4 March 1991.
83. B. Jacobs, 'Elections in China', *The Australian Journal of Chinese Affairs* (January 1991), No. 25, 199.
84. Ibid. 182–5; and McCormick, *Political Reform*, 142.
85. *CD*, 1 April 1991.
86. *Wenhui pao*, Hong Kong, 9 April 1991, *SWB*, *FE*/1042/C1/4, 10 April 1991.
87. Yuan Ma, 'The Development of an Administrative Procedure System in China', *Renmin ribao* overseas edition, cited in Amnesty International, 'China: Punishment without Crime: Administrative Detention', September 1991, ASA/17/91, 56–7. A more optimistic assessment may be found in R. Munro, 'Criminal Justice and the Rule of Law', *China Now* (Summer 1989), No. 129, 8–10. See also Wu Naitao, 'A Long Step toward Democratisation', *Beijing Review* 34 (29 April 1991), No. 17, 16; and Huang Jianshe, 'Zhongguo de "Xingzheng Sukong Fa" ji qi zai shenpan zhong shiyong de jige wenti' ('The Chinese Administrative Litigation Law and a Few Problems in its Judicial Application'), Paper delivered at the Chinese Studies of Australia Association Conference, June 1991. For an excellent discussion of this new law, see A.H.Y. Chen, *An Introduction to the Legal System of the People's Republic of China* (Singapore, Butterworths Asia, 1992) 176–84. Although often translated as Administrative Procedure Law, its more literal translation is Administrative Litigation Law.
88. Issues of 30 July, 31 August, and 28 September 1991, cited in Australian International Development Assistance Bureau, *Recent Population Policy in China*, Sector Report 1991 No. 4, by Terence Hull (Canberra, Commonwealth of Australia, 1991), 43–4.
89. See Wu Naitao, 'Offence Reporting; An Important Channel of Mass Supervision', *Beijing Review* 33 (15 January 1990), No. 3, 25–8; and 'Rules to Protect People Who Report Crimes', Xinhua 8 May 1991, *SWB*, *FE*/1073/C1/1–2, 16 May 1991.
90. Gong Xiangrui, 'Constitutional Protection of Human Rights: The Chinese View Under the Notion of "One Country, Two Systems"', Paper presented at the Hong Kong Bill of Rights Conference, The Faculty of Law, University of Hong Kong, 20–2 June 1991 (an edited version by the Organizing Committee, which has not been approved by Gong Xiangrui).
91. Economic and Social Council, United Nations, 'Question of the Violation of Human Rights and Fundamental Freedoms in Any Part of the World, with Particular Reference to Colonial and other Dependent Countries and Territories: Situation in China, Note by the Secretary-General', Forty-sixth session, Commission on Human Rights, Agenda Item 12 (30 January 1990), E/CN.4/1990/52.
92. Text provided by the Department of Foreign Affairs and Trade, Canberra.
93. Ibid.
94. *Australia Tibet Council News* (September/October 1991), 5.

95. Governing Body, International Labour Office, Case No. 1500 (China), 270th Report of the Committee on Freedom of Association, 245th session (Geneva, February–March 1990), GB.245/5/8, 92.

96. Asia Watch, 'Chinese Workers Receive Harsh Sentences: ILO Reports on 91 Cases' (New York, 13 March 1991), 2.

97. Ibid. 2–24.

98. J. Mirsky, 'Publishers Condemn China's Human Rights Record', *Observer News Service* (23 April 1991), No. 57591, 1.

99. P. Van Ness, 'International Sanctions and Human Rights: the Case of China', in J. Girling (ed.), *Human Rights in the Asia-Pacific Region* (Canberra, Department of International Relations, Australian National University, 1991), 19.

100. For effects of this debate, see J.V. Feinerman, 'Deteriorating Human Rights in China', *Current History* (September 1990), 268–9, 279–80.

101. 'The 'Most Favoured Nation Status' Debate', *Australia Tibet Council News* (September/October 1991), 4.

102. A. Kent, 'Human Rights in China: the Formal Framework', Briefing for the Australian Human Rights Delegation to China, Ministerial Policy Seminar, (5 July 1991), unpublished paper, 10.

103. *Report of the Australian Human Rights Delegation to China, 14–26 July 1991*, (Canberra, Department of Foreign Affairs, September 1991), citations at 3, 44, 51, 53, 58–61, 63, 66, 68, 74; La Mission de Juristes Français, *Justice Repressive et Droits de l'Homme en République Populaire de Chine* (Paris, October 1991) citations at 9, 10, 16, 19, 22, 25, 31, 37, 43–4.

104. G. Barmé, 'Travelling Heavy: The Intellectual Baggage of the Chinese Diaspora', *Problems of Communism* XL (January–April 1991), No. 1, 94.

105. W.L. Chong, 'The Chicago Congress: Recent Activities of "the Front for a Democratic China"', *China Information* IV (Autumn 1989), No. 2, 1–27.

106. Ibid. 3.

107. Barmé, 'Travelling Heavy', 97. The following description is based on this article, 92–112.

108. Text in Reuter News Service, 5 Nov. 1991.

109. See also assessment of INGOs' role by P. Van Ness, 'International Sanctions and Human Rights: the Case of China', 24–5.

110. Among reports of Amnesty International, see *China: the Massacre of June 1989 and its Aftermath* (London, Amnesty International, 1990), ASA 17/09/90; and 'People's Republic of China: List of People Detained for Activities Related to the 1989 Pro-Democracy Movement' (16 May 1990), ASA 17/24/90. Among reports of Asia Watch, see *Punishment Season: Human Rights in China after Martial Law* (New York, 7 February 1990); 'Torture in China' (New York, July 1990); 'Prison Labour in China' (New York, 19 April 1991); 'Two Years after Tiananmen: Political Prisoners in China (New York, May 1991); and 'Persecution after Prison: Problems Faced by Released Chinese Dissidents' (New York, 7 November 1991).

111. *Wenhua dushu zhoubao* ('Shanghai Reading Weekly'), 11 May 1991, review of Dong Yunhu et al (eds.) *Compendium of Human Rights of the World*, (Chengdu, Sichuan renmin chubanshe, 1991), cited in G. Barmé, 'Human Rights and Political Wrongs', Briefing to the Australian Human Rights Delegation to China, Ministerial Seminar, July 1991, unpublished paper.

112. Zhongguo tongxun she, Hong Kong, 20 June 1991, *SWB, FE*/1107/B2/6.

113. 'Renquan shouxian shi renmin shengcun quan guojia duli quan' ('The Primary Human Rights are the People's Right to Subsistence and National Independence') *Renmin ribao (People's Daily)*, 15 April 1991.

114. Text in *Renmin ribao*, 2–5 November 1991; and in *Beijing Review*, 34 (4 November 1991), No. 44, 8–45. Citations are from Information Office of the State Council of the People's Republic of China, *Human Rights in China* (Beijing, November 1991), at 6, 8–12, 15, 22–6, 28–9, 32–3, 35, 45, 57–8; for Chinese

version, see Zhonghua renmin gongheguo guowuyuan xinwen bangongshi, *Zhongguo de renquan zhuangkuang* (Beijing, Zhongyang wenxian chubanshe, October 1991).

115. For an alternative critique, see 'White Lies on Mainland's Human Rights', *Ming pao*, 13 November 1991, reprinted in *Inside China Mainland*, Special feature on Human Rights, 14 (January 1992), No. 1, issue 157, 3–6.

116. US Department of State, 'China', *Country Reports on Human Rights Practices for 1991*, Reports to the Committee on Foreign Affairs, House of Representatives and the Committee on Foreign Relations, US Senate, (Washington DC, US Printing Office February 1992), 830–1.

117. *Report of the Australian Human Rights Delegation*, 54.

118. cf. ibid. 62–72; M.C. van Walt van Praag, 'Tibet: A "Colony of China"', *Freedom at Issue* (March 1987), 31–4; C. Jansen and S. Cooke, 'Tibet: A Part of, Yet Apart from China', *The Canberra Times*, 10 and 11 October 1981; D. Thwaites, 'Sheng Shicai and the Political System in Xinjiang' (November 1991), unpublished paper; M.C. Goldstein and C.M. Beall, 'China's Birth Control Policy in the Tibet Autonomous Region: Myths and Realities', *Asian Survey* XXXI (March 1991), No. 3, 285–303; 'On the Margins: China's Other Peoples', *China Now* (Winter 1990), No. 135, 6–32; and T. Heberer, *China and its National Minorities: Autonomy or Assimilation?* (New York, M.E. Sharpe, 1989).

119. Xinhua, 'Principle of Tibetans' Right to Self-Determination Challenged', 14 May 1991, *SWB, FE/1073/B2/4*, 16 May 1991.

120. US Department of State, 'China', 828.

121. See A.R. Khan, K. Griffin, C. Riskin, and Zhao Renwei, 'Household Income and its Distribution in China', in K. Griffin and Zhao Renwei (eds.), *The Distribution of Income in China* (1993, forthcoming).

Notes to Conclusion

1. K. Hartford, 'The Political Economy behind Beijing Spring', in T. Saich (ed.), *The Chinese People's Movement: Perspectives on Spring 1989* (New York, M.E. Sharpe, 1990), 62.

2. See also B. L. McCormick, *Political Reform in Post-Mao China: Democracy and Bureaucracy in a Leninist State* (Berkeley, University of California, 1990), 127–9.

3. M. Weber, *Economy and Society: An Outline of Interpretive Sociology*, G. Roth and C. Wittich (eds.) (New York, Bedminster Press, 1968), Vol. 2, 754–5.

4. Ibid. 755.

5. Ibid. 652–3, 809.

Select Bibliography

Amnesty International, *Political Imprisonment in the People's Republic of China* (London, Amnesty International, 1978).
—— *China, Violations of Human Rights: Prisoners of Conscience and the Death Penalty in the People's Republic of China* (London, Amnesty International Publications, 1984).
—— *China: the Massacre of June 1989 and its Aftermath* (London, Amnesty International, 1990).
Asia Watch, *Punishment Season: Human Rights in China after Martial Law* (New York, Asia Watch, 7 February 1990).
Bailey, P., *Human Rights: Australia in an International Context* (Sydney, Butterworths, 1990).
Bao Ruowang and Chelminski, R., *Prisoner of Mao* (New York, Coward, McCann, and Geoghegan, 1973).
Barmé, G. and Minford, J. (eds.), *Seeds of Fire: Chinese Voices of Conscience* (New York, Hill and Wang, 1988).
Baum, R. (ed.), *Reform and Reaction in Post-Mao China: the Road to Tiananmen* (London, Routledge, 1991).
Bodde, D. and Morris, C., *Law in Imperial China* (Cambridge, Harvard University Press, 1967).
Brodsgaard, K. E., 'The Democracy Movement in China, 1978–1979: Opposition Movements, Wall Poster Campaigns, and Underground Journals', *Asian Survey*, XXI (July 1981), No. 7, 747–74.
Bull, H., 'Human Rights and World Politics', in R. Pettmann (ed.), *Moral Claims in World Affairs* (Canberra, Australian National University Press, 1979), 79–91.
Chen, A. H. Y., 'Civil Liberties in China: Some Preliminary Observations', in R. Wacks (ed.), *Civil Liberties in Hong Kong* (Hong Kong, Oxford University Press, 1988), 107–49.
Cheng Chuyuan, *Behind the Tiananmen Square Massacre: Social, Political and Economic Ferment in China* (Boulder, Westview Press, 1990).
Cheng, J. (ed.), *China: Modernisation in the 1980s* (Hong Kong, The Chinese University Press, 1989).
Chowdhury, S. R., *Rule of Law in a State of Emergency: The Paris Minimum Standards of Human Rights Norms in a State of Emergency* (London, Pinter Publishers, 1989).
Claude, R. P. (ed.), *Comparative Human Rights* (Baltimore, The Johns Hopkins University Press, 1976).
Cohen, J. A., 'China's Changing Constitution', *The China Quarterly* (December 1978), No. 76, 794–841.
Cohen, R., 'People's Republic of China: the Human Rights Exception', *Human Rights Quarterly*, 9 (November 1987), No. 4, 447–549.

Cohen, P. A. and Goldman, M., *Ideas across Cultures: Essays on Chinese Thought in Honor of Benjamin I. Schwartz* (Cambridge, Harvard University Press, 1990).

Crawford, J. (ed.), *The Rights of Peoples* (Oxford, Clarendon Press, 1988).

Davis, D., 'Chinese Social Welfare: Policies and Outcomes', *The China Quarterly* (September 1989), No. 119, 577–97.

Davis, D. and Vogel, E. (eds.), *Chinese Society on the Eve of Tiananmen: the Impact of Reform* (Cambridge, Harvard University Press, 1990).

Donnelly, J., 'Human Rights and Development: Complementary or Competing Concerns?', *World Politics*, XXXVI (January 1984) No. 2, 255–83.

—— *Universal Human Rights in Theory and Practice* (Ithaca, Cornell University Press, 1989).

Dutton, M., *Policing and Punishment in China: From Patriarchy to 'the People'* (Cambridge, Cambridge University Press, 1992, forthcoming).

Edwards, R. R., Henkin, L. and Nathan, A. J., *Human Rights in Contemporary China* (New York, Columbia University Press, 1986).

Falkenheim, V. C. and Kim, I. J. (eds.), *Chinese Politics from Mao to Deng* (New York, Paragon, 1989).

Ghai, Y., 'The Rule of Law in Africa: Reflections on the Limits of Constitutionalism', Conference Papers, Ninth Commonwealth Law Conference, Auckland, May 1990, 495–9.

Girling, J. (ed.), *Human Rights in the Asia-Pacific Region* (Canberra, Department of International Relations, Australian National University, 1991).

Goldman, M., 'Human Rights in the People's Republic of China', *Daedalus*, Human Rights, 112 (Fall 1983), No. 4, 111–38.

—— 'China's Sprouts of Democracy', *Ethics and International Affairs*, 4 (1990), 71–90.

Goodman, D. S. G. and Segal, G. (eds.), *China in the Nineties: Crisis Management and Beyond* (Oxford, Clarendon Press, 1991).

Gurr, T. R., *Why Men Rebel* (Princeton, Princeton University Press, 1970).

Harding, H., *China's Second Revolution: Reform after Mao* (Washington DC, The Brookings Institution, 1987).

Henkin, L., *The Age of Rights* (New York, Columbia University Press, 1990).

Hou Meixian (ed.), *Zhenxi ni de quanli: gongmin falu quanli guwen* ('Value Your Rights – Advice on the Legal Rights of Citizens') (Beijing, Jingji guanli chubanshe, 1987).

Hsiung, J. C. (ed.), *Human Rights in East Asia: A Cultural Perspective* (New York, Paragon, 1985).

Hu Shi and others, *Renquan lunji* ('Collected Essays on Human Rights') (Shanghai, *Xinyue* shudian, 1930).

Hua Linshan, *Les Années Rouges* ('The Red Years') (Paris, Éditions du Seuil, 1987).

Huang, M., 'Human Rights in a Revolutionary Society: the Case of the People's Republic of China', in A. Pollis and P. Schwab, *Human Rights: Cultural and Ideological Perspectives* (New York, Praeger, 1980), 60–85.

Hunter, N., *Shanghai Journal: An Eyewitness Account of the Cultural Revolution* (Boston, Beacon Press, 1969).

International League for Human Rights and the Ad Hoc Study Group on Human Rights in China, *Massacre in Beijing: the Events of 3–4 June and their Aftermath* (New York, December 1989).

Jacobson, H. K., and Oksenberg, M., *China's Participation in the IMF, the World Bank, and GATT: Toward a Global Economic Order* (Ann Arbor, University of Michigan Press, 1990).

Joint Economic Committee, Congress of the United States, *China under the Four Modernizations*, Parts 1 and 2 (Washington DC, US Government Printing Office, 13 August and 30 December 1982).

Kamenka, E. and Tay, A. E. S., *Human Rights* (London, Edward Arnold, 1978).

Kent, A., 'Red and Expert: The Revolution in Education at Shanghai Teachers' University, 1975–76' *The China Quarterly* (June 1981), No. 86, 304–21.

—— *Human Rights in the People's Republic of China*, Discussion Paper No. 3, 1989–1990 (Canberra, Legislative Research Service, The Parliament of the Commonwealth of Australia, 1989).

—— *Human Rights in the People's Republic of China: National and International Dimensions* (Canberra, Peace Research Centre, Australian National University, 1990).

—— 'Waiting for Rights: China's Human Rights and China's Constitutions, 1949–1989', *Human Rights Quarterly* 13 (May 1991), No. 2, 170–201.

Koch-Miramond, L.; Cabestan, J.-P.; Aubin, F.; Chevrier, Y. (eds.), *La Chine et les Droits de l'Homme* ('China and the Rights of Man') (Paris, l'Harmattan, Amnesty International, 1991).

La Mission de Juristes Français, *Justice Repressive et Droits de l'Homme en République Populaire de Chine: Rapport de la Mission de Juristes Français* ('Repressive Justice and the Rights of Man in the People's Republic of China: Report of the Delegation of French Jurists') (Paris, October 1991).

Lawasia and Tibet Information Network, *Defying the Dragon: China and Human Rights in Tibet* (Manila, Lawasia Human Rights Committee, 1991).

Leng Shao-chuan, *Justice in Communist China: A Survey of the Judicial System of the Chinese People's Republic* (New York, Oceana Publications Inc., 1967).

Leng Shao-chuan, with Hungdah Chiu, *Criminal Justice in Post-Mao China: Analysis and Documents* (Albany, State University of New York Press, 1985).

Leung, Wing-Yue, *Smashing the Iron Pot: Workers and Unions in China's Market Socialism* (Hong Kong, Asia Monitor Resource Centre, 1988).

Lianhe bao Editorial Department (ed.) *Tiananmen yijiubajiu* ('Tiananmen, 1989') (Taibei, Lianjing chuban shiye gongsi, 1990).

Liu Guoguang, Liang Wensen, and others, *China's Economy in 2000* (Beijing, New World Press, 1987).

McCormick, B. L., *Political Reform in Post-Mao China: Democracy and Bureaucracy in a Leninist State* (Berkeley, University of California Press, 1990).

Nathan, A., *Chinese Democracy* (New York, Alfred A. Knopf, 1985).

Oksenberg, M. (ed.), *China's Developmental Experience* (New York, Praeger Publishers, 1973).

Oksenberg, M., Sullivan, L., Lambert, M., (eds.), *Beijing Spring, 1989: Confrontation and Conflict*, The Basic Documents (New York, M.E. Sharpe, 1990).

Prémont, D. (ed.), *Essays on the Concept of a 'Right to Live'* (Brussels, Bruylant, 1988).

Ramcharan, B. G., *The Concept and Present Status of International Protection of Human Rights: Forty Years after the Universal Declaration* (Dordrecht, Martinus Nijhoff, 1989).

—— 'Strategies for the International Protection of Human Rights in the 1990s', *Human Rights Quarterly* 13 (May 1991), No. 2, 155–69.

Report of the Australian Human Rights Delegation to China, 14–26 July 1991 (Canberra, Department of Foreign Affairs and Trade, September 1991).

Reynolds, B. (ed.), *Reform in China: Challenges and Choices*, A Summary and Analysis of the CESSRI Survey Prepared by the Staff of the Chinese Economic System Reform Research Institute (New York, M.E. Sharpe, 1987).

Schwartz, B. I., 'On Attitudes toward Law in China', reprinted in J. A. Cohen, *The Criminal Process in the People's Republic of China, 1949–1963: An Introduction* (Cambridge, Harvard University Press, 1968), 62–70.

Seymour, J., (ed.), *The Fifth Modernization: China's Human Rights Movement, 1978–79* (New York, Human Rights Publishing Group, 1980).

Shue, H., *Basic Rights: Subsistence, Affluence and U.S. Foreign Policy* (Princeton, Princeton University Press, 1980).

Strand, D., 'Protest in Beijing: Civil Society and Public Sphere in China', *Problems of Communism*, XXXIX (May–June 1990), 1–19.

Szabo, I. *et al.*, *Socialist Concept of Human Rights* (Budapest, Hungarian Academy of Sciences, 1966).

Tan, C., *Chinese Political Thought in the Twentieth Century* (New York, Doubleday and Co., 1971).

Teiwes, F. C., *Politics and Purges in China: Rectification and the Decline of Party Norms, 1950–1965* (New York, M.E. Sharpe, 1979).

Townsend, J. R., *Political Participation in Communist China* (Berkeley, University of California Press, 1967).

Unger, R., *Law in Modern Society: Toward a Criticism of Social Theory* (New York, The Free Press, 1976).

Vincent, R. J., *Human Rights and International Relations* (Cambridge, Cambridge University Press, 1986).

Walder, A. G., 'Wage Reform and the Web of Factory Interests', *The China Quarterly* (March 1987), No. 109, 22–41.

—— 'Factory and Manager in an Era of Reform', *The China Quarterly* (June 1989), No. 118, 242–64.

Wang Gungwu, *Power, Rights and Duties in Chinese History: the 40th George Ernest Morrison Lecture in Ethnology* (Canberra, Australian National University, 1979).

White, G., Murray, R., and White, C. (eds.), *Revolutionary Socialist Development in the Third World* (Sussex, Harvester Press, 1983).

Whyte, M. K., 'Inequality and Stratification in China', *The China Quarterly* (December 1975), No. 64, 684–711.

World Bank, *China, Long-term Development: Issues and Options* (Washington DC, Johns Hopkins University Press, 1985).

—— *China: Agriculture to the Year 2000* (Washington DC, International Bank for Reconstruction and Development, 1985).

Zhang Chunjin, *Renquan lun* ('On Human Rights') (Tianjin, Renmin chubanshe, 1988).

Zhongguo nianjian ('China Yearbook') (Beijing, *Zhongguo nianjianshe*, 1988, 1989 and 1990).

Zhonghua renmin gongheguo guowuyuan xinwen bangongshi ('Information Office of the State Council of the People's Republic of China'), *Zhongguo de renquan zhuangkuang* ('Human Rights in China') (Beijing, Zhongyang wenxian chubanshe, October 1991).

Index